Game Design
Complete

Patrick O'Luanaigh

Game Design Complete

Limits of Liability and Disclaimer of Warranty

The author and publisher of this book have used their best efforts in preparing the book and the programs contained in it. These efforts include the development, research, and testing of the theories and programs to determine their effectiveness. The author and publisher make no warranty of any kind, expressed or implied, with regard to these programs or the documentation contained in this book.

The author and publisher shall not be liable in the event of incidental or consequential damages in connection with, or arising out of, the furnishing, performance, or use of the programs, associated instructions, and/or claims of productivity gains.

Trademarks

Trademarked names appear throughout this book. Rather than list the names and entities that own the trademarks or insert a trademark symbol with each mention of the trademarked name, the publisher states that it is using the names for editorial purposes only and to the benefit of the trademark owner, with no intention of infringing upon that trademark.

Paraglyph Press, Inc.
4015 N. 78th Street, #115
Scottsdale, Arizona 85251
Phone: 602-749-8787
www.paraglyphpress.com

Paraglyph Press ISBN: 1-93309700-0

Printed in the United States of America
10   9   8   7   6   5   4   3   2   1

President
Keith Weiskamp

Editor-at-Large
Jeff Duntemann

Vice President, Sales, Marketing, and Distribution
Steve Sayre

Vice President, International Sales and Marketing
Cynthia Caldwell

Production Manager
Kim Eoff

Cover Designer
Kris Sotelo

The Paraglyph Mission

This book you've purchased is a collaborative creation involving the work of many hands, from authors to editors to designers and to technical reviewers. At Paraglyph Press, we like to think that everything we create, develop, and publish is the result of one form creating another. And as this cycle continues on, we believe that your suggestions, ideas, feedback, and comments on how you've used our books is an important part of the process for us and our authors.

We've created Paraglyph Press with the sole mission of producing and publishing books that make a difference. The last thing we all need is yet another tech book on the same tired, old topic. So we ask our authors and all of the many creative hands who touch our publications to do a little extra, dig a little deeper, think a little harder, and create a better book. The founders of Paraglyph are dedicated to finding the best authors, developing the best books, and helping you find the solutions you need.

As you use this book, please take a moment to drop us a line at **feedback@paraglyphpress.com** and let us know how we are doing and how we can keep producing and publishing the kinds of books that you can't live without.

Sincerely,

Keith Weiskamp & Jeff Duntemann
Paraglyph Press Founders
4015 N. 78th Street, #115
Scottsdale, Arizona 85251
email: **feedback@paraglyphpress.com**
Web: www.paraglyphpress.com
Phone: 602-749-8787

Recently Published by Paraglyph Press:

Game Coding Complete, Second Edition
By Mike McShaffry

A Theory of Fun for Game Design
By Raph Koster

Small Websites, Great Results
By Doug Addison

Start Your Engines
By Jim Parker

Looking Good in Print, Sixth Edition
By Roger C. Parker

Degunking Your Personal Finances
By Shannon Plate

Degunking Microsoft Office
By Wayne Palaia
and Christina Palaia

Degunking Your PC
By Joli Ballew
and Jeff Dunteman

Degunking eBay
By Greg Holden

Degunking Your Email, Spam, and Viruses
By Jeff Duntemann

Surviving PC Disasters, Mishaps and Blunders
By Jesse Torres
and Peter Sideris

Degunking Your Mac
By Joli Ballew

About the Author

After completing a degree in Cybernetics under the tutelage of the well known "Cyber-Professor" Kevin Warwick, **Patrick O'Luanaigh** has become a senior figure in the European games industry. He worked as Head of External Development at Codemasters, working on titles such as Micro Machines, before jointly heading up their internal design studio. He began their external development program, signing and producing titles such as *Operation Flashpoint*, *Prisoner of War*, and the Cannes Palm d'Or nominated title, '*Music*.'

In 2000, Patrick moved to SCi Games in London, where he designed the original *Italian Job* game, and he oversaw the two *Conflict: Desert Storm* games that have sold well over 3.5 million copies. In his role as Creative Director, he is responsible for the quality and game play of all products, as well as identifying and signing new products and licenses, and has worked with companies such as MGM, Miramax, Paramount, and Warner Brothers. Forthcoming titles include a game version of the cult movie, *Reservoir Dogs*.

Patrick has written several articles for *Develop* Magazine (the official magazine of the European development community) and *MCV*, the UK Games Industry trade magazine.

Acknowledgments

Of course, I'd like to thank my wife and soulmate, Tammy, for her constant support, and my beautiful daughter Charlotte for her never-ending giggles and animal noises. I'd also like to thank my editors, Keith Weiskamp and Ben Sawyer, for their enthusiasm and advice in getting this book off the ground. Ben encouraged me to write the book and provided a lot of assistance with the chapter on "Serious Games." Keith provided never-ending enthusiasm along with superb editing without which this book wouldn't have been possible. I'd also like to express my thanks to Judy Flynn and the rest of the Paraglyph team for their hard work.

My gratitude is also due to all the talented industry veterans who agreed to be interviewed. I am extremely grateful to them for taking the time to answer my questions, and for being so helpful. I'd also like to thank Bill Ennis and Jane Cavanagh for showing faith in me over the last few years.

Finally, I'd like to express my appreciation to Richard Darling, founder of Codemasters, who inspired me to become a game designer and taught me much of what I know. Without Richard, my career would almost certainly have taken a different and doubtless less exciting direction, and I owe him a lot.

So, enjoy the book, and I hope that you'll find some useful tips and tricks within these pages that you can put into practice straight away.

Welcome to game design in the real world…

Game Designers Featured

Game Design Complete brings together the tips, techniques, and expertise from a number of the top game designers and experts working in the industry today. By reading the interview at the end of each chapter, you'll hopefully learn invaluable design insight from the designers of hugely successful titles such as *Burnout, Indiana Jones* and *Ultima Online,* the creator of Lara Croft, and the lead game audio engineer from one of the biggest film and game recording studios on the planet.

Here's a summary of the people featured:

Noah Falstein is a computer game industry veteran with over 25 years of experience under his belt. Having designed and written for companies such as Lucasarts, 3DO, and Dreamworks, Noah is now president of The Inspiracy, where he does freelance design, as well as lecturing and speaking at major conferences. Noah has worked on a huge number of extremely successful titles, including *Indiana Jones and the Last Crusade, Indiana Jones and the Fate of Atlantis, Battlehawks 1942, Secret Weapons of the Luftwaffe,* and the *Secret of Monkey Island.*

Richard Leibowitz is cofounder of Union Entertainment, one of the hottest film and video game production companies in Hollywood today. Union is unique among production companies in that it also represents a number of the world's best video game development companies and specializes in packaging the companies it represents with content appealing to publishers, whether licensed or original. As the primary deal maker at Union, Rich is in constant contact with major players in the film and game industries and has a unique view of the link between films and games.

Ben Gunstone is a producer at revitalized global publisher SEGA. With a long history of producing high-quality games, Ben is most recently responsible for titles like *Virtua Tennis* as well as the superb *OutRun 2,* based on the arcade sequel to one of the most influential driving games of all time.

Tim Wright (aka "CoLD SToRAGE") is something of a legend within the games industry—and a man of many talents. As a composer and musician, Tim was responsible for the audio for over 50 games, from the Shadow of the Beast series to *Sensible Soccer*, *Lemmings*, and *Powermonger*. As senior sound artist on *Wipeout*, Tim revolutionized the use of licensed music in games. As cofounder of and creative director at Jester Interactive, Tim designed and produced the MUSIC and MTV Music Generator series. He has created games on almost every game format since the mid 1980s, with a hand in the design, programming, artwork, and music of a number of titles, most recently the superb *Wipeout Fusion* on the PSP.

Simon Andreasen is the creative director of Deadline Games, one of Europe's fastest-growing and most innovative development studios. Not only does Simon have a great deal of experience with games on various platforms, but his track record in professional television production has given him a unique approach to game design, resulting in highly cinematic camera work.

Dax Ginn is something of a rarity. He's an experienced game designer with a law degree. After deciding that games were more fun than law books, Dax started his career at Psygnosis in London before working at Travellers Tales on *Crash Bandicoot: Twinsanity*. More recently, he worked on titles such as *I-Ninja* at Argonaut before spending a large amount of time designing a launch PSP title. In the process of doing so, Dax has become one of the most experienced PSP designers in Europe, talking at the very first Sony conference on the subject. He is now working at Eidos on a number of new projects.

Toby Gard is one of the best-known British game designers and was responsible for designing stunning cyber-heroine Lara Croft when he worked at Core Design. Since then, Toby has created the critically acclaimed *Galleon*, which showcases one of the most innovative and fluid camera and control solutions seen in recent years. After *Galleon*, Toby moved to the United States to help reinvent Lara at Crystal Dynamics and is currently working his magic charting the future direction of the Tomb Raider franchise.

Andrew Oliver is chief technical officer of Blitz Games, one of Europe's largest independent developers. Blitz (formerly Interactive Studios) has been around since the start of the video game industry, and Andrew has worked on hundreds of titles, from the classic Dizzy series right through to its impressive next-gen title, *Possession*.

Raph Koster is the Chief Creative Officer for Sony Online Entertainment. For many years he has served as a lead designer for teams building online virtual worlds. His first job was as a designer working on persistent worlds at Origin Systems, where he was the creative lead for Ultima Online, opening the online persistent world market to the general gaming public. At Sony Online Entertainment, he was the creative director for Star Wars Galaxies: An Empire Divided.

Alex Ward is Creative Director of Criterion Games, and is the man behind EA's phenomenal Burnout series and the innovative *FPS, BLACK*. Alex previously worked at Acclaim, and has an outstanding track record as one of the leading game designers in Europe.

Chris Nuttall is in charge of game audio at Air Studios in London. Not only do Air Studios create video game audio, but they are also a key player in the film and music industries, with film credits such as *Gladiator* and most of the James Bond films, plus key albums for artists such as Coldplay and George Michael. Chris has worked on the audio of many major games including Harry Potter and *The Italian Job*, and is uniquely positioned to comment on the challenges of audio design.

Tim Heaton is Senior Development Director at EA Partners Europe. Tim has a strong track record, having worked at Gremlin and Warthog. He has been in the games industry since 1994, and is currently working with some of the best development studios across Europe.

Ian Baverstock is Business Development Director (and co-founder) of Kuju, and has been responsible for the continued growth and success of one of Europes' leading independent game developers. Ian is responsible for sales and business development at Kuju, including new business areas and creative strategy. He played a major part in the launch of Kuju Wireless, now one of the fastest growing wireless publishers in the UK.

Dr. Ian Bogost is a game designer, academic game researcher, and educational publisher. He is Assistant Professor at The Georgia Institute of Technology, where he teaches and researches on videogame criticism and videogame rhetoric. He is also co-editor at Water Cooler Games, the online resource about games with an agenda, and has published and spoken internationally. Ian is also the founder of two companies, Persuasive Games, a game studio that designs, builds, and distributes electronic games for persuasion, instruction, and activism; and Open Texture, a publisher of cross-media education and enrichment materials for families. Prior to his academic and game development career, Ian was CTO of one of LA's top interactive marketing companies, where he worked on early experiments in Advergaming.

Maryam Bazargan is the Founding Director of New Street Media, one of the leading players in the in-game advertising arena. They bring together publishers, developers, advertisers and gamers in this rapidly expanding industry. Publishers and developers receive the benefit by an additional source of income for their games, and advertisers are able to dynamically advertise to a vast audience of gamers or develop joint events and marketing campaigns. New Street Media are working with companies such as PlayJam, Sony Computer Entertainment, Eidos, Konami, Ubisoft and Vivendi Universal.

Contents at a Glance

Contents

Part II
Core Gameplay

Part III
Design Challenges

Part IV
A Smarter Designer

Part V
If All Else Fails...

Introduction

Designing for the Real World

After spending the past ten years working on a wide variety of games, something peculiar came to my attention. I'm not talking about the increase in global alcohol consumption due solely to games industry PR teams. I'm not even talking about the incredible feat of inverse alchemy which turned a sexy feline superhero into one of the most disastrous film and game combinations ever seen.

What I noticed was that a considerable gap has emerged between pure game design "principles" and real-world game design in practice. Advice for game designers working in the real world has become very difficult to find. Most of the material published in books and magazines isn't focused on the kind of challenges and constraints that are rapidly becoming a fact of life for anyone involved in today's games industry. What do I mean by that? I'm talking about areas such as working on licenses, designing sequels, using focus groups, incorporating in-game advertisers (without selling your soul), and even what to do when you are asked to turn around a game heading for disaster. Certainly, there are plenty of fine books and other resources that cover the theory of game design and some even contain good design techniques. But any game designer who works day-in-and-out in the industry knows that there are many critical design related issues that are only learned through the school of hard knocks. The problem with this is that as the games industry continues to become very complex and the cost of developing games reaches new heights, designers can't afford to learn the hard (and costly) way.

For this reason, I decided to write this book.

I started out by putting down on paper all of the things that I've picked up over the years. (And as you can imagine, this became quite a big list that I had to refine a little.) My goal was to select the topics that would help any game designer get a more "complete" picture of the skills and design techniques that any working designer would need to apply today. In titling the book we selected the title *Game Design Complete* not because the book covers every concept and theory related to game design but because this tile reflects the more complete or holistic industry approach that the book takes.

To help provide a broader view on real world game design approaches, I've included interviews with top game designers around the world. As you read each chapter, you'll learn how successful designers such as Raph Koster, Noah Falstein, Toby Gard, Alex Ward, and others approach their craft. I hope these interviews provide some refreshing additional perspectives on each topic.

Of course, I'm losing my writing virginity on this book, so there are bound to be a few places where I've left out something or I make about as much sense as a Scottish programmer after eight whiskies. (Having worked with several Scottish programmers, believe me, they don't make much sense even when they're sober). But hopefully you'll be able to put into practice the design tips, war stories, and "reality checks" that I have written to help you get inside the industry and deal with the real-world design issues that are likely to be part of any game that you design.

Who This Book Is For

I wrote this book for anyone who is currently working as a game designer or anyone who wants to learn more about the real-world aspects of game design. Even if you are new to game design, hopefully you'll still be able to follow along because the book takes a step-by-step approach and starts with the basics of game design.

How This Book Is Organized

The book is organized into five parts:

√ Constraints and Opportunities: Here you will learn how to work with the basic constraints that game designers work with and the opportunities that emerge from these. In particular you'll learn how to work with licenses, how to design with platform issues in mind, and how to deal with demographics and specialized game audiences.

√ Core Gameplay: This part of the book focuses on the core gameplay issues that all designers must master, including cameras, control systems, characters, game environments, and level design. You can think of these topics as a game designer's building blocks. The better you get at working with these elements, the better designer you will become.

√ Design Challenges: In this section, you will learn how to work with the design challenges that you'll face when creating more elaborate games. Here we'll discuss online gaming design issues, how to design sequels, advergaming and sponsorships, and audio.

√ A Smarter Designer: To help you round out your game design experience, this part covers market research and focus groups, how to work with design teams, how to create game prototypes and pitch your designs, and how to design serious games.

√ If All Else Fails…The final part of the book covers disaster management and ends with some practical tips on game design. Disaster management is a topic that most books skip over, but it is a really important topic that any game designer working in the field needs to be fully prepared for.

PART I

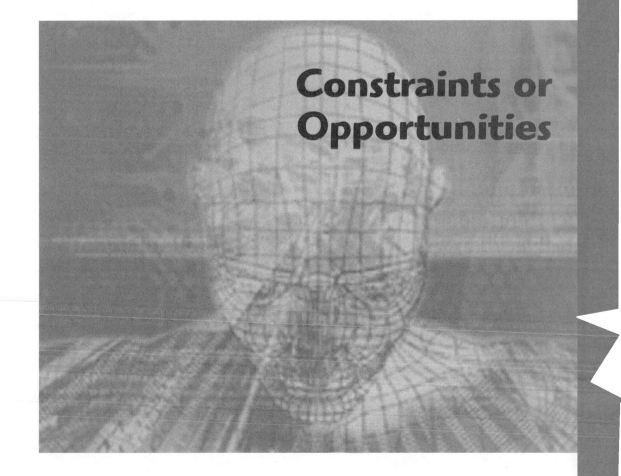

Constraints or Opportunities

Chapter 1

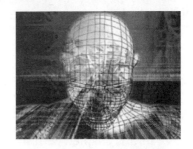

Getting Back to the Basics of Great Game Design

"In the beginning the Universe was created. This has made a lot of people very angry and has been widely regarded as a bad move."

Douglas Adams

I had the good fortune to meet the late, great Douglas Adams several years ago. I think that his quote on the perils of creating a universe is an apt way to begin a book about the challenges of real-world game design, especially when you consider that game designers are spread across the world designing new universes every day. I met him at a conference about artificial life, and he was fascinated by the possibility that computer artificial intelligence (AI) could become as smart and inventive as the human mind.

As you may have noticed, that kind of computer intelligence is still a long way off. Looking at the AI in some of the latest games that I've played, I think that my washing machine is probably closer to achieving it than some of the enemy soldiers, police cars, or gang members that play a central role in these titles. Even the block-buster games with sales in the millions haven't been able to get it right when it comes to simulating real intelligence.

Although *GTA: San Andreas*, *Half Life 2*, and *King Kong* may have pushed the bound-aries of gaming in many other ways, you can tell every time that the enemies facing you are not realistic, are not capable of adapting their behavior, and can't genuinely outsmart you. Hopefully, as the new generation of consoles evolve, more processing power will be available for more advanced and well-designed opponents that appear "believable." But the AI features are not the only ones that are flawed in recent game releases. Far too many games are still being pushed out the door lacking in the fundamentals of gameplay that make them realistic or truly enjoyable to play. Many of these games, for example, could benefit from better-designed character control, cameras, and vehicle handling. It's not always easy, but getting the basics right is something that I will be helping you focus on as a game designer throughout this book.

In this chapter, we'll start by looking at the key design elements that are necessary for real-world game design. You'll first learn that designing successful products for the real world involves getting past an "ideal" you might have in your head. Success derives from taking a hard look at what gamers in the real world really want. Succeeding in the game market is difficult enough, so the last thing you want to do is ignore what really works. As the chapter progresses, you'll learn how to live the life of a game designer, and then I'll help you learn some of the language that game designers speak. In the second part of this chapter, I'll introduce the 10 most important rules that I think all game designers should live by. Finally, we'll end by exploring how the fundamental techniques of gameplay are used to design great games. My goal in this chapter is to set the stage so that you can learn how to think like a successful game designer.

Real-World Design Isn't Idealistic Design

I've read a number of very fascinating game design books, and there are some really excellent bodies of work out there. Unfortunately, I invariably come across phrases like "achieving aesthetic purity" or "quantifying information efficiency" and then I find myself waking up an hour later with my face resting on the pages. So, what's that all about? Maybe I didn't get the memo. It's not that I'm clueless (or at least I don't believe so), but I feel that far too many game design books focus on the theory of game design, and they skip over the part where they are supposed to cover the actual practice of designing games "in the field." In other words, they don't provide the whole story. Perhaps part of the problem is that some of these books have been written by people who don't make a living designing games, or perhaps the authors who have the right experience get caught in the trap of spending too much time on theory.

My goal for this book, then, is to provide you with practical advice for designing games in the real world. We'll talk about how to do things like sticking Blu-Tak/Fun-Tak to your TV screen to help you work out how a specific game camera is behaving. I'll suggest what steps you can take if you find yourself working on the gaming equivalent of *The Titanic* and you've already hit the iceberg. I'll suggest ways to make practical use of focus groups and market research to actually improve your game rather than to play politics. We'll look at how gamers actually use the different controllers on the various gaming platforms, and we'll ride roughshod over game design taboos, like when to innovate and when to borrow and copy proven elements from other great games. Many design theorists seem to advocate designing everything from scratch and innovating each and every area of a game. In the real world, where we have tight deadlines, this simply isn't possible, and designers shouldn't be afraid of picking things that work in other games and using them as inspiration or simply copying them if appropriate. It happens each and every day within the industry, and if you're going to hit the ground running, you need to know the realities rather than the ideals. You'll need to know how to work with the constraints that you continually face as a game designer and how to turn challenging situations into opportunities.

In summary, we'll concentrate on real-world solutions and leave the theory to the other guys. As you work through the book, I hope that you'll find a number of useful ideas and techniques that you can apply to your game design work. And if you're not a working game designer at the moment but you want to be one, this book will hopefully inspire you a little and help you recognize which areas to concentrate on and how much you can learn by playing and analyzing other games. Throughout the book, I'll include special tips to help new or novice game designers avoid many of the common mistakes that I've made over the years.

Living the Life of a Game Designer

The life of a game designer is not always easy. With a few exceptions, almost everyone I've met in the game development industry has felt that they could be a successful designer, regardless of whether they are a programmer, QA technician, producer, artist, or musician! Everyone has their "dream game," and they think their idea is the one that will beat the pants off of all the other games that have been created.

Reality Check: It's very easy not to notice the contribution of a really good game designer when a game is doing well. The guys who write all of the tricky code or the artists who create the cool graphics tend to get all of the glory. A good designer is like a script writer for a movie—the person who works behind the scenes and creates the creative road map that turns imagination into reality.

Designers in general tend to be underappreciated. Admittedly, I'm a little biased on this subject, but I do believe it's true. There are some notable exceptions, normally at game development or game publishing companies that were founded by a designer. But quite often, designers can find themselves regarded as less important than programmers and artists. Steel yourself with the fact that this *will* change as the industry matures. Think about it: technology is becoming more and more powerful, programming languages and development platforms are becoming easier to use, and middleware is getting better and better. When photo-realism is present in every game, you won't be able to sell your game on technology—it'll be about the design. What will set games apart won't be John

Carmack's latest 3D engine (he's the technical genius behind games like *Doom* and *Quake*), but innovative, original, and superbly addictive gameplay. And that's where you come in.

Reality Check: If you don't think that games will become more dependant on design and less dependant on technology prowess in the future, just think about the motion picture industry. There was a time in the movie business when special effects and whiz-bang cinematic technology was the key to box office success. The rash of badly written but effect-heavy disaster movies in the 1990s was a direct result of finally having the technology to create realistic volcanoes, twisters, and meteor strikes. It feels to me like the game industry is hitting that same point with the new generation of machines, and in fact, I'm expecting to see a number of disaster games coming out over the next couple of years. But as the film industry has matured, screen writers and other creative talent (the designers) have started to take center stage. Movie buffs now seem to be more excited about a movie that is well designed and produced rather than a movie that relies on just the latest technology and special effects. In many ways, the game industry tracks the movie industry when it comes to the interests of the buying public, so don't count out the importance of great design!

To be successful at game design, you need to immerse yourself in games and live like a designer. As you play games or experience other forms of entertainment, try to think about the issues that the designers had to deal with and how they went about solving problems. Successful design is very much about problem solving. Consider carrying around a notepad or small sketchbook so that you can record what you find as you look at things that have been designed by others. You might want to ask yourself some of the following questions as you look at a successful design:

- What makes the design so unique?

- What are the obstacles that the designers had to overcome to make everything work?

- How does the design incorporate technology?

- What other designs might have influenced the design?

- How can the design be expanded upon?

- Are there any weaknesses in the design? If so, how can they be improved?

Creative Idea: The Power of Paper

Keep a notebook with you, and write down all the ideas you get, however crazy they seem. George Lucas kept a notebook handy while he was working on *American Graffiti*. In the film editing room he said, "Hand me R2D2" (which meant Reel-2, Dialog 2). He liked the way that sounded, so he wrote it down, and the rest is history.

Getting the Basic Terms and Concepts Together

If you're new to game design or self-taught, you'll need to learn the language that game designers speak so that you can interact with other designers. Like many other areas of design, game designers have their own special language that has evolved over the years. Here is a very short dictionary of game design terminology that will help you as you work your way through this book.

gameplay

The term *gameplay* is difficult to define. It refers to the combination of all the different actions that a player can perform, plus it involves the way a camera moves and how a character/car/object reacts to a player's controller. It consists of many game mechanics (see the next term). From my point of view, however, gameplay can be summed up very simply: If the gameplay is good, the player has fun; everything feels just right. If the gameplay is bad, the player gets frustrated and doesn't enjoy the experience. If you go to the electronics or computer store and see the games that really fly off the shelves, it's likely that all of these games have good gameplay. The games that are piled up in the bargain bin are those that have gameplay that sucks. Gameplay has nothing to do with the storyline, characters, flashy graphics, or great sound. It's about how the fundamental aspects of the game feel. So if you're playing a racing game, the gameplay is all about how driving the car feels. If driving the car in your game environment is great fun, everything else will follow. If driving the car isn't fun, no amount of stunning graphical effects and rendered cut scenes are going to save the game.

game mechanic

I know someone who seriously thought for many years that a game mechanic was someone you'd call if your PlayStation had a problem. In reality, we use the term to describe an individual aspect of the gameplay. For example, the fact that Mario can squirt water from his jetpack to wash away graffiti in *Mario Sunshine* (Nintendo, 2003) is a unique game mechanic. Likewise, the fact that he can jump off the ground and land on higher parts of the environment is another game mechanic (albeit one that is used in most character games, so it isn't unique at all).

GUI or on screen display

GUI stands for graphical user interface. In games, this normally means the on-screen interface: the 2D graphical bits around the edge of the screen that can show your score, weapon ammo, compass, a map, a speedometer, or any other useful bit of information.

front end

This term refers to the introductory screens and menus the players use to enter their names, select a game mode, and change any options. Traditionally, this has been a separate section to the main game and is shown largely in 2D (see Figure 1.1), although designers are now thankfully becoming more creative with the front end, and it is possible that the front end can be displayed partly or entirely in 3D (see Figure 1.2). Since games are often developed on tight schedules, the front end is often the part that suffers most when time runs out. Unfortunately, too many of them are thrown together quickly at the end of development without too much thought. A good front end is interesting, begins to immerse the player in the game world, and is simple enough to move through when the player just wants to get to the game quickly.

demographics

This term refers to the age range, sex, and income bracket, among other things, of people for whom a game is developed. For example, PC gamers tend to be a different demographic (older and more affluent) than console gamers. It's important that you understand the demographics of the average gamer out in the real world. I'll talk about

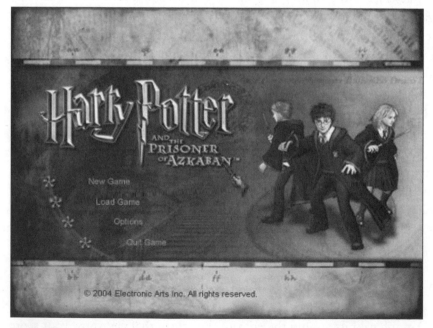

Figure 1.1
A fairly typical 2D front end.

Figure 1.2
·An example of a 3D front end.

demographics in much more detail in Chapter 4. For now, keep in mind that demographics is a key area for which any successful game designer needs to get a feel because it's becoming more and more important as the industry gets increasingly professional.

first person/third person

These terms refer to the perspective from which you view the game. First-person games (see Figure 1.3) put you behind the eyes of the character; you don't see your character in front of you, although you will probably see the character's arms (and any weapon or object the character is holding). Third-person games, on the other hand, are normally seen from a position behind and slightly above the character (see Figure 1.4). In third-person games, you see the character's body in front of you. Games such as *HALO 2* and *Doom 3* are first-person games, and the Metal Gear Solid series and *Mario 64* are third-person games.

USP

USP stands for unique selling point and refers to something about the game that makes it unique and sets it apart from other games on the market. Be careful not to confuse

Figure 1.3
A first person viewpoint.

Figure 1.4
A third person viewpoint.

this with a "game feature," which is a key aspect of the game that isn't unique. Overzealous marketers tend to confuse the two all the time! Proper USPs are fairly rare, but they can really help set a game apart in the market. For example, a USP may be that the player can superglue a door handle, and enemy characters will become stuck when they try to open the door. As far as I'm aware, this has never been implemented in a game before, so it is truly unique. An example of a key feature might be incredibly realistic water with a water level that can rise or fall. It may be a key element of your game, but *Waverace*, *Tomb Raider*, and many other games have all had water that could rise or fall and that their developers felt was extremely realistic. Bear in mind that the most important thing is whether the game-buying public will feel it is unique or not. If my game included a feature that had only been previously included in an obscure Tandy TRS-80 game that sold about 3,000 copies in 1986, I would call it a unique feature. There's no need to be too particular about what qualifies as "unique"!

mass market

This is an often overused term, but it is still critically important to understand. It's also an important aspect to bear in mind when you are designing a new game. If you're designing a big-budget game for a major publisher, you need to try to create a game that is going to appeal to the largest possible audience; a title that has the potential to sell well over one million copies. If you're working for a smaller publisher, or in a particular niche within the industry, knowing about the mass market may not be as important. But if you are aiming for a million sales or more, it's vital that you don't design games for yourself or your friends, but for the millions of average gamers who own the current biggest-selling platform, don't have much money to spend on games, and like licenses; the kind of people who love buying *FIFA/Madden* each year. It's really important that you move with the times, keeping an eye on the changing way these gamers play games. The millions of average gamers are the mass market, and if your game appeals to them, it stands a chance of selling in big numbers.

Reality Check: In my view, the best way to understand the mass market is to listen to it. Attend focus groups, listen to what people say, and read and watch other forms of mass-market entertainment. In the United States, *People* magazine is a mass market leader. In the United Kingdom, on the other hand, the *Sun* is the most read newspaper and the books in the Harry Potter series are currently the most-read books. So read these (at least every so often). Immerse yourself in popular culture, talk to average gamers, and you'll stand a chance of understanding the mysterious mass market.

Creative Idea: Top 20 Analysis

Take a look at the top 20 games in the bestselling chart at the moment. If you can't find the game chart in your country, just visit Amazon and use its list of top 20 bestselling games instead. Look at the games from a high level. How many of them are sports games? How many involve firing guns as the key element of the game? How many are violent? How many are sequels, and how many are new, original games? How many are based on licensed books, films, or TV series? The games industry changes over time, just like any other, and different styles of games become popular at different times. More sequels and licensed titles appear to be released in the run up to Christmas and also at the end of each generation of console. By keeping a close eye on what is actually being bought by the games public (as opposed to which games have the most hype), you stand a good chance of following how gaming trends change.

I.P. (intellectual property)

An I.P. is essentially a license, something owned by someone, normally a book, a comic, a film storyline, a TV show format, or a character. For example, "James Bond" is an I.P. that is licensed by Electronic Arts so that it can make computer games based around the James Bond world and films. Electronic Arts pays the people who own the James Bond I.P. lots of money in order to do this. An I.P. typically involves a large up-front payment (called a guarantee or advance) and a royalty (a percentage of all the profit made from the games).

immersion

This is a term that I tend to use a great deal. Immersion is the feeling of being dragged into a game world—forgetting the real world even exists and becoming totally immersed in the game. If you've ever played a game that sucked you in so completely that you forget to eat, drink, or sleep, you'll know what I'm talking about. Immersion is a very special feeling that is due in large part to the skills of great game designers—it's about achieving believability in the game, avoiding things like harsh transitions from 3D to 2D screens, and having a game that is so interesting that a player is even reluctant to leave to use the bathroom!

Realty Check: Immersion is a great concept and one that you'll want to aspire to for any game that you design, but when immersion becomes "extreme immersion," things can get out of hand quickly. Consider the case of the game-playing enthusiast in South Korea who died after reportedly playing an online computer game for 50 hours with few breaks. The 28-year-old man collapsed after playing the game *Starcraft* at an Internet cafe in the city of Taegu. The man had not slept properly and had eaten very little during his marathon session. I guess that, as with any form of media that sells to several million people, you are always going to get one or two who take things too far!

Ten Rules for Game Designers to Live By

Since we're dealing with the basics in this chapter, I thought I'd next give you what I consider to be the basic rules of game design. Tattoo these onto your forearm and don't ever forget them. We'll be coming back to them throughout this book.

Rule #1: Believe in Your Concept...

If you have an idea for a complete game, a game mechanic, or just some part of the design that you feel strongly about, stand up for it. Believe in your ideas, and don't be afraid to make them clear. Explain why you feel they are so important. It's your job to make sure any game you create is as enjoyable as possible, so don't let the fear of what others might say stop you from doing that job.

When you come up with an idea, try to write it down because that will make the idea more concrete. Don't be afraid to pass the idea around and get feedback from others you respect.

Rule #2: ... But Don't Be an Ostrich

Don't keep your head in the sand like an ostrich, refusing to listen to other people's opinions. While you need to believe in yourself, you also need to remember that you're not infallible and other people are also capable of having great ideas. And yes, some of them might even be better than yours. Listen to everyone's ideas and opinions, and keep an open mind about other people's suggestions. That way, you'll hopefully be able to find the perfect combination.

Rule #3: Tact Is Good

If designers have one common flaw, it is that we can be too forceful, too arrogant, and not tactful enough. As a designer, you need to tread a fine balance. Tact is an invaluable weapon in your armory. If you need to get people to agree to a change, be tactful about it. Explain to them what you want to do, and why. Don't just storm in and tell them how it's going to be; take the time to explain carefully. This may even mean on occasion pretending that you've listened to their thoughts more than you really have. I have a feeling that some of the developers I work with may enjoy reminding me that I wrote that, but on occasions it is true; sometimes it pays to listen to someone's idea even when you know after the first sentence that you're not going to use it. You'll find that using tact will win you much more respect from the team around you than blundering about like a loose cannon firing off your "design vision."

Rule #4: Pick Your Battles

If you manage to go through an entire project without some kind of design disagreement with your producer, you probably should phone up the *Guinness Book of Records* because you'd be the first designer to do so.

I believe that great games can often come from creative friction between the designers (always trying to make the game better) and the producer/project manager (always trying to get the game out on time and on budget). So, you're likely to have to fight several moderate battles over design ideas and features. Unless you're Will Wright (designer of The Sims series) or Peter Molyneux (creator of titles like *Black and White*), you're probably not going to win them all. So pick your battles, and be prepared to let go of certain ideas that aren't so important to you. It's about give and take, and your producer also has a job to do. Just because something is right from your design point of view doesn't mean it is necessarily right from the bigger picture of the project as a whole. Even the greatest film directors give in to movie executives over many things, saving their energy for the really important issues.

Rule #5: Don't Lose the Treasure Map

One thing that the great explorers always remembered (right after "don't try to pet the big cats with the large teeth") was to keep their map with them. Lose your map and you could lose your life. In the game world, your map is your overall design vision—your view of the final game and what you're working toward. As the lead designer, you are the torch carrier for the game. The best games are almost always a result of setting off in a particular direction and ending up there, even if it's two years later. Likewise, the worst games tend to be a result of starting off in one direction, changing direction halfway through, and then ending up somewhere completely different again. You're the navigator, and you need to hold onto the map and make sure you're always heading the right way. If someone tries to tell you differently, show them the map (your clear, well-written design document) and remind them of your objective. Then lock them up in the brig until the end of the voyage….

Reality Check: I have had bitter experiences with this issue a few times in my career. For example, on one project, which shall remain nameless, the marketing team agreed wholeheartedly with the original direction of the game, then changed their mind halfway through when a new person came on board. Rather than standing my ground and presenting a clear and strong reminder of why the game was headed in that direction (and why they agreed with it initially), I gave in, assuming that they knew more than I did. After the project was released, and flopped badly, one of the marketers confessed over a beer that the game would have been much better as originally planned.

Rule #6: Research, Research, Research

Never underestimate the importance of research. Play as many other games as you can. Try out all the gaming platforms. Play some online games also. Read gaming magazines, and figure out why games get bad reviews. Play all the games that will be competing with the one you're working on. Research your subject matter; if you're making a golf game, go play some golf and watch the major competitions on TV. The more research you do, whether general or specific, the more likely you will make the right calls when those important design decisions come along. Understanding the subject is vital to achieving believability and therefore immersion.

Rule #7: Always Remember the Magic 30 Minutes

The first 30 minutes of every game are of paramount importance. It's like when you meet a new person for the first time; your opinion of them tends to be made up very quickly. The same goes for a game, and it's especially true now that many people rent games before they buy them. It's doubly true for reviewers who see so many games that something needs to grab them quickly. Don't create your first level early on in development, when the teams aren't up to speed. Leave your first level until later, and throw in all the bells and whistles. Not everyone can afford to do an "E.A." (E.A., Electronic Arts, is the biggest game publisher in the world) and have a separate producer and subteam just working on the first level, but we can all ensure that the first half hour of our game is not a quiet introduction to the controls but an adrenaline-packed blast. Keep your gameplay simple for the player (it's important that your game starts off being fairly easy), but have lots of amazing stuff going off around the player, really showing off your game engine. Make the player's jaw drop; first impressions count.

Rule #8: Story Is King

Read *The Writer's Journey* by Christopher Vogler. It's a classic book that talks about the hero's journey—a classic mythical story structure that has been used in almost every film ever made. If you've ever noticed the similarities between Luke Skywalker's galactic quest from his humdrum life in the desert, Frodo's epic quest from his quiet life in the Shire, and Harry Potter's dramatic entry in wizard training after his boring life with his foster family, you'll understand why this book is so useful. Once you've read it, remember that just because we're making games doesn't mean that we can cobble together any sorry excuse for a storyline and it'll do. Games are getting increasingly professional, and we can help this process by using professional writers and making sure our stories have a proper beginning, middle, and end. Learn how a proper story is constructed, and try to use this knowledge to make sure that your game plotline is as strong and interesting as possible.

Let's look at a quick example of the difference between a weak plot and a strong one. A typical weak game storyline would be something like this:

Zane, a tough ex-special-forces soldier, is given a mission: locate and destroy the Hellcat gang who have kidnapped the president's beautiful daughter, Andromeda. Zane is given a briefing and then arrives at the enemy HQ with a huge arsenal of deadly weaponry. He survives a series of near-lethal attacks due to his athleticism and impressive military skills, eventually rescuing the girl and winning both her heart and the everlasting thanks of his country.

Here's an example of a much stronger storyline:

> **Bob, a fairly typical insurance clerk, is angry. He's fed up with the stress of traffic jams and modern life. Just as he's leaving work, he is kidnapped in a case of mistaken identify. He's beaten and left for dead when the kidnappers realize their mistake. But Bob isn't dead. He's alive and he's very pissed off. Bob has finally snapped, and now he's out for revenge. He's going to take every last kidnapper down, and they're going to see just how violently creative an angry insurance clerk can be....**

Hopefully you can see for yourself why the second story is richer and more three-dimensional than the first story, giving you a character who is interesting, flawed, and more identifiable for a player. It also lends itself much more to adding unusual, and therefore interesting, things to happen to the player as the game proceeds.

Rule #9: Plan for the Future

Unless you are designing a game that is clearly a one-off, you should be thinking carefully about sequels and where the game could go in the future. The only example I can come up with of a one-off game would be a film or book license that tied up all the loose ends, one in which all the key characters died or lived happily ever after. Other than that, you should try to build in a little room for a future product. Consider leaving some interesting unanswered questions or leaving the history of your main character a little vague so you can flesh it out in a prequel. Don't get carried away and feel that you need to do a George Lucas and design six complete games from day one. Just keep it in the back of your mind. If your game sells in huge numbers, the fans are demanding more, and your publisher gives you a huge down payment to create a follow-up game, you'll be the one stuck trying to figure out how your lead character actually survived the nuclear explosion in the finale to game 1!

Rule #10: Understand and Use Basic Human Instincts

This may sound a little theoretical and artsy, but it isn't. Mankind (and that means everyone who will play your game) has a whole load of primal instincts locked away beneath the surface. For example, there are reams of scientific research that shows that the hunter/gatherer instinct is at the core of much male behavior, and this is presumably one of the key reasons shooting games prove so successful with male gamers. But there are lots of other more interesting and less-often-used instincts that are worth investigating. Here are a few of them:

- *Collecting and Completion:* Many people like collecting things, and there is a basic human compulsion to try to complete a collection that has a few gaps within it. For many people, there is something strangely satisfying about completing things. I believe this is the reason why the Pokemon series sold so incredibly well; you could see from the beginning that there was a set number of missing Pokemon that you needed to catch, and as you began building up your collection, the desire to try to get every one increased.

- *Protecting:* Both men and women have a strong natural urge to protect their offspring, and some games have cleverly utilized this instinct. Sony's superb PS2 game *Ico* has the player leading around a smaller, less powerful character who is totally dependent on the player to survive. The player develops an incredibly powerful attachment to this character, which is something that is drawn on in the storyline later in the game. It may be that the protection instinct would be a great way to start a design that appeals to female gamers.

- *Fear of Nature:* Mankind has always been afraid of the natural elements. For example, thunder and lightning inspired such fear that they were traditionally linked to the anger of the gods. It's one reason so many classic horror movie scenes tend to happen during storms and the classic Transylvanian castle always has lightning forking above it. Why not use this instinct to your advantage by having a huge and intense storm grow as your game builds toward its climax?

- *Inquisitiveness:* Many people are naturally inquisitive. That's why we go into space, climb the tallest mountains, and blow particles apart to discover what they are made of. Why not play around with this instinct by hiding information from the player and arousing their curiosity. If I'm playing a first-person shooter and I walk past a door with a sign that says, "Do *not* enter this room," you know I'm going to really want to go in!

■ *Need for Shelter:* The need to find shelter is another instinct; watch how many gamers hug the sides of levels to avoid being in open ground when things are getting really dangerous. Games often use this instinct in a couple of ways. You can raise tension by forcing your player to enter a huge mysterious open area with some dramatic music in the background as they wait for the enemy to reveal themselves. The player should feel exposed and the tension will be twice as high. You can also assist by providing shelter points for the player to retreat into if the game gets too difficult, helping players regroup, recover, replan, and then continue.

If you want to find out more about this fascinating subject, I can recommend the book *Human Instinct* by Robert Winston as a good starting point.

War Story: The Power of Visuals

One of the hardest skills to learn as a designer is how to get the vision that you have in your head across to other people. However well you describe it, it's likely that other people will end up with a slightly different vision, as everyone makes different assumptions based on their varied experiences. Many people don't like reading long wordy design documents, so it's important to understand the importance of visual material.

We had this very problem with a project I was working on—the marketing guys just didn't get what we were trying to do, regardless of how many times we tried to explain or sat them down in front of a design overview. I decided to put together a short video, carefully selecting short clips from major films and TV shows that summarized the attitude, action, and gameplay that I expected in the final product. It worked extremely well and allowed everyone involved to "get" the final game at an early stage before any in-game code was created. I have since met a few other people who also do this, calling them "Ripomatics." So think about different ways that you can use Ripomatics or other visuals to enhance your design.

Using the Core Gameplay Fundamentals

There are many fundamental aspects to great game design that lie at the heart of every top seller. We'll cover the most important ones (the camera and control system) in later chapters. However, there are several other key areas that you need to be aware of, including using interaction, maintaining variety, avoiding frustration, incorporating replayability, encouraging drive and exploration, using difficulty levels wisely, incorporating the important element of fun, applying brainstorming, and using experts as much as you can.

Focus on Interaction

Interaction is what makes games interesting. Without being able to interact with the environment, objects, and characters, a player will get bored extremely quickly. If the player is driving a car, the interaction will probably be with street corners, other vehicles, pedestrians, barriers, tables, and even the classic stacks of boxes. If the player is controlling a character, the interaction will be with the world (for example, climbing up hills or hiding up a tree), with objects (such as opening boxes or climbing over a wall), and with other game characters (shooting at them, talking to them, or running away from them). As a designer, you should make a clearly defined list of all the types of interaction that your car, character, or whatever will be able to use. You'll probably find that this list forms the core description of your game.

Maintain Variety

Variety is fundamentally important. In the early days of video games, there was no option but to force the player to repeatedly play the same few minutes of gameplay with more enemies, at a faster speed, and with greater difficulty. Although there are modern games that rely on reusing the same gameplay over and over again (such as the excellent Super Monkey Ball series), even they have to create a wide variety of level types to keep modern players interested and challenged. Today, gamers are different as compared to early gamers, and they get bored much more quickly. Don't forget this, and don't fall into the trap of taking the easy option of repeating sections of a game without good reason.

Avoid Frustration

I am convinced that modern gamers are more easily frustrated by games than they used to be in the past. With classic games like *Pitfall*, you could expect the player to happily attempt the huge alligator jump many times before they got it right. You don't have this luxury nowadays. If a player is "killed" in the same place more than a couple of times, the player will start to get frustrated. This frustration is hugely increased if the player feels that it wasn't their fault. Having places where players cannot fail but die the first time they encounter them is just wrong. Players should always feel that they *could* complete the game in one go if they didn't make mistakes. I'll talk about blind gameplay tests later, but if you do test your games out on new players, watch them quietly or video record their actions. It should help you find out where their frustration points are.

One great way of helping with this problem is to provide hints to the player if the player has died in the same place more than once. I'm working on a game at the moment in which the player is able to purchase hints at any point that make the current level a little easier. Since purchasing hints takes up valuable money that would otherwise be spent on weaponry and cool objects, experienced players will likely avoid using the hints system. But for players who are finding the going a little tricky, the hints should be invaluable, and the player will always have enough money to be able to purchase them.

Of course, the ideal solution is to have a truly dynamic difficulty level that changes depending on how the player is coping with the game. So if the player is repeatedly dying because they can't make long jumps between platforms, the game would slowly increase the player's jump distance up to a fixed limit. The player wouldn't notice this happening. They would just find that the frustrating jump deaths became fewer in number and would enjoy the game more. It would never be altered for better gamers who weren't plummeting to their doom all the time.

Another way of implementing dynamic difficulty would be to slowly lower the difficulty of the enemy characters (or rival vehicles if you're designing a car game!) whenever the player dies and raise it every time the player manages to last 15 minutes without being seriously injured or challenged.

 Reality Check: Great games shouldn't be about trying to defeat the player; they should encourage the player to progress, scaring them half to death in the process and making them feel talented and skilful.

Think Carefully about Replayability

Your game will be played by many different kinds of players. Some will never finish; they'll play for several hours before finding themselves attracted to another title. However, many gamers still find the price of games very high, and they won't buy many new products at all. When they do, they want to get the most out of their $50. So think carefully about how to add replayability. If you're clever, you'll give people a reason to replay levels without having to create lots of new content. The Nintendo 64 version of *Goldeneye* is an excellent example from the past; it had a superb difficulty level, where new objectives within the existing levels would open up when you unlocked the next level of difficulty. Since this meant exploring parts of the level that you often ignored before, it gave the player a genuine reason to play the game through again. Think about unlocking a bonus mode that allows players to play through each level against a time limit, forcing them to play at a much faster pace. This is a very easy addition and it gives people a reason to try the main game again. Award your players bronze, silver, and gold awards for completing levels or sections in a certain way; this will encourage them to go back and try to get gold on everything. Hide special collectible objects around the world, and give players a reason to find them all. Or just unlock an extra item of equipment when they finish the game (such as the camera in *Metal Gear Solid*) and let them use that if they play through the game again, to add an additional twist.

Encourage Drive and Exploration

Players need a reason to want to continue with a game. Just completing a level and moving on to another one isn't a compelling reason; there must be something that they want to achieve, or to find out. Storyline is really important here; if your plot is strong, the player will want to find out what happens to their character. You might decide to tease your player at the start of the game by showing them a glimpse of a great weapon or some really jaw-dropping gameplay and then use that as a lure to drive them onward. Exploration is also an excellent way of encouraging players. The original *Tomb Raider* game did this really well. The areas that you came across were always so impressive and exciting (and full of hidden challenges) that players looked forward to what might be around the next corner. However you do it, it is really vital to make sure that the player has a really good reason to boot up the game again the next time they have some spare time.

Use Collecting and Completing Techniques

As I touched on previously, there is an innate desire within all of us for collecting objects and for completing things. A large number of kids and adults collect something in their personal lives. And everyone experiences the satisfaction of finally completing something that you've been working on for ages. Great games often draw on these almost subconscious feelings. You start *Pokemon* with a big (virtual) scrapbook with lots of empty spaces. As you fight and beat different kinds of Pokemon, this scrapbook slowly fills itself up. Trophy rooms in sports games work in the same way; you start by seeing the trophy room empty, with lots of spaces that need to be filled. As you begin to see the trophies and awards come together, there is a real desire to try to get them all. Remember to use collecting and completing techniques to enhance your game.

A very simple example would be to create a number of special bonus items and hide them around your game world throughout the levels. Make it clear to the player at the start that the bonus items are out there, and let the player see how many they have acquired at any point in the game. Immediately the player has a reason to explore the game world, something to encourage them to keep playing the game, and a tremendous feeling of satisfaction if they manage to find all the bonus items. Of course, you'll come up with some kind of satisfying reward for collecting them all, won't you?

Use Difficulty Levels Wisely

As I mentioned when I wrote about avoiding frustration, the best kind of difficulty level is one that has rarely been achieved in games—to automatically adjust the difficulty depending on how the player is doing.

Unfortunately, successful implementation of this ideal doesn't often occur for a multitude of reasons. In the real world, we're normally lumbered with fixed difficulty levels. My rule of thumb on difficulty levels is to always include them. Having watched countless focus groups, I have realized just what a huge disparity there is between hardcore gamers and some players who try really hard but find themselves struggling all the time; people who just aren't very good at games but still love them. Both types of player have paid for the game and therefore both deserve to be able to enjoy and complete the game. So use difficulty levels so that both types of players can enjoy themselves.

When I'm balancing a game, I like to think about three different categories of player and make sure I'm happy that all three will be able to enjoy and be challenged by the game:

Struggling Stuart

Struggling Stuarts would love to be good at games but don't have the skill. They are full of enthusiasm and buy quite a few games, but however hard they try, they still find games difficult; maybe they just don't have the mental or physical agility that other people have. But Struggling Stuarts have paid the same amount of money for the game as everyone else and deserve to be able to get through the game and enjoy it. Make sure you have a difficulty level for these players that is genuinely easy.

Average Joe

Average Joes are, (and it's not surprising), average gamers; they don't play games all the time, but they'll buy a good game every month, listen to recommendations from friends, and enjoy gaming as part of a balanced social life. They are pretty good at games, but it's very important that you remember that an average gamer isn't the same thing as an average game developer. If you create a game that is just right for you (thinking that you're probably average), it is likely that, as a game designer, you are actually better than average gamers and the game will be too hard. The only way to test out your game is to get average gamers in to play it! Average Joes will play a game for a long time to get their money's worth, and therefore, things like replayability are important.

Hardcore Harry

Hardcore Harrys are really good gamers; they spend long hours playing games and tend to buy more obscure games than the Average Joes. The game must be really high quality, with some unique features, and there must be a strong challenge for these guys, who are very talented gamers. Having a "difficult /hardcore" skill level is important for these players; some of them will want a really tough challenge. Hardcore Harrys are the people who will want to unlock bonuses and beat the game. But they will only do so if the game is of a very high quality.

Reality Check: One thing that you should consider seriously (and unfortunately this doesn't happen as often as it should) is allowing the player to change difficulty level during the game without forcing them to restart again. If you've spent two hours struggling through the first few levels before realizing that "normal" is too tough for you, you'll want to be able to drop the difficulty level down to "easy" without restarting the entire game. In my view, a great game will allow you load an existing game save but change the difficulty level. At the end of the day, the player has paid good money for the game and deserves to enjoy it.

I mentioned focus groups and this is something that we'll touch on later in the book. It's really important when you're balancing the difficulty levels that you get both hardcore and casual gamers who haven't seen it before in to play the game. There is no better way to find out where your game is too hard or too easy and where there are still moments of frustration. In my view, you should be aiming to get the difficulty of your game to match the graph shown in Figure 1.5. What tends to happen is that the difficulty levels of your game look more like the one shown in Figure 1.6. Here, there

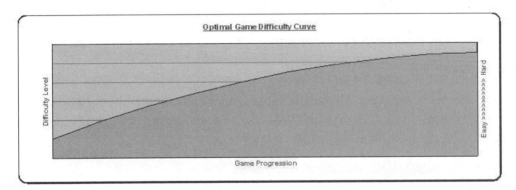

Figure 1.5
A perfect difficulty level.

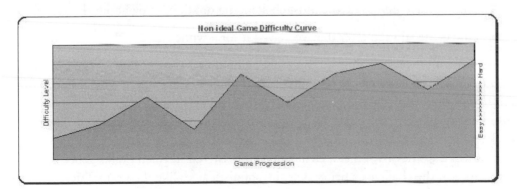

Figure 1.6
Common difficulty level problems.

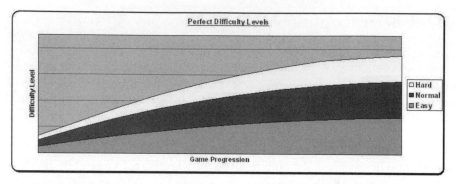

Figure 1.7
Multiple difficulty levels.

are a number of frustration points where the difficulty is hard enough to cause some people to stop playing the game. Get fresh players playing your game (and include people that are not great gamers) and they will really help you iron out your game difficulty and end up being close to the ideal. Figure 1.7 shows how multiple difficulty levels should fit together in a perfect game.

Don't Ever Forget *Fun*!

Repeat after me: Games must be fun. It's a very obvious statement but one that can get lost when you are knee-deep in game mechanics and level design. Get people to play the game and then ask them the following questions:

- Do they enjoy it?
- What annoys them?
- What bores them?
- What do they find to be the most challenging or stimulating about the game?
- Is the game still fun after they've played it for a while?

Raph Koster, in his fascinating and best-selling book *A Theory of Fun for Game Design* (Paraglyph Press, 2004), analyzes what it is that makes games fun. He believes a significant reason that something feels enjoyable is that it meets the human desire to master patterns. To be able to solve puzzles is vital, whether they require thinking or just the quick application of the controller to dodge a fireball or aim at an opponent. People want to feel that they have met a challenge and mastered it. Koster talks about the importance of the challenges being rich and sophisticated, like the best stories. Once a game is mastered, it stops being fun, so it's vital that you continue to challenge a player and introduce new elements to the challenge once a player is getting good.

Don't Forget Brainstorms

Remember that the best ideas normally come when people work together. Involve other people in your team (particularly other designers) when you're trying to come up with new directions and original gameplay. When the best sitcoms are written, they are created by small teams of talented writers sitting around a table, bouncing ideas off each other. You can hold your own brainstorming session in exactly the same way with other designers.

Try to set aside several hours, go into a quiet room, and put up a big A1 pad of paper. Explain what you'd like to brainstorm, and then get everyone to pitch in ideas. Write everything down, regardless of how stupid it sounds. The fundamental rule behind brainstorming is that no idea should be ruled out at this stage; put everything down on paper.

So, for example, you might have a main character who flies around using a jetpack (we'll meet this idea again later in the book). The objective of your brainstorm might be to come up with some unique and exciting game mechanics for him. So, start talking about what you could do with a jetpack. Where could you go? What is a jetpack made of? Could you use the jet flame to do something else? Maybe set something alight? Could you use it to burn other characters or objects? Is there a height limit? What happens when you run out of fuel? Can you put different types of fuel in? You get the idea.

If you're running out of ideas, try a different tack. If you wanted to destroy someone with a jetpack on, what would you do? Maybe you'd shoot the fuel pipes. Maybe you'd fire a heat-seeking missile at the exhaust fumes? How about if the character can take off the jetpack and drop down to the ground? Could you strap explosives to a jetpack, aim it at an enemy, and let go?

Only when you're completely out of ideas can you go through the list you've generated and see what might be useful and what really won't work.

Use Experts

However talented you are, the odds are that you're not an expert at everything. Making games involves many different skills, so don't be afraid to enlist the help of experts in other areas to help you out. If you can persuade people to help without being paid, that's great. But please don't be afraid to push for paid expert advice when you feel it is needed. We had an ex-SAS solider who had been on the ground in Iraq advising us with *Conflict: Desert Storm*. He helped us with character animations, mission structures, what Iraqi army positions looked like and showed us the best tactics to use. We never lost sight of the fact that we were creating a game that had to be fun, but his help was extremely useful. Similarly, when I've worked on rally driving games, we've employed experienced rally drivers and engineers to help us out with the car handling. Use expert scriptwriters, cut scene directors, and anyone else that you think will help make your game better. You're unlikely to regret it.

And Finally...Break the Rules When You Need To

Remember that you are free to break the rules. Don't assume anything. Think laterally and don't be afraid to try something different. As with anything in life, if you don't step out of your comfort zone and take a few risks, you're never going to be truly successful.

Summary

I've tried to cover what I consider to be all the basic elements needed to be a really good game designer. If you understand the terminology, appreciate the importance of the 10 basic rules of design that I've laid out, and understand the core gameplay fundamentals that we've gone through, I reckon you now have an extremely solid foundation to build from. Remember these when you're working on a project in the real world and you shouldn't go too far wrong.

This chapter has been about the basics. Things get even more interesting when we get into the details. Next up, we're going to look at licenses and the fascinating game design challenges they involve.

An Interview with Noah Falstein

Noah Falstein is a computer game industry veteran with more than 25 years of experience under his belt. Having designed and written for companies such as Lucasarts, 3DO, and Dreamworks, Noah is now president of The Inspiracy, where he does freelance design, as well as lecturing and speaking at major conferences. Noah has worked on a huge number of extremely successful titles, including *Indiana Jones and the Last Crusade*, *Indiana Jones and the Fate of Atlantis*, *Battlehawks 1942*, *Secret Weapons of the Luftwaffe*, and the *Secret of Monkey Island*. With such a strong track record, Noah is the perfect candidate to ask about the fundamentals of game design.

What do you think are the most important skills that a game designer should have?

NF: A love of learning. Every successful game designer I know is curious about almost everything, and most can run circles around your average TV quiz show contestant on all sorts of subjects. You don't get that way by specializing, so a desire to keep learning new things throughout life is critical. Also critical is a fascination with how things work and the underlying principles behind them. And a good ability to communicate those ideas is important, too—preferably verbally, written, and graphically, although few designers manage to be good at all three of those.

Are there any basic rules of game design that you feel ought to be drilled into every new designer coming into the industry?

*NF: Dozens! That's what my monthly column in Game Developer magazine is about, and along with Hal Barwood—who came up with the concept, we've been putting together a list of such rules. I'll be putting them on my Web site at **www.theinspiracy.com** in early 2006. Like any creative pursuit, it's important to know the existing rules before you break them. Some people balk at the very mention of the word "rule," so sometimes I say guidelines or principles, but it's really a semantic distinction.*

Do you have any tips for coming up with creative and original ideas for a new game?

NF: Perhaps paradoxically, I recommend a deep familiarity with other games, past and current, as well as a good knowledge of both classic and popular culture. Most good game designers have played many hundreds of games, and are also as comfortable quoting Homer's Odyssey as Homer Simpson. I've often had people tell me that they make a point of not knowing much about what has gone before "so their ideas will be fresh," but invariably they end up proposing stuff that's been done before—sometimes dozens of times. You need to learn to think beyond what's been done, sometimes at right angles to existing trends, to make something fresh. You also need to keep grounded in what's been done before so you know what players may expect, and how to best diverge into fresh territory without losing them. Having some good brainstorming partners is very helpful; it's possible to do it on your own, but much easier with talented colleagues.

What is your favorite ever game (of all time), and why?

NF: That would have to be the original Civilization by Sid Meier. A breakthrough game in many ways, and certainly one of the most compelling and addictive games ever made. In particular, the balance of the different types of units, buildings, and wonders of the world is quite marvelous, and hard to appreciate unless you've tried to do something similar yourself.

Can you name a few classic games that you would recommend new game designers dig out and play?

NF: Well, for Civilization, much of what makes it good has been carried through into its sequels, so you don't have to go back far. There are so many great games, I'd have to break it down by category. For instance, if you're doing a sports title, the original FIFA Soccer game was groundbreaking, whereas for any comedy-based game I'd have to recommend the collected works of Tim Schaefer (most recently Psychonauts) and Ron Gilbert (who "discovered" Tim) with his first two Monkey Island games. And everyone should play Tetris. It is the epitome of that Einstein quote, and a great apparent exception to so many conventional assumptions about games.

What do you think is the biggest game design mistake that people regularly make with games?

NF: Trying to do too much. I call it the "Kitchen Sink Approach." It's much better to do a few things very well, perhaps with many subtle variations, than to try to cram 3 or 4 different games into one. Blizzard is very good at finding their core focus and sticking with it. Diablo and Diablo II seem too narrow to be interesting, but are incredibly compelling once you start playing. There's an Albert Einstein quote I love that sums it up: "Everything should be made as simple as possible, but no simpler."

What are you most proud of in your career so far?

NF: If I had to pick a single game, it would probably be Indiana Jones and the Fate of Atlantis because it was so much fun to work on the game with Hal Barwood and I think it remains one of the better blends of story and interactivity, as well as one of the few original titles based on a movie character that was a big success. But on a personal level, I'm probably proudest of the help I've been able to give to others in their games or their careers.

If money and technology were unlimited, what kind of game would you most like to see made?

NF: This is where most people start going on about the Holodeck... but personally I'm happier with smaller, beautifully polished games than ever-larger special effects extravaganzas. I've probably put in more hours playing Advance Wars 2 on the GBA than any other game, in part because I use it to get me through my weekly workout routine (on a recumbent bike machine at the gym) but also because it is such a beautifully balanced little strategy game.

I think a holy grail of game design is creating games with believable and emotionally compelling characters, which is more limited by design and imagination than by money and technology.

How important is getting the difficulty level(s) right for a game, and how do you personally go about it?

NF: That's quite important, and tends to be an area where the art of game design comes in, as opposed to the science of it. I have often found that I need to twiddle with a bunch of numbers in the underlying equations of the game to find one key variable that most clearly makes the game feel harder or easier. It can be a different thing for each game, or at least each type of game, and then just test the hell out of the game, tweaking that variable up and down. When you start changing too many things it can ruin the balance of the game.

What do you think is the biggest challenge facing game designers as we move forward?

NF: The increasing pressure towards homogenization, as so many recent games look or feel just like each other. That, in turn, is a consequence of the growth in budgets, as publishers are increasingly unwilling to take chances with straying from game mechanisms that are untried, or to original characters or storylines. I fear that with the next gen consoles being even more expensive to develop for, we'll see an implosion, with sales of software dropping significantly in late 2006 and 2007. I don't think it will be as bad as the 83–84 crash (which I personally experienced, and it wasn't as hard to weather as people like to make it out to be) because the casual, downloadable market as well as mobile phone games and other areas like serious games provide good outlets for developers to keep in the industry. And of course I could be wrong, and 2006 will be a banner year.

And finally, if you had one piece of advice to give to a game designer who was just starting out, what would it be?

NF: Don't give up. If I meet two budding designers and one is talented but not persistent, and the other is persistent but not talented, the latter one is much more likely to get a job. Of course, having both is even better, but even if you're incredibly talented you need something to get you through the dry spells. All of my favorite designers have had their fallow periods or dud games, so persistence is definitely the thing!

Chapter 2

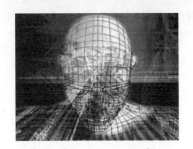

Licensed to Thrill

"My movie is born first in my head, dies on paper; is resuscitated by the living persons and real objects I use, which are killed on film but, placed in a certain order and projected on to a screen, come to life again like flowers in water."

Robert Bresson

There are not many aspects of the game industry that create such a strong reaction from people as licensed games. And in my experience, the reaction is very different depending on whether you're in the industry or a gamer looking for a new title in your local software store. A large number of people within the industry (particularly within the game development side) seem to turn their noses up at licensed games. I regularly hear comments such as these:

"They're all crap!"

"There's no innovation!"

"Licensed games are killing creativity!"

But licensed games continue to be among the biggest selling titles, and mass-market gamers around the world love licensed games. In fact, they can't seem to get enough of them. Look at the sales figures for the Harry Potter or Lord of the Rings games, which reached the number one spot on almost every platform best-seller list. These licenses also continue to spawn new games. The general quality of licensed products has been improving rapidly over the last few years. And if you want to be a well-rounded designer, I believe you need to understand and appreciate the unique challenges that licensed games provide.

Designing games based around licenses is one of the most important and least under-stood areas of game design. Here's the big challenge: How do you successfully convert a well-known film, book, or TV show to a video game? Many designers have done this very badly over the years. To be fair to the designers involved, game publishers used to be far too quick to slap a license onto a weak game to try to increase the sales. Believe it or not, this happens with less frequency now; today the problem is that we rush licensed games out in an incredibly short time frame to hit a movie release or, in some cases, a book release. I can understand this madness to ride the wave, considering their large marketing budgets. Consider Electronic Arts's (EA's) *Catwoman* game, where a huge team had around eight months to get the game mastered and out the door. This was all done for a movie that itself was a failure—perhaps if the game had more time it could have rescued the movie (grin)! Some publishers never learn…

In the real world, we can't all go after Harry Potter and James Bond, and only a few companies are willing to spend many millions of dollars on a license before they have even started making or marketing the game! So you're going to learn about what kind of licenses you might aim for if you're on a budget. You'll also learn about how to identify a bargain and how to make the most from a "B-list" license.

In this chapter, I'll explain how to avoid the common pitfalls that affect licensed games. At my company, we've successfully utilized licenses. When it's done right, there shouldn't be any kind of stigma attached to the use of a license. This chapter will help answer questions such as these:

- How can you tell which licenses will work well as games?

- How do you create original and exciting gameplay while staying true to the license?

- What are the best methods to help ensure a smooth working relationship with licensors?

- How do you go about adding new content to existing licenses in order to turn a 2-hour film into a 15-hour game?

- How does the approval process normally work with licensors?

- What rights should you push for when you're signing a license?

- How can you obtain strong licenses on a sensible budget?

Before we get into our discussion, I should just quickly clarify a couple of terms for people who might not be used to licenses. A *licensor* is the company that owns the license and sells you the rights—often a movie company, an author/publisher combination, a rights agency, or a corporation that owns a specific brand (e.g.,Lego, DC Comics, or Ferrari). The *licensee* is you—the company or developer that has licensed the game rights. Licensees generally pay an advance and royalties to licensors, and licensors generally sit back, approve or disapprove things as they come along, and almost without exception take longer to answer your queries and questions than they should! In fact, as a result, I suggest that all schedules for licensed games should not be cast in stone. I recommend that your producer add around 25 percent more time for the approval process than would normally be added. It's unlikely that this extra time will be wasted!

The History of Licensed Games

Licensed games have a very patchy track record. For every successful licensed game, there have traditionally been vast numbers of poor quality rubbish. (I almost used a four-letter word there because of my anguish at how many talented people have wasted so much time on some of these titles.) The legendary Atari VCS game *E.T.* is the perfect example. It was not only a very poor game (and if you don't believe me, take a look at almost any book about the history of the games industry), but the publisher managed to manufacture more cartridges than there were consoles in existence. Add these two facts together and it's no surprise that they ended up burying around two million cartridges in a New Mexico desert. One day in the distant future, some archaeologist, no doubt a citizen of the United States of EA, is going to unearth this mass of decomposing plastic and circuitry and wonder exactly what the game designer was thinking.

I believe the first licensed game was probably *Indy 800*, which was released by Atari in 1975 and was an eight-player racing game. I use the term *licensed* loosely here because I doubt that Atari paid any money for the rights even though the term *Indy* in the game's name refers to the Indianapolis racing circuit. This was closely followed by the game *Death Race* a year later, which was inspired by the movie *Death Race 2000*. Again, no money changed hands as far as I can tell. Being able to use brands like this can really help the game-playing public recognize your game as they associate it with other properties that have been established using someone else's marketing dollars.

It wasn't until the early '80s (1982 and 1983 to be precise) that big film licensing started to become more prevalent. *Tron* (see Figure 2.1) was the original film-licensed game and still stands as one of the better licensed games ever made. It was followed soon after by the Atari arcade coin-op game, *Star Wars* (see Figure 2.2), which was an incredible experience, allowing gamers to relive the dangerous Death Star trench run in cutting-edge vector graphics (which basically means lots of lines).

Toward the end of the '80s and the start of the '90s, Electronic Arts began its rise to the top. It did this by recognizing the value of sports licenses before anyone else and released games such as *Madden*, *PGA Golf*, *NHL Hockey*, and *FIFA Soccer* (see Figure 2.3) that started steadily in huge numbers and were updated on an annual basis.

By the early '90s, it was possible to slap a license onto an average game and sell a really large number of units. I think this was because, as games moved into more mass-market channels, new customers hadn't quite worked out that a big name didn't necessarily mean a great game and we were all a bit more gullible than modern gamers. This still happens, but it's less common. Gamers are a little more aware nowadays, as tiny sales of relatively poor titles like *Catwoman* show (although in that case, there is an argument that if the film had done well, the game would have sold many more copies, regardless of the quality). Fortunately for all of us, ever since the dawn of video games, there have always been games that showed just how well licenses could work. We'll take a look at

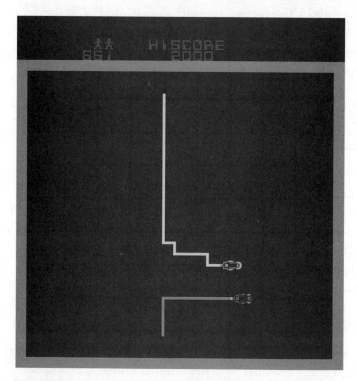

Figure 2.1
Tron, one of the first games created from a film license.

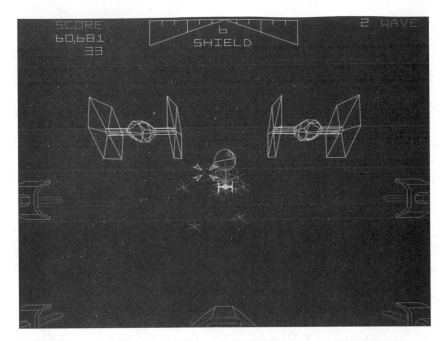

Figure 2.2
Star Wars, another successful film license.

Figure 2.3
EA's *FIFA Soccer*.

some of these later and examine how you can ensure that your licensed game ends up in this category rather than in the Wal-Mart bargain bins.

Top Five Licensed Games

A number of really excellent licensed games have been created that you can learn from. It's a good idea to play with some of your favorites and take a close look at how the game designers approach using the licensed properties to create their games. In this section, I've managed to narrow down the competition into my favorite five licensed games of all time.

Goldeneye (Nintendo 64)

Arguably the best first-person console game ever made. This game provides superb gameplay, highly original design, and the perfect balance between originality and use of a big film license.

Star Wars (coin-op)

One of the first ever licensed titles, and still a superb piece of game design amidst huge limitations. The thrill of piloting an X-Wing down the Death Star trench is something you could never forget, and for the first time, gamers felt that they could actually experience what their hero did in the movies!

Aliens vs. Predator (PC)

The use of very different gameplay mechanics for the aliens, predators, and humans, along with unique vision modes, made this a really superb game that combined two films licenses into one product. This game was so good that a movie was created called *Aliens vs. Predator*. This game provides a good example of how different licensed properties can be combined to create a popular game.

Spiderman (PlayStation 1)

Neversoft came up with a really great new control system that allowed Spidey to swing from building to building, climb walls, and hang from ceilings, and it still felt very natural. It's a really superb example of how to be original with a big license.

Dune 2: The Battle for Arakkis (PC)

A revolutionary game from 1993 that defined a genre that is still going strong today. It was the predecessor to the first *Command & Conquer* game and showed how well suited the PC is to strategy, war, and resource management titles.

Worst Five Licensed Games

There really were too many to mention; in fact, I think I could write a separate book on all of the bad games. Here I've managed to narrow down the list to five particularly appalling examples of how not to design a licensed game.

Superman (Nintendo 64)

Pretty much any of the old Superman games would do, but Titus's Nintendo 64 version managed to sink lower than any other. Gamespot's Joe Fielder says it all: "It serves no purpose other than to firmly establish the bottom of the barrel." If you ever want to experience how bad a control system can be, get a copy of this game and prepare to be amazed.

Ed Hunter: The Iron Maiden Game (PC)

Even a die-hard Iron Maiden fan described this game as a "human turd." A PC game so devoid of gameplay, graphics, and fun that it was little more than an interactive CD with annoying moments of button bashing between the songs.

Big Brother (PC)

A European publisher picked up the rights to one of the world's most successful reality TV shows, *Big Brother*. If they'd been creative, they might have tried something along the lines of *The Sims*. Unfortunately, they decided to slap it onto a really poor 2D platform game. Aarggh!

Queen: The Eye (PC)

What is it about rock bands and video games? A game that was inspired by the music of Queen. If only the designer had been inspired by the gameplay of Shigeru Miyamoto rather than the contents of his toilet bowl.

Shaq Fu (Super NES)

An evil sorcerer from another dimension wants to take over the world. And who is going to stop him? A basketball player. Who thinks he's a martial arts expert. Enough said. The worst fighting game ever made.

Designing for Constraints or Opportunities

The initial mindset of many designers is that designing a game for a licensed property is going to be a huge constraint and involve a lot of money. If you had the freedom to create your own new design, you could do anything. With a license, you're seriously limited and are forced down unimaginative routes. There is a widespread belief that working with licensors is a nightmare; they tell you what to do, and they make you change everything. In short, working on a licensed game is only slightly more preferable to having your toenails pulled out with pliers while being forced to play *Daikatana*.

 Reality Check: Relax. It's not true!

I've worked on many licensed games, including working with film licensors such as MGM, Warner Brothers, and Lions Gate. I've also worked with TV companies such as Carlton and book publishers, authors, and even the estates of dead actors. Believe me; working on a licensed game can be the most fun you've ever had. Rather than limiting your creativity, licenses simply channel it. Sure, when you've got a blank sheet of paper, you can create anything. But it's hard to know where to start. With licenses, you have a framework. Within that framework, it's possible to create hugely innovative products. Look at titles like *Chronicles of Riddick*, which recently set a benchmark for licensed games. Then there is the ground-breaking Nintendo 64 title *Goldeneye*, which was spectacular and launched a series of decently received 007 games (right up until the poor remake of *Goldeneye* released in 2004). And what's more, there will be people who love your license and who will look forward to your game, people who can't wait to spend their hard-earned money on it. Working with licensors need not be a problem at all. If the project isn't well run, then of course there are likely to be issues.

 Reality Check: If you work hard at communicating with your licensor, involving them from the start and talking to them regularly, you'll find that they leave the design up to you. After all, *you're* the game designer. They're normally more concerned with how the logos, licensed characters, and music fit in.

The long and the short of it is that there's absolutely no reason why working on a licensed game can't be an incredibly enjoyable, creative, and painless experience.

Finding Licenses

If you're in the fortunate position of being able to influence or even decide which licenses your company is going to try to obtain, then how do you go about this? How can you tell whether a forthcoming movie is going to sink or swim? The answer to this, as with so many questions, is *research*.

Reality Check: When it comes to big-time licenses like Bond, *X–Men*, or *FIFA*, small developers need not apply. However, small and even independent developers shouldn't get discouraged that they won't be able to work with or find licenses. The world of comic books, books, movies, toys, and branded products is large enough that there may indeed be a license you can make use of, and one you can afford. The process won't change, with the exception that you'll probably need to work with a more obscure license. Before you think this is a downside, let me make two additional points. First, some big licenses are often available to multiple parties, like the rights to professional athletes' names for use in a sports game. Second, today's obscure license may turn into tomorrow's gems. You may have to take a bigger risk, but if you pick your license carefully and do your research, you may find yourself with a huge brand on your hands. Big publishers and developers will often refuse to take the risk on new movies, preferring to wait until the cast is on board and the director and budget guaranteed. This offers smaller players the opportunity to get in early, show enthusiasm, and snatch the rights to a potential future blockbuster. Just be careful; it's easy to get caught up in the "magic of the movies" or with a new novel from a big-name author.

To start your research, you must read the big trade magazines for the property you want to license. For the film industry, the key publication here is *Variety* (**www.variety.com**), which is a *must read* for movies, TV shows, and so on. A major toy fair is held every year in New York, and annual book fairs are held as well. The comics industry has trade magazines, and so does the sports industry. I suggest that you start first by identifying the shows and publications that will help you.

Once you find a potential license you'll want to contact the rights holder, which may be a company, a publisher, or the creator of the licensed property. If it's a big company, chances are good that you'll want to contact it and ask who handles licensing (likely someone in the legal department or an outside rights holders' agency). If people don't seem to know, I suggest talking to the legal department or the public relations department. With individuals (such as authors), you'll want to track down their agent or track them down directly if you can't find an agent.

Creative Idea: Start with the Impossible

Some of the best ideas come from challenging yourself. So think of a type of game that has never been done, something about which most people would say, "You can never make a game like that!" Then think about all the different ways you could design it and also see if you can come up with a licensed character, brand, or movie that could be incorporated into it. You may find that an idea comes out that leads you to a strong concept that *is* possible.

Evaluating Licenses to Use

If you are looking at new movie licenses, find out how serious the film company is. In what stage is the project? Has a well-known director been attached? Are any major actors involved? One thing is for sure: *you must read the script.* This will normally involve signing a nondisclosure agreement and going in to the film company's studio for a script reading in a quiet room. Take your time and ask yourself the following questions:

- Does the script lend itself to being made into a game?

- Are the characters interesting and believable?

- Do you care about the characters?

- Are the characters strong enough to be adapted into a game?

- Does the main story arc provide enough room for a 12- to 15-hour game?

- If not, can you create your game world before or after the story from the film or run it in parallel?

- Are there areas of the plot that leave room for you to expand upon them in more detail in the game?

- Is there much action in the film, or is it all about relationships and touchy-feely stuff?

- Is there scope for a sequel? This may not be necessary, but if your game is a success, it can be really useful to have a foundation in place upon which a sequel can draw (see Chapter 10 for more about this).

Try to find out from the film company whether a budget has been drawn up for the film yet. The worst thing you can do is pay money for the game rights and then find out that the film isn't going to be made after all. In some circumstances, you might be signing the rights to a script before it even gets the proverbial green light, in which case all you need care about is how strong the script is and how suitable it is for an original game. But in all other cases, try to get an idea about how strongly the licensor feels about the property. This may well give you an indication about how seriously they will push the brand in other areas.

If you're looking at existing licenses (such as older movies, books, or comics), you need to do a different kind of research. Ideally, you need to perform some market research in the key gaming territories to find out how many gamers are familiar with and like the license. Doing this in multiple territories is very important. In the United Kingdom, we understand that our view on things isn't necessarily the same as the French, or the

Japanese, or our American cousins over the pond. In the same way, U.S. designers need to remember that their game needs to sell not only in the United States, but certainly in Europe, and ideally, in Asia as well. If you can't afford proper research, contact foreign gamers on chat boards and ask their thoughts. Phone up friends you have overseas. And don't forget to ask the licensor for as much information as possible—just remember to double-check it!

Licensing on a Budget

So how can you find a license for your game without paying more than the GDP of a small country? Well, clearly you're going to have to steer clear of the big blockbuster films, books, and brands. There are four key pieces of advice that I suggest you follow when looking for a license on a budget.

Think Differently

Forget trying to play in the same arena with big Hollywood movies or the latest best-selling novel. Think carefully about other forms of media that you could license. Could you license a famous actor and build a game around him? How about using a cult actor/actress—maybe someone who is no longer alive, like James Dean? Could you use a big sports brand or business brand as a license, such as a company or organization like Sky/Fox Sports, Apple, or NASA? How about using a well-known story or character that is out of copyright? Take a look at well-known novels or early movies that may be reaching the point at which their copyright expires and they're in the public domain. I could come up with many more examples. The key thing to remember is to think differently and find some kind of brand that people are familiar with.

 Reality Check: Your job as a designer is to find a unique property that others might have overlooked and adapt it into a good game. If you pick a brand or licensed property that works well, the brand will do the marketing for you.

Go for Strong Content, Story, and Characters over Just Recognition

Look for a license because it has a fantastic storyline and great characters instead of just focusing on how much recognition it has. There are hundreds of fantastic books that must be perfect for games, yet because they haven't been huge sellers, they are skipped over. Use the license as a way to guarantee a brilliant story and save yourself a fortune on scriptwriting.

Go for Shock Value or Controversy

Make the most out of a cheap or free license by spinning the publicity to help create a real controversy. It's a little-known fact that almost all the games that end up on the news because they are being targeted by senators or government officials end up selling many more copies than they were originally forecast to sell. While I in no way endorse the game, *JFK Reloaded* was a fascinating title that took a free license and a simple premise (examining the truth behind the JFK assassination by "allowing" the player to fire sniper rifles from various places) and then courted a whole load of negative publicity. SCi's *Carmageddon* game was hugely successful because of the enormous controversy it caused when it first came out. And there are many other examples where controversy has helped sell games in big numbers.

Go Early and Take the Risk

The bravest way to get a big license is to approach authors or film companies really early on and get close with them while a new project is just getting off the ground. You'll often find that it's not the big film distributors, but much smaller film development companies, that actually start new projects. If you can convince them that you share their values and believe in the brand, you may be able to sign up the rights at a sensible price very early on. Of course, if the film never gets released, or the book fails to sell any copies, then you may have a problem!

How Broad Are Your Rights?

Signing up a license isn't a binary thing. One lesson I leaned very quickly about licenses is that there is often a gray area. For example, you may have the rights to use a film name but you may not have the rights to use the actors, their faces, the film music, sound effects, and so on. So as far as game design goes, this is what I'd recommend you push for:

- **The name of the license and the main logo.** You want to make sure you have the ability to use this worldwide and promote it on TV, radio, in cinemas, and online.

- **The key actors/actresses.** You'll want their likeness rights and time in a recording studio for voiceovers, and the marketing team may also want some appearances or help with game PR.

- **The author/director.** For a major book, the involvement of the author can be really useful. This is certainly true for marketing purposes, but it can also be very true game-design wise. Being able to ask an author or director questions and understand some of the back story can greatly enrich your game. Getting a director to critique your cut scenes will help make them shine. Being able to work closely with director Peter Jackson helped the team previously responsible for the excellent *Beyond Good and Evil* to create a *King Kong* game that is very close to the movie.

2

- **The music.** This is especially true if the license has very well-known or distinctive music. Make sure your rights cover TV advertising and online promotional videos, as well as magazine demo discs.

- **Other aspects, such as key sound effects or getting models and animations from a special effects team.** Personally, I'm determined to use a cinematographer on a game at some point soon, so you might like to consider signing up other people from a show; even a stunt coordinator or cameraman to help your game feel more real.

Reality Check: It's important that you prioritize the licenses you want to try to obtain. Unless you (or your publisher) have an extremely large budget, it's likely that you won't be able to get everything you want for the money you can afford to spend. I suggest you work out what is most important; it may be that you don't really care about getting the original music as long as you have the movie star's likeness in the game and on the box. On the other hand, if the music is well known but the original star isn't quite as cool now as he once was, your priorities for obtaining licenses might change.

War Story: Get Your Faces Right

For one of the licensed games that I worked on, we unfortunately couldn't get the rights to use the real actors' faces. But we wanted to make the characters in the game look as much as possible like the people in the movie. If you get artists to create new faces that look a bit similar, you run a very real risk of getting into trouble. What we did was to invite members of the public to send in their photographs if they wanted to be in the game. We received about five hundred photos, and we selected five for the main characters in the game. The people were pleased and happy to sign a piece of paper giving us permission to use their likeness. We were also very happy, as we were able to select people who looked fairly like the original actors. But since we were licensing real people who actually existed, we were on pretty safe ground legally. Obviously, you will want to have all the actors licensed for the game you're designing, but if you don't, you might want to consider going down this route (after checking it out with your legal advisors).

Designing for Licenses

You're now probably wondering, once you've acquired a license, where do you begin? Well, as always, it's vital to start by doing your research. Find out as much information about the license as possible. Read the book, watch the film, play with the toy (and watch other kids play with it!), talk to the screenwriters. You should also visit fan communities and ask them what they like about it. Hassle the licensors for as much information as possible. Only then can you begin to do a proper job on the game design.

Reality Check: Using the Web can also be a very effective technique for doing research on a licensed or branded product. Use a search engine like Google and try to locate sites where users of the product or brand talk about their experiences with it. This will give you a lot of "behind the scenes" insight into how the property you are licensing is perceived. It could help you avoid a costly mistake of developing a game around a licensed property that you later find out has certain flaws that could turn people off from buying and playing your game.

Should You Remain True to the License?

One of the biggest challenges you'll face is steering a path between being completely accurate to the license (which may well make a boring game) and going too far away from the license (which may result in a game that doesn't bear any resemblance to the license). The best starting point is to discuss this issue with the licensor face to face. Although you might not believe it, many licensors will be very happy to support you in moving the game away from the source material. They may feel that you can enhance the license by adding new elements, rather than by simply copying what has been done before. Explain to them that games are different than films, books, or TV shows and that you'll need to create 12 to 15 hours of gameplay from something that may only last 90 minutes!

 Reality Check: When it comes to the world of game design, developers are increasingly interacting with parties outside the industry. This requires us to explain our industry, processes, development and marketing strategies, and so on to them in order to enlist what support we need from them. I suggest you consider developing a good presentation on this subject, as it will aid you in not only your license recruitment, but also in other aspects of your game design.

If you get your licensor to buy into a slightly original take on the license from day one, it will make your life much easier. Don't be afraid to follow prequel or sequel storylines or to run your game story in parallel with the license. But make sure that whatever you do stays true to the license in its fundamental aspects. A great example is the game *Chronicles of Riddick*. It takes place a long time before the film, but it contains the key character, his unique attitude, and the style of the film. Although the storyline is very different, the game works alongside the film because the main character and the overall universe are very accurately portrayed. Another great example is the first *Knights of the Old Republic (KOTOR)* adventure game by Bioware. So many recent *Star Wars* games hadn't really moved away from the license in new ways but *KOTOR* did and was well received. In fact, many *Star Wars* fans liked the writing in *KOTOR* more then they did in either of the first two prequels!

Which Character(s) Should You Use?

One common element in books, TV shows, and films is that they tend to involve a number of key characters and the action often jumps around between them. You need to decide at a very early stage whether your game will have more than one controllable character. The player can empathize much more with just one main character. But it limits you to one main story arc. Of course, you can show other plot threads through cut scenes or clever in-game storytelling, but the arc of your main character will become more important than it was in the license. On the other hand, you might want the player to control multiple characters over the course of the game. Although this adds variety, it can mean that the player has to get used to controlling different characters and may not feel a strong affinity for any of them, something that is key in encouraging players to continue playing and find out what happens next.

When I have seen the multicharacter aspect done well, I usually see several key attributes used:

- The player controls a small set of characters (four or fewer).

- The characters all stay together and act as a team.

- Regardless of whether the game has split levels (i.e., a single character used per level) or multiple characters on each level, there is usually a lead character around which the majority of the action revolves.

- Each character is not just unique in style and story but is also used for a unique purpose in the game. If the character doesn't provide a unique gameplay purpose, they are best relegated to the background.

Reality Check: No matter how attached you might get to a cool character that you license, don't forget that games rely on interaction. A movie or a book uses characters to tell a story, but a game must adapt its characters to engage a player into a world of activity and immersion. When you evaluate characters for licensing, try to look for characters that will engage players in some type of back-and-forth action. Also, make sure that you properly understand the characters from the original license. There is nothing worse than a game that has shallow two-dimensional representations of characters who were rich and deep in the original book or film. Make sure you keep the flaws that make characters so interesting; no one likes playing a hero who is either perfect or a stereotype.

Expanding the License—Content Generation

The worst licensed games often feel like they have a few hours of content that has then been brutally stretched out by the designer to last much longer. When I see games like this, I have to wonder why the developer even bothered to use licensed properties. Perhaps the only reason for having the license was to have more marketing clout. The problem with this is that players see through this very quickly and your game will likely get very bad reviews.

War Story: Your Licenses Must Fit Your Game

I have fought against the problem of adapting a license that wasn't ideally suited for a game several times in my career. I worked on a game based on the classic movie *The Great Escape* and it proved tricky to create enough content for an entire game. Players were forced to play through parts of the story that they didn't recognize, and we had to work hard to create a number of prequel missions showing how the characters arrived at the prison camp. I've learned to try to avoid "one-off" movies—the kind of movies that have a clear beginning and end, where nothing interesting is likely to have happened before or after the time period shown in the movie. Licenses that are more interesting are those that feature a "world" and those that give you the freedom as a designer to play around without sticking to a strict story.

You *must* be able to create enough original and exciting gameplay to last throughout the game; I normally aim for 12 to 15 hours worth of gameplay. And this is not always as easy as it sounds. Most movies last a couple of hours, so if you're working on a film license, you need to create another 10 hours of content from somewhere! There are a number of techniques that you can use to do this. Table 2.1 shows some of the better methods that designers use.

Table 2.1 Techniques for approaching a difficult licensed storyline.

Technique	What it involves
Fleshing out the storyline	This involves using a professional writer (someone who has considerable experience doing this). Keep to the key plot points, but expand on what happened within the time frame of the movie. Take the film The Godfather, for example. The story often jumps forward a few weeks, months, or years. It's easy to see how you can add interesting fights, events, and even gang wars within these gaps while sticking to the facts from the movie.
Creating a prequel	Depending on the license, you could add a new dimension to the story by setting your game before the events in the license. If the main character(s) are mature and have a mysterious past at the start of the book/movie, this can be perfect for exploring and creating as much new game content as you want. Just remember to make sure the prequel storyline fits in with the license and the characters are in keeping—and get a professional writer to create all the dialogue for you.

(continued)

Table 2.1   Techniques for approaching a difficult licensed storyline *(continued)*.

Technique	What it involves
Creating a sequel	In a similar way, you may decide to explore the events after the story from the license has ended. This is particularly ideal if the license left plot threads and story elements open, yet a sequel to the film/book was never created. Again, ensure you use a professional writer for at least the dialogue creation, if not the whole new storyline.
Having a parallel story	If you are having trouble building a game around the existing storyline, why not create a parallel story that runs through the events in the license. Pick a minor character and flesh out their story. Or create a new character who lives within the world of the license and maybe meets or passes the existing characters. If done carefully, you can create a new storyline that picks up on key events from the existing story and feels like it remains true to the license, yet is more ideal for a game than the existing storyline.
Using flashbacks	Flashbacks can be a great technique for jumping to things that happened in the past that may have been mentioned or discussed in the main story. Media such as movies often needs to be shortened to fit a specific time range, but in your game you can expand on elements that the movie likely had to cut out.
Using multiple viewpoints	You might want to consider having multiple playable characters within your game. Films often jump between the viewpoints of a number of people, and doing the same within your game may be the only way to make sense of the plot. If you want to do this, make sure each character is rich and interesting enough and that the actions and abilities you give each character are different enough to make them varied and exciting.

Whichever route you choose to go down, discuss it with your licensor as early as possible, and get them to buy into the direction that you feel is best.

Avoiding Common License Problems

Developing a game using licensed properties can be a costly venture, and thus you want to do everything that you can to avoid making mistakes. Let's look at some of the common traps that designers and developers fall into.

Designing by Numbers

Unfortunately, I have played far too many licensed games that feel like the designers couldn't really be bothered. They'd rather save their creativity for their "epic original project" (that they'll never get to make), and so they designed their licensed game by numbers, making it just like other games in the same genre and doing everything that you'd expect. If you go to the movies regularly, you know that the most interesting films are those in which you're unable to predict what is going to happen next; you think you know what's coming, and then the plot takes a massive twist. Games are the same; not just in the storyline specifically, but also in what you do and where you go. If you're just copying another game, and doing exactly what the player would expect, you're doing it wrong. Innovate and do something a little differently. Your review scores and sales numbers are likely to rise accordingly. Even though you are using licensed properties that have been created by others, there is no reason that you can't put your own spin on things and take what you have to work with into new directions.

Licensor Disagreements

Unfortunately, disagreements with licensors do occur. If you begin communication early and talk to them as often as possible, you'll have a better chance of keeping this from happening. But however brilliant you are at keeping them informed, there is always the chance that you'll both disagree over something fundamental. Creative people from other industries often feel as if they know exactly how computer games should be designed. Sometimes they have interesting and insightful thoughts, and sometimes they just don't understand the specific challenges of game design. At the end of the day, the licensor probably has approval over the game, so you won't be able to ignore them and hope the problem goes away. The best way to win them over is with facts; explain carefully why you think their idea is wrong. Show them other games to demonstrate problems that would be caused by going down this route. Do a quick focus group with a few gamers and present them with both views. Use facts.

If you think you might have disagreements over critical issues, try to get the issues on the table as soon as you can. That way you can manage your resources better and avoid the trap of going down a path from which you might have to retrack later in your design process. For example, let's assume you license a character and story line from a popular book. In your game, you start to change the character in ways that you know might bother the licensor, even though you have really good reasons for doing so. It might be that you need to change the character and the storyline to make it more interactive, which is important to create the best gameplay for your game. If you take your dilemma to the licensor early on and explain the situation and provide examples, you might have a better chance of winning them over. But even if you lose, you'll be in a much better position, because then you'll know where the boundaries are before you waste valuable resources.

Reality Check: Focus group research can provide valuable ammunition in disagreements, providing you're right and you don't try and prejudge or bias the results. Chapter 13 deals with focus groups and market research in much greater detail. But don't be afraid to admit it if you're wrong. Even the best designers make wrong decisions occasionally. What makes them the best designers is that they can see when someone else's idea is better and they're not too proud to admit their mistakes. Being able to see the potential in other people's ideas and build on them is the mark of a strong designer.

Being Too Close to the Original

Some licensed games run into problems because their designers have stayed totally faithful to the original and have not properly understood that games are a very different medium than books, films, comics, and TV shows. A brief comparison of the different types of media is shown in Table 2.2.

Table 2.2   Comparing how different media is designed.

	Video Games	Films	TV Shows	Books
Typical length	12–15 hours	2–3 hours	10–22 x 30 minutes	3–15 hours
Development time	12–30 months	6–24 months	6–18 months	3–60 months!
People involved	20–150	50–500	20–100	2 (author & editor)
Format	Interactive	Linear	Linear	Linear

Let's imagine for a second that you've been asked to design a game based around the superb Oscar-winning film *Titanic*. The easiest mistake to make would be to follow the film storyline exactly; with Leonardo DiCaprio's character (Jack) winning a ticket, going on board, and dying at the end (sorry if I ruined it for you—it hit an iceberg, in case you missed it…). Your game would certainly be true to the license, but you're going to have enormous problems making the game interesting enough, long enough, and varied enough. Standing on the prow, painting a soft-porn picture, or getting cozy with Kate Winslet inside a carriage just isn't going to cut it gameplay wise. The only point at which you've really got a game is after the iceberg has hit. The gameplay at this point becomes much more interesting—swimming through submerged decks, avoiding rising water, dodging panicking people, being chased by a guy with a gun, and sliding down the deck as the boat sinks. But if you just play this section as Jack and stick totally to the story, it's going to last about 15 minutes, maybe an hour at a push. So don't stick too close to the original if it means you're not going to create a constantly exciting and challenging game.

As an aside, if I had to design a game around that license, I'd probably allow the player to control a whole load of different characters between the time the iceberg hits and when the boat sinks. I'd give each character an objective and allow the player to skip between them, helping each character achieve their goal. A middle-aged man might need to rescue his daughter from a flooded deck. A woman might want to reach the last lifeboat on the other side of the boat. Using physics, with objects and people flying around, a game designer could make this game quite an exciting experience while retaining the emotional power of the film by following a whole load of different personal stories. Another idea might be to play an explorer going down to the sunken *Titanic* and entering into a flashback that includes the story of the person associated with a unique object they find. This of course is part of the movie itself, but it could be played out uniquely a dozen times and include historical true and fictionalized stories of survivors or those who didn't make it.

Being Too Different from the Original

At the other end of the scale, I have seen some games that are so unlike the original license that they are pretty much worthless. If you want the game to review well and appeal to fans of the license, you need to understand and remain faithful to the key fundamentals. Consider the *Titanic* example again. If you set the game in modern times, allow everyone to survive, or (God forbid) get rid of the iceberg, you'll end up with something so far removed from the original that the product will sink faster than the ship itself. Additionally, the music in the film was very recognizable, so whatever route you go down, you'd probably want to include it.

The worst example of this problem in a real game was from the *Big Brother* TV show. A company bought the rights to the reality show, which has been really successful around the globe, and instead of doing something creative (maybe along the lines of *The Sims*), they decided to slap the brand onto—yep you guessed it—a basic run and jump platform game. The only licensed element was the characters' faces and the name.

 Reality Check: *No!* Don't do it. You know it's wrong. The business part of my brain wonders whether the development costs were so cheap that a game like *Big Brother* ended up making a small amount of profit, despite it not selling in big numbers. Still, again and again, I've seen that if you don't focus on quality, you don't succeed. If you lack the creative vision to develop a licensed property, consider doing something else instead.

Coming Up with Original Gameplay

Creating new original gameplay mechanics is one of the hardest and most important aspects of game design. There are very few hugely successful games that are just copies of other games. Great titles innovate and include original ideas and new twists on existing standards. The best way to come up with original gameplay is by brainstorming. Invite as many creative people in as possible, and toss around the characters, places, object, vehicles, and other elements of the license. Think about (and discuss) what could be done with them. Allow anything to be suggested, however crazy it may seem. Often some of the most original game design ideas come from crazy origins.

Here are some examples of original gameplay ideas that contributed significantly to the success of games:

> **"What if I could go anywhere and jump in and out of any vehicle in the city?"**
> *Grand Theft Auto 3*

> **"What if we allow the player to use slow motion for gunfights so he can see the bullets flying toward him?"**
> *Max Payne*

> **"How about we go into a third-person camera when you use objects or climb ladders?"**
> *Chronicles of Riddick*

> **"Let's give Luigi a sucking device that allows him to suck up almost anything in the room."**
> *Luigi's Mansion*

> **"How about we make a positive feature out of big car crashes?"**
> *Burnout 3*

Make sure your licensed game design contains some original and interesting elements that will make people go, "Wow, I wish I had thought of that!" If you do this, you'll have a great foundation for your game.

Creative Idea: Adapt a Book or a Movie in Your Mind

Pick a recent movie or book that you really enjoyed and think about what kind of game you would make from it. Would you follow the story exactly or take a more unusual approach? Also, think about what your perfect licensed game would be if you could work with any license. What would you do to make it so fantastic? Can you think of a unique gameplay mechanic that could help set the game apart?

Working with Outside Creative Talent

Any game created from a license will likely involve the cooperation of outside creative talent. This means that you'll need to get good at being cozy with celebrities, estates of famous actors or movie stars, and others such as producers. Let's take a look at some of the tricks of the trade for getting the most out of the creative talent that you might be working with.

Working with Celebrities

Dealing with celebrities can be really enjoyable, but to be absolutely honest, it can also be a nightmare. Some celebrities are superb; they are grounded, down-to-earth, and very excited to be part of a game. Others make thousands of demands, and they are never happy with their in-game likeness. These are the same celebs who don't show up at meetings and recording sessions, forcing you to constantly rearrange things. In my experience, quite a few well-known celebrities are used to having their lives planned out and organized in extreme detail. They will become distressed if things are not running like clockwork or if you ask them to do something unusual. Understand how they work, and agree upon what they are going to be doing in advance so there are no surprises. I could go on, but I'm sure you get the idea ….

 War Story: Timing Is Everything

My most embarrassing true story involving a celebrity was a very well known radio DJ who was promoting a game I was designing and producing. I was told to show up at his house early one morning to accompany him to a press event, and I eventually managed to wake him up after knocking and ringing for a while. I sat downstairs while he went upstairs to take a shower. While I was in his living room admiring his impressive décor and mantelpiece full of awards, his girlfriend came down the stairs, totally naked, to get a drink. She didn't know I was in the house and got quite a shock when she saw me. Fortunately, the DJ didn't mention it, but I reckon I was lucky to live to tell the tale since he was an awful lot bigger than I was!

From my years of experience in working with celebrities to develop games from licenses, I've come up with a couple of rules that have worked over and over. If you are designing a game that involves celebrities, pin these rules above your desk, or tattoo them on your arm if that helps:

> **Rule #1: Make sure there is a very clear and formal approval process with lots of spare time in the schedule.** As with all deals, being as clear up front is vital because most problems normally stem from confusion and changing requirements. Celebrities can have a limited attention span, and they can get quite busy with many people making demands on their time. You can't just expect them to

drop everything when you send them your game because you want them to review it. Plan out everything that involves the celebrities you are working with far in advance and make sure you let everyone know if the schedule changes. You could find yourself in the situation of needing a few minutes of your celebrity's time, only to find that they are unavailable for the next six months because they are on location in Morocco for their next blockbuster film.

Rule #2: Keep your fingers crossed, and hope your celebrity isn't going to be difficult! Most professional actors behave professionally, especially when they are involved with projects that can help their career. If you are having difficulty, try to get a few minutes alone with them and explain the situation honestly and openly. You can try going through their agents, but to be honest, they can often be overly concerned about offending the star (who makes them money) and therefore are not always the best resource for solving problems.

Reality Check: Actors and other celebrities are used to being pampered, but they're also used to working with professionals who get there on time, do their job really well, and make the most of their most valuable asset— *time*. The surest way to earn an actor's ire is to waste their time by not being prepared.

Working with the Estates of Dead Actors or Authors

As I've mentioned already, I had the good fortune to work on *The Great Escape* (see Figure 2.4), for which we had a deal with Chad McQueen, son of the late, great actor Steve McQueen. We put Steve's likeness into the game, used his image on the box, and even took some of his audio from the film and merged it into new FMV (Full Motion Video) sequences. His "estate" (essentially another word for his family) was superb to deal with, and I believe this is often the case with estates.

However, you need to remember one key rule when dealing with people who have died; tread carefully and with respect. You need to understand the boundaries, where you can and can't go. With *The Great Escape*, we were essentially re-creating a film, which simplified our work and our demands. But as games start to use famous dead Hollywood stars in new concepts, there is a much greater risk that game designers could use the characters in ways that the estate wouldn't like.

To avoid problems, make sure you first research everything carefully. This might sound obvious, but if the celebrity died in a car crash, you'll probably want to tread carefully around things like in-game driving sequences. Make it clear up front exactly what you want the character to do in your game before the license is signed. That way, the estate knows what you're planning, and it will help avoid nasty confrontations later in the project.

Figure 2.4
Steve McQueen's likeness in *The Great Escape*.

Working with Other Outside Talent

Sometimes you may find yourself working with "creative" people more directly involved with the licensor, such as a director or producer who wants to get involved with the game design and have real input into the process. You might also have to work with an author or scriptwriter who wants to make sure their vision is carried throughout the game.

Being honest, I think most people's instinctive reaction is to be protective and nervous about this; certainly that has often been my initial feeling. But it doesn't have to be a bad experience. If you can build a good working relationship with the creative talent and they are smart enough to understand where they can be useful and where they are overstepping the mark, then you may find that things work extremely well. It's great to be able to ask questions about the plot or ask why something was filmed in a certain way, and there are more similarities between the various media forms than most people think.

I would normally start by being as open and honest as possible. Explain what makes games such a unique design challenge. Talk about interactivity and the fact that the player needs to have the freedom to make their own choices. Explain how you would like the relationship to work, and how you feel the person can get the most out of the process. Listen to their ideas, but don't be afraid to be tough and explain why things aren't possible. For many people, it will be the first time that they have been involved with a game, and once they trust you, they may well just be keen to learn more about our fascinating industry!

Working with Licensors

As you learned at the beginning of this chapter, licensors are the guys who sell you the rights to make a video game from their license. They then approve various aspects of the game and receive a royalty from each copy sold (unless you are lucky enough to purchase a license with only an up-front fee). Licensors come in all different shapes and sizes; sometimes it might be a single creative vision holder who is passionate about the brand. Sometimes it can be a large team of businessmen who are just focused on the profit margin. The way that you deal with licensors will need to change a little, depending on what is important to them and who they are. Let's take a closer look.

The Approval Process

In theory, licensors want approval over everything. In practice, they are often very happy to let you worry about the gameplay and just want to tick off the look of the characters, the overall storyline, and the marketing assets. Some licensors want to be involved in absolutely every aspect, while others are happy to sign off on whatever you send them. Regardless of what kind of licensor you have, the key to everything is communication.

Realty Check: *Rule number one is always send your stuff in for approval well before you need it.* If you don't, you run the risk of the approval process taking too long and having a knock-on effect for the rest of your development cycle. In the worst case, you might not be able to hit your release date, and if your game is due out the same time as a film, TV show, or book, that's very bad news.

Let them understand how important quality is to you. Talk to them regularly. When you send something for approval, explain why it's important. If you can develop a good working relationship with the people who make the approvals, you'll find that things run much smoother. And don't forget that it's not a one-way street. They are there to help you as well. Ask them for assets. Get them to go through the archives and find the information you need to make your game even better.

Reality Check: Keep in mind that the licensor that you are working with is your business partner. If your game sells well, they really benefit. If your game fails, they also might look bad. If they object to something in your game, they might have a good business reason for doing this, so try to first hear them out.

Pick Your Battles Wisely

You won't be able to win on everything. Be smart and pick your battles to preserve your time and resources. Understand that if your licensor is complaining about something, there is probably a good reason for it. If he doesn't think your main character looks good enough, make the main character look better unless you really are pushing the limits of the technology. Just be careful not to let them try to do the job of designer. If their ideas are good, it's not a problem, but let's face it, there are reasons professional game designers and developers exist—they're good at what they do. Often when I've heard about the licensor meddling in the design too much, it can involve a specific person on the licensor side. This means it is often a personnel issue, not always a licensor issue. The best way to handle such problems is to maintain as many contacts as you can with a licensor, because if you don't, you will have no one to appeal to (up or down the corporate ladder). So the lesson is to not only pick your battles wisely, but also put some thought into who you pick a fight with.

Working with Film Licenses

Let's look at film licenses in more detail. The relationship between the film and game industries has never been more interesting. Companies like Union Entertainment (a company based in Hollywood specifically to put together movies and games) are blurring the line between the two forms of media, and film directors are thinking about how games can be made from their projects from day one. In fact, some directors and movie stars are getting actively involved in games. Vin Diesel had some involvement in the *Chronicles of Riddick* game via his own game company, Tigon Studios, and directors like Ridley Scott have been quoted as wanting to get heavily involved with a video game at some point. Steven Spielberg is now working with Electronic Arts on new games, and Peter Jackson is helping to make a movie from the *HALO* games.

Film licenses come in two distinct types: licenses for films that have already been released and licenses for new films.

Released Films

The key advantage to working with released films is that you know how successful they have been—they have an established popularity that you can measure. You can also get a sense of the type of audience a film attracts (which is really important for developing a game based on a film). Another advantage is that you can review all of the criticism that has been written about the film. You'll know how the film sells in different markets and you might even know if a sequel is planned for the film or if other films are coming out that might be trying to exploit the same theme. This all means there is less risk attached, and because the film has been completed, you can settle on your game design and storyline right at the beginning, without worrying about the film story changing. One key disadvantage is that you'll probably find access to materials, the director, and actors much harder to arrange than with a film that is currently in development.

New Films

The biggest advantage of working with new films is that they're current; if you can release your game alongside the release of a big new movie, you'll benefit greatly from the buzz that is created by all the movie advertising and promotion. You can also get much better access to the movie assets, which can be really important to a designer. You might even get the chance to visit the film set, talk to the key crew members, get all the actors in one place for recording sessions, and even use models, objects, and animations from the special effects studios.

The biggest disadvantage with a film that hasn't already been released is the risk; films can bomb badly, and the film might be heavily delayed, messing up your game schedule. The film may not even make it to a cinema release. And if the film release is delayed, you might have no other option than to delay the game. This can sometimes be an advantage if you can keep working on it to improve its quality (providing your publisher doesn't mind investing more money!). However, you may find that you have a completed game that will sit there, slowly dating as other games are released. This is not a good position to be in.

 Reality Check: When it comes to being on set with a film in production, everything takes a lot of coordination. Often the talent will require separate contracts to work on the game and the scheduling to meet up with them will be maddening. Once you do get the time allotted, be prepared. Furthermore, with the stress of release, DVD extras, behind-the-scenes crews, and now gaming, it can be a real juggle for the director/producers who work on the film. As a result, some of the talent balks at how much extracurricular activity takes place on their sets. Having a good relationship with a director can make a big difference, so be sure to see how they feel about a project before you sign on the dotted line for the license.

Regardless of which type of film you're working on, you have the advantage of a ready-made story with a beginning, middle, and an end. But don't be afraid to move away from this. As I have discussed, some of the best licensed games don't stick to the original stories, but instead build on them, run in parallel, or explore the past or future.

Working with TV Licenses

There have traditionally been far less successful TV licenses brought into the gaming world than film licenses. I think there are three key reasons for this:

- The film industry is much more tuned into games and better understands how to market its titles to games publishers.

- Only a small percentage of TV shows are successful on a global scale; they tend to be quite regional. When you're spending several million dollars on a game, you need it to sell worldwide in order to recoup your investment.

- The games industry doesn't understand the creative process that the TV industry uses very well, and hence tends only to look at a TV license once a show is already a huge hit. The problem here is that since a game will take at least eighteen months to complete, and there is no guarantee that the show will still be running in two years time.

- I believe that fewer TV shows are as appropriate for turning into games; lots of the most popular shows are either soap operas (like *Desperate Housewives*) or sitcoms (like *Friends*) that rely on great dialogue and character interaction, not on action and excitement.

Ironically, one of the most successful games to be spawned from TV was a quiz game, *Who Wants to be A Millionaire*, which followed the success of the show around the world. However, shows like *CSI* and *24* provide ideal content for games, given their themes and more action-based storylines. One developer, Legacy Interactive (**www.legacyinteractive.com**), has been particularly successful with its *Law & Order* games as well as it's *ER*-licensed game. As TV shows are watched worldwide thanks to DVD boxed-set sales and top-tier shows (think *24* or HBO's *Deadwood*) take on higher-production values, the TV licensing route may improve.

One of the biggest challenges with TV licenses is that they often consist of many 30- or 60-minute episodes. With a game, you ideally want a much longer storyline with a clear ending (unless you're making an episodic game, in which case the TV episode structure can be ideal). As with films, I'd recommend you use a professional writer to help convert an episodic TV format into a much longer and stronger game storyline.

 Reality Check: Using Moby Games (**www.mobygames.com**), you can search for writers that have successfully worked on games in the past. Some have professional TV or movie writing backgrounds in addition to their game work. While only a handful of such great game-design-savvy writers exist, depending on your license, it can be useful to track them down. My feeling is, as more scriptwriters grow up out of the gaming generation, finding writers who really understand gaming will be less of an issue.

Working with Book Licenses

Book licenses offer a unique design challenge, especially if the book is very popular. For the first time, you'll be putting images and graphics to characters and locations that readers have only ever imagined. Getting this right and understanding what was in the author's mind is key. If possible, you need to meet with the author and pick their brains. Draw up a big list of questions that will help you fill out the visual question marks. Talk to fans of the book, and try to understand what makes the book special to them. One big advantage with a book license is that you'll have a very clear storyline to work with, which is often much longer than a film script. As with all licenses, don't be afraid to adapt the book rather than stick to it rigidly. Games are a very different form of entertainment, and by adding in or removing elements or running your story in parallel to the book, you can often create something much more appropriate as the basis for your game design.

There are two more great things about book licenses. First, they are generally quite a bit cheaper than films or TV shows. Second, authors often write several books in a series, giving you lots of material to work from and a tailor-made choice of storylines for future sequels.

One of the most successful games based on a book series is, of course, the enormously successful Harry Potter titles (see Figure 2.5). EA worked closely with the author to make sure the game re-created her vision of the world, and they made the games extremely close to the stories, almost following them word by word. Arguably, they may have taken too little risk in terms of coming up with innovative gameplay, but they certainly did more than enough to happily satisfy fans of the books and sell many millions of copies.

Working with Sports Licenses

Working with sports licenses is very similar in many ways to working with films or TV. In my experience, the biggest single point of difference is that you're often dealing with some very gray areas, unless you have a massive all-encompassing deal. For example, with soccer games in Europe, despite the fact that you might have a license for a particular trophy or organization, there are still a whole host of legal issues about whether you can use player names in different countries, whether you can use the club's official kit, and so on. Some sports (particularly the smaller ones) have got their acts together, and when you buy their license, almost everything you need comes as part of that. But unfortunately, that is not normally the case.

Figure 2.5
Harry Potter.

So rule number one for working with sports licenses is to carefully examine exactly what the license allows you to do and to identify any areas that aren't covered and that will be important to the game design. Sports licenses by their very nature force you to design in a very tightly defined way; there is only so much you can do with a basketball game, for example. But that doesn't mean you have to turn off your creativity and design by numbers. Sports games can sell incredibly well and fall in two categories: evergreens and new creatives.

Evergreens

First, there are the evergreens that sell year in, year out. If you're working on one of these, creativity is definitely harder to achieve given the tight time frames, but one great idea can be incredibly important. Companies like Electronic Arts are always looking for a "killer feature" every year to help differentiate the game from last year's product. Coming up with this killer feature is tricky when you're on the 16th version of a game, but by utilizing increasing levels of engine power and technology (particularly when one generation of consoles transitions to another), it's possible to come up with features of a sport that just haven't been possible to simulate before.

2

For example, in a football game, greater levels of technology would allow you to simulate fans running down to the barriers and hurling abuse or praise as you run past celebrating a goal or a touchdown. I think it would be pretty cool in a soccer game to score and then taunt the opposition fans who have been giving you abuse and jeering you. Thinking about that leads me on to another idea—allow the player to decide how and where to celebrate rather than making it an automatic cut scene. This feature might be one worth considering in more detail. So, even for games that have been done so many times before, there are always new ideas to bring to the table, provided that your core engine technology keeps increasing.

New Creatives

The other type of sports games from my point of view are the "new creatives." These are not long-running brands, and they come out of nowhere. They sell because either the sport hasn't been made into a game before (or at least not in a while) or the game provides a fresh, interesting approach to the sport, offering something new to the players.

Designing this kind of sports game is even more exciting; you're trying to create something new and therefore you should be able to take a fairly unique approach. The most important thing you can do is to sit back and fully understand all the intricacies of the sport. What makes this type of sport exciting? What is best about the sport? Is there anything dull about the sport that you wouldn't like to simulate?

Finding sports that haven't been made into games before is obviously becoming extremely hard. However, there are always niche areas that you can fill, provided your publisher is happy to aim a game at a smaller marker. In Europe, there are companies that make successful "niche" sports games from rugby, cricket, and snooker. None of these are really the kind of sports that big publishers will touch—they're never going to be multimillion-dollar sellers. But there will always be a market for a really enjoyable game that is easy to control and captures the essence of the sport.

Challenging existing sports titles in a major sport is a more difficult proposition. You need to carefully analyze the existing titles on the market and identify a direction that will make your game clearly and distinctly different. Simply copying an established brand is never going to work and is pointless from my point of view. So, for example, if you're looking to take on *FIFA* and *ISS Pro Evolution* in the soccer world, you need to offer something new. Personally, I think it would be extremely tough to compete with these titles, but if I was going to, I'd explore a single-character football game along the lines of Sony's *Libero Grande* (where you play as an individual rather than a team) or focus on an online-only 22-player soccer game. Those examples are the kinds of major differences that will allow your game to get noticed and get people excited. But your game will also need to be incredibly enjoyable and addictive in its own right, and there lies the real challenge.

Summary

Hopefully you now have a good understanding of how to approach designing a game based around a license. I'm going to summarize the key guidelines that I recommend you try to follow when working on licensed games. Remember them, and you'll be much more likely to create a great licensed game that excites both the players and your licensor.

- **Be original.** Make sure you add original gameplay.

- **Work closely with your licensor.** Make sure you talk to your licensor right from the start, and have regular clear and open communication.

- **Research, research, research.** Research the license properly—know your property inside out.

- **It's good to talk.** Talk with the key people involved with the license, including authors and directors.

- **Don't be rigid.** Don't be afraid to adapt a storyline rather than stick rigidly to it.

- **Know your rights.** Know exactly what license rights you have and don't have.

In the next chapter, we're going to look at designing games for the various gaming platforms, from the smallest mobile to the latest next-generation console.

An Interview with Richard Leibowitz

Richard Leibowitz is cofounder of Union Entertainment, one of the hottest film and video game production companies in Hollywood today. Union is unique among production companies in that it also represents a number of the world's best video game development companies and specializes in packaging the companies it represents with content appealing to publishers, whether licensed or original. As the primary deal maker at Union, Rich is in constant contact with major players in the film and game industries and has a unique view of the link between films and games.

What do you think is the most common problem with film-licensed games?

RL: I've spent a large part of the past few years helping developers make film-based games and feel well qualified to say that our industry sells packaged goods rather than works of art. As a result, publishers, for the most part, don't license film properties, regardless of how great the underlying content or development talent attached. They license the mega-million-dollar film marketing and advertising campaigns and the brand awareness that comes along with it. For instance, anyone who's ever tried to sell a film-based game to E.A. Partners (EAP) knows that EAP will only consider games based on sequels of films that earned more than $100M in U.S. box office, regardless of the compelling nature of the content or the development talent attached. Many publishers are wary of film-based games for a variety of reasons, not the least of which include fear of missing release dates and relenting creative control:

- *Release Dates: The simple facts of the matter are that it takes longer to make a game than a film and today's game buying public won't support short-cycle "license slaps." So, even if a publisher is intrigued by the film and its gameplay possibilities, it may pass on the opportunity to publish the film-based game simply because there's no way to develop a quality game in time to take advantage of the film's prerelease marketing spend.*

- *Creative Control: Despite the game industry's long-standing, albeit tumultuous, relationship with Hollywood, film producers and studio executives may have unrealistic expectations with regard to the scope of game development in the short development cycle, have difficulty accepting whatever changes/compromises need to be made to make the property more appropriate for games, or, in general, are simply overprotective of their properties and often use their "licensor approval" rights to dictate the game's creative direction, all to the ire of publishers.*

Make no mistake about it, though, publishers covet the high-profile film licenses to anchor their product lineups regardless of product quality (although that seems to be changing) and will spend big bucks to acquire them.

Film licensors often have a reputation for being hard to work with. Is this true, and how can game designers help build better relationships with film companies?

RL: We're working on several projects with film talent and, although film producers and studio executives may have earned their reputation for being difficult, the creative talent involved in our projects has been great to work with.

Film talent wants to work with us and the developers we introduce them to because we provide them with an additional creative outlet for their projects, an opportunity to establish their project as an existing property, a better chance to set up their property as a film, and a chance to earn additional fees as a property owner, game producer, and/or game writer.

If someone is designing an original game concept, is there anything they should bear in mind if they want to have the best chance of selling it to Hollywood as a movie?

RL: With respect to games, movie studios seem interested in high-profile existing properties and original concepts.

■ Existing Properties: Studios are interested in established franchises and their accompanying built-in consumer bases (e.g., Tomb Raider, Resident Evil).

■ Original Concepts: Studios are also interested in untapped original concepts, whether they're from novels, comics, games, or elsewhere.

That being said, games are different than films (interactive vs. passive) and each is a specialty. Rather than single-handedly attempting to develop both games and films, I suggest game designers concentrate on what they do best—develop unique gameplay elements—and team up with a film producer to attach film talent (e.g., screenwriter) to develop the game story and resulting feature film.

Are there any film-licensed games that you think worked well?

RL: There are two ways to define success: financially and critically.

■ Financial Success: Obviously, the Pixar movie games (e.g., Finding Nemo, The Incredibles) have performed well for THQ, as have the DreamWorks movie games for Activision (Shrek 2). Activision's Spiderman and LucasArts's Star Wars games have also sold well. EA has made a habit of licensing huge movie properties and publishing successful games like Harry Potter, the James Bond games, and Lord of the Rings.

■ Critical Success: Critically speaking, Chronicles of Riddick: Escape from Butcher Bay is my favorite case study. Although the movie didn't perform well, the underlying content was great for games, and VUG partnered with film talent (i.e., Vin Diesel and Tigon Studios), hired a great developer (i.e., Starbreeze) and employed a "director" (i.e., Peter Wanat) to make a state-of-the art Xbox game.

Can you give any good examples of game IP that have worked well in Hollywood?

2

RL: Tomb Raider and Resident Evil both generated more than $100M in box office sales, an impressive achievement regardless of source material. There are other properties, like Namco's Dead to Rights at Paramount, Midway's Spy Hunter at Universal, and Prince of Persia at Disney, that exemplify studios' interest and investment in movies based on top-selling games.

We all talk about films a great deal, but what is your view on the relative lack of TV licenses in games?

RL: Actually, there are plenty of TV licensed games, just not on console. Check the PC section of your local game store and I think you'll be surprised how many hit shows have been made into games (e.g., CSI, Law & Order).

Games on console are a different story, though. Publishers are often weary of developing such games for two reasons:

- *Lack of Marketing Event: As mentioned earlier, publishers are most interested in high-profile film licenses because of the M&A spend and resulting brand awareness. Television properties don't receive the same kind of treatment and, thus, aren't that interesting to publishers.*

- *Timing: To make up for the lack of marketing event, television properties must build brand awareness (e.g., 24, Alias, Buffy, The Shield). Thereafter, the interested publisher must determine how popular the show will be by the time the console game is ready to ship a year or two later. No publisher can easily make such predictions and they all want to avoid what happened to Fox and VUG re: Dark Angel—a seemingly successful show is canceled just weeks before the game's release.*

Do you personally play many games?

RL: It's no secret that I spend more time working than playing games. I'm lucky, though, to have some gamers around me that can't help but play games as often as possible. So, even though I don't play a lot of games, I get to see a lot of them being played. In fact, I watched Dan Jevons finish Riddick in a day, Doom 3 in two days, and Half-Life 2 in about the same time.

What is your favorite ever game, and why?

RL: Tiger Woods Golf. I can school my friends, win some money, and walk away with bragging rights, all in an hour or so. If I really had to tee it up, I'd have to drain my wallet for the privilege of wasting an entire afternoon dodging hackers' errant shots (LA County courses) and settling my bets. I like other EA sports games, too, including NHL 2005, Madden, and SSX3. My favorite non-sports game has to be Halo (I haven't finished Halo 2, yet). The guys at Bungie designed a game that even a non-gamer like me can't put down.

What do you think is the biggest game design mistake that people regularly make?

RL: Game designers and their companies often fail to prototype core gameplay systems early enough in the overall development process. While a design idea may look good on paper (e.g., new style of control or innovative game mechanic), you'll never know how great or not so good the idea is until you build the prototype. Failure to do so may result in wasted production time, decreased net profits, and/or cancellation of the project altogether.

If money and technology were unlimited, what kind of game would you most like to see made?

RL: I've been extremely impressed with Half-Life 2, not only for the great graphics and physics, but also for the story-driven campaign and the desire of non-players to watch players play the game. As time goes by, games will appear more lifelike, stories will equal gameplay mechanics in importance, and players and non-players alike will be emotionally invested in games as entertainment. So, one way to answer your question is to say that we've established Union to produce story-driven games with unique gameplay mechanics that will be released on the heels of the related movies' marketing campaigns.

What do you think is the biggest challenge facing game designers as we move forward?

RL: My first reaction is risk-averse publishers. The game press has rightfully pointed out that publishers are extremely risk averse and the game industry is currently steeped in sequels and high-profile licenses that appeal to a wide audience. As a result, game designers don't often get a chance to showcase their talents and design unique and compelling gameplay. That being said, as games become more accepted as mainstream entertainment, more private money will flow into the game industry and more designers will have the chance to showcase their talents. I believe the biggest challenge facing game designers in the future is how to balance unique gameplay with compelling stories that engage players emotionally.

And finally, if you had one piece of advice to give to a game designer who was just starting work on a major film license, what would it be?

RL: Try to understand the core essence of what makes the film license unique, and then figure out a way to distill that essence into gameplay.

Chapter 3

The Art (and Challenge) of Designing for Game Platforms

"Computers in the future may weigh no more than 1.5 tons."
Popular Mechanics, 1949

As if designing games wasn't complicated enough, we have to factor in the differences between the various platforms that we are required to run them on. There is often a large disparity between the platforms, not just in the technology, but also in the demographics of the users. For example, the average PC owner is considerably older than the average PS2 owner (according to *Future* magazines in 2005, the average *PC Gamer* reader is 30, whereas the average *Official PlayStation 2* magazine reader is 23). This age difference has a major impact on the kind of games that work well and sell best. Also, each platform has is own unique controllers and input methods. For some platforms (e.g., mobile phones), the interface is largely limited to a small number of digital buttons that make fast "twitch" action gaming very tricky. The technology difference between the platforms can also be dramatic. Imagine designing a game to work on both a high-end PC and a mobile phone—not an easy proposition. But don't worry, I'm not going to recommend that as an exercise in this chapter!

Because of all this disparity, game designers are forced to construct very different game designs for each platform. It's hard enough if you're creating a design for just one individual console, but often you'll be required to design a game to work over a number of platforms. So how do you go about doing this and getting the most out of each format? The aim of this chapter is to help point out the differences of each key platform and give you some advice on how to approach them. I'll talk about the platforms that are hugely popular as I write this, but I will also cover the next generation of consoles, the ones that are about to launch (and may be old hat when you read this). I'll try to cover them in as much detail as possible, but since they are not currently released, please forgive me if I make any incorrect predictions. I'm sure it'll be much easier in hindsight!

Creative Idea: Play as Many Versions of a Game as You Can

Go out and rent a copy of the same game on as many different platforms as you can. Try to pick a game that has been released on as many formats as possible, from the latest next-gen console to a small handheld, or even buy the mobile version of the same game. Play each version for an hour, and take a look at what differences there are. Is the gameplay different or have they kept it the same? Does the game have the same levels on each platform, or has the game been fundamentally redesigned? Have the designers overstretched the weaker platforms by forcing the high-end design onto them? Try to guess what the designers were thinking, and why they made the decisions they did.

Striving for Platform-Independent Design

The ultimate way to design games for multiple platforms is to have a different development team on each version. That way, you can design each version independently to be the best game possible on that platform without having to make any compromises. You'll end up with the best quality results for each platform.

Unfortunately, the economics of the games industry normally dictates that this isn't possible. Making a game across three platforms would cost three times more than making it for one platform using this methodology. In reality, by sharing a common code base, and often much of the art and level design assets, it is possible to make a three-platform game for a relatively small additional cost over a single version. But if you're doing this, you'll need to design your core gameplay very carefully. You can't properly create one shared game design for three platforms. I think you need to identify a platform around which to create the initial game design and only then tweak that game design for the other platforms.

So how do you decide which platform to build your initial design around? I recommend you consider three ways of approaching this problem:

- Design for the most advanced system. Design your game for the most technologically advanced platform, and then cut back your design for the less-complex platforms. The advantage of this approach is that your game will look stunning since it will fully support the most impressive hardware. One disadvantage is that the other platforms can suffer, and there will often be lots of work involved in creating new lower-detail artwork and models. Also, you're spending lots of time on the most complex hardware, which normally requires more work and more people. Therefore your development effort and cost will generally be a little higher than in the next two options.

- Design for the most popular platform. Design for the system with the biggest installed base and then add or subtract assets and gameplay mechanics as necessary. Of course, this may be the same platform as in option 1, in which case, your choice is easy. However, using the last generation of consoles as an example, the PlayStation 2 has a bigger installed base than the Xbox. By designing your game specifically for the PlayStation 2, you are more likely to create a high-quality game for that platform. Other versions will suffer (especially more technically impressive platforms) since the game won't fully support all the extra memory, processor power, and features it can offer. But if you can only make one platform perfect, it makes sense for it to be the platform that will sell the most units (at least that's what your publisher will tell you!).

- Design for the most appropriate platform. Design your game for the system that suits your game idea the best, and then alter your design accordingly for other platforms. From a designer's point of view, this option makes perfect sense; your game idea will probably be more appropriate and suitable for one platform than another, so designing the main game with that platform in mind will surely make the best game. Sadly, you'll often find that not many people see things from a designer's point of view, and this approach is often not acceptable to the men (or women) with the money. Having said that, there are many types of games (for example, complex role-playing games, detailed real-time strategy games, and flight simulations) that generally work and sell better on PCs. The same is true with certain game types on other platforms. So if your game design is a flight simulator, you may find that potential sales are higher on PCs than on consoles. It's a complex issue, which is why sales staff from a publisher can be a great asset and carrying out research is vital.

Creative Idea: Pretend That Technology Is Here

Imagine that you had the ultimate console in your grasp. With an infinite amount of computing power, what would you use it for? When you've thought of an idea, see if there is a way to create that effect with current technology. For example, the technology behind PlayStation 2 games like *Dynasty Warriors* and *State of Emergency* does a great job of simulating hundreds of people on-screen at once. Although it isn't actually quite that many, it's a superb demonstration of how you can use old technology to make a world feel packed full of people. So imagine a game without limits, then challenge your programmers to create that effect within the limits. All platforms have a finite amount of power and memory, even the Xbox 360 and PlayStation 3, so make sure you push your programmers to challenge these limits, whichever platform you are working on.

What to Look for to Create an Independent Design

Later in the chapter, we'll discuss how you can work your design around specific platform features so that you can maximize the full potential of a platform. This is especially important for creating games that can make the most out of the technology that we have. But it's also wise to think abut some of the game design elements that operate independently, more or less, of the features of a specific platform. For me, there are five key areas where you may be able to share the same design over all the platforms that you may need to support. If you can share these elements across all the different platforms, the games should have the same feel even though the technology, size, and scope might be quite different.

Overall Design "Hook"

Every game needs a "hook"—a one-line description that summarizes what makes the game special and the key unique feature that will make people want to buy it. If you have a different hook for each platform, it will be really hard to get a common message through to the gaming audience and it will make it more difficult for the people marketing your game. So try to get a consistent hook (for example, "nonstop action with the most realistic fire effects ever seen in a video game"). Make sure this hook forms the basis of your design on all platforms. Although the mobile phone and Gameboy Micro platforms might not have the graphical power of a PS3, you should still focus on nonstop action and fire and make the fire look better and more realistic than in any other game on each platform.

Interface

Try to get a consistent interface and front-end design across all your platforms. Although the text and positioning will no doubt need to be changed a little for smaller screens, if you can get a common interface style across all your platforms, it will help define your brand and link the different versions together. Ideally, get your marketing creative guys in from the publisher early on, and define a single graphical design that works across the interface/front end as well as the box, manual, and point of sale material (which means posters, "shelf talkers," and other physical objects which will go into the stores when your game is released).

Gameplay Mechanics

It should be possible to take a few key game mechanics and implement them across every platform. So in the example I used earlier, having fire that can spread and quickly engulf a complete building is a cool, unique selling point (USP) that could form part of a key gameplay mechanic—the need to escape from a burning building and find the route out in a limited time while combating smoke and flames. On a PS3, Xbox 360, or PC, it is possible to make this look incredibly realistic. But there is no reason you can't use the same mechanic even on basic mobile phones. I can imagine a 2D platform game with spreading fire that could also work really well. So try to settle on a few key mechanics, one of which should form your "hook" that can be used across all the platforms.

Storyline/Characters

You should be able to have a consistent storyline with the same key characters across all platforms. You may need to shorten the story or simplify it for the less-complex devices, but you should still try wherever possible to have a single, powerful storyline regardless of which platform the player is using. Again, it will help your game to present a consistent message, and people playing it on a less-powerful platform won't feel like they're getting a bad experience.

Graphical Style

Although the various platforms will undoubtedly vary in their capabilities graphically, it should be possible to keep the same overall style regardless of whether your game engine is throwing around many millions of polygons or a few hundred 2D sprites. You may not be able to keep the same amount of graphical variety on mobile phones in particular, where memory space available for graphical textures is very limited, so try to identify the "key" graphical identity of your game (i.e., which of the levels is your "lead" level that gamers will associate with the game) and make sure that this style comes through on all the platforms.

Know Your Technology

Some people say that technology shouldn't affect game design. They think that game design should be a pure art form without being dirtied by real-world hardware limitations. I don't believe that this is true at all. Take a look at the classic games that have come out of Japan (like many of the Mario and Sonic titles) that have been designed entirely around a new platform. The designers have taken a clear knowledge of the new technology and used it to try things within the game design that haven't been attempted before. To be a truly great game designer, I believe that either you need to have a decent understanding of the technology behind the platforms or you need to be able to bounce ideas off someone who does. I don't mean you need to know how to program the processors, or even how much video RAM they have available, but you'll want to have a knowledge of what the platforms should be able to achieve and what each platform is best and worst at.

Technical issues like the polygon count (how many triangles the platform should be able to throw around at once) are not just for artists. By having an idea of how graphically powerful a platform is, you should be able to work out whether it will support your design for 32 enemies on-screen at once, for example. Having a rough idea of the memory available can help you decide how big your world should be and whether the programmers will need to stream level data from the DVD (which means loading new bits of level while you're playing, but in the background so the player doesn't notice). It's also useful to have an idea of the processor power, which will give you a rough clue to how clever the artificial intelligence can be. If you want 16 super-smart squad members climbing over obstacles and supporting the player while looking clever, you'll need quite a bit of processor time. Other aspects worth knowing are the music and audio capabilities of the platform, how online gaming works with the platform (play a few examples of online games to get a feel for this), and so on.

War Story: Make Sure You Have a Name You Can Use

One of the most fascinating platform launches ever was the "Enterprise 64." Rumor has it that the original name was going to be the "Elan Enterprise." Just before launch, with many of the consoles made and most of the launch marketing in place, the manufacturer found out that they couldn't use the name Elan because it was owned by someone else. In a desperate panic, they decided their only option was to call it the Flan Enterprise and file off the bottom of the *E* from the casings they had already made! One failed launch down the road, they then decided to drop the first name and call the computer simply the "Enterprise." But it was too late, and the platform failed to be a success. There is a lesson there— make sure a trademark search is done for the name of your new game (or platform) before everyone gets too attached to it and the product is about ready to ship! If you have a game name that hasn't been properly checked, you may find that early magazine previews and PR work is wasted if you have to change the name later. We now try to use obviously incorrect placeholder names (such as "Project K" or "Game 2") to avoid this very issue; otherwise, an "okay" temporary name might end up being the real name!

Table 3.1 provides a summary of key technologies and how these technologies can impact game design.

Table 3.1 Technical features and how they affect game design.

Technical Feature	Game Design Use
Graphics power (polygons per second)	This gives you an idea of how detailed the in-game environments can be, how many characters/objects you can have on-screen at once, and how many graphical effects you can have going at the same time.

continued

Table 3.1   Technical features and how they affect game design (*continued*).

Technical Feature	Game Design Use
CPU power	This gives you an idea of how much artificial intelligence you will be able to get running and how clever it can be. It also determines how powerful features such as physics can be; if you want to have very advanced physics in the game, for example, with lots of items flying around, you will need lots of CPU power to do the math.
Video memory	This gives you an idea of how many textures you will be able to have in a game. This is not necessarily an issue for a designer, but if your game engine can't stream new textures from the CD/DVD/cartridge, your game levels will be limited in size (unless you want repetitive textures everywhere).
Graphics chip features	Every graphics chip has its own cool technical features, and by reading what these are, you can come up with novel game mechanics that exploit them. For example, if a graphics chip can easily make glass that refracts things behind it (which looks very impressive), you might want to include a use for glass in your game design. When designing games for specialized chips, however, you should be mindful of the compatibility issues. If certain chips are not widely used, you could end up creating a game that would not run properly or have performance issues on machines that were lacking the chip.
Main memory	The amount of memory that a platform has will affect how big your levels can be without streaming and how much you can store on the platform. This is normally much more of a problem with consoles than on PCs, where there tends to be a larger amount of memory available. Memory size was widely regarded as the most limiting factor on the PlayStation 2. It's not really an issue you need to worry about unless you're designing enormous open worlds full of objects, in which case, you should check this out with a programmer who specializes in each platform you're designing for.
Disc/cartridge size	This could be a CD, DVD, UMD, Blu-ray, or cartridge and will determine how big your entire game can be in terms of memory size. For example, if you want a soundtrack of 100 songs, along with a huge amount of in-game speech, video cut scenes, and levels, you may run out of room on the storage device. With storage sizes increasing rapidly, it shouldn't be a problem that you need to worry too much about, but if your game is going to be especially enormous in terms of videos, sound, and music, you'll need to mindful of the storage issues.

continued

Table 3.1 Technical features and how they affect game design (*continued*).

Technical Feature	Game Design Use
Online functionality	What can the platform do online? Does it have its own matchmaking system to allow players to meet up or do you need to create your own or use an off-the-shelf system like Gamespy? Do players have headsets so they can talk to each other? Does the system support online video feeds so players can use a camera to see each other? Does the platform support downloadable content, micro-payments, and episodic games?These are all questions that you need to start asking yourself as you evaluate the potential of a platform for developing onlne gaming features.
Controller layout	What is the controller like? Every controller is unique and has buttons that work better than others. What are the default buttons that are easiest for people to use when they pick up the controller? Try to take a look at what other games are using and whether there is a "standard" control system. Which buttons are analog and which are digital? Is there vibration or force-feedback? Can it tell where the controller is in space, and how it is being rotated, like the Nintendo Revolution controller? Also check whether you have enough buttons to control all the functionality you want to put into your design.
Number of controller slots	How many people can play at the same time? If people have to buy an adapter to use more than two controllers simultaneously, will enough people have these to merit including four-player simultaneous play within a design?
Memory card size	Knowing how big the memory card is should rule in or out massive save games. For example, if you want to save player-generated audio or pictures for any reason, these will eat up save game space quickly. If you want to store huge amounts of data (for example, in a football management game), the save game space may fundamentally affect how detailed your design is.
Hard disc as standard?	Does the platform come with a hard disc? If it is an optional add-on, you need to decide carefully whether to support it since that will stop many gamers from playing your title. Some games rely on having a hard disc (for example, if you store long replays or if you have a rewind time mechanic or similar aspects). Also, if you rely on downloadable content for a future revenue stream, a memory card might not be enough to store this kind of thing.
Music/audio memory	How much memory is available for storing audio and music? If your game doesn't support streaming, you'll need to fit a whole level's worth of music and audio into memory. If you are using surround sound encoded audio files and lots of rich multilayered music, you may have issues if the platform doesn't have strong sound hardware.

continued

Table 3.1 Technical features and how they affect game design (***continued***).

Technical Feature	Game Design Use
Surround sound support	Does the console support full surround sound?
Other built-in sound features	The platform may provide audio effects like occlusion (walls and objects deadening sounds) and custom environmental effects (like echoing hallways) within the hardware. This means you should take full advantage of these features within your design since you essentially get them for free, without taking up any time from the main processor(s).

3

Common Platform Design Mistakes

I thought it might be useful to spend a little time examining some of the common mistakes made by game designers as they try to create games for multiple platforms. Hopefully, knowing about some of these real-world mistakes made by others (including myself!) will save you from making the same mistakes and wasting valuable resources. Trying to support multiple platforms is a challenging endeavor, and the more you think through your goals and plans, and the more you are aware of the pitfalls, the better off you'll be.

Don't overdesign: Here, a game gets designed for the most impressive and powerful platform, and then this high-end design is shoehorned onto the less-powerful platforms. This often results in slow frame rates, a clearly visible "edge of the world" where you can see the game environment popping in, and a generally suboptimal game on the lower-end platforms. In reality, the game design and scope should be carefully planned for each machine, otherwise the designers will end up throwing a complicated design at a platform that simply can't properly cope with it. This is often one of the big causes of delays in the industry.

Don't underdesign: Surprise, surprise—this is the reverse of overdesigning. In this case, a game has been designed to work well on the least-powerful platform, and then that design is moved onto all other platforms. On the most powerful platforms, even if the artists can improve the visual detail and effects, the player will still not be able to take full advantage of all the horsepower and features that the platform has to offer. Game players who have the version on the high-end platforms will think that the game is worse than other games because it won't take advantage of the unique features that the platform has to offer. This is a surefire way to ruin a really good game and rack up really bad reviews.

Don't make the different versions too different: Some multiplatform games are designed in complete isolation by different people for each platform. For example, the PSP version might be completely different than the PS2 version, which might in turn be completely different than the Xbox 360 version. There is a real danger with this approach because your consumers get misled. The marketing team won't want to send out mixed messages, so they will naturally focus on the most powerful version (Xbox 360 in this case). When gamers get excited by the advertisements and buy the PS2 version, they will likely be extremely disappointed when they realize that the game is nothing like the one they thought they were buying; maybe it isn't even the same genre or the same storyline or has a different main character!

Don't ignore the less-powerful platforms: A common trait among almost everyone in the games industry is to get excited by technology. The lure of the newest and most exciting platform is hard to resist, and many multiplatform games have bucket loads of attention lavished on the newest and most impressive formats, whereas the older less-glamorous versions (which ironically are often the ones with the biggest number of potential customers!) get relatively ignored. There is a genuine danger that designers can slip into the feeling of "Well, it's not great, but it'll do—it's only an old platform after all." You need to make sure you continue to push older platforms—gamers never want mediocre games, and the fact that your next-generation version is stunning isn't going to mean much to a gamer on an older platform.

Pushing Each Platform

In the first section of this chapter, we looked at the basics of how to design games so that they could work with different platforms. The goal is to take the elements that are common between platforms and emphasize that aspect in your designs. But each platform has its own strengths and weaknesses, and it's important that you try to push each version of your game to include as many of the platform's strengths as possible. The design challenge is that you need to be able to design for the unique features of a specific platform to get the most out of it but still create designs that will work for other platforms. It's really a two-layer approach; the inner layer, or the "core," is all the key stuff that is the heart and soul of your game. These are the things you try to take onto every single platform. The outer layer is the platform-specific stuff, which you can redesign and change to make it as perfect as possible for each format.

When you are supporting several platforms at the same time, it might not be possible to have enough people on each version to fully utilize all the strengths. But it's important to try to hit as many as possible, and when developing for consoles, you will be pushed hard into doing this by the manufacturers (currently Sony, Microsoft, and Nintendo dominate the market). On the PC platform, it's vital that you try to make your PC version as PC-friendly as possible; otherwise, you run a very real risk of being badly received by PC gamers and the PC press for simply releasing a poor console port.

War Story: Avoid the Console Port

One of the biggest platform challenges I run into regularly is designing the same game on a console and the PC. Since console games tend to sell in bigger numbers than PC games, we tend to focus on the console versions, making sure they are as perfect as possible. Unfortunately, due to the fact that there is only a limited amount of time and developers to work on a project, it doesn't always seem possible to spend enough time working on the PC versions as we should. At times they have often ended up being too similar to the console versions, which hurts in the marketplace. It's very easy to talk about pushing each platform, but this involves a great deal of discipline and organization to make sure that you have PC specialists on your team and that you spend enough time thinking about small changes and improvements to make a great PC title rather than a console "port."

I want to run through all of the main platforms that are around as I write this and take a look at what specific areas you should keep in mind when you're trying to maximize your design for each platform. I've also included the new generation of consoles, although given the fact that I'm writing this in 2005, it is very early for these platforms. In fact, as I write this, the big debate is whether Microsoft can do enough with its new console to generate an equal market share with the new cell-based PlayStation. Nintendo is going down the route of innovation, not competing in terms of raw horsepower, but instead coming up with a genuinely unique controller that should encourage very different kinds of games. Nintendo seems happy to watch the big mainstream battle from the sidelines while offering its own unique take on video gaming.

Designing for the PC Platform

PCs provide a unique challenge because you're not designing with a fixed technical spec in mind; your game will be run on a large range of different PCs, some of which will be more powerful than others. This needn't affect your design too much, but it is certainly something you should bear in mind. You need to work out which areas can be reduced in quality by users without affecting the gameplay. As a quick example, if the resolution of in-game textures is reduced to fit into the memory of a particular graphics card, your 3D in-game noticeboard, which provides the player with a vital clue, might become unreadable. Here are some things to think about when designing PC games:

- To maximize your design, you need to make sure you have really thought through the mouse and keyboard control. Many PC gamers expect to have fully definable keys.

- You may want to think about giving your gameplay a more strategic and tactical slant on the PC and maybe adding a little more depth to your PC version. PC gamers are, on average, a little older and more inclined to play games that require them to think, at least a little.

- You should also think about offering a level editor and giving players the ability to "mod" the game. Modding a game essentially means allowing players to customize it and create their own maps, game types, graphics, and sound. The mod community can be enormous for many games, and as a developer or publisher, it's important to keep in mind that it can extend the life of your game and keep fans of your game happy while you create the next installment.

- You should have a clear and quick installation process for your game.

- The game should provide help and advice about downloading the latest graphics drivers. It should also support both the latest graphics cards (for high-end PCs) and the lowest specification that is sensible. This will enable the largest number of PCs to run the game well as possible. This may not sound like a design issue, but your design decisions at the start of a project will have a large effect on the final minimum spec PC that it runs on.

- It is important not to release a buggy version of the game with the view "we'll patch it later." PC gamers are becoming increasingly frustrated by this (it seems to occur far too regularly).

- You need to think carefully about online gaming because it is such a key part of so many PC games. Can your game support online play, and if so, how can you make your PC online gameplay unique and stand apart from other titles?

The Future of the PC

The PC is a fascinating platform because it continues to evolve all the time. As I write this, Microsoft has just announced a renewed focus on helping build the PC as an even stronger gaming platform after several years of ignoring it in favor of its Xbox console. The big question for me is whether PCs will eventually find a place in the living room as the center of entertainment and media or whether they will remain on the outskirts, as they are now. It will also be interesting to see whether the traditional strategy and simulation games that have helped keep the PC such a unique platform will properly move over onto consoles. If consoles offer wireless mouse support, they could be a real threat to the PCs' long term future as a specialized gaming machine.

Creative Idea: Play the Leading Games on Every Platform

It sounds obvious, but it is important that you make the time to play the leading games on every platform so you get firsthand experience. This also means playing online games on each platform, both short and sweet one-off online games like *Battlefield 2* and persistent world online games like *Guild Wars* or *World of Warcraft*. Without firsthand knowledge of how the latest games are pushing each format, it will be very hard for you to design your game properly.

Designing for Sony PlayStation 2

The PlayStation 2 is currently the biggest-selling console in the world with a huge installed base of around 100 million units. Consider these points when designing a PlayStation 2 title:

- You will need to provide a careful and thoughtful implementation of the PS2 DualShock controller, including use of the analog buttons if possible and built-in vibration.

- It's obvious, but you should push the graphical level of the PS2 as high as possible.

- You will need to think about a memory card save system and consider using the PS2's online functionality (while remembering that this is still very patchy across territories such as Europe).

- Consider using the EyeToy camera peripheral as an additional gameplay feature— maybe capturing the player's face and using it within the game or allowing the player to play a subgame with it.

- Most high-quality PS2 titles now include Dolby Pro Logic surround sound, and you should try to make sure your audio design reflects this.

- If you are used to designing for the PC, remember that this generation of consoles is very different in terms of the display they use. The screen resolution is smaller, meaning you'll need to think carefully before porting a PC GUI to PS2. Sony has strict guidelines about how close to the edge of the screen you can place useful information because different television sets cut off different amounts from the screen edge.

The Future of the PS2

The PS2 has been a phenomenal success for Sony, and with so many consoles out there, PS2 game sales will continue for a good few years yet. But as publishers and developers start to switch their attention to the next generation of platforms, there will undoubtedly be fewer original titles, more sequels, budget titles, and licensed games that push the PS2 further. The good news is that this won't happen until the end of 2006 at the earliest. So 2006 should be a great year for the PS2; the machine should finally achieve maximum performance, and PS2 games should still be widely available throughout 2007 and 2008.

Designing for the Xbox

The Xbox was Microsoft's first attempt at creating a game console. It has been pretty successful (at least outside of Japan), especially in the online arena, where it has staked a dominant position. Here are the kind of things you should bear in mind when creating an Xbox-specific title:

- It's important to try to use all the additional on-chip graphical features that the Xbox provides over the PS2, which is one reason it's easier and quicker for developers to make stunning looking games for the Xbox as compared to the PS2.

- You'll need to give careful thought to the Xbox controller, which is noticeably different than the PlayStation 2 controller. Trying to use exactly the same system on the Xbox doesn't work well because there are two triggers rather than four and the black and white buttons are in a very unique position. Unlike the two extra trigger buttons on the PS2, you can't press them while using the two analog sticks at the same time.

- The Xbox offers you a hard drive, and Microsoft wants you to use the hard drive to speed up reloads. You may also want to consider using the hard drive to provide a unique gameplay feature. For example, you can use it to store lots of replay data, rewinding time, and so on.

- You should definitely try and use the Xbox Live online system for gameplay or, at a minimum, for updating scores to a high score table. Microsoft has a better and stronger online implementation than Sony in this generation, and you should try to take advantage of it.

- Most key Xbox titles support Dolby Digital surround sound, so you should try to make sure this is implemented.

- Consider the specific demographics of Xbox owners (who are considered to be more hardcore gamers than PlayStation 2 gamers). Mass-market games haven't fared very well on Xbox, and although Microsoft is trying very hard to change this situation with it second console, it's not a good idea to rely on strong sales of a mass-market family title on the first Xbox.

The Future of the Xbox

The future of the Xbox looks decidedly less rosy than the future of the PS2. Sony has a superb track record of supporting its older platforms for a long time, but there is a feeling within the game community that Microsoft will focus almost all its efforts on the Xbox 360. It is rumored to be losing quite a lot of money on each Xbox it sells, and it doesn't appear that it can launch a cheaper, smaller version like Sony has been able to do. So my instinct is that while PS2 games will still be selling well right through 2007, the original Xbox might be a fairly dead platform by that time.

Designing for the Gamecube

As with most Nintendo consoles, the Gamecube is unique in terms of its design, technical specifications, and the kind of games and game players that it has become associated with. Nintendo also has an unusual approach to third-party games and publishers (third-party just refers to other publishers that are not connected to and don't work directly for Nintendo). Whereas Microsoft and Sony are good at courting publishers and developers, helping them out and making it easy for them to work on their platforms, Nintendo doesn't have the same mindset when it comes to supporting these third parties. At least in Europe, it's difficult to even get much information and support from Nintendo, and the company seems to be much more focused on creating its own first-party games. If you're creating a Gamecube title, think about the following:

- The controller is very different from both other console platforms, so you need to think carefully about the Gamecube controller and how your game works with it, especially the smaller number of buttons available to you. It essentially has three trigger buttons, which can make for an interesting challenge if you are porting a PS2 game.

- The Gamecube has quite a unique graphics system, so speak with your Gamecube programmer and try to support these strengths as much as possible.

- Game saves are made to the Gamecube memory card in a way that's similar to how they're made to the PS2.

- It's important that you consider the specific demographics of Gamecube owners. They are a very hard bunch to pin down; they tend to be slightly younger and more hardcore at the same time! Designing the game to appeal to them as much as possible is an important consideration. Quality is more important to Nintendo customers than to any other platform (this can be seen by the much higher correlation of sales to review scores with Nintendo games than the other platforms), so it is much harder to get away with anything less than superb products.

3

■ It is important to support Dolby surround sound, which is normally Dolby Pro Logic on the Gamecube.

The Future of the Gamecube

As I write this in late 2005, we are currently only making the occasional Gamecube title, and these are primarily for the U.S. market, where Gamecube sales are still fairly good for the right product. However, I expect this to continue to dry up over the next 12 months.

Designing for the PSP

The PSP is a superb piece of hardware, but only certain types of games really show off its full potential. You really shouldn't expect to port a game from the PlayStation 2 and assume that it will be fine. Here's what you should consider if you are designing a PSP title:

■ Think about screen resolution, which is smaller than standard console games. You'll need to think carefully about your GUI and on-screen messages. The fonts you use will need to be readable on a relatively small screen.

■ Think about the problems with streaming, which is dynamically loading sections of the environment, graphics, and sound from the disc while the player is playing the game. Streaming is a process that is done in the background so the player isn't aware of it. However, it eats battery life, something that the PSP isn't blessed with. Therefore, you'll need to think about creating smaller, self-contained levels. This in itself isn't necessarily a bad thing. On portable devices like the PSP, players want to pick up and play games for much shorter amounts of time than on a console. For example, you might be on a train for 10 minutes and want to play through a quick level. Streaming is allowed, but Sony definitely prefers games to limit streaming wherever possible.

■ You need to think about the save system and the structure of your game. You should allow people to play it in quick chunks and ideally save whenever they want to or else use closely spaced checkpoints at which the game is saved automatically.

■ Think about the control system. There are a limited number of buttons, and the analog stick doesn't move and operate as it does in traditional console game pads. There also isn't a second analog stick on the right, and there are only two trigger buttons.

The Future of the PSP

I believe the PSP has a fantastic future ahead of it. After a fairly successful global launch, and with some really heavy-hitting titles now appearing on it, the PSP has the potential to become one of the most successful handheld game devices ever developed. When you add in the MP3 playback, the ability to display photos and films, and the undoubted visual appeal of the unit itself, you have a very unique piece of hardware that turns heads. I have very high expectations for the PSP over the next five years and I'm certain that the quality of games can improve dramatically as well. I'm anxiously waiting to see what the next generation of developers will be able to get out of the hardware.

3

Designing for the Nintendo DS

As with many Nintendo devices, the DS is a truly unique portable gaming system. It uses two screens (one of which is touch sensitive), which provides some great opportunities. The use of two screens also introduces a design constraint because you really need to think of a special use for the bottom screen. Here's what you should consider when designing games for the DS:

- Decide how you want to use the bottom screen. So far, the typical approach has often been to use it for something fairly dull, such as using it to display information that is normally shown on the main screen (health, score, and so on) or as an additional set of rarely used controls (for example, moving the camera or triggering special moves). What is more interesting is that it actually works pretty well as a main controller in its own right, either with the stylus or the plastic finger pad that is part of the carry strap. It can be quite daunting using it as a main controller, especially given that it is directly below the main screen, so I'm currently not sure whether enough people will be happy using it to make it a sensible choice for fast-action games. But for more unique titles, such as *Warioware*, which is packed full of short, snappy mini-games, it's perfect. EA's *Tiger Woods* game demonstrates how it can be used to allow new control systems; in this example, a fluid stylus input acts as your golf swing. It's also nice to use it for menu selection (just touch what you want).

- As with the PSP, you need to think about the limitations you are given, which are even greater in the case of the DS, both in terms of overall technology (which is considerably lower than the PSP) and the lack of an analog stick.

- The DS also doesn't have the power to display full-quality fast-moving 3D images in both screens directly. This is why the lower screen is normally 2D when the top screen is being used for 3D. Bear this in mind with your design, and try not to confuse the player by requiring them to look at both screens at the same time!

The Future of the DS

The DS is already proving itself a breath of fresh air in the gaming market with its innovative design and some superb new titles. Games like *Nintendogs* show the biggest strength of Nintendo—creating addictive games for the masses that are unusual and yet hugely compelling. In my mind, there is definitely room for the DS and PSP to coexist. They are aimed at different people, and the DS is unashamedly a cheap gaming machine rather than an expensive multimedia device. I think the DS has a strong future ahead of it if Nintendo can continue to improve its support to third-party companies.

Designing for the Microsoft Xbox 360

The Xbox 360 is the second Microsoft console and has online gaming at its heart. It's an extremely powerful machine capable of stunning visuals and superb audio. Here's what you should bear in mind when designing games for the Xbox 360:

- Fundamentals: There are a number of fundamentals that Microsoft insists you have in your games, including support for high-definition television, wide-screen (16:9) screen format, and surround sound audio.

- Online: The Xbox Live system has been greatly extended to provide all sorts of new functionality. Make sure you use online elements in your game wherever possible, and plan to provide downloadable content to help support your customers.

- Make sure you utilize the huge amount of raw processing power available in the next-generation consoles. Don't fall into the trap of assuming that your gameplay will be the same as before, but with nicer graphics. It will be possible to move gameplay to a new level. A simple example is a fighting game where the extra horsepower allows you to have a large number of characters, proper deformable environments, full and detailed physics on everything, and realistic cloth, hair and other animating objects. It will be possible to create gameplay that simply wasn't possible before. For example, imagine a huge bar-fight with thirty people all fighting each other, throwing each other into furniture and gradually destroying everything in the room. This kind of experience has never been a feasible proposition in real-time until now.

- Microsoft is promoting the use of the 360 as a multimedia machine, so think about whether you can incorporate photos, audio tracks, and video footage from the console in your games.

- Remember that the basic 360 model does not come with a hard drive, so if you create a game that relies on a hard drive, you will be limiting your audience. It may be that Microsoft insists that all 360 titles run without needing a hard drive.

The Future of the Xbox 360

Microsoft has a battle ahead of it to usurp Sony as the leading game console manufacturer. But early feedback on the 360 has been encouraging, and this may be the machine to help Microsoft gain an equal share of the marketplace. Until the PS3 sees the light of day, it is hard to tell whether the rumors about it being more powerful than the 360 are true in practice. What is apparent is that Microsoft is hitting the ground running; it is clearly the leader in the fast-growing online gaming market, and it is absolutely determined to take first place. With its resources and superb support of third-party publishers and developers, I wouldn't bet against Microsoft.

Designing for the PlayStation 3

The PlayStation 3 is an extremely powerful multiprocessor console, with more brute force than the Xbox 360. As I write this, none of the next-generation consoles have launched, so it is difficult to distinguish too much detail between the Sony and Microsoft consoles. My advice here is similar to the advice I gave about the Microsoft Xbox 360: remember the fundamentals of high-definition video and audio support, and think about creating new gameplay that hasn't been possible before. With regard to online gaming, it is likely that Microsoft will continue to have an edge in this regard, but a majority of PS3 titles are likely to make major use of online gameplay.

The Future of the PS3

Sony is a great company, and there is no doubt that the PS3 will be an incredibly powerful machine. It will be fascinating to see when it launches and how Sony responds if the Xbox 360 launch is a big success. With the track record of the PlayStation and PlayStation 2 behind it and deals in place to have exclusive periods (where rival platforms cannot be launched) with brands like *Grand Theft Auto*, Sony will no doubt enjoy continued success. Whether it can restrict Microsoft from making inroads into its market domination is the big question. Another big question is how easy it is to develop games on the hardware. The PS2 was considerably more difficult to get the most out of than the Xbox, and Sony has been working hard, bundling tools and middleware to make things easier for developers. But the proof of the pudding remains when final debug kits go out, and as I write this, programmers are only just finding out how much of a beast the PS3 is!

Nintendo Revolution

Other than the stunningly original controller, little has been announced about the Revolution. It's clearly less powerful than the two competing consoles, so you'll need to think carefully about the scalability of your game if you are creating it for the Revolution as well as the Xbox 360 or PS3. But the Revolution doesn't seem to be about power; Nintendo seem to be steering away from a direct technology battle with Sony and Microsoft, and are instead positioning themselves in a very different space. The Revolution isn't a multimedia machine; it's a games machine with a real difference: the controller.

The controller is where the Revolution will come into its own, and it should make for some extremely unique control systems. The standard controller comes in two parts: a remote-control style unit which you hold in your right hand, and a small trigger/pad unit which you hold in your left hand. The two units are attached via a cable. What makes it special is that the remote control style unit can detect how it is being moved and rotated. So if you wave it around, the game can tell exactly where it is in 3D space, and how you are turning it. This should make for some truly intuitive gaming. Wave your controller like a sword, and your in-game sword will move in the same way. Use the controller as a baseball bat and smash in-game pitches into the distance. Point the controller at the ceiling to reload a gun. The possibilities are endless.

Techniques for designing games for this kind of control system would fill an entire book, but I would advise you to think carefully about how best to control your game, and throw out all your preconceptions before you do so. Tradition says that first-person shooters are controlled using one or two analog sticks; but with the Revolution controller, the player can point the remote in the direction they want to look or move, which might making aiming even more intuitive than with a PC mouse.

Nintendo has proved very adept at thinking a little differently than its competitors, and hopefully the Revolution will be such a "revolution" that people will want to own both it and another more mainstream console. The fact that the controller looks like a traditional TV remote control, and that players don't need to be adept at using two sticks while pressing a multitude of buttons should make this platform attractive to a new audience. There are many people who are scared of game controllers, and these are the kind of people who enjoyed the Sony Eyetoy or Singstar, which allows them to take part very easily. Hopefully, the Revolution will hit this potential audience head on.

Apple Mac

Apple Macs have had a patchy record in terms of games support, but as sales continue to grow with smaller and cheaper models, Mac games are becoming more important with publishers. The links between the Apple Mac and the forthcoming Xbox 360 may also help this process (the first Xbox 360 development kits came in the form of modified Apple Mac PC's!). In terms of technology, Apple has a unique position in the marketplace. The Mac is not often changed or customized by its owner, which means that on average, Mac gamers do not have as powerful machines as PC gamers. However, the nightmare of having seven billion different combinations of graphics cards, memory sizes, processors, and sound cards is not an issue with the Mac. This obviously makes QA testing much easier. The best starting point would be to identify the specs for the Mac that will be current when your game is due to launch and build your design around that level of power, although Mac games most often are almost direct ports of PC games! Also remember that most Macs have only one mouse button, which is a real challenge in terms of mouse control for games.

The Future of the Mac

With a stunning new operating system, Tiger, and the huge success of the iPod/iTunes, there is a real feeling that the Mac is really making inroads into the home (and no longer being predominantly a professional art/music/video production tool). More and more games are being ported to the Mac (often by third-party companies specializing in this process). If Apple plays its cards right, it's possible that the Mac could end up as an important platform just as the PC is, and this might be one of the reasons why Microsoft is renewing its commitment to support PC gaming!

Mobile/PDA Gaming

The gulf between high-end consoles and the bottom-end mobile phones and PDAs is simply enormous. Fortunately, the days of WAP (Wireless Access Protocol) gaming (pretty much dreadful multi-choice text adventure games) are long gone, and the latest mobile phones feature support for some decent 3D games. Designing games for mobile phones is a fascinating challenge. It's very hard as the range of phones is enormous. At the low end, you have no 3D and you are limited greatly by the basic graphics performance. At the high end, it's possible to do some quite impressive 3D titles. Regardless of the technical power of the phone, you have to remember the major limitations that you must work around.

War Story: Count Your Blessings

One mobile developer told me that he was creating a game for 210 different phones, each of which was slightly different and had to be tested and debugged separately. When you're worried about coping with a console game on three platforms, remember what the mobile developers have to put up with!

One of the toughest challenges facing mobile game designers is the huge breadth of technology. You will often need to design a game at least twice—once for the high-end phones and again for the more basic (but also more common) models. Another major challenge is the input. You are stuck with a poor digital stick (if you're lucky) and some poor digital pads with numbers on them. This makes the situation a real nightmare if you are used to console game design, and you have to create your game accordingly, not penalizing the player for a taking a little longer to press a button and not expecting the player to press multiple buttons at the same time. You also have a fairly low-resolution screen, which means that on-screen displays and text need to be carefully planned; don't expect to be able to show too much at once. Finally, many mobiles currently have very little storage space, which means that games often need to be no more than 100 to 300kb in size! Compare this to a new console game, which can be anywhere from 4 to 12Gb! This means you might have to create a game that is 48,000 times smaller!

Having said all that, it's often a case of looking back to older games from the early days of video games. The limitations don't mean that you can't create something that is fun; it will just be very different than the same game on other platforms. One ray of sunshine is that mobile technology is expanding rapidly. One generation of consoles might last five to seven years, whereas most people buy a new mobile phone every year or two. I fully expect mobile games to be at the level of Gameboy Advance or even Gameboy DS within a few years. I just hope the guys who design the mobile phone handsets think more about user input!

Creative Idea: Base Your Idea on a Great Retro Game That Hasn't Been Reinvented Yet

Play through some old games that have been created for retro consoles or home computers. When you find a game you really like, ask yourself why you like it. See if there is a gameplay mechanic or an idea that you can take and apply to modern-day gaming. Truly great ideas rarely go out-of-date. By spending a bit of time taking a close look at what has been done in the past, you might gain a better perspective on the elements that go into designing great games that stand the test of time.

Designing for Future Platforms

In the final chapter of this book, I will take a look at the future and what it might hold for video game design. In terms of platforms, increases in technology will continue to keep the game business at the cutting edge in almost every field. More processing power means that we'll be creating the most advanced AI in almost any industry. Greater graphical power means that we'll be creating true CG-quality scenes within 15 years (the kind of things you see in the latest movies). Sounds will continue to be richer and more lifelike as everyone starts to use surround sound and true occlusion and reverb find their way into games. In short, the challenges ahead are going to be incredible. But technology will reach a limit. After all, when graphics become truly lifelike, what can you do next? When sound is perfect, where do you go next? Games won't be able to rely on technical prowess to make them best-sellers. What they will need more than anything else are talented game designers to come up with unique concepts and novel gameplay. That's where you come in.

Summary

In this chapter, I've tried to provide an overview of the platforms that are currently used by gamers. We started out looking at the best ways to design games so that they can be developed for multiple platforms. Then we looked at the major platforms in a bit more detail to flesh out some of the important design considerations. In the next chapter, rather than looking at different kinds of platforms, we're going to be looking at different kinds of gamers and how you can design a game for specific groups of people.

3

An Interview with Ben Gunstone

Ben Gunstone is a producer at revitalized global publisher SEGA. With a long history of producing high-quality games, Ben is most recently responsible for titles like *Virtua Tennis* as well as the superb *OutRun 2*, based on the arcade sequel to one of the most influential driving games of all time. With *OutRun 2*, Ben has experienced and mastered the challenges associated with converting a successful arcade game to console.

What do you think is the biggest difficulty when converting an arcade game to a console?

BG: By far and away, the biggest challenge is taking a fantastic 3- to 5-minute arcade experience and then giving it enough longevity for console users. A straight arcade conversion just isn't enough in today's marketplace.

Why do you think that *OutRun 2* has got such strong reviews? It must have been hard meeting the high expectations that fans of the arcade game had.

BG: It has reviewed extremely well throughout the U.S. and Europe. It helped that the arcade version was so spectacular; we were building from a very solid base. All we needed to do was find some magical longevity to complete the full package. I always knew OutRun 2 had a strong following; it was a favorite of my own youth. But I never quite realized the strength of that following. In a way, we picked up on this in our advertising as well, with the tag line of "Let the love affair begin... again." My main objectives, however, were not to reach the fans' expectations but to meet AM2's (the Japanese-based SEGA Arcade team). They have probably the highest quality levels that I have ever worked with before. You know that if it passes AM2's critical eye, the fans would be definitely pleased.

Did you refer to the original *OutRun* arcade game, or did you base your game solely on the sequel?

BG: The conversion contains the original OutRun classic as a hidden unlock. We felt this was a definite must and everyone we spoke to about this project asked if we were going to include the original. I suppose the way the mission structure is laid out harkens back to the original game as well. It is set up in a 15 mission pyramid grid exactly as you would race through the stages in the original.

How did you address taking the same gameplay and visual style onto a very different piece of technology? Was there anything you wanted to do that you couldn't?

BG: Technology was easy (says the non-programmer!). OutRun2 arcade was running on the "Chihiro" board. This board is basically an Xbox with 128MbRAM. All Sumo (the development team) had to do was compress the memory usage down to 64Mb RAM and hey, bingo, we had a game. This is where SEGA Europe's choice of Sumo Digital really paid dividends. Sumo managed to not only compress the original levels to fit into 64Mb by utilizing some nifty lighting techniques and rewriting the memory manager, but they also managed to show eight cars on the screen at one time (the arcade version only ever did four). The reason why so many reviews state the game looks so much like the arcade is because it damn well is!

The only thing we couldn't do in the time frame was to get traffic into live play. The arcade machines were designed to play four-person multiplayer but linked through 100Mb direct connections. Therefore, lag or packet loss was never an issue. Obviously, when playing over the Internet, this is an issue and the traffic system just couldn't cope with it.

Was it hard reproducing the feeling of the arcade game using a console joypad?

BG: Again, we have AM2 to thank on this count. Leading up to E3 of 2004, we were hard at work tying a demo together. This was to be OutRun2's first public appearance and we had to make sure the handling was spot on. Sumo had tried to get the handling right but it never quite hit the mark. Having worked on a few driving games, you get a feel for the handling more from other players, especially ones who haven't played the version before, as after a while it can become difficult to judge for yourself—you almost get used to the handling quirks. After the fourth or fifth handling tweak from Sumo, I would get comments from users about it being a bit heavy or light or a bit too easy to pull off a power slide. What Sumo did then was open up the handling parameters into the front end. We sent this build off to AM2 and a week later, the magic numbers came back. Sumo implemented the numbers and, hey, presto—not another sound came from our testers; everyone was very happy. In a way it felt like AM2 sprinkled a bit of "magic gameplay dust" over the game at that point but that actually diminishes what was done. A designer at AM2 sat down and played the Xbox version, tweaking numbers until he got it exactly right—no mean feat!

What are you most proud of in your career so far?

BG: OutRun2 has definitely got to be my career peak so far. But working for SEGA Europe also puts me in a position where I can work on a number of very high profile SEGA IPs (all of which have a strong fan following).

What is your favorite ever game, and why?

BG: Probably the game I have played the most is Everquest. Saying that, it's probably not my favorite as it was a sort of love/hate relationship (anyone who has played EQ for any length will understand this feeling). As for the game that I think back most fondly of... probably Black Bass Fishing on the NES. It was a cracking game that combined the fun of fishing into a level gaining game (i.e., catch so many pounds of black bass to get to the next lake where bigger fish await).

What do you think is the biggest game design mistake that people regularly make with games?

BG: Mixing up game rules with real-life rules. You wouldn't believe the number of times I hear "Well you can't do X in real life." In the end, the game has to be designed to be consistent with its own rules.

If money and technology were unlimited, what kind of game would you most like to see made?

BG: A game where you can interact with everyone and everything, where every decision you make has a real knock on effect to the world you inhabit.

What do you think is the biggest challenge facing game designers as we move forward?

BG: Managing the players' expectations. As consoles become more powerful, I think users will expect to see more than just prettier graphics. They will want total immersion with the product they buy.

And finally, if you had one piece of advice to give to a game designer who was tasked with taking a game from one platform and moving it onto another, what would it be?

BG: If it's a straight conversion, I'd tell him to get another job as we don't need him. If the conversion also involves adding more content, the rules really need to be followed. You have got to know the game inside out and you must treat it almost as if it is a new game again. Follow those two rules, and make sure you don't trip up any set rules from the original, yet allow yourself enough room to add something really new into the pot.

Chapter 4

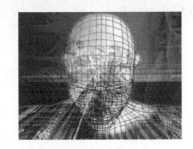

A Break from the Norm

"No one would think of denying that video games are big, but few grown-ups outside the business have an understanding of just how big they've become."

Jonathan Dee

Gone are the days when a game designer could think about a cool game idea, sketch it out in the back room, have it developed, and create a blockbuster game. The fierce competition, high stakes development costs, and demanding public have drastically changed the dynamics of the industry and how games need to be designed. In many ways, the games industry has evolved as the movie industry has. A designer now needs to consider age groups, market segments, niche topics, and a host of other factors in order to be successful.

This may sound suspiciously like "publisher speak" if you're working for a developer, but it's true. The good news about the games industry today is that it has expanded to such a degree that a designer can be successful in creating games for unique audiences such as women gamers or people interested in using games for serious learning and training. The bad news is that as a designer, you really need to understand these different markets. Hopefully, I can give you an overview of these areas and help you understand the design opportunities and constraints that they offer.

In this chapter, I'll give you ideas on how to design your games for different kinds of people, as well as how to create unusual types of games and applications. I have divided the chapter into two parts. In the first part, we'll look at how to design games for different demographics. Here I'll discuss important techniques for creating games for specific types of people, whether the focus is on young or old gamers or female players. In the second part of the chapter, I'll discuss how you can create unusual and highly innovative games, as well as how to use game technology for non-game applications. We'll look at techniques for designing budget games, and then I'll discuss how to use game technology for other areas, such as creating films, an area known as Machinima, which has really taken off over the last few years. Another field that is growing rapidly is the area of "serious games." It's such an interesting and relevant area of game design that I've given it its own chapter (see Chapter 15).

What all of these topics have in common is that they involve a need for game designers to step out of their comfort zone. As designers, we need to learn how to think a little differently and to target games at areas that aren't traditionally addressed by typical game developers.

Designing for Demographics

You might be wondering what demographics is all about and why you need to care about it. After all, what do demographics have to do with the real issues of designing and making games that gamers want to play? Let's start by looking at a dictionary definition of *demographic*.

> **Demographic (dem·o·graph·ic) *adj*: Relating to the study of the characteristics of human populations, such as size, growth, density, distribution, and vital statistics.**

Understanding demographics is especially important if you want to design a game for a specific targeted audience, and in particular a non-core game audience. In plain English, I'm talking about games for older gamers or very young gamers. Other specific and important niche areas are "serious" business/educational games and games for people with particular handicaps. It's also important to look at the issues involved in designing games specifically for women, although as you'll see in a minute, women are now playing almost as many games as men and are rapidly becoming a huge and important part of the existing gaming audience. Many women play games that have been designed with men in mind, but this is something that is changing and will continue to change as the industry gets increasingly more professional. Some women will play typical male-oriented titles, but many more women will play titles that have been created with them in mind. Games like *The Sims* and *Nintendogs* demonstrate how original female-friendly titles can also be extremely high-quality games with much broader appeal.

The majority of games are designed for the mass market. But most people in the industry have their own unique interpretation of what the phrase "designing for the mass market" means. For me, it means aiming your game at the average age, average gaming skill level, and most common sex of video game buyers. In other words, the goal is to reach the largest game-playing audience as possible. You may be surprised at how old the average gamer is. A survey compiled in the United States by the Entertainment Software Association (ESA) and released in 2004 found the average age of people who play games is 29, and 36 is the average age of people who actually bought the games. Men make up 59 percent of gamers, meaning that a surprisingly large 41 percent of gamers are female. This tells us that the mass market audience for males is approximately 21 to 35. The age is going up annually, and it is therefore unsurprising that more and more Mature-rated games (18+ in Europe) are being released by game publishers. I should also point out that I have seen figures from Sony and Microsoft that indicate that their platforms are targeted for an average age that is a little younger than this, but even for consoles and excluding PC gamers, average game players are 23 or over and increasing each year.

4

There is a fairly well-defined split between people who were kids or teenagers when the very first home computers and video games came out around 1980 and those older than that. As I write this, in 2005, someone who was 18 in 1980 is now 43. The number of gamers older than this is still very small. Many more people younger than this play video games, and the percentage increases as you get to people currently in their mid-thirties, most of whom were brought up with video games in the house or knowing someone who played home computer games.

Reality Check: The age when video games were just for kids is truly over, and although many older people still mistakenly believe this is true, year by year the people who grew up with the early home computers are still buying and playing games and raising the average age even higher. In 20 or 30 years time, there will be whole new areas that have opened up as games are being created for a booming 60+ audience! By 2035, there should be very few people around who haven't played a video game at some point in their life.

War Story: Identifying the Next "Big Thing"

I've been fortunate enough to be able to judge the likely commercial success of a game within a few minutes of picking it up and playing it. I'm not always right, but I tend to get pretty close to the mark. Each year a few key titles become massive commercial successes because they are very innovative. If you're lucky enough to be given the freedom to design the next big thing, nine times out of ten you should be aiming to do something that hasn't been done before and if possible, reach a market demographic in a unique way that hasn't fully been exploited. If your design doesn't involve a long prototype phase in which you are trying out a mechanic that is new, it's very unlikely that you will have a groundbreaking hit on your hands.

I'll use two examples from European developers that I saw at a very early stage. *Battlefield 1942* was originally a poor-looking game with superb gameplay. It had multiplayer up and running from day one and the ability to leap into any vehicle and fight against each other. It was genuinely the first time that these features had been incorporated into a game. EA managed to sign the game and spent a long time working with the developers on the graphics. But since the gameplay was there, it always had an excellent chance of succeeding, and EA recognized this. Around the same time, I saw *Operation Flashpoint*. Again, the game was very rough around the edges, but its scope, scale, and realism were unique. As a single player war game, it offered something that hadn't been done before. *Battlefield* got away, but I signed up *Operation Flashpoint* and it went on to sell over a million units on PC alone. In comparison, I've signed games that look fantastic and have great technology, but their gameplay needed work. It's much harder to get a huge hit from this kind of title, unless you have the time to play around with the gameplay until you get it just right. Not every game can be a groundbreaking genre-defining title, but if you really want to create one, focus on prototyping the gameplay that is genuinely original from day one and worry about the other elements later.

As the game market continues to expand, more and more successful games will emerge that are developed for different demographics. Today, you can design games for 2- to 4-year-olds, college-educated adults, or any age in between and reach a wide audience. With each age group, you need to consider a number of factors, such as game context, manual dexterity required, interface issues, and so on. We'll look at the design issues in more detail as this chapter progresses, but for now, let's look at some age distinctions to get an idea of some of the design constraints that are involved. Table 4.1 presents some of the critical issues you need to consider when targeting games for certain ages. You also need to consider ESRB ratings in the United States and PEGI ratings in Europe and how they can affect how your game is sold. Games that receive a Mature or "18" rating as compared to those that that receive a broader Teen or "15" rating may not have smaller sales at the moment, but as the ratings system becomes more widely used by the general public and retailers, a more limited rating could hurt your sales, especially if you are targeting your game for a younger audience. Talk with the ratings people about your game design early on and you should get some clear guidelines on what to avoid if you want to hit a particular age rating.

Table 4.1 Age considerations in gaming.

Early Preschool (ages 2 to 4)

This group has problems controlling the mouse, keyboard, and other complex input devices. They can't type or read. So how do you design a game for them? Preschool children can use the arrow keys and find single letters on the keyboard, and they can use a mouse if you design the hotspots to be very large. In fact, the hotspots should be no smaller than about 1/12th of the screen. Speech is the easiest cue for early preschool games. Here are some rules for using speech wisely for this age group:

(continued)

Table 4.1   Age considerations in gaming (*continued*).

- Your game should be so simple that it does not require instructions. *Do not* use spoken instructions as a substitute for an obvious interface. That said, do use simple phrases to lead the child through the game.

- When there has been no input activity for a while, play a phrase telling the player what to do, like "Click on the cat" or "Press the *A* key."

- Use speech as a payoff. After the child has performed a task, say, "That's great," "Good work," or "You did it!"

- Have the characters in your game talk. This age group especially likes silly noises and words. (Come to think of it, I like silly noises and words too!) Young children like bright colors and simple shapes. Unfortunately, publishers like detailed, high-resolution graphics because their adult taste is quite different. Adults tend to equate complexity with a high price and thus quality. Your job as the game developer is to somehow satisfy both constituencies.Do not make the interface too busy and complicated. The early preschooler's brain has not yet had a lot of experience making sense of complicated and detailed pictures. Use surprises such as pop-ups, random animation, clever sounds, and so on. Your players last year thought peekaboo was completely entrancing and now love jack-in-the-boxes. Avoid frightening images. Children of this age are not ready to handle concepts like injury, death, separation, violence, monsters, witches, and bad guys. In fact, almost anything that is not friendly should be avoided.

Preschool (ages 4 to 6)
Many of the principles that apply to early preschool apply to this age group. These children are becoming more coordinated and can recognize words (although you can't count on reading). Some have become experts with the joystick and can manage a mouse better, so simplified arcade games are within their abilities. However, it is still a good idea to provide a keyboard interface as well as joystick or mouse controls. I'm embarrassed to say that I remember my younger brother Tom playing *Doom* with a PC keyboard on his fifth birthday. He was actually pretty good at it, and fortunately it hasn't turned him into a violent rampaging thug as the press seems to believe happens to everyone who plays a game involving guns. But I wouldn't recommend this course of action, and I'm sure at the time he actually preferred playing games that were a little more appropriate!

Early Elementary (ages 5 to 8)
At this age, children may enjoy monsters and other bad guys as long as the enemies are "safe." For example, in the game *Word Rescue* by Karen Crowther, the enemies are blobs that the player "slimes." However, in *Treasure Mountain*, the pixies are friendly and humorous, even when they are sneaking up on the player to steal a coin. It goes without saying that violence, injury, blood, and gore really aren't great for this age group.

Elementary/Middle (ages 7 to 11)
These children have reached "The Age of Reason." They are starting to develop their own peer culture and can think for themselves. At this age, kids begin to identify with the group that is older than they are. You, the designer, must be careful not to present material that is too "babyish." Your

(continued)

Table 4.1   Age considerations in gaming (*continued*).

characters should be just a little older than your target player. You can assume that this group reads, although not fluently. There is some controversy over whether the vocabulary should be watered down so that it is well within the child's resources or whether one should aim higher. There are arguments on both sides; use your best judgment. You are on solid ground whichever philosophy you choose to follow.

Teens (ages 12 and up)

At this point, you're dealing with full-fledge gamers who are pretty much ready to play most any game available unless their parents intervene. "Cool" is king with this group. Boys are most taken by games like first-person shooters and fighting and racing games where they can indulge in testosterone feats. Girls are more interested in social activities; sitting down at the computer is not often high on their list. The Internet and its social connotations have helped tremendously with the female segment of the market, but still the focus for this group is sans computer—which is the major challenge to overcome! Online games with social aspects seem to hold a great deal of promise in terms of appealing to girls as products like *EverQuest* and *The Sims* (online and off) have shown.

Adults (ages 17 and up)

These players tend to be well educated adults, although as games have broadened demographically, the adult segment is now not just those high enough on the socioeconomic scale to own a computer. Their ability to enjoy and deal with more sophisticated stories and content allows you to pursue nontraditional themes—storylines that would garner a PG-13 or R rating in a movie. Despite the recent call for ratings, there is far more opportunity to create adult-level content than there was in many earlier instances of the games industry. As a small level of distinction (and this is a bit of a guess), the 17-to-25 market is also heavily dominated by college-bound kids. Therefore, online games (i.e., MMOGs) and multiplayer games (like *Quake* and *CounterStrike*) are interesting. Most universities and dorms are packed with high-speed access, and students, despite studies, have more free time and fewer responsibilities then those who've hit the workforce and parenthood. (Sadly, I know this from bitter experience!)

Seniors (ages 55 and up)

We haven't reached a point at which lots of retirees are playing computer games, but this time is coming. Just think of all of those bingo-card-carrying members who love their game, and then think about how the population is aging, and thus we are likely to have a demographic that will increasingly be among the fastest growing for games. It is difficult to tell at this point what the important design issues will be, but I can see that physical issues such as text size, speed, and interface components will be affected. For example, *Knights of the Old Republic* would work fine, but the ending is very tough for the non-dexterous. Up until the end, it was pretty much a strategy game that was easily manageable by those without arcade-like command of their Xbox controller or PC mouse.

Designing Games for Older Gamers

Let's start by discussing how games can be better designed for older gamers. As you're probably aware, this is a tough demographic to design for. Although I've noticed some very real differences between different age groups of older players, I'd like to run through some generalizations that I hope may be useful.

Action/Thinking

Market data across the world shows that the average age of PC gamers is significantly higher than of console owners. Older gamers are slightly less interested in fast-paced action games. On the other hand, they enjoy games that encourage them to think and use their intelligence to solve problems. This is supported by the success of titles like *Myst* and the Sims/Theme games, which are popular with older players. It also helps explain why more successful PC games tend to be more strategic or are what we call "God" titles (games where the player plays the role of an all-powerful "controller," as is the case in games like *Sim City, Theme Park,* and *Black and White*). However, this doesn't mean that older gamers don't play action games. From my own experience with games like *Conflict: Desert Storm*, older players tend to enjoy the tactical elements of the game; for example, they enjoy splitting up the four-man squad of soldiers, using the sniper to cover the advance of the other characters, and so on. Younger gamers, on the other hand, more often pile in and assault enemies head-on.

Dexterity

Younger gamers are attracted to games that have fast action because they have the dexterity to keep up with the challenges of the game. As people get older, they think and react to situations at a slower pace. Because of this, games that are especially designed to give the player an adrenaline rush can sometimes be a turnoff to older players. If the player doesn't have the manual dexterity to keep up with the game's action, they will likely get frustrated because the game will make them feel bad. And sometimes older players can cope with the dexterity but just don't find "twitch" gaming, which is all about reactions, as enjoyable as a more adventure- or strategy-based title where they can exercise their brain cells as well as their nervous system!

Playing Time

Older gamers in general have less time to play games because they have to work or look after children. Therefore, being able to play games in short chunks of time is more important. Older gamers are more focused on the gameplay and won't be as wowed by fancy cinematics, great music, or fancy FMV (Full Motion Video) sequences. They've experienced the gloss, and they know that what counts is whether a game is fun to play or not. This also makes older gamers loyal to brands. If they have really enjoyed one game, they are likely to buy a sequel.

Licenses

It's obvious really, but older gamers are attracted to licenses they know and put off by licenses that are clearly aimed at younger gamers. So the latest WWE wrestling title is never going to be a big hit with 30- to 50-year-olds, whereas a game based on a classic film like *The Great Escape* or a big 1980s TV show like *The A-Team* might be popular. Finding a license that covers multiple demographics is the Holy Grail of game licensing, and that is one reason companies like EA pay so much for brands such as *Lord of the Rings* and *James Bond*, which sell very well as a result of this broad appeal. If you're designing around a license, research which age group it particularly appeals to and make sure your game is aimed at this market.

Design Approaches

Let's look at an example of how we might go about tailoring a design to an older gaming audience. Let's take a fictional Mafia game that has been designed for a younger or more general audience, a game in which we have organized crime gangs and need to gain control of a city. With just this simple premise, it is possible to take the game design in a number of different directions. For a younger audience, we could create a first- or third-person action shooter, where the player takes on the role of a new gang recruit, starting at the bottom of the chain. The player is sent out on missions and drives cars fast, shoots rival gang members, smashes up shops, and generally causes mayhem until they finally rise to become the "Don" of their gang. This approach would make for a very fast-paced action game in which the player is directed most of the time, shown where to go, and then let loose to have fun completing the missions.

For an older gamer, the setting gives huge opportunity to create some more tactical gaming. Rather than giving the player control of just one character, I'd allow the player to be the Don, ordering his team members around, keeping one step ahead of the other gangs and the cops. We could let the player take control instantly of any of his gang members to keep an element of action within the gameplay, but the overall aim would require much more thought and strategy. Another option would be to create a massively multiplayer online game with hundreds of people playing as rival gang members, creating new gangs, and maybe also playing as the cops that hunt the gang members down. By giving players the freedom to play as they like, younger gamers could happily fire guns and cause huge explosions, while older gamers concentrate more on building their crime family up, outthinking the other players, and interacting with other people. The older players could even double-cross allies and create traps. As always in this chapter, I'm trying to highlight the differences between the age groups, not state an iron-cast rule; some young gamers love games that involve strategic thinking, and some older gamers love action games! The advantage of the approach I'm introducing here is that you could evolve your design ideas into a game that would appeal to both older and younger audiences. The strategic planning would quickly appeal to older players and the action in the game would entice younger players to play the game. The game could also provide a path so that younger players don't outgrow it. As the younger players gain more experience playing the game, they can get more involved in some of its more strategic aspects.

 Reality Check: Even though your goal may be to target a particular demographic, such as older players, there's no reason that you can't broaden the market for your game by designing it so that it also appeals to other audiences. You can often achieve this by including features that allow players to "grow up" as they master the game or act younger and not feel foolish.

4

Designing Games for Children

I'm not an expert in designing games for children or younger teenagers, but I have picked up a number of tips that may be useful if you need to design a game for this age group. The kids market is a strong one, covering a range of different types of products, from basic educational games and games for very young kids to more sophisticated titles such as *Lego Star Wars*, which appealed to a huge range of players, including many adults. Most educational games tend to be released on the PC platform, and many outlets that sell games have a specific PC kids section. On consoles, kids games tend not to be educational as such and are often licensed. Licenses seem to work extremely well with kids, and if you take a look at the best-seller lists and at successful E/3+ rated titles, I think you'll be amazed at how many are licensed by a film, TV show, or toy brand. Anyway, let's look at are some tips that should help if you want to design a game for children.

Test Your Game Concept on Children

For younger kids (10 or under), the single most important element is to test your game on players of that age and listen to their feedback. It's impossible for an adult to properly understand the exact level of complexity and difficulty necessary without a huge amount of experience.

Assuming you don't have this experience, getting kids to focus-test your design and early versions of the game is definitely the best way to succeed.

Make Things Clear (but Not Patronizing!)

In general, kids need to be told exactly what they are expected to do, and the difficulty of your game needs to be carefully balanced. Clear, understandable on-screen instructions and simple controls are important. However, equally important is to not patronize your audience by making the game too easy and devoid of any real challenge. I believe the same approach is probably true if you are designing educational software for children. You should always test your design and early versions of your software on kids of the appropriate age and carefully note their feedback. If they find the software too simplistic or too complex, you need to deal with it.

Kids Aspire to Be Older

Older kids (11–15) aspire to be 18, and this age group will be clamoring to play the *Grand Theft Auto*'s of this world. My recommendation for designing games to appeal to this age group is to make games for this age group feel edgy and adult-like without actually getting a teen or mature age rating. Games like *Driv3r* picked up quite a number of sales in the teen market because they were seen to be "like GTA" but weren't 18 rated.

Design Approaches

Let's take a quick look at the highly successful *Lego Star Wars* game, which came out in 2005. In terms of game design, the developers did a number of key things very well. First, the game was designed to be very simple to pick up and play, even though it had a lot going on all the time. So many games are incredibly hard these days, and Travelers Tales (the developer) didn't fall into this trap. Second, it allowed a second player to drop in and drop out. This makes the game ideal for households that have more than one child or when a parent would like to play the game along with their kid. Online gameplay is an important component of gameplay, especially when looking at the future, but games that allow more than one player to play in the same room will likely be stronger sellers for this audience than purely multiplayer games. This is particularly true if you are targeting your game for international markets such as the United Kingdom or Europe. Third, *Lego Star Wars* offers a huge amount of collectibles and things to unlock. We've talked already about the importance of the collecting instinct, and this game fulfills this instinct very well. Finally, and maybe most important, this game is very entertaining. The first time you see the well-known *Star Wars* scenes shown with Lego people and Lego environments, it makes you laugh, and you know it's going to work really well. In my view, this game is almost a perfect kids game and well worth playing if you're interested in designing for this age group.

Designing Games for Women

This is a very tricky section for me to write as a man, and I want to avoid generalizing too much. However, I've learned two things that I guess are pretty obvious in retrospect. First, if you want to design a game specifically for women, it's a good idea to have a female designer on board. You just can't beat having someone heavily involved who is actually part of the audience you are designing for! (This is a good point to keep in mind as you are designing games for any demographic.) Second, and even more crucial, make sure you focus-test your idea out on women. It's very easy to fall into a patronizing, male view of what women want. In other words, shopping, ponies, and fashion won't cut it! By asking questions and paying attention to what elements of your game design women like and dislike, you'll learn more about what makes modern female gamers tick.

The phenomenal success of The Sims series is due in large part to its attraction to female gamers, which make up a large proportion of players. Titles for younger gamers, such as *Barbie Fashion Designer*, have demonstrated that you can sell games designed specifically for girls to a large audience. (*Barbie Fashion Designer* sold over 600,000 copies on the PC platform in its first year.) Don't lose sight of the fact that many female gamers want to play games that are very similar to those currently available. Sometimes it might just be a case of changing the advertising to highlight slightly different elements of the game. But there is no doubt that a large percentage of women don't play games, and therefore as an industry, we are probably not creating the right products for this audience.

I'm now going to risk eternal damnation from all my female friends, colleagues, and readers by giving you my view on a few general trends to bear in mind if you want to design a game with female players in mind. As always, these are generalizations; not every male gamer is the same, and so it is with women.

Competition Is Less Important

Men seem to be a little more competitive than women, and hence female gamers are happier having less-competitive goals and playing cooperative game modes. In her excellent book *Gender Inclusive Game Design* (Charles River Media), Sheri Graner Ray talks about the reaction of female gamers to the traditional consequence for failure in a game: immediate death and a "Load last save game?" box. Killing and being killed is a structure that underlines the vast majority of games and isn't the most female friendly mechanic to include. Sheri wonders whether the player should actually be punished for wrong decisions. Titles like *Myst* (another very female-friendly title) simply prevent the player from continuing until they successfully solve a problem or carry out the right action.

My advice is to leave out the notion of "boss battles" at the end of your game levels and focus more on a rewarding and intriguing storyline that encourages players to continue onward. Think about whether the player should be killed for failure or whether you can keep the player alive and encourage her to try another way forward.

Story and Characterization Is More Important

An average female gamer cares more about the story and characterization than an average male gamer. Make sure your storyline is professionally written, rich, and emotional. Spend time making sure your story flows properly. Heck, you should be doing this anyway, but it's doubly important if you want female gamers to buy into your concept.

Women Care More about the Character They Are Playing

Guys often couldn't care less about the character they are playing as long as he has a big gun, and hence there have been a huge number of first-person titles in which the main character is pretty much a nonentity. Now it is argued by some that designers should leave the main character deliberately blank so that the player can impose their own personality on him/her. I'm not a big fan of this theory.

Give your main character a strong personality, and make him/her likeable but flawed. You can build up the main character even in a first-person game; take a look at titles like *Chronicles of Riddick* that switch to third person when the player performs an action and other games that use mirrors and cut scenes to highlight the main character. If you want female gamers to feel at home in your title, offer a female character, and please, don't give her 34DD breasts and a skimpy bikini.

Women Like Playing Online and Interacting with Other People

Until artificial intelligence gets so good that you can realistically interact with other characters in a single-player game, women seem to have a definite bias toward playing games online and playing cooperatively with other real people. It is also true that women like talking more than men.

Reality Check: Make sure your game has strong online gameplay, and include really good chat facilities and headset support; allow players to interact with each other.

Use Appropriate Difficulty Levels

Focus groups that I have carried out have strongly hinted that, at least for the moment, the average female gamer is not as adept at fast "twitch" gameplay as the average male gamer. I'm sure this will change and is due to the large number of new female gamers who just don't play traditional fast action-based games. But it appears to be a fact for now.

 Reality Check: Make sure your game supports multiple difficulty levels and that you don't make your core gameplay really hard.

4

As I said before, I'm certainly not an expert on female gamers, so I'm just passing on what I have learned from observing women playing games. I currently work with an excellent female designer and producer, and I hope that in the future more women will work within the games industry. I'm especially looking forward to working with female designers who come into the industry because of titles like *The Sims* and can bring in a mass-market female view on what they want from games. Unfortunately, many women in the industry at the moment have had no choice but to like and design masculine games.

 Reality Check: Try to think outside of the usual sexual stereotypes. Challenge traditional ideas such as female characters always wearing skimpy clothes and the need for your character to carry an AK47. Female gamers are a reality, and designers who take this audience seriously and try to make sure their games appeal to them (as well as to male audiences) will be the ones who are really successful in the next decade.

More Tips on Targeting Gender Considerations

When it comes to dealing with gender issues in games, there are two critical questions to ask: How do you target women gamers, and how do you target women gamers without losing male gamers? There are no easy answers here. At this time in our culture, women are not as attracted to games, competition, and technology as men are. This doesn't mean large amounts of women don't like and play games. In fact, a recent survey by the Entertainment Software Association showed that women over 18 who play games outnumber male gamers in the age range of 6 through 27. Of course, this doesn't mean that they purchase the same amount of games, but this does show that there is money to be made by targeting female players. If you don't believe me, you obviously don't have access to Will Wright's (creator of *The Sims*) or the Miller brothers' (creators of *Myst*) bank accounts. (Of course, I don't actually have access either, unfortunately, but I'm pretty confident their investment advisors are smiling).

Here are some useful tips to consider for developing games that can directly appeal to women or at least span the two genders:

■ Consider having women help design your game, and try to involve them in the entire process. In his analysis of why *The Sims* worked so well for women gamers, Henry Jenkins, the leader of EducationArcade.org and a professor at MIT, pointed out that Maxis had women in key positions throughout the entire product development process. It really does make a difference.

■ Games should have both male and female protagonists. Some even allow the player to choose whether to play a male or female character. A male gangster or ex–Navy Seal may appeal to many men, but women are not going to want to play *as* them. They may want to play *with* them, but that's another story...

■ You should not feature significant blood, gore, or fighting if you expect to appeal to a general female demographic.

■ Try to avoid gender stereotypes; the male should not always be the leader, and the female should not always be portrayed as a sex symbol or someone who is weak or powerless. These kind of stereotypes are very out-of-date.

■ Try to include humor (but not gross-out bodily function humor). Humor tends to appeal equally to male and females.

■ Join and read the IGDA Women in Development list. This group provides good insight into how to design games for women.

■ Women tend to learn about and evaluate products by using them and not by reading feature lists. Thus, try to provide samples of your game to demonstrate its gameplay. This is one reason why I think casual online games do so well with women. Not only are they free, but you can try them before fully committing. Make sure your female-friendly game gets onto the console magazine demo discs and that a PC demo (if applicable) goes out on the Internet.

■ Read a book on the subject by Sheri Graner Ray (who has held many positions in the games industry and is currently working on *EverQuest*) titled *Gender Inclusive Game Design* (ISBN 1584502398) from Charles River Media. Unfortunately, the book has a lot of typos, but the content is decent.

Races and Sexual Orientations

One area that is very rarely addressed is how to design games for specific racial groups or for people with a specific sexual orientation. Several games have now featured a black protagonist; *GTA: San Andreas* is one of the most obvious examples. In many cases, I can't help feeling that the black characters have been included by white game designers simply because the main character is a gang member and the designers' view of the world assumes that gang members are more often black than white and that they believe this will attract more black gamers to their title. This kind of typecast design is pretty lazy, and I hope we'll see more games with intelligent, positive black and Asian lead characters in the future. I believe that black and Asian gamers need strong, talented, and above all, heroic main characters to look up to, just as everyone else does. I'm really looking forward to seeing the first Bollywood-inspired Indian game, with a great story, strong characters, and superb musical sequences. With the rapidly improving game development industry in India, this will happen sooner rather than later, and I hope I'm involved in some way when it does!

With regard to sexual orientation, I'm absolutely convinced that there will be a game designed specifically for gay men or gay women at some point soon, and providing the game is really strong, the first example is going to sell a lot of copies. But persuading the people who ultimately control the budget to finance such a game is a different story. If I was going to design a game with a gay audience in mind, my first step would be to get some creative gay men and women involved in the design. Just as it's almost impossible for a man to design a game for women, I imagine the same is true with sexual orientation.

As more and more people continue to play games (with gamers getting gradually older), these kind of targeted products *will* appear. Watch this space.

Cultural and National Differences

Another demographic issue to consider is one that relates more to culture and international markets. There are two main issues to think about here. First, gamers in different countries can tend to favor different genres and types of games. Second, there are various laws regarding game ratings in each territory, and what is allowed or not allowed in relation to violence, religion, and historical references can change significantly. It is important that you have a fairly good idea of both of these issues because you don't want to design a game only to find out that your publisher can't sell it in many countries, and you don't have a fallback option. Let's look at both of these in a little more detail.

Gaming Preferences

When designing for a global market, you should be aware that certain types of games perform better in one region than another. For example, Japanese customers don't seem to go for hardcore simulations as much as North American audiences do, and fast-moving first-person games really do make many Asian gamers feel ill and therefore don't sell nearly as well there. Meanwhile, many anime-style titles don't do as well here, and of course Rugby titles sell better than *Madden Football* in Australia and Europe. There are so many different kinds of preferences for every single country that there isn't room to try to list them out. For example, German gamers have a much stronger tendency toward thoughtful strategic gameplay, and hence, real-time strategy (RTS) games and PC titles have a much larger share of the market in that country.

Creative Idea: Research the Market

Decide at the start of your design the key territories in which you need to succeed. If you don't have much knowledge of one or more of the territories, take a week to do some thorough research. Beg, borrow, or steal information about the best-seller lists, and compare the titles that are doing well. Speak to people from that country if possible, or at least to people that understand the market fairly well (such as sales managers from your publisher if you have one). Pick a title that has performed badly in that territory but did well elsewhere. Try to find out why that title didn't perform; was there something about the design that turned off the gamers in the country you're looking at?

Laws/Ratings Issues

The second big issue relates to laws and rating systems in the various territories. You'll be amazed at the differences that can crop up, and it is easy to design a game that can get banned! For example, Germany has very strict laws about showing Nazi symbols and swastikas, so you must make sure that nothing like this appears in the German version of a game. Having red blood, the ability to kill people, or decapitations in your game can instantly make the game a Mature/18+ rating in certain places and in some countries may cause it to be banned. Some countries are very sensitive about religion, so if you have your mercenary character hunting down cardinals in the Vatican, you'll likely get into really hot water. In my experience, the rules are always shifting around a little, and what is acceptable one year might cross the line the next year. Even in the United States, the reaction to violent games can swing rapidly as public opinion changes. I would advise that you make a clear list of each element that could prove a major problem and have a fallback option available. For example, you could turn the blood color in your game to green if necessary for certain versions or penalize the player by reducing their score if they kill innocent civilians. Don't go over the top and sanitize your game too much, but you'll need to keep an eye on the big risks. Most of the smaller regulation issues shouldn't limit your design too much.

War Story: How Big Are the Risks?

My favorite story about controversial game design is about Jon Hare and the guys at Sensible Software, a well-known British developer that created some superb titles such as *Cannon Fodder* and *Sensible Soccer*. They created a game called *Sex, Drugs and Rock & Roll* that was designed not just to push the boundaries of taste and decency, but to smash them down. I was told that one of the opening scenes involved a nun taking hard drugs on a toilet while performing oral sex, with a crucifix in the background. You may not be surprised to learn that the publishers at the time considered the game a little too risky and it never saw the light of day!

Designing Nonstandard Games and Applications

In this section, we'll focus on the issues and techniques involved in designing unusual kinds of games and how to use game technology for different applications. We're going to start off by looking at how to create extremely unusual and innovative games and then how to design games specifically to be sold at a budget price. I'll finish the chapter by talking about the current rapid advances in using game engines to create movies and TV shows.

Creating Unique and Unusual Games

A few times every year, a stunningly original and off-the-wall game comes along. It normally comes from Japan (where the local appetite for unusual games allows developers and publishers to take bigger risks), and it normally sells fairly well and wins lots of awards in magazines like *Edge*. And most game designers see the game, and think one of two things:

"I wish I'd designed that—that is *so* cool"

Or

"There is no way in a million years that my developer/publisher would green-light that game design"

On the assumption that you want to create a unique design (despite the fact that you'll find it very hard to get funded, at least in North America or Europe), how do you go about coming up with something crazy yet brilliant? How to you convince the people that you work with to support the idea? There is no magic formula for coming up with unique game designs, but there are ways to help you arrive at a great off-the-wall concept.

Let's start by taking a look at a few examples of these kind of games.

Parappa the Rapper by Sony Computer Entertainment

This game is a dancing/rapping game featuring two-dimensional characters in a 3D world (see Figure 4.1). How could this ever work? But it did; the gameplay was fun, and the visual style was totally unique. It single-handedly spawned dancing and rhythm titles like the equally unique *Space Channel 5* by SEGA.

Rez by SEGA

Like *Space Channel 5*, this game was developed by SEGA's developer UGA in Japan (see Figure 4.2). It was the world's first "music-shooter." At its heart, it's a shooter in

Figure 4.1
Parappa the Rapper.

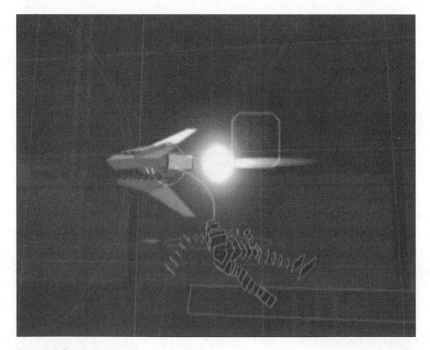

Figure 4.2
Rez.

which you fly through cyberspace blasting things into oblivion. But the way it is presented, with a highly original vector graphic style alongside a truly unique musical element, the game stands out miles apart from other shooters. The music builds up as you shoot items, adding different instruments and changing the rhythm. Playing *Rez* almost sends you into a trance; it's a fascinating and unusual combination.

Warioware by Nintendo

The Wario games offer a completely fresh approach to gaming, where each mini game lasts 5 to 10 seconds. It's addictive as hell and a perfect multiplayer "after the pub" game (as we say in the U.K.). Bucking the trend of one long story-driven game, *Warioware* is the ultimate pick up and put down title (see Figure 4.3).

Figure 4.3
Warioware.

Katamari Damacy by Namco

Let's get this straight. You play as a tiny alien who rolls a ball around. And everything sticks to this ball. And it starts off tiny, picking up drawing pins under tables, and ends up so big that you're collecting houses and trees? Can you imagine being given the green light to develop this? And it works beautifully. It's like a breath of fresh air amidst a sea of games with guns, stealth, and secret agents (see Figure 4.4). Fantastic.

Figure 4.4
Katamari Damacy.

The Sims by EA

You may be surprised that I've included this game (see Figure 4.5), but when it was first announced, it was an extremely different and unusual concept. It took a while to get over the pleasant shock that a huge publisher was backing something so original (it turns out that Will Wright apparently had to invest a large amount of his own money and time to get the game advanced enough to be signed). It's a superb demonstration of a completely different kind of game that hits a much wider audience than traditional mainstream titles. Even more impressive, it has been extremely successful commercially. As far as I'm concerned, Will Wright is a genius and one of the most innovative designers around at the moment.

EyeToy by Sony Computer Entertainment

Again, this may be a surprising addition to the list, but the idea of bundling a cheap hardware camera with a game that allows players to effect on-screen objects by waving their hands and kicking their legs is a superb one (see Figure 4.6). Many argue that only someone as big as Sony could have pulled this game off, but there is no denying just how successful the *Eye-Toy* has been and how many new gamers it has encouraged who had never played games before. Created in its London studio, Sony has shown how

Figure 4.5
The Sims.

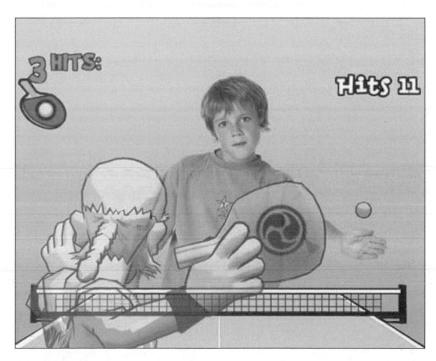

Figure 4.6
EyeToy.

rewarding it can be for console manufacturers to give designers the freedom to think outside the box. It's also an excellent example of a game that appeals to the whole family, from young kids to grandparents!

So how do you go about creating original ideas like these?

Well, from my point of view, the answer to this question is to have proper, organized brainstorming sessions. I'll cover brainstorming in more detail later in the book, but the basics are as follows:

- Get a bunch of creative people into a room and shut the door.

- Get a whiteboard or lots of large sheets of paper and lots of pens.

- Start tossing ideas around and writing down everything that is said.

- Investigate "What if" scenarios. For example, in the case of *Rez*, the designers may have talked about the various elements that make up a game and arrived at music. The conversation could easily have been something like this:

  "Okay, so music. What could we do differently with music?"

  "What if music wasn't just played over the top of a game, but you could actually alter the music as you play the game?"

  "How would that work?"

  "Well, maybe you could punch or shoot stuff to trigger different samples."

  "How about building up the intensity and tempo of the music as you progress through a level?"

  and so on…

- Keep the flow of ideas going. When I'm doing brainstorms, I like to prepare lots of different things I want to explore in advance so that if things go quiet and people run out of ideas, I can keep things moving by going down a different avenue. As an example, if I was trying to come up with a highly original design, these might be some of the avenues to explore in a brainstorm:

  - Can we come up with an original graphical style that hasn't been done before?

  - Can we come up with a way of controlling a character or object that is unusual? What if we don't use the controller in the normal manner?

  - Could we set the game somewhere very unusual?

  - Is there something cool we could use the latest physics technology for?

- If we could bundle any kind of controller or technical add-on to the console/PC, what could we create?

- Are there any major types of film, TV shows, or books that aren't really being explored by video games at the moment?

- How can we attract female gamers to our game?

- Can we make a first- or third-person shooter without having guns in the game? What could we fire at the targets/enemies?

and so on…

4

Creating highly original game ideas is tricky, and creating highly original game ideas that are commercially viable is even harder. If you don't work in the Japanese games market (which is known for its love of quirky and unusual games), the best chance you have of getting your unique game design made is to tie it into a theme that is commercial and think carefully about how you present it. If I had designed *Rez*, for example, and wanted to get it green-lighted at a major U.S. or European publisher, I would take the unique elements and put them into a more relevant setting. For example, I would have a modern police officer running through a rioting city taking out the bad guys, with rhythm, instrument samples, and maybe even elements of rap triggered by what you hit and when, in the same way as *Rez*. I know some designers will argue that by altering your original vision at all, you're selling your soul as a designer, but this book is about designing in the real world, and in the real world, we want our games to get made and to sell well.

Designing Budget Games

Although not obviously a demographic issue, designing a game specifically for a budget price point is a challenge. Broadly speaking, I believe that the people who buy budget games fall into two separate camps. The first group consists of people who simply can't afford to pay the full retail price, and the second group are those who can afford full-price games but like to make impulse purchases when they come across a good deal that will save them some money.

Obviously, many budget games were originally sold at full price and have come down in cost because either they are a little dated or they have struggled to sell at a higher price and the publisher has dropped the price to try to generate more sales. However, there are many games that are designed to launch at a budget price from day one. So what types of differences are there between full-price games and budget games? If you have a decent number of people present, try splitting the team up into subgroups, and then reconvene to present your ideas to each other.

Niche Topics or Very Specific Areas

A budget price allows you to target very niche or specific areas, particularly areas where you would struggle to create enough content to justify full price. Examples might include niche sports (such as fishing or pool), card games, basic music sequencers, cheap-and-cheerful point-and-click adventure games, and a whole host of other genres that simply wouldn't sell at full price against the likes of *FIFA*, *Halo*, *GTA*, *Metal Gear Solid*, and so on. Take a trip down to your local game software store and look at the variety of budget games available. You'll see that there are several successful companies that specialize in creating budget-only game software. You may also find budget software sold in unusual places, such as specialty catalogs or gas stations.

Creative Idea: Watch Movies and Pay Attention to the Camera Work

Really do take a trip to a game store and check out the whole shop, looking at pricing in particular. See how many second-hand games are sold compared to full price. Look at whether the store has any budget sections, and if so, make note of the platforms. Are these budget titles simply old full-price games, or have any of them clearly been created to sell at a cheaper price? By keeping an eye on retail, you will pick up any new trends quickly and can watch what the competition is up to.

Smaller, Shorter, and Cheaper Games

Designing a game for a budget price allows you to get away with a much shorter and smaller product, often at a dramatically lower development cost. A full-price game would be expected to provide 10 to 15 hours of gameplay, whereas a budget game could offer 4 to 8 hours. The quality bar is also lower for budget titles; people don't expect the games to look as good as the latest cutting-edge title, so life is easier if your development team is not as big or as experienced as the big guys. It's also possible to develop games much quicker at a budget price. Niche areas are generally quicker to create product for anyway, since you don't have lots of competing titles that you need to beat feature-wise. But even when you're creating a budget game in a competitive genre, the development time can be cut dramatically if you're making a game with only half the content of a full-price title.

Reality Check: One other great reason for doing a small, short game development is that it allows you to move very quickly, which you might want to do in order to tap into a new craze or to get a game out rapidly in time for a TV show or film. Many people look down on games like these, but they have their place in the world, and they often sell very well. As I write this, there is a craze for a game called *Sudoku*, which is kind of a numerical crossword. Within three months of this craze making its way into the national newspapers, a game was on shelves taking advantage of it. Although the game is clearly very simple, you have to admire the company involved for turning a product around so quickly!

Add-on Packs

Creating add-on packs for existing games is an interesting design challenge. You're treading a difficult line between creating enough new content to justify people paying for it and completing the pack in the shortest time possible. The usual direction taken by designers is to use exactly the same game engine and mechanics and to create a whole load of new assets, including new missions, new FMV, new dialogue, and a fresh storyline. There are many examples of successful add-on packs, which seem to sell anywhere from 10 percent to 50 percent of the numbers of the original game. For example, *Half Life* has had a few great add-on packs, as have many PC strategy games. The all-time record must have been set with *The Sims*, which seems to have spawned several hundred different add-on packs with extra characters, furniture, and locations to play with. *The Sims* is without doubt the perfect "add-on pack" title.

Updated Versions of Older Games

It's also possible to update an existing game, giving it a proverbial lick of paint, polishing off the rough edges, upgrading the graphics, and releasing it at a budget price. This is an attractive option if the original title is hard to obtain, yet the core gameplay was excellent. This is also a strategy worth considering when you have an original game that filled a niche that still hasn't been saturated with competing games.

Opportunities with Machinima

Another fascinating use of game engines to reach people who might not necessarily play games is Machinima. Machinima has been around for many years now and basically involves using game engines to create short films, full-length movies, and TV programs. To do Machinima properly, you need a game engine that supports modification, ideally one that allows you to use your own customized character models, textures, objects, and even animations. The director plays the game, capturing the output as a video file. Normally some way is found to detach the in-game camera and either place it in a static location to mimic a real-life camera or set it up as a free-roaming camera moving on virtual tracks or a virtual crane as if it were in an actual film set.

Creative Idea:

How you use cameras is a very important part of Machinima. Much of the "language" of films comes from how directors place and move cameras within the scenes, and different directors often have unique camera styles that become associated with them. If you want to create Machinima, watch a couple of movies by your favorite director (I'd personally recommend Alfred Hitchcock, Christopher Nolan, and James Cameron) and analyze what the director does with the camera. Is the camera always moving, or is it often static? Does the director often use wide angle lenses? Do they like close-ups or distant shots? Where are quick, fast paced edits used, and when does the director/editor choose to linger over one long shot? Do they use handheld cameras, or are all the movements smooth and fluid? Take the elements you like, and try and copy them within your Machinima, while feeling free to create your own style. Remember that you have the freedom to create shots that real directors can only dream of, since you can move cameras anywhere!

When clips are edited together and sound and music dubbed over the top, it is possible to create some excellent pieces of work. For the reasons mentioned earlier, Machinima is often created using PC-based graphics engines such as the *Doom/Quake* engines, the *Unreal* engines, and *Half Life* engines. The "modability" of these pieces of technology allows for a high level of customization. It's also possible to use the multiplayer aspect of these titles to have multiple players running around within the game engine, essentially having multiple actors on-screen at once.

Hopefully, Machinima will progress to the stage where multiple people are "shooting" a movie over the Web, all in headset communication, with a number of actors, a director, and some cameramen. The director will be able to record everything as data (like a replay in traditional games) and then play it back later, allowing him to capture all the live actor movements and actions and then experiment with different lighting, cameras, and so on.

If you want to find out more about Machinima, I suggest you visit **www.machinima.com,** which is an excellent starting point. You might also want to get a copy of the book *3D Game-Based Filmmaking: The Art of Machinima* (Paraglyph Press) written by Paul Marino, one of the founders of the Machinima organization.

Summary

Hopefully, this chapter has given you a glimpse into some very different kind of games—games that are designed for specific types of people or unique and unusual games that totally break the mold. By constantly challenging what kind of people you should be designing games for, and by keeping a close eye on the rapid progression of technology and the advent of areas like Machinima, you stand a better chance of coming up with the next *Sims* and making a game that really is groundbreaking! In the next chapter, we're going to go into a bit more detail and focus on an incredibly important area within game design that is often rushed or overlooked—the game camera.

An Interview with Tim Wright

Tim Wright (aka "CoLD SToRAGE") is something of a legend within the games industry—and a man of many talents. As a composer and musician, Tim was responsible for the audio for over 50 games, from the Shadow of the Beast series to *Sensible Soccer*, *Lemmings*, and *Powermonger*. As senior sound artist on *Wipeout*, Tim revolutionized the use of licensed music in games. As co-founder of and creative director at Jester Interactive, Tim designed and produced the MUSIC and MTV Music Generator series. He has created games on almost every game format since the mid 1980s, with a hand in the design, programming, artwork, and music of a number of titles. He now runs Tantrumedia, a company specializing in multimedia solutions for the games industry, and has recently contributed music to the superb *Wipeout Fusion* on the PSP.

4

What do you think are the most important skills that a game designer should have?

TW: Originality, spontaneity, good communication skills, and a working knowledge of the target platform's limitations. They should know how to be part of a team and on occasion act as a buffer between the producer and the rest of the development staff. They should balance a firm stance with encouraging the team to buy into and improve upon the design. The best designers retain artistic integrity without alienating everyone all around them. It's all about balancing desires, practicality, and egos.

Do you find that you have to think about different age groups when you design for different platforms?

TW: To a certain extent, yes, but platforms tend to pass naturally through the age ranges as they mature. New systems can be prohibitively expensive and are purchased by adults or younger enthusiasts. As the retail price drops, along with the price of software, maturing platforms find a younger audience as they are either passed down to siblings or sons and daughters or are purchased new in more affordable bundles.

Having said that, there are definite demographics, for example when dealing with the likes of Gamecube versus your average Xbox or PS2 player. Nintendo has always garnered a younger image than the cool 20-something marketing techniques of Sony with its PlayStation range.

With the MUSIC/MTV Music Generator series, did you hear from many people outside the traditional 10–25 gaming age range?

TW: Absolutely. The peak of the bell curve in terms of age range was a lot higher than the average game, with the peak in the 20-somethings. We received e-mails and letters from people in their late 50s who had rediscovered their musical leanings after coming across a copy of MUSIC in their local supermarket. As well as being broadly embraced in terms of age range, we found it to be a long-term "evergreen" in terms of sales, too, instead of peaking a week after launch as many games tend to.

Do you ever think about designing games with the female market in mind?

TW: While at Jester, we toyed with a couple of titles for the teenage girl market. We always felt it was difficult to make a design that was appealing without being condescending or demeaning. An office full of males attempting to fathom and buy into designs for a product aimed squarely at the female market always seemed a little odd. So we canvassed opinion from wives, daughters, and female friends. The responses were very positive, but sadly, they hinged upon Sony hardware that was never released outside Japan.

What are you most proud of in your career so far?

TW: That's a really tough question. I have been lucky enough to have so many amazing opportunities in such short space of time!

I am proud that I have accomplished what I set out to do with the MUSIC products—to have someone who started out by penning tunes on MUSIC become a successful recording artist in their own right. And truthfully, this has gone beyond my wildest dreams. There are local radio stations in London that broadcast urban music tracks composed solely using the MUSIC products.

I am proud to have been involved in a groundbreaking title such as Wipeout. Indeed, this came full circle of late, with some of my new music being licensed for the new PSP launch title Wipeout Pure. I have met so many of my childhood heroes and famous personalities in the music industry through the music products I have designed and worked on. It really will be something to tell my grandchildren.

What is your favorite game (of all time), and why?

TW: That is such a hard question to answer! It would have to be either Paradroid or Hired Guns. Paradroid had different gameplay elements all rolled into one—sheer genius. Hired Guns (Amiga) was just so atmospheric and polished in terms of playability, level design, sound design, and was totally addictive, especially in multiplayer mode. More recently, I've loved playing Freelancer and the reinvented Doom series. If you push me, it would probably be Hired Guns.

Have you found that you need to make differences to a game for the U.S. market as opposed to Europe?

TW: In terms of marketing and presentation? Undoubtedly. In terms of content? Yes, to a degree. But core functionality or product design, basically the intrinsic part of a product that gives it that edge, seems to be pretty universal. It might need to be dressed in a different way and the content tweaked to suit, but the core elements generally suit all.

What do you think is the biggest game design mistake that people regularly make with games?

TW: The designer can get too close to the product. You really do need to take a step back and look at things with fresh eyes on a regular basis. Getting too close, you can lose the bigger picture. Something that seems perfectly obvious to the designer can be unfathomable to the newcomer.

Good design needs to be a narrative. You need to take the player/user by the hand and lead them through the new world you've created. Don't let the ride get bumpy unless you're ready to catch them should they fall. My top tip when designing is... don't assume anything about your target audience, except their love of enjoyment. What might be obvious to you is not necessarily obvious to others.

If money and technology were unlimited, what kind of game would you most like to see made?

TW: I would like to see a game that evolved with the player. Let me give an analogy. As a child, I was into the music and bands of the time, and as I've grown, so have they. Their music has evolved and I have followed their progress, buying each new album. Some hits, some misses. But the point is, the musicians age with you and match your change in tastes and interests. As they mature, so do you. A multiuser, evolutionary game that could have the appeal to last years instead of weeks would be the ultimate form of entertainment.

Most of us have fond memories of playing a game on a now-defunct system. We look back through rose-tinted spectacles and reminisce about the good old days and the fantastic times we had. Upon inspection we find that these old computer systems aren't that great and the games are blocky and too difficult to play. But imagine an experience that lived alongside your life, a Matrix-style environment that you could dip in and out, a world where there are basic rules, but the story unfolds as the players explore. No doubt there would be chaos for a long while, but people eventually tire of this and would form alliances to bring order and a sense of belonging. I guess this could be called unreal life? Somewhere to escape to for an hour or two.

When you're finding music for a game, how do you go about making a cohesive set of tracks while trying to appeal to people who invariably will like different kinds of music?

TW: This is essentially a no-win situation. The best thing to do is not to try to appeal to taste, but to suitability. You have to consider what type of music will invoke the right response from the user. Cinema has the luxury of fully orchestrated scores, which are universally accepted mood controllers, hence, we see their use more and more in games. Other titles simply dictate a style of music; for instance, the Wipeout series simply cried out for futuristic style electronica as opposed to any other fast-paced style.

What do you think is the biggest challenge facing game designers as we move forward?

TW: *The ability to work as part of a team of designers, each with their unique area but also partial responsibility for the entire game. This will be a key skill. Chips will have to be removed from shoulders at the door before entering the workplace.*

Having original ideas accepted and acted upon will become less likely as budgets rise yet again for development on more powerful platforms. Recent estimates on development costs for the new iterations of Xbox and PlayStation will mean even less risk-taking and more dependence on expanding established genres such as first-person shooters and racing games.

And finally, if you had one piece of advice to give to a game designer who was just starting out, what would it be?

TW: *Be firm but fair from the outset when dealing with other would-be designers. They tend to sit in chairs labeled producer, programmer, or artist. Design by committee generally ends in disaster, so don't be railroaded by strong personalities, but do accept criticism graciously. If someone has a genuinely good idea, don't be afraid to take it on board and give credit where it's due.*

PART II

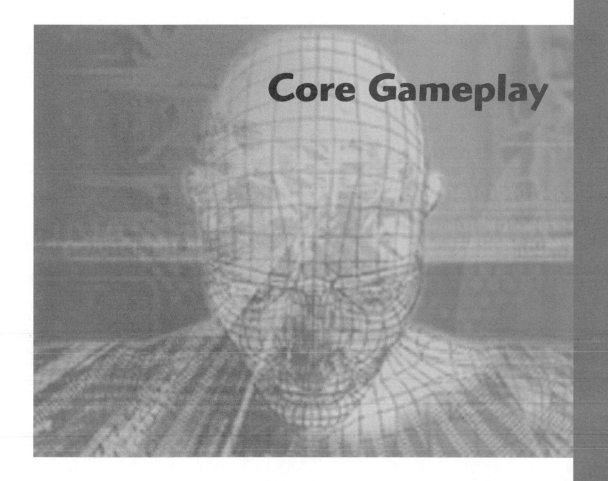

Core Gameplay

Chapter 5

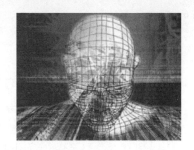

Designing Camera Systems

"Who would believe that so small a space could contain the image of all the universe?"

Leonardo da Vinci (talking about the pinhole camera)

In the first part of this book, we explored many of the background issues related to designing games for different markets, platforms, and real-world constraints and opportunities. This has set the stage for more detail in the second part of the book, in which you'll learn how to handle core gameplay features as you design your games. This involves dissecting components such as camera systems, control systems, characters, game environments, and level design. All of these elements are fundamental parts of the foundation behind all great games. Get any of the aspects wrong, and your game will never reach its true potential.

In this chapter, we'll start with the techniques for using good camera work to improve the playability of your games. We'll look at why camera work is so important in creating a good game, and you'll see some examples of games that get it right and those that don't. We'll then look at the basic camera principles that game designers draw on to create their games, such as center of rotation, the importance of fluidity, using cutaways, and so on. We'll also explore the four important styles of cameras that are used in games: third-person cameras, first-person cameras, vehicle cameras, and God/strategy cameras. As you work through this chapter, you'll learn how to go through the process of determining what type of camera system is best suited for the type of game that you are designing.

The Importance of Good Camera Work

The in-game camera represents the players' eyes. It's something that is used every second that they play the game. Yet far too often, it isn't given nearly enough attention. There is no excuse for this; designers that don't take time to think about their in-game camera should be locked up in a dark room and forced to play *Catwoman* for the rest of their natural lives.

I've played too many titles in which the camera behaves like it's been strapped to an insane ostrich. (Close your eyes and imagine, just for a second, what it would look like if you stuck a DV camera to the head of a mentally unbalanced ostrich.) In bad games, you'll find the camera bouncing around, jerking, and getting stuck behind objects. You might be attacked, but you can't properly see who has attacked you because the camera has wandered off and is now bisecting a rock and your character's ear.

Bad cameras ruin games. It's difficult to explain without using video clips to demonstrate, but there are many examples of games with poor camera systems, and one or more of the following problems usually come to light:

- The main character obscures what you want to see (see Figure 5.1).

- A third-person camera is set at a strange angle or a position that makes the game hard to play (see Figure 5.2).

- When you turn around within an enclosed space, the camera goes crazy and starts moving in strange directions or goes through the walls of the environment.

- The camera is locked too tight to the player or vehicle, making it feel like it is attached to an invisible iron rod. This makes the camera feel jerky, because every small bump or gradient change on the floor will instantly alter the camera quite sharply.

- The camera is too loosely attached to the player or vehicle and tends to wander off, drifting too far away or suffering too much lag when it rotates, so you can't see what is in front of you until it catches up.

- Fixed static cameras are badly positioned so that when you are being attacked by someone a meter in front of you, the camera is looking down on your head from above and you can't see a thing (see Figure 5.3).

The annoying thing is that the difference between a good camera and a bad camera can be a couple lines of code. It can be half an hour's work if you know what you're doing. But the failure to spend half an hour fixing a bad camera can make a bigger difference

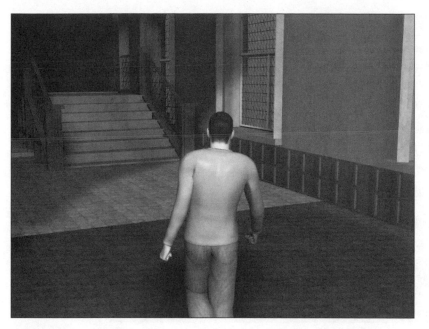

Figure 5.1
A badly positioned camera that causes your character to block important items in front of you.

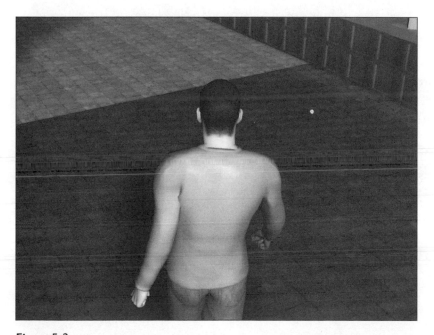

Figure 5.2
A poorly positioned third-person camera that stops you from seeing where you are going.

Figure 5.3
A badly placed static camera that prevents you from seeing an attacker directly ahead.

to your game than thousands of hours of great artwork or level design. If you're an aspiring game designer and you want to avoid the most common and damaging design mistakes, make it your goal to understand how good game cameras work.

War Story: Camera Work Can Make or Break Your Game

To emphasize the importance of this chapter's topic, let me tell you about a game that I was lucky enough to work on in the past. When I got involved with the project, the gameplay was in quite a state. It felt awful and played badly, and everyone pretty much agreed that it was destined for review scores of about 40 to 50 percent. In fact, there was a real case for canceling the project at that point.

Immediately, we made a few alterations to the way the camera behaved and a couple of control changes. The gameplay was literally transformed. Instead of feeling frustrating, the game had become really enjoyable overnight. Just moving around and interacting with the game world was great fun. The game ended up getting 80 percent review scores, sold almost a million copies, and won two awards. I'm not telling you this to blow my own trumpet (God knows, I've worked on a few nightmare projects as well), but just to show you how important the cameras and controls are. Combined, they are the single most important element of a game. Get them right and you've got a fantastically strong foundation to build from. Get them wrong and your house is going to fall down. They will make or break your game; it's as simple as that.

A Library of a Thousand Different Cameras

Hopefully, this chapter will help give you a good idea of what to think about when you're designing the core gameplay for your next project. But nothing beats experience. Borrow or rent as many games as you can. You only need to play the first 10 or 20 minutes of each game to analyze the way its camera works (and weigh up the strengths and weaknesses of its control system, which we'll discuss in the next chapter). Don't be afraid to use other games as examples when you're trying to get your gameplay right. This book is about the real world, where we look at other games to see what worked well and what didn't. A pure designer might want to lock themselves away in isolation and create the perfect system without looking at any other games. But this isn't how the real world works. If I had a hundred dollars for every time someone referred back to a Mario or Zelda game, I'd be a rich man. There are thousands of games out there; think of these as a library of a thousand different attempts at camera and controls. Some of them work brilliantly; some of them don't. Learn which ones work well and why.

Five Examples of Excellent Camera Systems

Before we get into specific camera techniques, let's look at some games that use great camerawork. I'll tried to select different types of games so that you can gain some insight about how the camerawork can make a big difference in different syles of games.

Legend of Zelda: Ocarina of Time by Nintendo

This game is a superbly crafted game, with a camera that allows you to see exactly what you want to see. The game deals very simply with small internal environments and big open exteriors. It's a real benchmark title for many reasons, and you could do much, much worse than base your game camera on the Zelda camera system.

Tony Hawks Pro Skater by Activision

This was one of the only times that I've noticed a new camera solution that genuinely made my jaw drop. It premiered in the very first Tony Hawks game (and was retained in subsequent ones and copied by many other titles). I'm talking about the way the camera flies up above the skater when you leap into the air. No one had done it before, and the camera technique worked so well. The transition from behind the character to above is perfectly smooth and perfectly timed and makes the jumps feel infinitely more exciting than they would otherwise. Pure genius.

Max Payne by Rockstar

This is a superb example of allowing the player to control a third-person camera using the right analog stick. It works extremely well, and the player always feels like they are in control of what's going on. Despite some quite tight and narrow environments, the camera very rarely has any problems at all. In slow motion "bullet-time," for example, the camera feels perfect. If you're creating a third-person camera for a shooter, you could do much worse than copy *Max Payne*.

Galleon by SCi

If you get the chance to play *Galleon*, take a close look at the camera system. It's a unique approach where you control the camera rather than the character, without it feeling strange. It works very well and helps allow some extremely fast and frantic gameplay.

Metal Gear Solid by Konami

A superb third-person camera system that allows the player to see exactly what is needed to use the great stealth gameplay while showing off the awesome graphics to their very best. The camera moves around a great deal but always remains smooth and intuitive. It's a really superb example of camera design.

Five Examples of Bad Camera Systems

Studying games that have bad camera work can also be very beneficial, and hopefully, it will help to keep you from making mistakes that have been made by others.

Fantasic Four by Activision

This game has a poor camera system which suffers from the unusual problem of being too low most of the time. This means you often can't see what you want to see, as your view distance is too short. The camera occasionally gets stuck between people's legs, which looks painful, and certainly doesn't help the gameplay! Poor camera collision is a common problem with third-person cameras, and can really damage gameplay.

Death, Jr by Konami

This PSP title is a very average game with a dreadful camera system that tends to focus on entirely the wrong spot at exactly the worst time possible (when you're being attacked by large numbers of enemies and are on the minimum health level possible). At precisely this moment, the camera wanders off and decides to focus on a wall, or someone's foot. I have no idea what the designers and developers were thinking.

Charlie and the Chocolate Factory by Take 2

This game has all the hallmarks of a rushed license which was developed in an extremely short time to try and coincide with the movie. In terms of the camera, most of the action takes place from fixed camera views. Unfortunately, the cameras seem to have been placed at random, and hence solving many of the puzzles is often rather like pulling your own teeth out.

Sonic Adventure 2 Battle by Sega

A strong game let down by a constantly bizarre choice of camera angles and a horrible choice of camera system in general. It's a great game to play if you want to see what a huge effect a poor camera has on an otherwise enjoyable game.

Dino Crisis 3 by Capcom

This game provides another example of the perils of fixed camera positions. Not only are many of the cameras placed extremely poorly, but you often find the switch between one camera and another happening in the middle of a complicated jump. There is nothing more frustrating than pushing left, and just before you push the jump button, the camera switches so that continuing to push left now moves your character to the right!

5

Understanding Basic Camera Principles

Using cameras effectively in your games requires that you master the basic principles of how cameras operate, how they can be controlled, and how you can change them. We'll start with the basic techniques, such as center of rotation and the importance of fluidity. Later in the chapter, we'll look at how cameras can be controlled in other ways, such as using first-person or third-person cameras in a game to produce different kinds of effects. I'll try to provide you with as many examples as I can for the various techniques so that you'll be able to better visualize how the camera operates.

The Center of Rotation

Unless a camera is static (as used at times within horror games like *Resident Evil* and the classic *Alone in the Dark*) or runs along splines (as seen in linear platform games like *Crash Bandicoot* and *Peter Pan*), the in-game camera will follow your character/vehicle and will rotate around a certain point. This point is called the center of rotation (see Figure 5.4). It will often be the center of the character's head or body. If the camera is tracking a vehicle, the center of rotation is often a point somewhere between the front and the center of the vehicle. Changing the center of rotation can make a big difference to the feel of a camera. For example, if you are creating a driving game, try changing the center of rotation from the front bonnet/hood to the middle of the car and then to the rear. You will notice a dramatic difference in how the game feels and whether the car looks cool or just weird! In fact, you may consider using this difference to highlight the kind of car you are driving. By moving the center of rotation a little forward for front-wheel-drive cars and a little backward for rear-wheel-drive cars, you might help the player subconsciously feel how they are driving.

Figure 5.4
The center of rotation.

To Control or Not to Control?

One of the key questions you need to consider up front when designing your camera work is: Should you give your player the ability to move the camera and rotate it around your character? Games are generally split between those that do and those that don't. The advantage of giving the player control is that they can look at parts of the environment that they want to see. This is useful for games that involve exploration and finding secrets. The big disadvantage is that it's easy for less able players to get confused with the controls and run around with the camera facing their feet. It also means that you can't decide exactly what the player is looking at, which means the player might miss key set pieces and events. You should also consider whether to auto-center the camera when the player starts walking/running forward. This can be a helpful addition for many players, who use the freedom of camera control to look around when stationary but don't want to have to manually move the camera back into exactly the right place when they are running through a level again.

The Importance of Fluidity

It is vital that a camera feels fluid and springy. There should be no jerks, and the player should never notice the camera "lock" into place when it reaches a limit. You should use simple momentum on the camera and basic spring/damper math to ensure that the camera accelerates and decelerates smoothly in all axes and for translations (movement), as well as rotations. This rule holds true for cut-scene cameras as well as for in-game camera work. More and more game designers are copying the camera work from great films. To feel realistic, many cameras now include cameraman shake and physical effects. For example, if an enemy fires a shotgun toward your character, you might like to make the camera recoil and wobble slightly in response, as if it were hit by the blast. Touches like this can really add to the feeling of immersion generated by your game.

To Cut Away or Not to Cut Away

There are generally two schools of thought regarding video game camera design: you either allow the camera view to change and show something else in the middle of the gameplay (called cutaways) or never interfere with the camera while the player is playing the game, and stick with end-of-level full motion videos (FMVs) or cut scenes. The advantage of doing cutaways during the action (often pausing what the player is doing in order to show something else) is that you can give the game a really dynamic and cinematic feel. Let me highlight a few examples:

- The *Prince of Persia* games (particularly the most recent versions) often pause the action and switch to a new camera view to show a wall collapsing or a chandelier dropping down to crush an enemy as a result of the player's actions. The camera then returns to normal, and the player continues with the game. This makes the game feel very intense, as if there is always something going on, and the camera work mimics the MTV style of television, with quick cuts and nonstop action.

- I worked on a game based on the original *Italian Job* movie (see Figure 5.5), and the player was driving Mini cars from a third-person camera view. When the player hit a ramp and launched the car into the air, we cut to a cinematic camera

Figure 5.5
The original *Italian Job* game, with a cutaway camera showing a jump.

positioned below the jump, showed the car flying over the jump, and then switched back to the third-person camera just as it landed. The player remained in control, but since there isn't much you can do while a car is in the air, it worked very well and helped deliver the feeling of huge and dramatic car jumps.

Where problems can occur with this methodology is if the player is just about to do a time-critical action (like cutting off the head of a monster, which needs to happen at just the right moment). If the game cuts away just before this happens, the player will feel frustrated. When the game cuts back, the player will almost certainly need a second to readjust, and therefore his opportunity to decapitate the monster will have passed. So you need to think carefully about when you let the camera cut away, and maybe have it happen at certain checkpoints in your level where you know the player will not be doing anything other than walking/running.

On the other side of this argument lies games like the Half Life series, which brilliantly demonstrate how designers can create an entire game without leaving the first-person camera once, even for cut scenes or FMV sequences. All the cut scenes happen in real time around you, so you can look and move through them while they occur. Because the game never once breaks from player control (other than unfortunate brief "loading" screens), the game is incredibly immersive; it's easy to forget you are playing a game and to get dragged into the world the developers have created. If they had the camera cutting to external events, it would have made it a totally different kind of game and, in this case, I think a worse game.

 Reality Check: As you have probably guessed, my view is that both of these approaches can work very well, and both have their places. If your focus is building the main character and making the game feel cinematic, then cutting away to show cool things happening or to feature a dramatic set piece in which you can see your character's face is a good idea. But if you are creating a game in which you want to focus on immersion and creating a world that sucks the player in, you may want to consider completely avoiding cutaways.

Styles of Cameras

Now that we've discussed some of the basic techniques that apply to the different types of cameras used in games, let's dig a little deeper and look at the palette of cameras that are available. As you probably know, there is no "one size fits all" camera technique for every game, but there are camera decisions you can make early on in your game's design to greatly enhance the player's experience and create more compelling gameplay.

So how do you choose which style of camera to go for? I have split the cameras broadly into four types:

- Third-person cameras

- First-person cameras

- Vehicle cameras

- God/strategy cameras

We'll look at each of these in detail in a moment. If you want to create a vehicle-based game, you'll obviously want to use a vehicle camera, which is designed to maximize the sensation of speed and the ability to slide a vehicle and drive it fluidly from either behind or within the cockpit/driver's seat. If you are creating a game in which the player isn't in control of just one character but many different characters/units, you may want to consider a God/strategy camera, which allows the player to have a bird's-eye view of the action, zooming in and out, selecting various units, and ordering people/objects around.

If the player is going to control one main character, you will probably want to consider first-person or third-person cameras. First-person cameras are excellent for immersion and for shooters. This is the case not only for PCs (where the mouse makes aiming first-person games extremely intuitive) but also for consoles, as the HALO series has shown. Other than the Timesplitters series, the PlayStation 2 hasn't had a great deal of success with first person titles, but I suspect this is likely to change on the next generation of systems. The disadvantages of a first-person camera are that you can't see the main character and you also can't see the area to the sides and behind your character. If your game involves lots of platform elements (such as leaping up walls, jumping from ledges, or swinging from ropes), it will be really hard to do this from a first-person perspective because you don't have the required field of view.

Field of View

In real life, our eyes are capable of picking up movement from almost a 180-degree field. So when you are looking forward, if someone moves to your right or left, you will notice that movement. Within games, camera field of views are normally much smaller. When you sit a few meters away from a TV, it looks best when you show between 60 and 100 degrees of vision. This is one reason it's much harder to perform complex feats of agility in first-person games. With a third-person camera, you can see all around your character because the camera is behind and above the character even though it is still showing a 60- to 100-degree field of view. It's worth noting that you can change the field of view for dynamic effect. For example, you can select a turbo mode in a racing game, and if you widen the field of view slightly, everything will feel much faster. Also note that if your field of view is too small in a first-person game, it becomes incredibly difficult to orient yourself within the environment. See Figures 5.6 and 5.7 for examples of what a narrow and wide field of view look like from the same position in the same environment.

Figure 5.6
A narrow field of view.

Figure 5.7
A wide field of view.

The more agility you require of the player, the more ideal a third-person camera view can be. We've discussed cutaways, and for some reason, it feels more natural to cut away from a third-person camera than a first-person camera. If you want lots of cinematic cutaways during your game, again consider a third-person viewpoint. Choosing which to use is a big decision, and I recommend that you play some of the best examples of both types (starting with *Half-Life 2* and *Prince of Persia 3*) before you decide which to use.

Reality Check: It is also worth mentioning there is no law that says you need to stick to just one camera, and as we move on to the new generation of platforms, I suspect many games will have different cameras for different sections. For example, why not use a God/strategy-style camera to control the tactical situation in a war and then leap straight into a first-person camera to play individual soldiers within that battle. Or you might have a game where you switch between first- and third-person depending on what the player is doing (something that was done to a small extent with *Chronicles of Riddick*).

Using Third-Person Character Cameras

One major choice that you need to make with any third-person camera is whether to make it screen-centric or character-centric. What do I mean by this? If a camera is screen-centric, pressing up on the controller will make your character/car move toward the screen (away from you). In a character-centric game, pressing up on the controller will make your character/car move in the direction it is facing. This won't necessarily be into the screen. With many games where the camera is locked behind the main character, this difference isn't very noticeable. It does, however, make a huge difference if your camera isn't locked behind the character. See Figure 5.8 for a comparison of some popular third-person games, and where their default camera positions are.

Figure 5.8
Default camera positions for some popular third-person games.

There are three general types of third-person camera systems that I am aware of. Let's explore them next.

Behind-Character Camera

The most common third-person camera is the behind-character camera, where a floating camera follows the character from above and behind. Often this camera remains at a fixed distance behind the character, only moving closer when an object (such as a wall) gets in the way.

The advantage of this camera is that once it is working, it should work anywhere in the game world, so no extra time is required to set up lots of individual cameras. It also gives the player a large amount of freedom; they can see whatever they want to by simply rotating the character (or the camera, if you allow the player to rotate the camera using the right analog stick). The main disadvantages are that it doesn't allow you to use camera positioning and movement to create atmosphere, and it is hard to make these cameras work perfectly in small tight areas when the player backs into walls or turns around quickly.

Toby Gard's excellent game *Galleon* introduces an unusual twist. Although in effect the camera remains behind the character, you are able to point the camera where you want to go and the character will move a little left and right in order to reach that point. So, for example, if you want to move to the other side of a canyon and there is a narrow plank of wood running diagonally from your side to the other, you can point the camera at the other side and walk toward it. Your character will automatically track the plank of wood and move along it in order to end up where you're pointing.

Static/Rotating Camera

Several games use fixed-position cameras (often high up in the corner of rooms) that either are stationary (with the character moving around the screen) or rotate (and sometimes zoom) to track the character. Games like *Alone in the Dark* used these cameras to great effect, and you'll see them in many horror games, as well as adventure games where the designers want to use a particular camera view to create an atmosphere or to highlight certain objects within the scene. The disadvantage of this camera system is that it can be hard for the player to see what is ahead and it takes away the freedom of being able to look where you want to look, which many players must get used to. The highly successful Resident Evil series also tends to use this kind of camera.

Spline/Tracking Cameras

The third common option for third-person cameras is to have them moving but fixed to invisible rails that run through your world. These rails can be straight but are more often spline curves, which make the camera move in a much more believable (and smooth) way—very much like sweeping film shots where the camera moves along on rails or a crane. These cameras work best in contained environments, and some games switch to this kind of camera when indoors and use a behind-character camera for outdoors. More advanced versions of this system allow for tracks that split and join, allowing the camera to change paths depending on what the player does. The advantage of this camera system is that the camera will never become stuck; it's always where you want it to be. It's also good for creating atmosphere because you can direct the camera farther away or into a particular place for effect. The main disadvantage is that it's harder for players to control their characters, especially when they want to turn back on themselves; it can get quite confusing.

By and large, I would almost always recommend making your camera screen-centric.

Using First-Person Cameras

Traditional first-person cameras are generally easier to implement, although in recent games, designers are coming up with some excellent additions. The traditional first-person camera is set at head height (between the eyes of your character) with only the lower arms of your character (and any associated weaponry) visible. Additional little touches can make first-person cameras a little more interesting and involve the game player more. These include things like very subtle movement as you run around, simulating the bob of a character's head. In driving games, a "driver's helmet" camera is sometimes included, which is essentially a first-person camera within the vehicle. This camera is subject to physics forces, so when the car brakes hard, the camera will dip forward slightly. Keep these effects very subtle and they will really enhance your game.

The excellent *Chronicles of Riddick* game showed how well transitions between first-and third-person cameras can be handled. Before this game appeared, it was assumed that flicking quickly between different kinds of cameras would break up the feeling of immersion that the game builds up. But done at the right time (in the split second when the player doesn't have control of their character, when pressing a button or starting to climb a ladder), it actually works and solves one of the key problems with first-person cameras: that you can't see your character. It is for this reason that many license-based games use third-person cameras; you want the player to see and realize that they're playing a famous character and that is really hard to do in first person. *Duke Nukem 3D* solved this by having lots of mirrors within its levels, but that might not be a solution for your particular design.

Using Vehicle Cameras

I'm always amazed by the differences that have developed between vehicle- and character-based games. One of the key things that people now expect in driving games (because it has always been done this way) is multiple cameras that the player can select.

Personally, I blame the fantastic *Sega Rally* arcade games with their four camera buttons, which influenced every racing game designer from then onward. Anyway, players are now used to the fact that they can choose their camera and have therefore developed favorite driving cameras. Some people like to drive from behind their car, while others won't play anything without a full-screen bumper cam.

Reality Check: What frustrates me as a designer (and forgive me for the massive generalization that I'm about to make) is that many people in PR and marketing honestly believe that the more cameras you have in a game, the better. A marketing phrase such as "'Fifteen different camera views" is something they can stick on the back of the box. But it just isn't true. As designers, it's up to us to provide players with cameras that work well. One great camera view is better than five bad ones. Throwing in lots of extra cameras that aren't very usable is a waste of time, and it will take much more time to toggle between the various cameras to find the one you want. I recommend using no more than four cameras in vehicle games.

The most effective cameras that can be used with vehicles include the behind-the-car camera, the bonnet/dashboard camera, the bumper camera, and the driver cam.

Behind-the-Car Camera

This camera (see Figure 5.9) is one that is placed above and behind a car, normally several meters away. I suggest using only one behind-the-car camera and placing it in a position that allows you to see the whole car, but ensures that the car body doesn't

Figure 5.9
Behind-the-car camera.

obscure your view of the road ahead. Have it low enough that you can see the wheels. Rotate it around a point anywhere between the center and the front of the car. If you want, allow it to move slightly farther away when the car is accelerating and move slightly closer when the car brakes. Allow it to lag rotation-wise behind the car when the player turns the car to the left or right, (although I'd suggest that you don't allow the camera to lag more than 45 to 60 degrees at any time). All camera movements must be smooth, using momentum.

Bonnet/Dashboard Camera

This view (see Figure 5.10) may be a standard bonnet view (situated at the rear edge of the bonnet, with the 3D bonnet filling the bottom third of the screen). Alternatively, you might like to move the camera back a little and show the windscreen and the bonnet. If the camera is fixed rigidly to the car, your bonnet or windscreen will look like a rendered 2D bitmap, so you should try to allow your camera to rotate and move very subtly to simulate real life. If you stuck a video camera onto the bonnet of a car, you'd definitely notice camera bounce and shake when the car traveled at speed. Add this effect into the game and your camera will feel 10 times better.

Figure 5.10
Using a bonnet camera.

Figure 5.11
Using a bumper camera.

Bumper Camera

This camera (see Figure 5.11) is essentially a very low camera that is placed directly ahead of the front bumper. You won't see any part of the vehicle, and the key to this camera is giving the player the feeling of speed because it is so low. Ideally, the camera will be literally attached to the bottom of the car bumper, allowing you to experience the car bouncing on the road surface and get a feeling for the intensity as the car tilts left or right. In my view, the worst bumper cameras stay a fixed height above the road and float along smoothly. I suggest you place this type of camera as low as you dare without causing graphical problems or polygon clipping.

Driver Cam

If you're trying to simulate real life, you might want to include a driver camera (see Figure 5.12). This can be as simple as placing a camera in the position so that the driver's eyes can show the player the dashboard, windscreen, and bonnet. Or it may be as sophisticated as modeling the g-forces on the driver's head (so if you brake sharply, the camera will move forward and tilt downward). You might also want to experiment with turning the camera toward the road ahead, which will give the player the sensation that the driver is turning their head into the corners. This can really assist the player when turning sharply.

Figure 5.12
Using a driver camera.

Strategy/God Game Cameras

Strategy, sim, and God games use very different camera systems compared to the cameras used in most other kinds of games (see Figure 5.13). I define a "God" game as a game in which the player sees the world from a camera high above the ground and can't control an individual character.

The player often has much more control of the cameras for these type of games since they often need the freedom to look anywhere in the environment and zoom in or out of the game world. The kind of camera systems you use will depend greatly on exactly what kind of game you are making. Sim games often track a particular character, and the cameras are fairly basic, looking down on the character from an angle and giving the user a number of different zoom levels. When the character goes inside a building, you can deal with these cameras in a number of ways, by switching to an internal camera, making the walls of the building semi-transparent, or not drawing the walls and roof of the building at all.

Real-time strategy games are tricky; having a fixed isometric-style camera feels quite dated now, but giving the player full 3D control over the camera can result in the player getting lost, especially if they rotate the camera and get disoriented. A good solution is

Figure 5.13
A typical strategy/God game camera.

to allow some 3D movement, but to keep the orientation the same (so that up is always north on the map).

Using Other Camera Techniques

Using cameras isn't just a question of picking the right type of camera and being done with it. There are a number of really interesting places in most games where you can use camera work in an interesting and cinematic way to add style and polish to the experience. Let's take a look at a few examples.

Cut Scenes

In-game cut scenes and FMV sequences are getting ever more elaborate and professional. In the past, it was possible to get away with a fixed-position camera pointing at your characters with some basic lip-syncing. However, players expect much more nowadays, and you need to think like a film director when composing your cut scenes. Moving cameras, interesting editing, and intelligent scene composition are important to make your cut scenes and FMV both exciting and dynamic. Consider involving a proper director or editor to give your cut-scenes some real polish. Alternatively, you could read a few books on directing cameras in films to give you an idea of the vocabulary of film. There are many different types of shots that are used to give different effects. A simple example is that filming your character from low down makes them look heroic and strong. Filming a character from above has the opposite effect. Cut scenes don't need to be consistent with the in-game camera, but it does help to ensure that the cut scenes don't jar too much with your in-game camera work.

Creative Idea: Watch Some Classic Films for Inspiration

If you want to give your game a particular style, watch classic movies with a similar theme and make a note of what the director does, how the camera moves, how often the camera cuts, whether a wide-angle or narrow lens is used, and so on. For example, if you're making a horror game, why not watch some classic Hitchcock films and use his camera techniques in your cut scenes? Not only will it be a refreshing change to the large number of dull and lifeless cut scenes around, but it may also remind players of the movies and help your game develop tension, fear, and atmosphere.

Using Cool Camera Effects

One of the best ways to make your in-game cameras more exciting is to use some effects to make them feel realistic. This can give your game real style. Here are some examples:

Explosions: When an explosion happens near your camera, make it physically shake the camera and cause it to sway and move slightly.

Damage: You could make the lens crack or shatter when damage occurs to the character or vehicle in your game or if an object hits the camera. This can fade after a while if you don't want an image of a crack obscuring your game for long. If an object hits the camera, make it recoil before gently returning to its original position.

Swaying when sprinting: Make the camera sway slightly or bounce up and down gently when your character is running fast.

Tilting: If your vehicle or character turns a corner sharply, why not tilt the camera a little bit before it recovers? This was done to great effect in the *Starsky and Hutch* game.

Lens debris: Have objects collect on the lens of your camera. They can fade out over time to avoid getting the camera too opaque. You might include bug splats, rain drops, drops of oil, dirt, and so on.

Handheld cameras: Why not emulate the handheld cameras that you see in many TV dramas or reality TV shows? *NYPD Blue* was a great example, where the constant use of shaky handheld cameras gave it a very raw and edgy feel. You could do the same thing in-game, rather than relying on the normal, perfectly smooth camera system.

The Religion of Blu-tak

In an age where many people are unable to contemplate leaving home without at least three handheld electronic devices and even our pens have USB connections and data storage, it is a strange truth that one of the most important items in the game designer's toolbelt is a large ball of Blu-Tak.

So why is a substance usually used for sticking posters to the wall in student bedrooms such an important element of game design? It's because you can stick it onto a TV/ monitor without damaging the screen. This allows you to notice some very subtle aspects of the core gameplay:

- It lets you see exactly which point the camera rotates around.

- It lets you see how the camera moves around the world.

- It allows you to see whether your main character moves around the screen or stays locked in position relative to the camera.

Regardless of how the programmers think the camera system is working, you should always check it out for yourself, and this is a great way to do so.

Checking Camera Movement

So, how can you use Blu-Tak to check how your camera is moving and rotating? First, let's look at third-person cameras and how you can quickly answer a few important questions.

Is the Character Central?

Place the Blu-Tak in the center of the screen and see how your on-screen character is placed in relation to it. This is easy on a monitor, but bear in mind that on some televisions, part of the image may be clipped off the side. You should either use the game's built-in screen-centering option (if it has one) or else use the on-screen display to measure the proper center, stick a piece of Blu-Tak there, and then compare your character position to that. Note that you might not actually want your character to be directly in the center of the screen (this can get in the way of aiming reticules), but you can use the stationary Blu-Tak to check that your character remains exactly where you want as you play the game.

How Does the Character Move and Respond to Control Changes?

Place four small bits of Blu-Tak onto the screen at the top, bottom, left, and right sides of the character when the character is stationary. Then run around the world, trying to make the camera behave in the most extreme ways possible. Run fast and then stop suddenly. Move into the corner of rooms and turn around. Jump onto objects. The Blu-Tak allows you to easily see how the camera moves and rotates around the character. Hopefully, this will help you identify any camera problems that are present within your game. Try it because it really works!

Let's take a look at how to do similar things with vehicle games.

How Does the Car Rotate?

Place a piece of Blu-Tak directly above the center-front of the vehicle when it is stationary. Then drive fast, and steer from left to right, trying to make the car turn as sharply as possible. Make a note of exactly where the center of rotation is. Is your car rotating around the front or a point in the center? In my experience, you'll probably want the vehicle to rotate around a point somewhere between the front and center of the car, probably closer to the center.

How Does the Car Move?

Again, place four small bits of Blu-Tak onto the screen at the top, bottom, left, and right sides of the vehicle when it's stationary. Drive, fly, or sail around the world, and notice how the vehicle moves in relation to the Blu-Tak. Does the camera lag behind the vehicle when you accelerate? When you brake sharply, does the camera move closer to the vehicle?

Remember that you can use the Blu-Tak process with other games. Put on a classic game, and use it to identify exactly how the camera system differs to your title. Some designers use masking tape in exactly the same way.

Summary

Your game camera system is vitally important. Play the best games in the genre, and compare your camera system with theirs. Try to give detailed and specific feedback. Use your imagination with your camera and don't be afraid to try out different effects, and even jump between different camera types at different times. But remember to keep everything smooth; jerky camera movements and cameras that snap into place will turn people off to your game immediately. Learn what makes a good game camera and your title will have a really solid foundation to build on.

Equally important to having a brilliant game camera is having a superb control system, and that's what we're going to look at in the next chapter.

An Interview with Simon Andreasen

Simon Andreasen is the creative director of Deadline Games, one of Europe's fastest-growing and most innovative development studios. Not only does Simon have a great deal of experience with games on various platforms, but his track record in professional television production has given him a unique approach to game design, resulting in highly cinematic camera work.

So Simon, what do you think is the most common problem with in-game cameras in modern games?

SA: The most conservative games have only one player-controlled, first- or third-person camera and a lot of badly edited and directed cut scenes. A lot of developers could certainly learn a great deal from film and television people.

Where do you stand on the issue of first-person versus third-person cameras? Can you see yourself designing a first-person game at some point?

SA: The difference between first-person and third-person camera work in games is no more than the difference between a story or film told in first or third person. Very few stories or films are actually told from either perspective, and I'm exited to see more and more games picking this up and playing around with cameras. A recent experience for me was playing Chronicles of Riddick, which, even though primarily being first person, is so well told and executed that the character stands out as if it was a third-person game.

My first game was a first-person adventure game and—even though I have made more than five third-person games since then—I still dream about making a first-person game... soon!

Are there any games where the camera or control system has made you go "wow!"?

SA: My major "wow" was "Metal Gear Solid. It did something with the PlayStation which the machine was not intended for—creating true in-game-rendered, truly cinematic and dramatic experiences with very little space, power, and help from the machinery. Metal Gear paved the way for the whole generation of games like Splinter Cell, Hitman, and a hundred other similar cinematic games.

My next big "wow" was GTA with a minimalist control scheme and a large complex super-fun sandbox game world. Like Metal Gear, GTA challenged the machine and did what the machine was not intended for.

It will be really interesting to see how developers will challenge the new machines. With only half a gig of RAM and more processor power, it's easy to see where Microsoft and Sony want us to go. But hey, the winner will most probably go in a direction they'd never thought about. The big guys need us small folks... just like Hollywood needs John Woo, Tarantino, and Coppola.

Has your background in TV and filmmaking given you a different approach to the cameras that you use in your games?

SA: Only few games benefit from the full use of cinematic camera tricks. I guess it is because only a few developers have had hands–on experience making films. Developers could learn a lot from looking at the masters of cinematography and having one talent responsible for al the camera work in a game—that being cut–scenes or in–game cameras.

One example of a trick that can be used (with great results in games) is the vertigo effect developed by Hitchcock's cinematographer Robert Burks, who shot the Vertigo film. It is great for short and effective zooms (less than 3 seconds), for shocks, and for dramatic cuts. The trick is super easy: you change the FOV to a wide angle while you dolly in on an object. This trick gives the illusion that the camera is moving backwards and you get a creature right up in your face. Spooky!

5

What is your view on static or spline-based tracking cameras (the kind of thing often seen in horror games)? Is there an argument for using cinematic-type camera positions and movements even though they can be a little confusing?

SA: In early games with 3D rendered cut scenes, people were so fascinated with long trackings and overdid them a lot. But now I see very cool ways of using them in context in the game, where the player can choose to activate tracking strategically and even take partial control of a tracking. An example of brilliant use is in Mark of Kri, where the player meets a bird and can choose to get a glimpse of the level he is about to enter by letting the game camera follow the bird.

What are you most proud of in your career so far?

SA: In all of the games I've made, I have emphasized that the games can be played by different player types and cater to more than one gaming style.

Four years ago, I was assigned to make a Trivial Pursuit–type of game for the PC called Globetrotter. The publisher wanted the target audience to be from 10 to 40 years old. Imagine trying to make a game which has to be fun both for a 10-year-old CounterStrike geek, a 13-year-old teenage daughter, a competitive 40-year-old father, and a computer-phobic 40-year-old woman. Well, we did. The game was released in Europe and got an average of +80% rating in the hardcore gaming press, all major newspapers, and even women's magazines. And it outsold all other games in the Nordic countries but Diablo2 that year.

What is your favorite ever game (of all time), and why?

SA: I am not sentimental and my favorite game is always the last fantastic game I have been playing (or are playing). I just left Burnout 3 and I am just crazily in love with it. The Criterion guys just do so many things right: graphically, physics, control-wise, diversion, and the progression is just perfect.

A list of favorite games through the last 20 years includes Pac-Man, Haunted House, Dungeons, Elite, Prince of Persia (the old PC version), Lost Vikings, Wolfenstein, Sim City, Indiana Jones (the early LucasArts games), Full Throttle, Doom, Wipeout, Carmageddon, Grim Fandango, Metal Gear Solid, Resident Evil2, GT, Final Fantasy7, Warcraft2, Heroes of Might and Magic, Commandoes, Myth, Diablo, Half-Life, SSX, Max Payne, GTA, Mafia, Hitman2, ICO, Metroid Prime, Mark of Kri, Total War Shogun, Knight of the Old Republic, and Burnout.

Next game to play: God of War.

What do you think is the biggest game design mistake that people regularly make with games?

SA: The single big mistake designers often make is bad controls. You can never test controls early enough. Bring in hundreds of people and observe them playing. Let them rate the controls so that you can evaluate the tests through the full production. In my opinion, control trimming never ends.

The major overall mistake many developers make is that they create games for themselves and forget the gamers. This results in games that are too hard to control; too hard to get into; too hard of a learning curve; too black, dark, monochrome, and gloomy environments; too zombie, sci-fi, and trolls and goblins; and are just very hardcore and niche.

If money and technology were unlimited, what kind of game would you most like to see made?

SA: Here I am very egocentric. My biggest wish is to make or see somebody make a U.S. remake of my first game, Black Out from 1996 (only published in the Nordic countries). The game system has many similarities to the "play as good or bad" ideas of Knights of the Old Republic and Fable. But in Black Out, there's more to life than good or bad and the game takes place in a gritty contemporary setting (think Seven).

The structure of the game is a murder mystery in which you are the central character. Unlike previous games, the key is not to be found in "a cigarette butt left on the scene of the crime," but in the psychological profile of the murderer. By exploring the city in which you can move around, and through a series of memories and flashbacks, you will realize early on in the game that you are the murderer.

The point system in Blackout is unique. It is kept concealed from the player and operates by noting the player's choices and categorizing them according to four temperaments, described by the four elements: earth, water, fire, and air. In the course of the game, the player is presented with a number of choices. Each time an answer to a question is given or a choice is made, it is registered by the game. The personality that dominates at any given time is decisive for how the game responds and which pieces information the player gains access to.

What do you think is the biggest challenge facing game designers as we move forward?

SA: I think the biggest challenge for developers is not gameplay-related or creative in any sense. There is so much great talent out there and more are coming with the new generations.

The biggest challenge for game designers is the pressure created by a continuous demand for higher production values. A lot of great studios have gone bust the last few years because they simply couldn't handle large-scale productions, big budgets, and couldn't keep the creative idea intact through productions lasting up to three or four years. Also, publishers have a great responsibility believing in the creative talent and strong individuals. If we do not keep this in mind, the industry will just be pumping out an endless line of clones. And, in the end, this will be very bad for all of us.

And finally, if you had one piece of advice to give to a game designer who was just starting out, what would it be?

SA: Don't think you can do everything yourself. Listen to your colleagues (artists, level designers, animators, coders, and producers) and use their input—they are the real experts.

5

Chapter 6

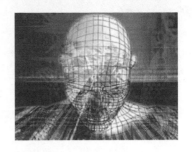

Control Systems

"What man's mind can create, man's character can control."
Thomas Edison

In the previous chapter, you saw just how important the in-game camera is. Getting it wrong can ruin a potentially great game. But the in-game camera has an equally vital partner—the control system. Together, this dynamic duo are responsible for the "feel" of your game. The control system is how your playable character(s) or vehicle responds to the player when they press a button, move an analog stick, move their body in front of an EyeToy camera, or even wave the controller around in the case of the Nintendo Revolution. Get the control system right and you're on your way to creating a masterpiece.

Creating Gameplay Magic

Many people believe in love at first sight. When you meet that special someone, you know immediately. The chemistry between the two of you feels just right. Even if you don't believe in that, it's a scientific fact that we make up our minds about strangers within the first few seconds. We get a gut reaction; an instinct. First impressions count. (If you'd like to read a good book about how this instinct works, check out the best-selling book *Blink: The Power of Thinking Without Thinking* by Malcolm Gladwell.)

It sounds obvious, but the same is true of control systems. When you pick up a great game for the first time, it's "love at first sight" with the right control system. It instinctively feels right. When you use the controller, your character moves just as you'd expect. There is no difference between what you want your character to do and what the character actually does in response to your input. You can see exactly what you need to do within the game world. The gameplay and controls feel smooth, fun, and intuitive. You can't wait to explore the level you are playing and get into the game. You enjoy playing so much that you don't want to stop, even though you have other important things tugging at you, like going to work or getting something done around the house.

Compare this with a bad game. Right away your character doesn't feel responsive. He looks like he's not really connecting with the environment. You can't get your character facing the right direction. You want to stop moving, but his animation carries on for a second too long. It feels like you're fighting with the controls. You're attacked. You try to get a weapon out, but it is hidden behind a horrible inventory menu that takes several seconds to understand. You get killed and you have to wait for a 20-second reload before you can restart. Your first impressions are awful. Having this experience is the gaming equivalent of going out on a blind date and meeting a psychotic bunny-boiler who likes dressing up as Attila the Hun; you're going to be out of there faster than you can say, "Sack the designer."

 Reality Check: Making great and intuitive gameplay isn't magic. It's a science, and I believe that pretty much all the great games have been carefully designed to be that way; the magic rarely comes by accident. And the control system you use is absolutely fundamental to this. If you're an aspiring game designer and you want to avoid the most common and damaging design mistakes, make it your goal to understand how intuitive control systems are created.

A Library of a Thousand Different Control Systems

As I mentioned in the previous chapter, borrow or rent as many games as you can. Analyze the strengths and weaknesses of their control system. Use other games as examples when you want to get your gameplay right. There are thousands of games available. Think of these games as a library of a thousand different attempts at control systems. Let's next look at some examples of games that have great control systems.

Mario 64 by Nintendo
In my view, this is one of the greatest games ever developed. *Mario* demonstrates the perfect one-stick control system for a third-person platform game.

Ico by Sony
Try really hard to get ahold of a copy of *Ico*. It deserves its status as the PlayStation 2's hidden diamond. It disappeared without a trace at retail, yet it does so many incredible things in terms of game design. The control system, particularly the way you get to interact with the second character, is absolutely jaw-dropping.

Goldeneye by Nintendo

Goldeneye on the Nintendo 64 was one of the first truly great console first-person shooters. It proved that first-person titles could work well outside of the PC platform. The controls were simple and intuitive and they fit perfectly with the gameplay.

EyeToy: Play by Sony

A extremely unique title that came bundled with its own small camera. Plug the camera into your PS2, put it on top of your television, and it becomes an input device, tracking changes in the image to allow you to hit virtual objects by waving your arms around. Pure genius.

Basic Control Design Techniques

I already mentioned that the best control systems are intuitive. But this doesn't mean that every part of the control system needs to be intuitive; great games have unique features, which means that there may be some new actions to learn. These actions, however, should be simple to pick up, and the player should be able to get comfortable with them very quickly. A good example is the original *Tomb Raider*, and in particular, the combat controls. The combat was implemented with a simple technique that works beautifully—one button is used to pull out your weapon and one to fire. The aiming is taken care of for you automatically, but you can clearly see where you are aiming and what you are aiming at. Since the key element of the game is about where you are moving your character, and not about aiming, the designers kept the game very straightforward. Had they put in a second stick aiming system, forcing you to try to aim at the same time you're moving, the control system would have been way too complex for most players. If they made it so that you could only fire ahead of you, the game would have been fiddly and frustrating. As it was, the control system used was an intuitive one that fit the gameplay perfectly.

 Reality Check: A great way to try out different control systems is to get new players to test them out. If they are struggling after several minutes, chances are your control system isn't intuitive and is therefore going to cause problems for your players. Control systems often take a long time to get just right, so don't get demoralized if your first attempt doesn't meet with universal approval. Keep testing the controls on a random selection of new people, listen to their feedback, and go back and tweak things. After doing this a few times, you should find you have something that works well.

In the following sections, we'll take a close look at the elements that make up a control system.

Understand What People Are Used To

I used to be a believer in the purity of game design; if you can create the perfect system, then it doesn't matter what any other games have done before, and it doesn't matter what people expect; they'll love your game regardless. You could sit in an isolated room never having seen any other games, but if you were a good enough designer, you could create perfection regardless.

Unfortunately, in my experience, this is a fallacy. Players get used to control systems, and different kinds of controls become the norm. If you're creating a first-person shooter for PCs, you should seriously consider allowing the players to look around using the mouse and move their character using the W, S, A, and D keys. Players are so used to this control setup that it would be crazy to try to offer the same functionality in a different way and force them to learn something new just for your game. In the same way, many first-person console games offer a twin-stick control system with turning/ aiming on one stick and movement on the other. So if you're creating a game that isn't in a unique genre of its own, it is definitely worth playing other big-selling games of a similar type and seeing what control layout they use. If most of them use the same system, and the games have sold and reviewed well, chances are this system is pretty much a standard. Only change it if you have a really good reason and you think you can create something even more intuitive.

Aiming Up and Down

It is a strange fact of life that around 50 percent of people like to push up on a stick to move a camera/cursor up on the screen and the other 50 percent like to push down in order to move it up, much as you would the controls of an aircraft. Actually, I suspect that more of the public prefer the first method (known as non-inverted) but that more people in the game industry prefer the second method. I must admit that I've never gotten around to actually measuring this split scientifically, so if anyone has done so, please let me know. Regardless, almost every game includes a "invert Y-axis" option. The method that is used as the default one tends to be determined by the person who can shout the loudest. I'd strongly recommend making the default setting non-inverted, not just because it is how I play, but because in my experience, it is how more mass-market gamers play. A number of games (most notably *HALO*) actually ask the player at the beginning to look up at the ceiling and then note whether the player instinctively moves up or down on the stick. The game then recommends an inverted or non-inverted control, depending on the player's instinctive movement. If you can do this well, it's a really elegant way to help players get the control system right.

Control Options: Lots or Few

Many games feature a whole host of different control options for the player, often allowing them to choose between 10 different controller configurations, many of which are totally unplayable. The ironic thing is that the vast majority of players will only likely use the default control system. Other than allowing players to invert the y-axis, I would strongly recommend having only one control configuration on console games and making sure it's really excellent. Multiple control configurations always smacks to me of designers who didn't really know what the best way to play the game was. You should have multiple configurations only if you're really not sure of the best method and your QA team is split on which they prefer.

Things are different on the PC; players often have their own individual preferences in terms of keys, since the keyboard can be used in so many different ways. For PC games, I generally suggest allowing players to redefine all the controls if they want to, in part due to the nature of PC gamers, who like to be able to tweak their experience much more than console gamers do. However, you should still spend plenty of time making sure the default setup is as close to ideal as possible. If you are having trouble coming up with the ideal default settings, try to let your players decide. After all, they usually know best. Assemble a few groups of players and give each group a version of the game with different default settings. After they have had time to play the game for a while, check in with them and see if there are certain settings that most of the players like the best.

6

Two Sticks versus One

Deciding on a control system for modern console games can be difficult. One of the hardest decisions is whether to base your character control around one analog stick or two. These are two fundamentally different ways of controlling your character, and different people seem to prefer one or the other. In my view, there is no correct answer; the two types of controls are more and less applicable to different types of games, so it really depends on the style of game you are making.

One-Stick Control

A one-pad solution gives you control of the character on just one pad, normally the left one (see Figure 6.1). Assuming you're using a third-person camera, pushing up on the stick makes the character move away from the camera.

Pulling down on the stick makes the character run toward the camera, pushing left makes the character run to the left, and so on. Often, when you run to the left or the right, the camera will slowly rotate around the character until it is behind again. Or the user must press a button to return the camera to a position behind the player.

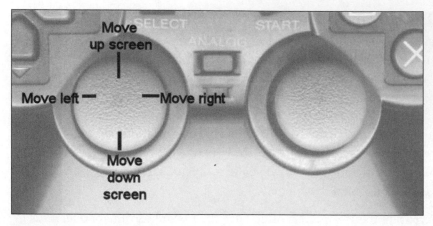

Figure 6.1
Using a one stick control.

With a one-stick control system, a second stick is normally used to allow the player to manually rotate the camera for moments when they want to look around the environment. But it is still a one-stick system, because for the majority of the time, the player needs to use only one stick.

Twin-Stick Control

With the twin-stick approach, one stick handles forward and backward movement and the other handles rotation. There are two main varieties of twin-stick control:

- *Twin-stick character control:* Here the player always controls the character (see Figure 6.2). So regardless of whether the character is stationary or moving, the left stick moves the character forward/backward and strafes left and right. The right stick rotates the player left and right and often has no effect if you move it up or down.

- *Twin-stick camera control:* Although this seems very similar, it is a fundamentally different approach (see Figure 6.3). The player technically guides the camera. The left stick works in the same way character control works. When the character is stationary, the right stick spins the camera around the character, both left and right and above and below, normally rotating around the center of the character. When the character is moving, the control changes and the character and camera both rotate left and right at the same rate, effectively making it feel as if you're now rotating the character. The up and down movements still rotate the camera around the character, allowing you to look down and up at the environment.

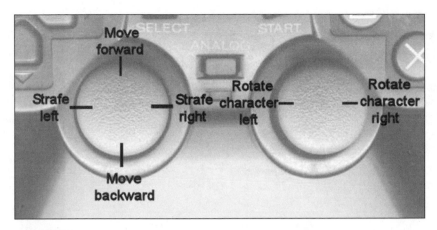

Figure 6.2
Using a twin-stick character control.

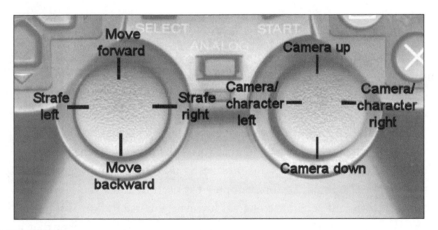

Figure 6.3
Using twin-stick camera control.

PSP One-Stick Control

With the Sony PSP, only one-stick control is available (See Figure 6.4). If you want to implement a control system similar to a twin-stick, it's possible to use the X, Triangle, Circle, and Square buttons as forward, back, left, and right, with the stick controlling where you look. I haven't seen this used on other platforms, but it's clearly possible, even on the PS2. The biggest disadvantage is that it dramatically reduces the number of buttons available to use for other things, but it is a very intuitive way of controlling FPS games on the PSP. It can also be very handy when porting a PS2 control system to the PSP.

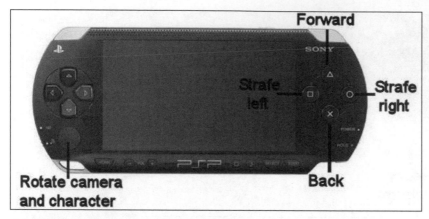

Figure 6.4
PSP twin-stick control system using only one stick.

Digital Pad

All of the current consoles include a digital pad as well as one or two analog sticks. So what should you use the digital pad for? Well, in many games the digital pad is an identical mirror of the left stick. People who don't like using analog controls (and there are many people like this, especially when it comes to driving games) can use the digital pad instead. Making a digital pad behave in a similar way to an analog stick isn't always an easy task. It often involves using nonlinear conversion tables, so that holding the digital pad down longer will result in an accelerated turn. Fortunately, as players are getting used to analog sticks, the digital pad is now being used for more interesting options. In the Conflict series of games, for example, it is used to allow the player to quickly switch between different squad members. However you use it, don't forget that it is digital, so it works best for on/off actions and toggle selections. Remember that it is there and provides a great place for you to put four related options you want to give the player quick access to.

Dealing with Complexity

Think carefully about how complex you make your control system. It's great to have a game that has depth, but you need to make sure that new players are gently introduced to that depth. It doesn't matter too much if some of the more complex controls (which aren't needed until later in the game) are hidden away on your controller using combos or submenus as long as the core controls that you need from day one are as simple and obvious as possible.

Keyboard Control

Keyboard control can be a real pain in the neck. It's by far the worst controller for games in common use. You run into problems if you require the player to press more than three keys at the same time. Certain key combinations can trigger off all sorts of Windows functions. Add to that the fact that there are different layouts of keyboards, especially in different territories. Obviously, the keys are digital, and different people have strong preferences for different key combinations. However, the light at the end of the tunnel is that a standard has become apparent—using W, A, S, and D as the core movement controls and the mouse to look around. Keys like E for performing an action, space for jump, Shift for walk, and Ctrl for crouch are also becoming common-place. Whatever you decide, I strongly suggest that on all PC titles, you make the controls completely user definable so that everyone can set up the game in a manner that suits them best, given the tricky nature of using a keyboard.

6

Mouse Control

The mouse is normally used for looking around and rotating characters in first- and third-person games. In strategy and God games, the mouse is normally used to move the camera around the environment. Most mice now have scroll wheels in the center, which are useful for zooming in and out of the screen (or gun sight). A mouse provides a superb interface for first-person games; it is much more intuitive to use than game controllers once it is picked up. However, you can only rely on it having two buttons, and therefore for most games, it can be used only in combination with the keyboard.

Third-Person Character Control

You've seen the arguments for using the one and two analog stick control methods. Either method will work in a third-person character game. From my experience, more complex games that involve combat and fine aiming work better on two sticks. Simpler games, especially platform games and games for a younger audience, are far better suited to using just one stick for character control.

First-Person Control

Most modern console games use the dual-stick approach with forward/backward movement and strafing (moving sideways) on the left stick and rotation on the right stick. This is close to becoming a standard in terms of console first-person shooter (FPS) titles. However, it is possible to successfully control a first-person game using just one analog stick, the best example being *Goldeneye* on the Nintendo 64. The default system in *Goldeneye* relied heavily on the player not having to aim up and down too much; the one stick basically had forward/back and rotate left/right on it. The advantage of this system is that it's very quick to pick up. The disadvantage is that the game levels need to be predominantly 2D. If you need to look up and down too much, this system just won't work because either your up/down movement needs to be on the other stick (which doesn't feel right) or, as in the case of *Goldeneye*, you need to press and hold down a button and then use the default stick to aim. This can break up the game flow since you remain stationary.

This game also had a second control system that could be selected, an early version of the dual-stick system that used the digital pad to replace the left stick.

For PC games, of course, the mouse and keyboard combination is such a strong standard that it makes sense to stick with this as your default control setup for first-person games.

Vehicle Control

Vehicle control has been implemented many different ways over the last few years. However, as with FPS games, there is now a fairly clear standard on each of the platforms. Let's look at consoles first. Using the left stick to steer (often with the additional option of the left/right buttons on the digital pad) is fairly obvious. In terms of acceleration and braking, things get more platform specific. On the PlayStation 2 controller, the X and Square buttons are traditionally used for acceleration and braking (although this is different in Japan). On the Xbox controller, the left and right trigger buttons are traditionally used for the same purpose. I strongly recommend not using analog sticks for acceleration or braking; it just doesn't feel intuitive. Whether you opt for trigger buttons or the traditional buttons on the right-hand side of the controller, make sure you make full use of the analog functionality. It can really enhance your control of a vehicle if you are able to apply the throttle or brakes gently or harshly. One trick is to make sure that full acceleration or braking is not dependent on the button reaching 100 percent of its movement because this will cause players to get extremely sore thumbs! Make the maximum occur at about 75 percent of the movement range so that the game is more comfortable to play. In terms of other vehicle controls, the most common ones are handbrake and manual gears.

Gears are often on the trigger/shoulder buttons (although they can be found on the A, B, X, Y buttons on the Xbox controller). If you're using a handbrake, it can be put pretty much where you like as long as it is accessible while the player is steering and accelerating. So if your acceleration is on a trigger/shoulder button, put a handbrake on one of the buttons on the right of the pad and vice versa.

Reality Check: On the PC platform, you need to support as full a range of steering wheels and joysticks as possible. Don't ever use the mouse to try to steer a vehicle (although you might just about get away with controlling a plane on the mouse). Traditional keyboard controls for driving games are still the cursor keys, although as I have previously mentioned, you should allow PC gamers to reconfigure the keys if they want to.

Advanced Control Techniques

Hopefully, you now have most of the basic knowledge you'll need when you're deciding what control system to use. I'd like to move on to some more advanced techniques and cover some areas that are not often discussed, such as supporting a video camera as a control system and porting control systems from one platform to another.

Linking Displays and Controls on the Same Side

There is a relatively small thing that many designers don't realize can help make game controls feel intuitive. This involves using buttons, sticks, triggers, and keys on the right-hand side of the controller to control things shown on the right-hand side of the screen. And in the same way, you can use buttons, sticks, triggers, and keys on the left-hand side of the controller to control things shown on the left-hand side of the screen. Using the PlayStation 2 controller as an example, in the Conflict series of games, your current weapon and a sliding inventory are on the right-hand side of the screen. The inventory button is on the right-hand side of the pad. On the left-hand side of the screen are the characters, showing you who you currently control. The character selection is on the digital pad on the left-hand side of the controller. Although most people won't notice, having things on the correct side really helps them subconsciously feel at ease with the game.

Analog Buttons

Believe it or not, many people don't know that the buttons on modern console controllers are analog. So I suggest going down one of three routes when you're deciding how to use the analog nature of controller buttons:

- Don't make variable pressure of the buttons a requirement. For example, in most racing games, you can still play the game fairly well if you just press the buttons down fairly hard all the time, but you get increased response and control if you vary the pressure you use on the buttons.

- Implement some kind of tutorial to explain that the buttons are sensitive. For example, you might tell the player that the harder they press on the "shoot" button, the less accurate but more often their machine gun will fire.

6

■ Make the analog use completely subconscious. For example, players tend to hit buttons really hard when they are stressed or panicking. If you detect a sudden extra-hard button press, why not play a slightly different character animation or piece of speech to indicate this. The game may then be able to pick up on the player's mood in a very small way!

War Story: Making Controls Too Challenging

I worked on a game called *Richard Burns Rally*, which was an extremely realistic rally driving simulation. The control system made such good use of the controllers that we found real rally drivers would actually achieve quicker lap times than our driving-mad QA team. This was particularly true if the drivers were given a steering wheel with force feedback built in! Of course, the downside of this was that many average gamers found the car was just too difficult to control; they didn't want to have to use the brakes!

Evil Buttons

There are a couple of buttons on the current versions of both the PS2 and Xbox controller that are just plain evil. These are the "stick down" buttons (known as the L3 and R3 buttons in Sony terminology). They are digital buttons that are engaged by pressing directly down on the analog sticks. Why do I call them evil? Well, there are two reasons. First, my research has shown that a large percentage of gamers don't know that they exist. Therefore, they're not intuitive, and gamers can easily fail to notice their functionality. Second, and more important, it is extremely easy to press them by accident and fairly tricky to press them without causing the stick to jerk slightly in one direction. For this reason, I strongly advise not using them if at all possible. The only circumstances in which you should consider using them is if all the other buttons are used and you have a function that needs to be performed when you're stationary. For example, some games use these buttons for switching to a sniper view, which makes some kind of sense because you really need to be stationary when sniping. Still, I'd suggest avoiding these buttons if you can.

Unusual Control Systems

This chapter covered most of the common control systems and issues that you will come across. However, these controls by no means represent a comprehensive list; since games are so diverse, there are also an enormous number of different control systems. If you're creating a DJ game in which tracks are mixed, or a cooking game in which the player is chopping up food (this really exists!), your standard first- and third-person controls won't help you. The key thing to remember is to make your controls intuitive and easy to use. Think about which controls the player will need to use simultaneously, and make sure that these actions are fairly easy to use at the same time. Fight the urge to give the player control of every little feature in the game, and try to keep the controls simple and effective. Automate features that the player doesn't really care about. Many games automate jumping rather than having a jump button (you just push against a wall or run toward a gap and the game will automatically jump for the player). If you haven't seen this working, try playing *Zelda: Ocarina of Time*.

Creative Idea: Use Different Peripherals

Consider using different peripherals to enhance your game. For example, you could consider using a dance mat (which many people now have) in a very unique way (perhaps to trample aliens underfoot, or to run a 100-meter sprint in an athletic game).

EyeToy/Cameras

One of the most unusual control interfaces available at the moment is the Sony EyeToy (see Figure 6.5). This is essentially a camera that connects to the console. The camera feed can be used by games as a control system. This is done by comparing consecutive frames of video to see what has changed. Usually, the only parts of the image that have

Figure 6.5
The Sony EyeToy camera.

changed are where things are moving, such as the player's arms and legs (unless the camera is facing a window, in which case everything goes horribly wrong as cars and people go past and mess up the game!). You can also get a camera to connect to the Xbox consoles, and of course PCs have had cameras available for some time now. Using a camera to register player input opens up a whole host of possibilities. From washing your car in a racing game right through to fistfighting terrorists, you should consider whether using a camera allows you to do something really special that wouldn't be possible otherwise.

Using Controllers in Unusual Ways

If you are creative, it is possible to think laterally and create unusual things you can do with the controller. A great example of this was *Metal Gear Solid*, in which you met a character called Psycho Mantis. The character had psychic abilities and demonstrated this by asking the player to place the controller on the ground and then making it move by turning on the rumble mechanism. In the battle against this character, the player eventually realizes that the only way to defeat Psycho Mantis is to pull the controller out of slot 1 and put it into slot 2, thereby stopping the enemy from knowing in advance what the player was doing.

 Reality Check: There are other ways to make the controller become part of the gameplay. One idea I had was to flash simple Morse code messages to the player using the LED on the Dual Shock controller, as if a character within the game was trying to silently communicate for help. Admittedly, it would be a bit of a pain if you didn't know Morse code, but hopefully it might set you off to create an even better idea.

Working on Multiplatform Control Systems

It can be a real design challenge to make a control system that works well on one platform work equally as well on another. Moving from one console to another isn't too tricky, although you must remember that Xbox and PS2 gamers do have slightly different standards that they have become used to. The big issue comes when you're moving to console from PC (or vice versa). And it's an even bigger problem when you're moving to a handheld device from a console. Let's look at three examples in a little more depth.

PC to Console

PC games tend to have quite a lot of controls. I've worked on several PC games that had a huge amount of depth and used a correspondingly huge number of PC keys. In a couple of cases, the developers had incredible problems moving the control system over to a console platform, mainly due to the limited number of buttons on the controller. A great example of this is *Operation Flashpoint* from Codemasters. Five years after the original, I'm looking forward to seeing how they finally solved the problem of getting the PC control system onto the Xbox. PC games that involve mouse control can be a huge problem on console controllers; moving a cursor around with the analog stick is a real nightmare. If your PC game is too complex and has too many controls, you really have no option but to simplify the game. Try to take away the less-enjoyable elements and automate as much as possible while keeping the core gameplay as close as possible to the original version.

If your PC game uses a mouse cursor (as many RTS games do), you have a few options (none of which are ideal, in my opinion). You could use one stick to move the cursor around, using the analog nature of the stick to affect the speed of the cursor (so if you move the stick hard left, the cursor moves rapidly, whereas a gentle nudge to the left will allow you to move the cursor slowly for accurate aiming).

You might want to have specific places to which the cursor jumps. So when you push up, the cursor jumps to the closest vertical unit or object that you can select.

Finally, you might want to try a sticky cursor system, where the cursor slows down when it moves over objects that are selectable, which can help stop the player from spending ages trying to move the cursor exactly over the target. An alternative to that system is to make all the selectable objects have a kind of gravity that attracts the cursor to them when it is close.

Console to PC

In general, moving a console control system to the PC isn't really an issue. The most common problem is that too many developers port the control system over without pausing to think whether it could actually be improved for PC gamers. You could consider having a mouse-controlled first-person view on PC when porting a third-person console game, or maybe adding shortcuts on the function keys to bring out the depth and complexity of your game. (This is a major generalization, but PC gamers tend to prefer more depth, freedom, and complexity than console gamers.) Think about putting shortcuts to often-used inventory items or special moves onto the keyboard. Put instant access to all your weapons onto the number keys at the top of the keyboard.

Console and PC to Handheld

Other than the Sony PSP, I just don't believe it is possible to convert a proper console or PC game onto current handheld devices and retain exactly the same control system and gameplay. My advice is to forget the console/PC game and work out what will be the most fun for the handheld device you're working on. Obviously, try to make it as close to the original game as you can, but *fun* is the key word. You may well need to use a completely different control system (and change the gameplay quite significantly) in order to make a great handheld game. Don't be afraid to do this. Even with the PSP, you will almost certainly need to make changes because it has only one analog stick. Can you automate the camera so the player doesn't need to control it? Can you use one-stick control player movement rather than two?

Summary

Together with your game camera, your control system will form the basis for your gameplay. Get your control system right and your game will feel fluid and intuitive. Get it wrong and it'll feel clunky and frustrating. Learn from other great games with a similar system, and don't be afraid to copy elements that work well.

An Interview with Dax Ginn

Dax Ginn is something of a rarity. He's an experienced game designer with a law degree. After deciding that games were more fun than law books, Dax started his career at Psygnosis in London before working at Travelers Tales on *Crash Bandicoot: Twinsanity*. More recently, he worked on titles such as *I-Ninja* at Argonaut before spending a large amount of time designing a launch PSP title. In the process of doing so, Dax has become one of the most experienced PSP designers in Europe, talking at the very first Sony conference on the subject. He is now working at Eidos on a number of new projects.

What do you think are the most important skills that a game designer should have?

DG: I have worked with a lot of different designers and I think the most effective ones are those that have the ability to communicate well with all the varied personalities that they come into contact with during a project. This means having a balanced combination of technical under-standing and artistic instinct and a good eye for gameplay. It also helps to have unlimited enthusi-asm about your ideas and the vision you have of your game. A big part of design is motivating other people and getting their "buy in" to your concepts. If you aren't visibly overflowing with excitement when presenting your ideas, there is very little chance that the coders and artists that are tasked with implementing your vision will go that extra yard to make it happen.

What are the key things to consider when you're coming up with a control system for a new game?

DG: Here are three tips I can provide:

- *Keep it as simple as possible. Regardless of how hard core your intended audience is, a simple control system will always benefit the gameplay experience. Every button that you can get rid of, while still designing an interface that is simple and intuitive, is a fantastic gain in accessibility.*

- *Encourage self-expression. The control system is the only way that the user can express them-selves in the game world, so your interface design should allow and promote self-expression. I think that is a big part of the appeal of the Eyeloy; it's a control system that is really driven by self-expression.*

- *Focus-test. It is inevitable that during the years of development of your game, you will get used to the control system and become blind to any flaws in your design. It is so important to regularly give the controller to someone who has never seen your game before to see how long it takes them to get the hang of it. If they get confused or aren't enjoying themselves, look at ways to simplify your control system or refine the "feel" of it to promote greater scope for self-expression.*

What is your view on the best way to control a third-person character; do you favor using one or both sticks for character movement?

DG: This really depends on the kind of game that you are making. If you are creating a third-person shooter, I don't think you can go past a first-person setup with the left stick controlling character movement with strafing assigned to left/right and the right stick controlling the cross-hair. A platformer, melee combat title, or character-driven title (where you want the user to see the character's face) really demands all character movement to be done with the left stick, with the right stick controlling the camera.

My personal preference is for the first setup, because I find it more intuitive from playing so many first-person shooters. It would be interesting to implement this style of control system into a non-shooter game.

Do you prefer using a mouse or control pad for first-person games?

DG: I have to go with the mouse and keyboard setup for first-person games, not only because they traditionally came from that kind of interface with Doom and Wolfenstein, but there is so much targeting assistance that needs to go into a console FPS to get the feel of it anywhere near that of a PC shooter. A mouse just works better than a stick.

Do you have any advice for people with regard to using the analog nature of controller buttons, something which is often ignored?

DG: I think that it's ignored for a good reason—no one gets it! Analog functionality on the sticks and shoulder buttons has brought about a total sea change in current gen control systems, and I think this has happened because you can feel the analog nature of a stick in its sweep. The distance between the extremes are appreciable enough for the user to use strategically whether it's for accelerating a vehicle or aiming a weapon. The face buttons, on the other hand, still feel digital, so there is no "play" between not pressed and pressed, between on and off. Short of raising the buttons an inch off the pad, I don't think that buttons will ever take full advantage of analog functionality.

What are you most proud of in your career so far?

DG: I have spent a lot of time talking to students and visiting schools to tell kids about the highs and lows of game development. The most rewarding thing that has come out of these visits is the raw excitement that so many kids have for the games that they are playing. These products that we spend so much of our working lives creating have a real impact and meaning to the people playing them. This is the thing that gives me the greatest sense of pride, that millions of people are playing the games that I help to create and really enjoying them.

What is your favoritegame ever, and why?

DG: *Tetris. It is a master class in simplicity but a totally addictive game design at the same time. It's a game that almost everyone on the planet has played at least once and never gets tired of. The control system is as simple as you can imagine, but it still has massive scope for self-expression. Being able to accelerate the drop speed of a block, or cheekily slide a block into a hole at the last millisecond to fill a side hole, these are all features that allow the user to play* Tetris *with flair and express themselves through the interface.*

I think the next block preview window is genius as well. Imagine how much less strategy there would be in Tetris *if you didn't know what shape was coming next.*

What do you think is the biggest game design mistake that people regularly make with games?

DG: *Too many designers make games for themselves. This can really only be solved by frequent focus testing to help designers work out what their audience thinks of their game rather than what they think. It's too easy to overlook the difficulty of a game because you know it inside out. Before you start your design as well, you should be sure that the desired gameplay experience that you have in your mind is shared by a decent chunk of your target audience. There is no point making a game that only you will buy.*

If money and technology were unlimited, what kind of game would you most like to see made?

DG: *I would like to see a game about love—one that expresses the ideas and emotions that poems, movies, and books do so well, but in a game. I don't think that you would need unlimited technical and financial resources to do a simple game like this, but I think a fully immersive virtual reality interface would help somewhat. It is just not traditionally the sort of game that developers go for, but sooner or later games will become truly emotional journeys as well, and surely a deeply engaging interactive love story would be as popular as noninteractive portrayals of love.*

What do you think is the biggest challenge facing game designers as we move forward?

DG: *The games industry has matured so quickly that we have lost sight of the essence of a game and instead we are trying to create theater. I don't think that games are ever going to be better than movies in telling a story, so I get annoyed when I see game titles advertised as being cinematic or having a great story but have little in the way of gameplay. Really we should be focusing on what makes games different to movies, moving away from Hollywood and forging our own unique identity. And that is delivering an engaging interactive experience that can be revisited time and time again. Chess has no story but is a fantastic game that I will play as long as I live, and the same can be said for almost every card game, board game, and playground game that you can think of. Games, according to their heritage, should be designed to be played and replayed, whereas movies are meant to tell a story and then be shelved.*

6

The challenge for designers is to return to their roots and focus on creating games that reinforce our interactive identity rather than titles that are only appealing due to the fact that they are the game of the movie.

And finally, if you had one piece of advice to give to a game designer who was just starting out, what would it be?

DG: My advice would be to never forget that moment when you had an idea and believed that it was a good idea. As you think about a concept, you get overexposed to it and start to doubt if it is any good at all. Too often you will bin it and go in search of something else, not because it is better, but because it is different. Really good ideas are the heart and soul of any good game, so when you have one, make sure you see it through to implementation and don't ditch it because you are not excited by it anymore. Chances are, when the player sees that concept in action, they will feel the same way that you did when you conceived it.

Chapter 7

Designing Characters

> "You cannot dream yourself into a character; you must hammer and forge yourself one."
>
> *James Froude*

Creating a unique game character is a major challenge. Nine out of every ten new characters disappear pretty much without a trace, and very few ever reach the lofty heights populated by Sonic, Mario, Lara, or Crash. If I had a dollar for every chisel-jawed counterintelligence operative or ex-special-forces mercenary in the gaming world, I'd be a rich man. But can you remember any of their names? I can remember Sam Fisher from the *Splinter Cell* titles, but I don't recollect anything particular about him, and I played through the first two games!

If you want to create another "me-too" hero, you might as well skip to the next chapter. If, on the other hand, you want to create an unusual character, or a flawed and interesting hero—one that your players will be able to remember—you've come to the right place. A large portion of this chapter will concentrate on how to create an unusual main character for your game. To get there, I'll begin with a more standard task—creating a human hero or heroine who isn't two-dimensional. You'll quickly learn why memorable game characters aren't perfect and how to go about designing characters that have the right balance of flaws and other interesting attributes. In the last part of the chapter, I'll walk you through a fun project in which we'll create some characters for a sample game.

Heroes Aren't Perfect

One of the most common flaws with many game characters is that they have no flaws! Watch any good movie or read any great book, on the other hand, and without fail, you'll find three-dimensional characters who have an edge to their personality. They're never perfect.

To be successful at designing great characters, you'll need to take the time to flesh the characters out. Every character you develop should have some type of background that you dream up and refine. To help you determine a character's background, here are some questions to consider:

- Where have the characters come from?

- What mistakes have they made?

- What aspects of their personalities are appealing?

- What are their biggest flaws?

- What makes them so unique?

- What features will people remember about them?

If you need help, use a professional writer to help you get your characters right. If your game is a success, the characters may end up being around for many years, so they deserve to have some time spent on them at the start. If you get stuck, think about interesting people that you have met during your life and exaggerate certain characteristics about them a little. If you're interested in creating interesting characters and writing powerful game storylines, I would strongly advise that you buy a copy of the book *The Writer's Journey: Mythic Structure for Writers* by Christopher Vogler (Michael Wiese Productions, 1998).

Creative Idea: Use Your Friends and Family!

If you get really stuck when trying to come up with a new character, think through all the people you know (whether friends, family, or just casual acquaintances). Many of the greatest comedy characters have come through this route (for example, Basil Fawlty from *Fawlty Towers* was based on a hotelier that John Cleese met). Toby Gard based Lara Croft partly on his sister, and Mihoko from *Galleon* was based on his girlfriend!

Creating Unusual Characters

Designing a game around an unusual main character is one approach that was extremely common in the early days of computer games, when designers would often find themselves controlling frogs, eggs, and even babies. More recently, we've had successful titles featuring an earthworm and a bandicoot and several games involving monkeys. But this is starting to occur less and less; the majority of main characters nowadays are fit human adults who can sprint across a walkway, jump across a rooftop, and fire two semiautomatic handguns, all without pausing for breath. One reason for this is the increasing emphasis on immersion. With more cinematic cameras and the growing popularity of the first-person perspective, many designers want to make people feel as if they are actually in the game world. And that's something that seems much easier if you're controlling a 20-something male or female. However, I believe that there is a real opportunity to set your game apart and make your lead character someone other than a highly athletic ex-special-forces soldier working for national security.

Reality Check: Regardless of whether you are asked to create an unusual kind of character or you decide to create a unique hero yourself, there are lots of things you need to consider. The key is to try to forget the existing assumptions and work from the ground up. Don't take anything for granted.

Examples of Great Character Design

Before we start to look at the types of characters that can be used in games and the types of emotions you can use to bring life to your characters, let's look at some characters that I've selected as being standouts.

7

Sonic the Hedgehog

From the Master system to the PS2, Sonic (see Figure 7.1) is a great-looking character with great athletic abilities and above all, speed. He may not have a rich background or deep emotions, but he's really distinctive and his shape and form fit his function perfectly.

Solid Snake

Snake (see Figure 7.2) is a totally cool character from the *Metal Gear* games. He's a flawed hero who always comes out on top. He smokes, he's rude to people, and he's a ruthless killer. Yet as a player, you want him to win, and he makes a great lead character. His bandana and combat suit give him a highly original look

Lara Croft

Probably the most famous gaming character of all time, Lara's rise to success was amazing. A female Indiana Jones, Lara (see Figure 7.3) is a sexy, brave British adventurer with a sense of humor. The balance between sex appeal, skill, and practicality in her design is perfect.

Lemmings

In a very similar way to the modern-day Worms franchise, these tiny on-screen creatures (see Figure 7.4) were brought to life by some great animations and brilliant use of

Figure 7.1
Sonic the Hedgehog, a very well-known character.

Figure 7.2
Solid Snake.

Figure 7.3
Lara Croft.

sound and voices. Clicking the Self Destruct button was always hilarious. It's a great example of how superb sound can bring characters to life.

Dog's Life
This is a highly original title featuring a dog as the main character (see Figure 7.5). The designers pulled it off extremely well. The game lets you do every canine action you'd ever want to do, and the animations and controls are superb. It's a great example of how to have a realistic animal as your main character while keeping the game entertaining and funny.

Determining the Type of Character You Want
The most likely constraint that you'll be dealing with is the type of character that you're creating. It could be an animal, an inanimate object, an alien, or just a human that acts in an unusual way. I can't remember seeing a game in which you control an old person with a zimmer frame, but it's certainly possible, although I doubt it would make for

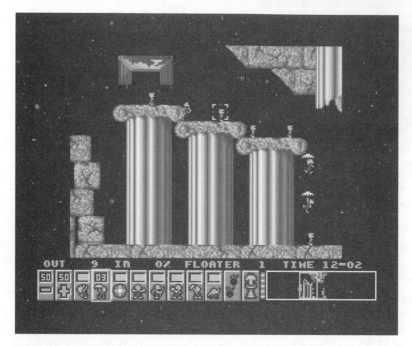

Figure 7.4
Lemmings.

Figure 7.5
Dog's Life.

particularly engrossing action. Let's consider the various categories of characters that you are likely to come across.

Animals

You need to decide from the outset whether you are aiming for a realistic simulation of a particular animal or whether you are going to indulge in anthropomorphism (endowing animals or inanimate objects with human characteristics). Making your character anthropomorphic can be a positive approach, and it allows you a range of actions and interactions that wouldn't be possible otherwise. Note that having an anthropomorphic character may well make your game feel rather quirky, and some people would say that having cute talking animals is a very "Nintendo" kind of design, which may or may not be what you're after. (Using such a character may seriously limit the appeal of your game with older game players.) Of course, there is no reason why you can't go down a design route with your ninja kitten that helps it appeal to older gamers. For example, giving the character a grenade launcher might be a good start. The important thing to keep in mind is that an anthropomorphic character could make your game look or feel "kid-like."

Your choice of animal will also have a significant impact on the kind of game mechanics you can use and the overall tone that you give the game. It is worth carrying out some kind of market research (even if the research involves just a few well-chosen friends and colleagues) to gauge people's first thoughts when they hear the name of the animal. A kitten is cute and cuddly to most people, which allows you to either go down the cute and cuddly route or take the opposite approach and make your kitten the meanest and ugliest son of a gun ever to hit the gaming world. Some animals are easier to endow with human qualities. For example, giving a wood louse an endearing human personality will be trickier than giving a personality to a dog or a bear. Having said that, I remember playing a game called *Mister Mosquito* that let the player take on the role of a blood-sucking mosquito, flying around a house targeting the people who lived there. It was a very interesting title, although I'm honestly not surprised it didn't sell very well!

If you want to take the realistic approach, make sure you do your research. Read a few books on your chosen animal, and pick up on the most interesting aspects of its behavior. For example, meerkats communicate very well as a community, and if an attacking animal (such as an eagle) comes near, this fact is quickly passed around by stamping and loud screaming noises before all the animals dart into their holes. This might lead you to make your meerkat a brave but nervous soul who has to survive many set piece events as larger and larger predators attack, generating suitable panic and mayhem as the warning cries scream out and the animals dart around looking for safety.

Example: Animal Crossing

Animal Crossing (see Figure 7.6) was a fantastic title for the Nintendo Gamecube that allowed the player to take the role of a cute animal, buy a house, carry out favors for other animal characters, and generally live in a friendly, happy animal world. The characters were very humanoid in their actions; they wore clothes, walked on two legs, talked, wrote letters, and bought and sold objects. But each character you met had its own personality; some were kind, others were often grumpy and selfish. It's a superb and addictive game well worth looking up.

Figure 7.6
Animal Crossing.

Objects

Objects are even harder to approach, and the only real choice is to give them human qualities. The main exception to this is a robot; you could go the realistic route or base them on what you think will be realistic in the future. Even then, robot designers tend to use anthropomorphism as a tool of the trade. I remember a great story I heard in the cybernetics department at Reading University. They made a little robot that was able to move around at random. They allowed it to play a number of audio recordings of small animals in pain (don't ask me where they got them!). They then invited people to come and hit the robot with a rubber mallet. "No problem—that's easy" was the normal response to this request. As the robot sensed the approaching hit, it darted out of the way, normally receiving a glancing but harmless blow, at the same time emitting a loud pitiful yelp. It then backed away slowly from the nearest object (normally the person with the mallet) emitting short soft cries. Most participants refused to carry on after this point, despite the robot being nothing more than a few circuits and some electrical hardware! A few samples and a predefined movement had convinced them that this robot had feelings. There aren't many games I can remember with objects as the main character, although films like *Chitty Chitty Bang Bang* and the Herbie series show how powerful this approach can be if you manage to create empathy with the object in question.

Example: Thomas the Tank Engine

Finding an example of using an object as a character in modern games is tough. Many games (such as the Wipeout series) don't have a main character and instead let you select a vehicle, but very few of them give the vehicle any personality! Atari's successful series of Thomas the Tank Engine games (see Figure 7.7) has done well and shows how anthropomorphism can work well with children. Of course, all the hard work in character design was done beforehand by the author of the book (Reverend W. Awdry).

7

Figure 7.7
Thomas the Tank Engine.

Weak Humans

People are very used to playing games with strong, ultra-cool protagonists. In the film industry, it isn't uncommon to see films in which the lead character is weak in some way, but games rarely reach this level of sophistication, probably because of the belief that people are less keen on interacting with a flawed character. This shouldn't be the case; in film scripting, the quickest way to guarantee a two-dimensional character is to give the character no flaws.

Having a physically weak character will probably lead you to using puzzle-solving techniques and mental challenges or strategy over fast-action "twitch" gameplay. But having a weak character may just mean that they avoid head-on confrontations; it doesn't necessarily mean that they can't run fast or use agility to get themselves out of trouble.

Slow humans have their own set of design problems; if it takes ages to move around the environment, the player is going to be bored very quickly. I'd recommend that you avoid using very slow characters unless you can come up with a creative way of engaging the player as the character moves.

Example: Fahrenheit

Quantic Dream's excellent adventure game *Fahrenheit* (see Figure 7.8) has four main characters, and the player gets to control each of them during the course of the story. Apart from a male and female cop, the other two characters are fairly weak; the murderer is a normal guy who had a moment of madness, and for most of the game, he is very passive, trying to avoid getting into any more trouble and finding out what happened. You also play as his brother, a priest, who is physically weak and quite a long way from a typical game hero. The game *Ico* included a weak and powerless female character who you had to look after throughout the game, which worked incredibly well.

Superheroes

Superheroes often seem like the easiest characters to design; they can do anything, so surely you are free to do what you like? Well, actually, you may find that superheroes can be one of the hardest types of characters to work with because you need to be able to restrict them with your level designs. It's all very well to have a hero who can teleport from place to place at will, but how do you stop the character from leaping straight to the climax of the level or teleporting in behind the main bad guy and shooting him in the head? Superman can effectively teleport because he can fly at superfast speeds from one location to another. He can punch through steel and concrete, so how do you keep him within your level? In other words, what do you use as barriers? If your superhero can fly,

Figure 7.8
Fahrenheit.

how can you stop the player from flying anywhere on the entire level that he wants? If you're creating a new superhero, you have the luxury of designing his (or her) capabilities with this in mind, but if you are using an existing licensed character, you will need to think carefully about how you can limit the character in your level design.

Example: City Of Heroes

City of Heroes (see Figure 7.9) is a superb online game in which you get to create your own superhero and fight crime, ganging up with other heroes to save the world. The developers at Cryptic have done a great job of allowing players to create an almost unlimited number of different heroes while providing plenty of superpowers and allowing players to build on them throughout the game, which helps prevent lots of the problems I just mentioned. For example, by limiting the amount of time players can fly and how fast they can fly, it's possible to provide realistic challenges and progression.

Other Character Types

There are many other kinds of characters, ranging from imaginary creations (such as alien creatures) to ghosts or poltergeists. If you are creating an imaginary character type, you are free to hone the character to your specific requirements. It's harder when there

Figure 7.9
City of Heroes.

is a volume of historical information that creates expectations from your audience. For example, people believe that ghosts can walk through walls. So if you're making a ghost game, you'll need to come up with a convincing reason why your ghost can't do this. Or if you decide to let your ghost pass through walls, you'll have the same problem you have with superheroes; namely, how will you constrain your level enough to provide sensible goals and a route from start to finish? One obvious mechanism in this instance is to use energy; moving through walls takes effort, and the character can move through only a certain number of walls without replenishing their energy. Some walls are likely to be thicker and harder to pass than others, so steel walls may be a great way to stop your character until they become more powerful later in the game. But you do need to think of every possible angle and come up with some clear and sensible rules that gamers can understand.

Creative Idea: Don't Throw Away Characters or Designs

Don't ever throw away your character or game designs unless there is nothing remotely strong about them. Mark any strong ideas, interesting characteristics, a unique game mechanic, or an original setting. Then file it away. Later, if your new game design needs spicing up, go through your files and see if any idea or character would fit into the new concept. For example, you may have a design that has been rejected, yet has an innovative camera system that everyone liked. Or you may have come up with a really unique villain who just doesn't work for the game you're working on currently. Store it away; you never know when it might come in handy.

Incorporating Unusual Emotions Or Goals

Once you've determined the type of character you want to use, you'll need to incorporate unique emotions to bring your character to life. Otherwise, you're character might seem one-dimensional to your player. In using emotions, however, you need to be careful. Strong emotions can lead you to create actions and interactions that are out of the ordinary, but they can limit what you allow your character to do. Let's take a look at some of the most common emotions that your character might have.

Anger

Imagine Michael Douglas's character in the film *Falling Down*—a middle-aged man who has snapped and is incredibly fed up with life and what fate has dealt to him. This isn't the kind of character who is going to sneak around in the shadows. This isn't the sort of person who would collect gold stars and find keycards to open doors. This kind of character is going to be extremely angry and is going to inflict damage and pain on anything that gets in the way. The animations, actions, and interactions ought to reflect this. For example, don't allow him to gently open a door; he should kick it down. Put lots of physics objects in the character's way that the player can knock over to show his rage. Inject a sense of dark humor if you like, by allowing him to pick up and use unusual everyday objects as weapons. But be true to your character. If he's angry, show it, and make him the angriest game character you've ever seen. Just resist the temptation to fall back on standard game mechanics. Instead, ask yourself how you can fulfil a similar function in an exciting and relevant way.

Example: Mr. Angry

It was hard finding games which featured a truly angry character. For sure, characters like Duke Nukem and his parody twin, Serious Sam, get quite upset at the stream of dangerous enemies attacking them, but neither is truly pissed off. The closest example I could find is a Commodore 64 game called *Mr. Angry* (see Figure 7.10), in which you play a photographer sneaking through a hotel. If you wake Mr. Angry up, life becomes very difficult for you because he is *really* upset! But there is definitely an opening for a game with a really angry main character. Over to you.

Figure 7.10
Mr. Angry.

Fear

Making the player feel scared is a key design goal in many games. But rarely does the main character properly exhibit fear and pass on that tension to the player. So, if you decide that the player will be controlling a scared teenage girl, for example, make sure the actions and interactions that she can carry out are relevant. She's not going to be firing weapons in both hands, reloading instantly, and scoring head shots. If you want your character to fire a gun, make her nervous about it. Make it take slightly longer than normal to reload so the player sees her struggle to get the bullets loaded. Make her gun hand shake when she's walking along with it. Use gameplay in which she doesn't tackle dangerous enemies head-on but instead the player is encouraged to outthink the game and use stealth and problem solving to move forward. If you want to see a great example of in-game characterization, watch the female character in *Ico*. You feel protective toward her, not because of cut-scene storylines, but because of in-game actions and animations.

Example: Sanitarium

An impressive PC adventure game from the late 1980s, *Sanitarium* (see Figure 7.11) lets you play as a female amnesia patient struggling to hold on to reality. It's a very scary title, and the main character experiences and shows real fear throughout the game as she struggles through sinister hallucinations and very real and dangerous enemies.

How am I supposed to get there?

Figure 7.11
Sanitarium.

Reality Check: If your main character needs to be scared, show it. Watch some of the classic horror movies and note what the directors do with camera angles, pacing, and sharp cuts. Notice that the horror is very rarely shown; the danger is suggested. Remember that the player's imagination is often far more powerful than the most graphically detailed creature that you can create!

Revenge

Revenge and anger should work in a similar way, except that with revenge your character will have one sole focus that should override all others. When other characters in the game are worrying about lesser matters, your character should be sweeping them aside with a single unstoppable purpose. Make sure the player understands just how driven the character is, and if you can, make the player feel the need for revenge as well. This is a tough but extremely powerful trick. If you can get your player attached to someone in the game and then have that person killed or captured by your bad guy, hopefully the player will feel angry too and have their own personal need for revenge! This is something that some films do very well: sucking the viewer in and getting them to share in the emotions generated within the main character.

Figure 7.12
Fable.

Example: Fable

The excellent Xbox game *Fable* (see Figure 7.12) is a great example of a game in which revenge is the primary motive for the player. In *Fable*, you play briefly as a small boy (as the game elegantly introduces the mechanic of letting you decide whether to be good or evil). The village is then attacked by a rampaging hoard of barbarians who brutally kill your family. It's a real shock beginning to the game (after only about 10 or 15 minutes of gameplay). It sets up perfectly your desire for revenge while leaving it up to you to decide whether that revenge moulds you into a noble hero or a violent psycho!

Escape

Maybe you are setting out to create a game in which the sole aim is to escape. In this scenario, don't waste time on aggressive game mechanics; think about the kind of things that an escaping character would do. Can you knock objects over to gain yourself time? Can you hide until the danger passes? Getting away is all that counts, so your character may become desperate. The character might be tempted to steal objects or cause diversions. If you want a big confrontation, spend time setting up the final battle, so that when the player has no option but to face their foe (and they have gained enough items or strength to be able to do this), they know that it is the moment of truth.

Example: Conflict: Vietnam

Many games over the past 25 years have had escape as their main driving force. One fairly recent example is *Conflict: Vietnam* (see Figure 7.13). The four-man squad finds itself stuck deep behind enemy lines in a highly hostile area, and most of the game portrays their struggle to fight their way back home to safety. Other good examples include *Prisoner of War* and *The Great Escape*, both of which require the player to break out of prisoner of war camps and get back home. Even the unparalleled *Half-Life 2* is essentially an escape game, as you spend most of your time being pursued by the evil government forces.

Figure 7.13
Conflict: Vietnam.

Other Emotions

There are other emotions that you may be required (or choose) to focus on. Giving your main character a deep inner sadness can make the player desperate to know what is behind it. Resolving this problem, and ending the game with a happy character, can be very rewarding. Starting your character with a sense of real confusion can be a useful tool for drawing players into the storyline because they want to find out what is going on. Whatever emotion you need to use, put yourself in the role of the character in the same scenario. What would you do? What feels right?

Maybe your character has an unusual goal in mind; they won't be happy until they've saved someone's life or ended their own life. Maybe they just want to find someone to love them. Think about giving your character a goal that is a little different from the norm and you might find that new types of gameplay become apparent to you.

Important Questions to Ask in Designing Characters

Regardless of what kind of character you're trying to create, and what the particular constraints are, there are some common questions that you need to ask yourself to understand your character properly. I've used the masculine pronoun *he* for the sake of brevity, but bear in mind that, as I've mentioned before, your character could be female, an animal, or an inanimate object!

How Does the Character Move?

Moving around an environment is the most important aspect of almost every game. Just think about the possibilities:

- How does your character move?
- Does he run around like a person?
- Does he roll like a ball?
- Does he hop or slide?
- How quickly can he move?
- Can he jump?
- Can he fly?
- How does he react when he is being pursued?
- How does he move when he is injured or low on energy?

Regardless of whether you're working on a side-scrolling beat-em-up game, an isometric RPG, a first-person shooter, or a complex third-person adventure, you need to consider exactly how the character will be able to move around the environment in all directions. A great example of this is the Metroid Prime series (see Figure 7.14), which offers something very different by allowing the player to switch between a bipedal robot and a metal ball. The ball enables access to narrow areas and also allows some fast-paced rolling gameplay as the player hurtles down inclines. Sometimes moving over particular

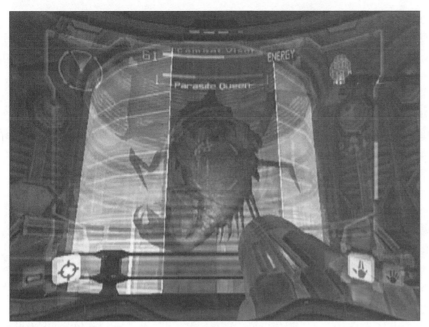

Figure 7.14
Metroid Prime.

7

objects or switches can cause them to operate, so that moving also becomes a way of performing actions. Consider what will happen if you move your character into an object. Will the object move or be knocked over? Think about all the implications of moving within your chosen environment.

Creative Idea: What Annoys You?

Think about characters that annoy you in games that you otherwise like. Pose the question: How could that problem be resolved? Some of the best ideas come from taking flawed ideas from other people and making them work properly. So if you love a character but think he's too perfect, try creating a similar character with a major flaw. By playing around with various ideas, you stand a better chance of coming up with something special.

One other quick thing I'd like to mention at this point is the variety of animations that you end up creating for your character. If the player is going to be staring at the back of the character running around the game world for many hours on end, make sure you have more than one run animation; otherwise, the gameplay will feel artificial. In real life, if you watched someone run for 10 hours, I guarantee you that his physical actions would change and would not repeat every one second; it would vary depending on terrain, the angle of the surface, whether the character is a little tired, and what he's carrying. Adding in little touches like leaning his hand on a wall when he's walking near it and putting his hand on the corner of a wall as he runs around it are also worth thinking about. At the end of the day, if you're unsure, watch someone doing the action in real life.

What Actions Can the Character Perform?

Most games allow the player to perform actions other than moving, although there are some notable exceptions (*Super Monkey Ball* being an obvious one, in which you use only one stick for most of the game, with no buttons needed at all!). Currently, the easiest thing in the world is to give your character a gun and allow him to shoot things. There is no doubt that guns and gun combat are extremely popular with gamers, but at least allow yourself a little time to ponder other options before barreling down the commercial highway. There are other obvious actions: jumping, crouching, looking behind you, and so on. But for every obvious action, there are many less-obvious things that your character could do. This is where you need to remember what kind of character you are creating and make sure that the actions you are proposing are suitable. Sometimes these can be clearly incongruous (such as giving your cute female survival horror protagonist the ability to head-butt seven-foot tall terrorists to death), but it isn't always clear-cut, especially when you become too close to your design. It is always useful to have someone else to bounce these kind of ideas off of. Some examples of more original actions that I'd like to see in a game sometime soon are using extrasensory powers to alter the behavior of enemies and feigning death in order to escape from a lethal situation. I've come up with both those in 30 seconds, so imagine what you can come up with over a proper brainstorm!

How Does the Character Interact with Its Environment?

In my mind, the difference between actions and interactions is that the player needs an external object or element of the environment to carry out interactions, whereas he can perform actions (like firing a gun) at any time regardless of where he is. As with actions, there are many common interactions that are used repeatedly—for example, climbing ladders, pressing buttons, and opening doors. But most game environments have something that sets them apart and offers clues to unique interactions that you can create for your character.

It's possible to create some fairly original environment interactions. For example, I'd like to see the player have the ability to build traps by moving and stacking objects (giving the player the freedom to make evil and cunning plans). You could also allow the player to cut power cables and touch them against metal objects (floors/gratings) to electrocute enemy characters. Just promise me that you'll set aside some time to think of something different before you reuse interactions that have been used hundreds of times before.

Does the Character Have Any Special Abilities?

Special abilities are the kind of things that generate "oh my god" moments when you experience them for the first time; for example, the moment in *Splinter Cell* when you realize that you can prop yourself between walls high in the air and watch clueless enemy guards wander around beneath you (see Figure 7.15). The trouble is that for it to be truly special, you need to come up with something that hasn't been seen before. The first game to feature a usable zip wire must have been pretty cool, but put your character in front of a zip wire nowadays and the modern player isn't going to be quite as excited. I don't want to give away too many of my ideas (I'm bound to need them), but one example might be allowing your character to leap off the edge of a building, free-fall down, and pull a parachute cord at the last minute. I'd certainly find that a pretty impressive gaming moment, and the ability to base-jump within a game would be a real unique selling point (USP).

7

Figure 7.15
Splinter Cell's "Wall-straddle" move.

What Is the Character's Goal?

What does your character want to do? The best films set the character up with a clear goal in mind that he achieves at the end of the film after a tumultuous journey. Whether it is finding that one special someone, killing a bad guy, rescuing a hostage, winning a competition, or just simply understanding himself better, you need to have a goal in mind for your character, even if he doesn't know what it is himself. You can then measure your level designs against the goal: Is this level moving my character a step closer to his goal, or is it an irrelevant distraction? Players often become bored when they don't feel they are progressing, and allowing players to move steadily toward the goal gives them a feeling of purpose.

Why Is the Character Doing This?

Why is your character pursuing his goal? Why doesn't he just put his feet up at home, crack open a beer, and watch a football game instead? You ought to have a real reason driving your character onward. Why does he want to go into the haunted mansion when he could just run out the door to safety? Maybe he needs to rescue his friend. Maybe he is driven with a desperate need to know what is going on inside the mansion. Whatever it is, make it clear to the player, and understand it yourself before you attempt to design the rest of the game.

Using Multiple Characters

Many games feature several characters on the side of the player, and these can be split into two main categories: noncontrollable teammates (which are always controlled by AI) and controllable teammates. With controllable teammates, the player can switch control between the characters; when the player is not in control of them, the teammates may also be controlled by AI, or they may just remain stationary.

Noncontrollable Teammates

Noncontrollable teammates may be at the player's side throughout the entire game, or they may be characters that you meet and stay with for a short period. There are many important areas that you need to consider from a design point of view.

Technology-wise, the pathfinding and movement of teammates are extremely important. Common problems include getting stuck behind 3D geometry, blocking the player's way, and moving into or through other teammates.

Creating believable and interesting characters is also another challenge. It is important that you understand that you need to achieve a balance between having lots of narration and dialogue with a teammate (which helps create a more developed character but can be annoying if it constantly interrupts your concentration) and having a predominantly mute character who has much less personality but never annoys the player. Finding ways to bring out the characteristics of the teammates can be important for story-based games, and this is often achieved using in-game cut scenes or FMV sequences. However, I'm definitely a fan of trying to bring more speech into the actual gameplay. For example, if you've had a fight and you then run to another location with a teammate following, this is a great time for an interesting piece of dialogue while the player is still controlling their character. And there is no reason both characters can't talk while the player is in control. As long as it doesn't occur during a time of frantic gameplay, but instead during a calmer moment, it can be a more fluid way of building your story and characters without the interruption of pausing the game for a cut scene.

War Story: Blind AI

In one of the games I worked on, we had one main player character and another half-blind AI character that the player had to lead to safety. Trying to avoid making this section of the game too dull was a real challenge because constantly telling someone to stop and go soon gets frustrating. The solution was to make the blind character fairly independent, providing that the player remain within about 50 feet of him. It was necessary to keep him close and keep an eye on him, but the player didn't have to spend too much time actually interacting with him. It's exactly the same with hostages in the online shooter *Counterstrike*. The designers initially gave the player the ability to start and stop them but soon decided that it was simpler all around just to let them follow the player intelligently all the way back to safety.

Controllable Squads or Teams

Having a squad of characters that the player can switch between can be a great way to add freedom and variety to the gameplay in your title. The Conflict series is a great example of this. One potential risk is that the player doesn't empathize with any character because they might not be any one character. In fact, they may end up feeling more like a god (as in many of 'sim' games) than getting immersed and feeling like a character. With multiple controllable team members, you need to decide how you will switch between the characters—do you allow the player to do this at any time, or is it forced on the player, or can the player change only at certain moments? There are some very creative ways of doing this—for example, titles like *Messiah*, which allow you to take over another character by entering his body like a ghost, or games in which you can see from the viewpoint from another character but not actually control them. Introducing characterization is even harder. Since you probably don't know which character the player will be controlling at any one point, it is harder to have in-game dialogue between the characters.

7

The Intensity Roller Coaster

In passing, I want to mention the importance of creating an "intensity roller coaster" for the player, with moments of frantic action interspersed with time to recover and prepare for the next one. If you watch great films, you'll find they mostly adhere to this principle, with bigger and bigger moments of excitement followed by calm, rising to a crescendo at the climax of the film.

There are several examples of games that deliver this roller coaster very well. *Half-Life* and *Resident Evil 4* are both examples of very well-paced games that give the player some intense action and then provide the player with a chance to catch their breath before hitting again even harder. Of course, it's much easier to create this roller coaster if your game is fairly linear, because you'll have a fairly good idea of when players will hit each new section. If the game is totally free-form, the player may end up making their own decisions on whether to take a breather or not.

Design Project: Mole with a Mission

To demonstrate some of the techniques and concepts that I have covered in this chapter, let's work through a sample game design that focuses on a unique character so that you can see firsthand the kinds of choices and design trade-offs you'll need to work with when you create characters for your games. As we go through the hands-on project, try to think about what you might do differently for one of your own games. I imagine that no two designers will end up with exactly the same character design.

Mole with a Mission

The boss is on the phone and he wants to create a cool new character to start a major brand. A few focus groups were held to present some ideas for different kinds of characters, and the feedback strongly suggests that the character ought to be based on a mole. The focus groups felt that moles are cute, "interesting" animals that haven't been seen in games before. Using this research as a starting point, our mission is to create a unique game design based on a mole. The game will need to appeal to all kinds of gamers, although it won't be a platform game.

We'll need to start by thinking about the biggest risks that we must face. Cute animals in games rarely appeal to older gamers, so we need to think of how to address this issue if we want hardcore and mature gamers to buy the game. We're going to deal with this on two fronts. First, we'll deal with the look and personality of the mole, and then we'll deal with the kind of game we're going to make.

Designing the Mole Character

The primary decisions to be made are how realistic to make the character and what kind of personality he will have. Do we go for a cartoon look, a more stylized approach, or an accurate re-creation of the real-life animal? Do we go down the most obvious route of a cute, half-blind character, or do we try something more unusual? My decision in this case is driven by the need to try to appeal to older gamers as well as younger ones. I think our mole needs to be cool, not cute. So we're going to have a heroic main character who is supercool (imagine a mole version of Tom Cruise from *Mission:Impossible*). I also want to make the mole very angry and focused. So imagine that human construction workers are digging foundations for new buildings and it's causing tunnels to collapse and totally destroying the mole community. Maybe our mole hero has got a family and his baby or wife is nearly killed. He goes off, steaming with anger to try to single-handedly stop the menace. We'll create a very stylized mole, giving him some human attributes without straying too far from what they really look like. Maybe we'll give him a pair of Ray-Ban sunglasses (and get our licensing team to get Ray-Ban involved) since it will help him look cool and it fits in with the half-blind image of moles (whose eyesight, as we know, isn't great).

7

Creating the Gameplay

Our main aim here is to create something fresh and original; we're not after a run-of-the mill platformer (even if done really well). This game has to be innovative. So we need to decide how realistic to make the mole's actions and interactions—do we stick to what moles do in real life, or do we go to the other end of the scale and allow our character to hold objects, fire a gun, and even walk on two legs? For this game, we want to try to make the character feel and act like a real mole as far as possible. So the key gameplay mechanic in this game is going to be digging.

Digging with Real Soil Physics

It's important, as a designer, to keep up with the latest technology and middleware so that you can use them when you need to do things that might not have been possible previously. In this instance, we want to use a physics system to create realistic soil and objects that collapse and drop with gravity. This will allow our hero to burrow underneath objects to cause them to fall over or sink downward. Using an extremely realistic representation of soil, it should be possible to make the tunneling feel very intuitive so that the player quickly understands what causes the ground above to collapse. If you've played *Worms* and used the tunneling device in that game, you'll understand the starting point. But in our game, the character tunnels much faster, with the player able to direct his mole up and down freely to alter the angle of the tunnel. Also, if he digs too close to a heavy object and creates a large cavern, he can cause the earth above him to drop down, causing knock-on effects for other objects above.

Camera/Control System

Tunneling in three dimensions is going to be tricky, so while it will make it much harder for the development team to make the game feel cutting edge, I think the gameplay needs to be largely two-dimensional, with our mole moving from side to side. However, to make this look as up-to-date as possible, the game world needs to be in 3D, and although the action takes place mainly in one plane, we'll move the camera around in some really cool ways to show off the fact that the environment is three-dimensional. Take a look at titles like *Viewtiful Joe* (see Figure 7.16), which shows that it is possible to make a really good-looking game from a mainly side-on or isometric view.

Figure 7.16
Viewtiful Joe.

Summary

Although I don't think that *Mole with a Mission* will ever make it into development (or sell many copies if it did!), I think the character and game design ideas we walked through will help you see a few ways of going about creating a character and integrating the basic gameplay.

You should always strive to make your characters interesting. Think carefully about what they're going to do, and make sure the player is going to want to play the role of that character. Several years ago, a young Toby Gard did exactly that and ended up with Lara Croft.

An Interview with Toby Gard

Toby Gard is one of the best-known British game designers and was responsible for designing stunning cyber-heroine Lara Croft when he worked at Core Design. Since then, Toby has created the critically acclaimed *Galleon*, which showcases one of the most innovative and fluid camera and control solutions seen in recent years. After *Galleon*, Toby moved to the United States to help reinvent Lara at Crystal Dynamics and is currently working his magic charting the future direction of the Tomb Raider franchise.

Can you recommend any good starting points if a designer is trying to come up with a memorable game character?

TG: Well, certainly not other game characters. If you want your character to be memorable then it will have to be different. That means looking at anything except other games for inspiration. Who is this character? is the first question. Once you know if the character is supposed to be a fisherman or a brain surgeon or a mutant hamster, you can start playing with ideas based on that theme. I tend to start searching for whatever reference I can that has any link to the character's central theme—reading stuff, looking up images on the Internet, going to the book shop. Then I just start putting ideas that seem interesting and cool together into a bunch of different sketches. If I'm finding myself stuck doing clichés, then I tend to do a bit of the old brainstorming shenanigans like putting completely bizarre unconnected ideas together with the base theme and seeing where it gets me or inverting some of the assumptions I've been making.

All the time, for me, I am looking at whatever I'm drawing and asking myself, "Is this cool?" If an element is cool it will stay alive into later designs; stuff that looks stupid doesn't. It seems like a bit of an obvious comment, but I honestly think some character designers don't ask themselves, "Is this character cool?" Instead, they are only interested in making something that is pleasing to their own eye, which is different. For instance, there appear to be plenty of male character designers who design girls wearing frankly impossible steel G-strings with obligatory thigh-length boots. I believe that those chaps really like looking at these sorts of characters, but I'm not convinced they think that the character is cool. A cool character demands respect and is defined visually by more than just how "hot" they are. I think it would be hard for anyone to arrive at a party wearing the costumes that some female game characters have had to wear and not illicit titters from the other partygoers. It's just not cool to wear that stuff. Really.

Anyway, eventually when I've got something I like, I do a bunch of really rough color compositions to see what works well. Then I make up a clean image, and Voila!

How important is the physical appearance of the character in relation to how they move and interact within the game environment?

TG: Psychologically speaking, first impressions really do last. For most people, the first time they will see your character is on a poster, the game box, or on the pages of a magazine. If the character

7

does not grab their attention at that point, you have already failed to a fairly large extent. Clearly once you are playing a game, you will be worrying less about what the character is wearing and more about what they are doing, but before then, you will try to judge the character as best you can from the clues you have at hand, and they are all likely to be physical. It's the same with real people. You judge them at a glance: what they are wearing, how they are standing, what age they are—that sort of thing. You make up an idea in your head of what you think that person might be like. I'd hope you still keep an open mind, but chances are, if you see someone who is dressed like a Goth, for instance, you are likely to have certain expectations as to what that person will be like (and rightly so; what you wear is a language, and many people are very fluent in communicating who they are through what they wear). Clearly most, if not all, of those expectations you form are likely to turn out to be completely off the mark, but the point is, people do judge each other that way, and they will judge your character design the same way, consciously or not. The bottom line is, you cannot be too careful with the physical appearance; it is incredibly important that it's as appealing as possible.

Is it important to flesh out the personality and history of your character?

TG: That depends on the game. I find it helpful regardless, or you will tend to make a relatively flat character. It's certainly important to know what motivates them.

Other than Lara, what is your favorite game character and why?

TG: Hmmn, maybe the King of All Creation from Katamari Damachi, or Ben Throttle from Full Throttle, both because they are hilarious.

How do you feel about titles like the Grand Theft Auto series that have almost no characterization in the main character but where the player is allowed to customize the character to look like them, effectively becoming their personal avatar in the game world?

TG: Oh that's great stuff. As a player, I like that the most, to be honest. I mean, many games are about slipping into a fantasy world, and slipping into someone else's fantasy character is not as easy as slipping into one of your own. I personally think that is the way forward. Maybe one day there will be a standard format for a character in games. You'll be able to set it up in game X, then after that adventure, take it to game Y, just keep letting it grow and grow. Portable avatars—that way, game developers don't have to worry about that whole side of it. They can concentrate on making the stories, the adventures.

What are you most proud of in your career so far?

TG: I've had the chance to work with some great people, and I've had the honor to meet some incredible game designers. That's cool.

What is your favorite game ever (of all time), and why?

TG: *It was Ultima Underworld, a truly, unbelievably well-designed game. Then, I played EverQuest and it blew my mind. Then, World of Warcraft just started sucking all the life juice out of me, it's so damn good. But right now, my favorite game of all time is Half-Life 2. That game is just a perfect example of what immersive interactive stories can and should be. I freaking love it.*

What do you think is the biggest game design mistake that people regularly make with games?

TG: *Too much copying of other games.*

If money and technology were unlimited, what kind of game would you most like to see made?

TG: *I'd like to see an epic kung fu odyssey. Not an ersatz one, but based on real Chinese kung fu literature and mythology. In fact, I'd like to make it. Shame I can't read Chinese.*

What do you think is the biggest challenge facing game designers as we move forward?

TG: *Adapting to managing teams of 100+ people.*

And finally, if you had one piece of advice to give to a game designer who was just starting out, what would it be?

TG: *If you love it, then do it, and don't take no for an answer.*

7

Chapter 8

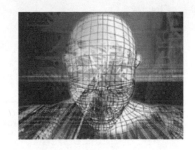

Game Environments
and Level Design

"A common mistake that people make when trying to design something completely foolproof is to underestimate the ingenuity of complete fools."

Douglas Adams

This chapter is all about designing the rich and immersive worlds in which our in-game characters or vehicles reside. These worlds are created in two steps, as you'll learn in this chapter. First, the lead game designer creates an outline where each level will be set, clarifying the overall game mechanics and specifying what they want to achieve with each level or section of the game. For the second step, a level designer is typically employed to create the layout of the level and implement it using a level designing tool. Good level design is a real art, and there are many level designers who are so good at their field that they should never do anything else. It's a real shame that there seems to be a design "hierarchy" in which level designers need to move up in a design team or company to become more general game designers. Hopefully in the future, top level designers will be rewarded for what they do best and not be encouraged to move away from what can be a very important and skilled role.

Although I'll be using the term *level* in this chapter to define a section of a game, it doesn't have to mean one specific linear section. It can also mean a chunk or area of a much larger open world. *Level* is a commonly used term within the industry, but games are increasingly becoming less linear as they provide the player with more freedom. If you are creating one large open-world city for your game, you will need to split it into manageable sections that can be shared between your level designers, and hopefully most of the things I'll say about levels apply to sections of a larger open-world environment as well.

Step 1: Creating the Blueprint

The first step to take before you start designing your levels is to create a level design blueprint. This is a top-level summary of what your game is, where each level fits into the overall story, what kind of things need to happen in each level, and so on. So what should you include as part of the blueprint phase? Let's take a closer look.

Know All Your Gameplay Mechanics

Before any levels are designed, it is vital that you have a complete game design document (see Appendix A for a game design document template) that covers all the gameplay mechanics you want to use in the game. I have seen levels created and only then the gameplay decided and shoehorned in. This is *not* the way I'd recommend doing it. If you know exactly what the player will be able to do in your level, you should be able to design and build the level to use these elements properly. If you take a look at any great level, it has been designed around the gameplay, not the other way around.

War Story: Wrong Way to Design a Level

A simple example of the wrong way to design a level would be to create a level for a character and then decide that the character is able to fly. Obviously the level will have been created without this in mind, and not only will it have lots of problems in terms of limiting the character (and stopping them from flying straight to the end of the level), but it also won't include anything that requires the player to fly. If you know the character can fly before you set about designing a level, you can create hidden areas to which the player can fly and therefore make it a mechanic that actually has a real and valid use.

Keep a Constant Set of Rules

It can be very disorientating to the player if the underlying game rules change between levels. What do I mean by an underlying game rule? An obvious example would be that your character can climb up rocky walls but not smooth metal ones. The player will soon get used to this rule. If one level designer isn't aware of this and allows the player to climb up metal walls, or doesn't allow the player to climb up a rock wall, the player will get annoyed and confused.

A more subtle example would be that you decide to use areas of yellow light to help indicate places that the player needs to go to (to help the player along subtly). As the player progresses through the game, they will start to realize that a yellow light means "come this way," and it becomes a conscious or even subconscious cue. The player will get confused if you use this rule in some levels and then break it in others (for example, by using a yellow light over a lethal trap). Once this happens, the rule is broken. You may want to break rules on purpose to help develop paranoia and discomfort, but I suggest that you only do so if you have a very good reason.

Give Each Level a Distinct Theme

You want people to be able to say, "I just got to the level with the massive tower" or "Did you manage to get past the crocodile swamp?" Every level (and ideally every half hour of the game) should include something unique and memorable. If in doubt, think, "How will a school kid describe this level to his friends in the playground?" If there isn't an easy way to describe the level, you have a problem.

Always Make the Player's Goal Clear

Some game designs are deliberately created to make players feel lost and bewildered to encourage them to explore and find their own solutions. But it's very hard to do this well, and I wouldn't recommend going down this route unless you have an excellent reason and feel you have the skill to carry it off. The vast majority of games are designed to try to make the player's goal crystal clear so that the player knows exactly what they need to achieve. This is especially important for the first hour of the game. New players need to be lead gently by the hand as you introduce them to the game and explain how it works and what is expected of them. For this reason, location-specific objectives are widely used within games. Essentially, these are goals that have a location attached to them. A map, an on-screen compass, or some kind of in-game indicator is used to point to the physical location. Some games have only one objective at a time, keeping it nice and clear for the player, but other games have multiple objectives and either allow the player to select which one they want to aim for or encourage a specific order while giving players the flexibility to do it their way. Also remember that players might save the game and then come back to it several weeks later. The player may not remember the cut scene that was shown just before the save point, so you need to make sure there is some way that a player can recap their goals and review what they are doing. However you do it, keep the player's overall goal clear so they never become lost.

Step 2: Designing the Level

Once you have defined your blueprint, (again, take a look at Appendix A if you'd like to see a template for this kind of document), you'll need to design each level or section within the game. While the gameplay fundamentals of your camera and control system provide instant feedback to the player, level design is the element that will define the player's experience with your game over the longer term. (Good level design is a real skill, and if you're really good at it, you might choose not to worry about any other aspect of design and concentrate on designing levels exclusively.)

8

Reality Check: The key challenge when designing levels is to keep the player wanting more. You should strive to push and surprise, challenge and intrigue, but never make the player feel frustrated, aimless, or confused. You want to keep the gameplay of the level just challenging enough so that the player doesn't get bored too easily, but not so challenging that that player will quit in frustration.

Start by making a huge list of everything that you know you'll be able to use within your levels. This list should include the following items:

- Objects that the player can pick up and use

- Unique locations

- Enemy characters

- Friendly characters

- Vehicles

- Animated objects, wildlife, or things to help the level feel alive

- The building/object/location where the player starts the level

- The building/object/location where the player finishes the level

There should be enough elements that you can keep introducing new things to the player throughout the game to keep things interesting. *Half-Life 2* is a perfect example. Just as you get used to what you're doing, the game introduces a new weapon, vehicle, or game mechanic (such as using bait to attract insects). It never feels dull or repetitive. If you don't feel that your game has enough interesting elements to introduce, talk to the rest of your design team about it. Having five enemy types across a typically 10-to-12-hour game just won't cut it. Let's next look at the kind of things that you should consider as a level designer.

Introduce Key Level Design Themes Early

It is often nice for the player to notice early on what makes each level different from the previous one. For me, the best levels are ones that the player can easily describe to his friends. For example, here are some of the comments you might hear:

"**It's the one with the huge collapsing aqueduct.**"

"**It's the one where you get attacked by a giant man-eating octopus.**"

As I've mentioned earlier, try to make sure every level has something that makes it unique, and try to give the player an idea of this near the start of the level, even if it is only a hint.

Reality Check: In the first *Tomb Raider* game, there was an enormous *Tyrannosaurus rex* that attacked the player in an extremely memorable section (see Figure 8.1). Ask anyone who played the game, and I assure you they'll remember this moment. It's a great example of how to make a level feel truly unique.

8

Figure 8.1
Tomb Raider T.rex attack.

Focus on the Magical First Half Hour

The first half hour of your game is vital. So if your level is the first one the player will play, in my view, it's by far the most important in the game. Try to create a blend of training and a stunning and dramatic introduction, showing off what your game can do while starting off easy. Play the *Medal of Honor* D-day assault intro level by EA, which is a perfect example of this approach. You need to wow people with the first 30 minutes of gameplay, making it exciting and intense while remaining easy to complete. The player needs to think, "This is amazing," as well as, "I'm pretty good at this, aren't I?!" It's the perfect combination.

Don't Use Everything Everywhere

Save enemies, objects, and special events so that they are special. Drip-feed new elements into the game as the player progresses. Ideally, you will have enough new elements to introduce. If not, try to persuade the producer to add more elements. If this gets nowhere, try to vary the existing elements. For example, if you've got a sword model, have two swords in the game, one more powerful than the other. Persuade an artist to create a slightly different texture for the new sword. Voila! This can give you instant additional content with minimal effort.

A good example of this is the game *Knights of the Old Republic*. The game allows you to collect different gems so you can customize your lightsaber to be more effective in different kinds of attacks and also to glow a different color. With little development effort (a few lines of code, an interface screen, and a few objects placed around the game), it delivers an extra gameplay element and something additional for the player to focus on collecting and customizing.

Try to Avoid Level Reuse If Possible

One of my biggest gripes with level design is when the player is forced to go back through a level, retracing their original path. I have seen this done well, but only if the environment has changed in a major way; for example, if there is a flood and now the environment is partly underwater, giving access to areas that were previously inaccessible. The original *HALO* game, despite being a great product, had this problem. At points in the game (and one point in particular), the level designers had reused an area again and again to make the level longer. It resulted in a section that became boring. My advice would be to not force the player to play through an area they have already seen, unless you are going to change that area in an interesting way and turn the fact that it has already been seen into a positive.

 Reality Check: There are occasions when, to create variety, it is quite nice for the player to dash one way and the other through a small environment solving puzzles, unlocking new doors, and using their knowledge of a contained area to work out how to move on. But I would still recommend keeping these to a minimum and making sure that most of your game doesn't involved the player backtracking through areas.

Expect the Unexpected

Games quickly become dull if the same things happen repeatedly and the player is able to predict what is coming up next. A great level designer will throw in the occasional shock, something totally unexpected that catches the player by surprise, but still feels logical and possible within the rules of the game world. What do I mean by logical and possible? Well, imagine you're playing a James Bond game and you've gotten used to shooting hundreds of enemy agents as you proceed through an underground chemical lab. The designer needs to shake things up a little. If you come around a corner and find a giant boulder rolling toward you that you need to run away from, that would feel out of place; sure, it's different, but it obviously destroys the illusion of breaking into a chemical lab. However, if you come around a corner and find a bomb ticking down that you needed to defuse by shooting a liquid nitrogen canister to freeze the mechanism, that would not only add variety (and a change of pace), it would feel more logical and possible.

The Process of Creating Levels

Now that we've discussed the basic steps involved in designing levels, it's time to take a closer look at how game levels are actually made. It's a little difficult to generalize too much when discussing the actual process of building levels because every game is a bit different. However, there are some important techniques that can be used as you are creating your levels from beginning to end. Try to incorporate these techniques into your own design and development strategies so that you create a process that works for you.

Get Your Level Down on Paper

You should always mock the level out on paper (see Figure 8.2). (It's much cheaper to make changes on paper!) Some people use quick and basic 3D packages (such as the excellent SketchUp) to do the same thing, but I find that paper is even quicker. The overall level shape is drawn out along with all the key places, objects, and enemies that the player will meet. Don't worry if you are not a great artist. What's important is that you get all of the important concepts and components down on paper. If it's a track or stage for a driving game, the shape is worked out carefully, giving the player a varied and exciting experience. Good designers will remember to put unique objects at places within the level to help players get their bearings. You should also remember that levels are 3D, and although it's hard when drawing a 2D design on paper, you need to remember to use height within the environment to make it more interesting. Also, try to be as ambitious and imaginative as possible. You can always cut something out if it isn't working, but if you're not really creative at this stage, it's not going to magically appear later on. If other levels have been created already, compare them with your paper design. Does it fit in? It is too similar? Does it look like it will be fun to play?

 Reality Check: Once you are reasonably happy with your paper layout, you might want to let it sit for a few days and then come back to it to review it. You might want to pass it around to the other people that you are working with or other game players who can give you some good feedback. Don't be in a hurry to rush to the next stage. It's easy to change things at this point, so try to be as flexible as you can and explore different design options.

Emotion Maps

One interesting area that I'm exploring at the moment is the idea of creating 'emotion maps' for game levels. These work in a similar way to typical level maps. The idea is that

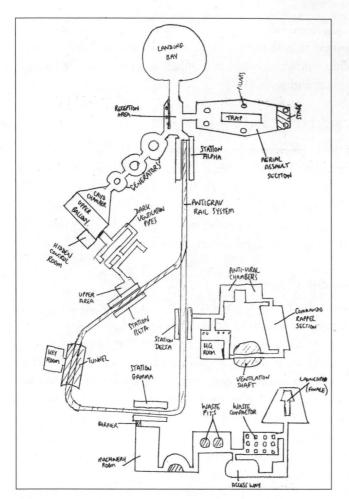

Figure 8.2
Rough paper level design.

you take a physical map of the level, and write down at key points in the level what emotional state the player should be feeling there. This is done with close reference to the storyline and in-game dialogue. When the level is designed, puzzles, the environment, set piece events and characters/objects can be created in a way to help highlight the desired emotion at each point. So if you want the player to feel scared, rather than just leaving it to the storyline, that entire section of the level is designed with that emotion in mind. So in this example, you might have the lights suddenly black out, a strange cry come from the distance and so on. The storyline might require that the player's character feels angry. So rather than just playing a cut-scene, the level around that section can be designed to build up this emotion. In this case, you might have another character die that the player feels attached to, causing the player to feel the emotion of anger. *Half-Life 2* is a superb game in terms of the storyline and making the player feel emotional, and I'm convinced that the level designers knew what emotion they were aiming for in every part of their levels. Anyway, it's something to think about – I haven't tried it out in practice yet, but will be doing so shortly.

Creating the Rough Geometry

Once you are set with your paper layout, you'll be ready to start creating the level by working with a level designer or an artist. If the studio has a strong level design tool, a level designer should be able to use it to create the basic geometry of the level. By this, I mean creating lots of simple rectangular rooms and corridors of roughly the right size, with door openings, slopes for staircases, and so on. This will give you a feeling of how big the level is, how long it takes to run through it, and whether the rooms are too big or too small. If your team doesn't have this ability, you could use a 3D graphic artist to take the paper design and create some rough level geometry using a program such as 3DS Max or Maya. At this stage, in my experience, the level is best left untextured to save time. It's likely that there will be many changes, and the whole process is quicker if an artist doesn't texture the level until it's more complete. Figure 8.3 shows a rough part of a level with basic geometry, and Figure 8.4 shows the same section in its final form.

First Pass Placement

The level designer will use the level design tools to place objects, enemies, weapons, vehicles, and other unique entities within the rough geometry. It's very important at this

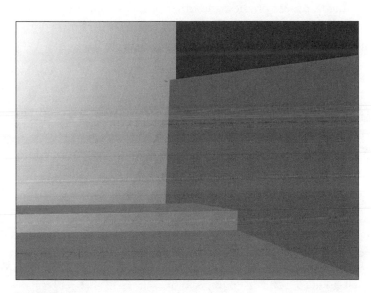

Figure 8.3
Rough section with basic geometry.

Figure 8.4
Final quality section.

stage to be able to play the game using this rough level. If you can only fly through the
levels with a virtual camera, it's very hard to judge how a level will play once you introduce
enemies with AI, moving platforms, proper physics, and other vehicles racing against you.
The more of these elements that are present (at least in an early form), the better your
chances will be of nailing the level early and not having to make changes later on.

Test-Play

The level designer will play the level (which will look very ugly at this stage) many
times to get a feel for how it is paced, whether it is exciting and interesting, whether
there is enough variety, if there are any dull sections, and so on. Generally, in terms of
pacing, you're ideally looking to create a roller coaster. Try to create intense adrenaline
rushes followed by calmer moments before rising back up into even more intense
moments. If you need to, plot out what the "excitement curves" look like.

 Reality Check: If you're unsure about how to create an "excitement curve," try the
following. Get someone to play the game for the first time, and ask them every minute to
give you a score from 1 to 10 for how exciting the game is at that moment. For each level of
the game, plot a graph of the excitement level. If your level is well designed, you should find
the graph looks a little like Figure 8.5, building up to peaks of excitement that get bigger
and bigger until the climax of the level (it sounds like something you'd read in the *Good Sex
Guide*, doesn't it!?).

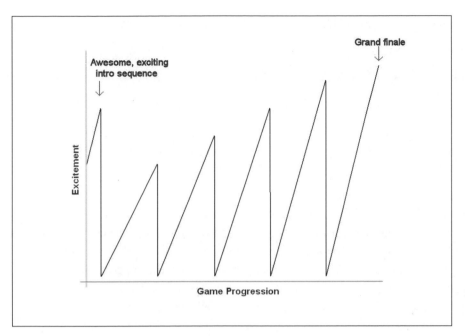

Figure 8.5
An ideal excitement curve.

8

If you are creating a stealth game, you still have intense moments when you sneak up behind a dangerous enemy hoping they won't turn round, so the same rule applies. Even with driving games, a perfect rally stage or car racing circuit will have moments when you can catch your breath, line the car up, and wipe the sweat from your brow before the next dangerous corner.

Fine-Tune the Geometry

Based on your test play, you will almost certainly need to change quite a bit of the geometry. Again, this may be done by an artist based on your level design feedback, or you may be able to do this yourself within a level editing tool.

Here is a checklist of some of the most common things you might do when you're fine-tuning level geometry:

- Create cover to help the player.

- Remove cover to make combat more exciting.

- Add alternate paths for the player where a section is too linear.

- Add in small, secret areas to place collectible objects.

- Remove dull sections completely.

- Add tall objects to prevent the player seeing so far.

- Create a "dogleg" within the level to help prevent visible clipping.

- Change the gradient of a slope to make a section more dynamic.

- Widen corridors and doors to stop camera problems.

- Raise ceilings and roofs to stop camera problems.

- Open up sections that are too cluttered and confusing.

Fine-Tune Object Placements

In addition to changing the geometry based on your first test play, you will almost certainly want to change the position of some of the objects and characters within your level, as well as alter their behaviors, the direction they face, what they are doing when the player meets them, and so on. At this stage, it's worth trying to balance the level roughly, setting up the attributes of the characters you meet. Often your tools will allow you to say how brave or scared characters are, how well they hear, whether they stay in their positions or are allowed to run at the player, and so on. This is a good time to experiment with different scenarios to see how they work.

Test-Play Again

Now that the geometry and placement has been changed to reflect your first feedback, you should play through the level again. At this stage, it's important to get feedback from other people who haven't played the level before. Be as tough with the level as possible. There are a number of questions to consider at this point:

- Are there any sections that are still not very exciting?

- Are any of the areas too difficult or too easy?

- Do you make full use of all the gameplay mechanics that were planned out in the blueprint?

- Have you placed secret pickups around the environment to encourage players who like exploring?

- Does your level feature enough variety in height, with slopes and vertical sections?

- Is there enough variety through the level?

- Does the level feel realistic (if that is what you're aiming for)?

Make sure you're really happy with the level at this stage. It's also important to compare your level with others in the game at this point, before lots of work goes into second-pass artwork. Make sure the level is not too similar to other levels in your game (or other games), and that you're not using the same puzzle as someone else. It's also worth thinking about difficulty levels. If the game is going to have multiple difficulty levels, make sure you know how these will work. Do you need to set up three different sets of enemy placement, one for easy, one for medium, and one for hard? Or will the enemies be made weaker and less accurate? Test the level on each difficulty level and make sure that it seems to be working at this stage.

Create the Second-Pass Artwork

At this stage, the level will take a huge leap from rough, untextured geometry to something that looks close to final artwork. The work at this stage is normally done by artists, but it may be done by the level designer, who places pre-created final-quality textures and models into the level using the tools.

Test-Play One More Time

At this stage, you should play through the level again. Is the level clear or confusing? Does the player know where they need to go next? Is it easy to get lost? For the first time, you're seeing the level almost as the final gamer will see it. Now is a good time to get more people to play the level. Make sure these are people who haven't seen it before. Don't give them direction; just leave them alone and see where they get stuck, what they find too hard, and which bits they really enjoy. The level needs to be really good fun at this point. If it's not, you need to cut out the sections that don't work and be ruthless.

Improve Placement

Again, improve the placement of enemies, objects, and vehicles. Make sure you've used everything that you were planning to use, and double-check to see if everything feels just right. Nothing should stand out as being stupid. For example, I've played a game in which you come into a police station parking lot and find a tank parked there. It feels wrong—what would a tank be doing in a police station lot? Maybe you should create the corner of an army base later in the level and have the player steal the tank and smash it through the fence, or you could have the tank abandoned in the street surrounded by dead soldiers who have been ambushed. Anyway, double-check to make sure the level is believable and exciting and meets all the objectives you identified when the blueprint was created.

8

Make the Final Pass on Your Artwork

The artists will do a final pass of the artwork, improving textures, playing the level themselves, and adding effects and detail until it hopefully shines. The level should now be complete in terms of geometry and textures.

Complete the Final Balancing

As you reach completion of the game, all the levels need to be balanced with respect to each other so that the game gradually increases in difficulty as you play through it. At this point, you may need to make your level a little easier or tougher, which is often done by making subtle changes in the number of enemies you encounter, their aiming accuracy, or if it's a racing game, the width of the hardest corners, the angle of a hairpin, or simply the skill of the AI drivers. The aim at this stage is to end up with a complete game, one in which each level gets gradually harder until the player has a tough challenge to complete the game.

Other Level Design Considerations

Of course, there are other things to think about when you're designing a level. Many developers have their own unique level design tools, which you'll need to learn, or you may find yourself using middleware editing tools which come with technology such as Epic's Unreal engine. It's also important to think about the kind of environment that you are designing; whether it's a busy city or a sinister jungle, you ought to make use of all the unique qualities that environment has to offer. So let's take a look at tool and environments in more detail.

Using Level Design Tools

One of the more frustrating issues of level design is that almost every development studio uses a different internally created level editing tool, each with its own nuances, pluses, and minuses. There are many reasons for this, but most developers develop their own level editing tools either because they need something that integrates seamlessly with their own technology, or because their game requires a very specific type of editor because it may be quite unique. Until EA bought RenderWare, it was looking as if more and more studios would be using RenderWare technology and therefore using its tools to design levels. The situation now is that other publishers are very nervous about using technology owned by their biggest rival and as many people predicted, it's looking like RenderWare will not be supplied to third-parties in the future. Therefore, studios tend to be split between using their own technology or licensing something like the Unreal engine.

Unfortunately, things seem unlikely to change quickly, and as level designers move from one company to another, they will almost certainly need to learn new tools.

Game Environments

Let's now take a look at some specific types of game environments and the challenges and opportunities that they each present to you as a game designer. When you're creating gameplay in a specific type of environment, it can be useful to consider in advance what the environment offers you and what its positive and negative aspects are.

Outdoor Environments: Cities

Designing games within cities is very popular at the moment. The biggest single challenge that you'll face is that a city is a very large open environment. Games like the GTA series allow you the freedom to explore an entire city, and players will expect the same lack of restriction in other games. If your technology isn't capable of rendering a large open-world area, you'll probably have to find reasons and ways to restrict the player—maybe road blocks or collapsed buildings. But you'll need to do it carefully because players are likely to find it frustrating.

Another challenge with cities involves consistency. Assuming that you're going to allow the player to enter certain buildings, the player will wonder why they aren't able to enter other buildings that look just as accessible. And as soon as you start putting massive metal locks onto all the other buildings, the realism breaks down. If you're allowing players to enter and drive vehicles, they will expect to be able to enter any vehicle unless there is a good reason why they can't.

It's also much harder to build a huge city and keep it exciting, diverse, and full of people and objects to interact with. When you are building more linear levels, you can create superb Hollywood-style set-piece sequences because you know the player will pass through a certain point in a certain direction. This is harder in a large open-world environment. Although you can (and normally do) force the player to arrive at a certain point in the city, you don't have nearly as much control about which direction they come from, whether they are driving or on foot, and what time within the game they reach that point.

However, there are also many positive aspects of using a city for your game environment. Most players are familiar and comfortable with the setting; they understand automatically the rules of driving (traffic lights, road signs, and so on) and how to navigate around an urban setting. You have a large environment within which you can place lots of missions, secret items, and people/objects to interact with. Because the

8

player isn't going to try to enter every building, it's easy to unlock buildings or areas as the player progresses through the game.

Outdoor Environments: Forests and Jungles

Forests and jungles create their own very unique challenges. Probably the biggest problem is that players can easily get lost. This is especially true if it's an open-world environment, where the players can travel within limits in any direction they want. When you're re-creating a jungle, you try to make it feel real, and therefore it's almost impossible to create a unique, distinct-looking area every 50 meters to help the player navigate. Games like *Metal Gear Solid: Snake Eater* are largely linear, so you're constantly moving "forward" through the environment. This helps develop the gameplay and keeps the player from getting lost, but it does feel constrained and limiting.

War Story: Don't Let the Player Get Lost

In creating the game *Conflict: Vietnam*, we quickly encountered the problem of the player getting lost. In order to make the gameplay flow, we needed to keep the game largely linear (although we had multiple paths through areas). The Vietnamese jungle is quite claustrophobic and narrow, and therefore it was very hard to create the freedom necessary for players to use their four squad members in a useful and creative way. All too often the squad gameplay was reduced to running through a linear section of jungle with the squad members following the player, acting more like extra lives than anything else. But if we'd tried to make an open-world jungle, where the player was allowed to reach objectives by whichever path they preferred (or to simply go exploring), it would have made creating set-piece events and ambushes much harder. Since action is the key driving force behind the Conflict series, it's fairly easy to see why the levels were kept quite linear.

It's also very difficult to come up with enough variety to make a jungle or forest interesting. Given that the player might be playing the game for 10 or 15 hours, that's an enormous number of clever ideas you need to come up with to make new sections of forest or jungle feel different. There are only so many ditches, rivers, huts, and tunnels that you can add to these kinds of areas. One area that has been largely unexplored is making the most out the environment in terms of weather. Moisture, dew, humidity, steaming clouds, and the sudden rainfall that can be heard on the treetops above are all things that make jungles unique. My feeling is that to do a jungle or forest justice in a game, you need to introduce proper weather, and maybe even a day/night cycle. Walking in a forest in the moonlight, scared as hell, with noises in the distance as the rain starts to fall could be a great setting for gameplay. Both jungles and forests can create huge levels of claustrophobia, tension, and fear. Think carefully about variety and how to keep your player from getting lost. Then, ramp up the audio, and scare the hell out of your player using mysterious sounds in the distance or the sudden crack of a stick behind him just as it starts to get dark!

Outdoor Environments: Snow and Ice

I believe that environments that consist of snow levels (normally set in the Arctic or Antarctic) are probably the hardest kind to create. My hat goes off to the designers on *The Thing* for creating a whole game in this setting. As with jungle and forest environments, one of your biggest challenges is keeping the player from getting lost. This is especially true if you are making use of snowstorms. One way of dealing with this is to make it part of the gameplay. You could give the player a large number of flares and let the player mark their own route. But it's not an ideal solution, and it's not realistic to have very distinct areas every 150 feet in the arctic. An even bigger problem is creating enough variety to keep the levels interesting. You've got even less to work with than you do in jungle environments, and you'll probably want to resort to man-made buildings every so often.

Graphically, snow levels are a nightmare. There is so little that the artists can spend their polygon budget on. You've got no option but to make the snow look incredible and add footprints and tracks as the player moves around. But in reality, these environments are essentially very white. And having a never ending white level isn't exciting and certainly won't get your PR team drooling when they're trying to capture a hundred different screen shots. My recommendation would be to try to avoid setting an entire game in a snowy environment and make it a unique and distinct section within the game.

Indoor Environments

Buildings and interior environments present a set of design constraints that you don't get with the outside world. If your game has a third-person camera, you'll need to plan for it early on in the process. It's very easy to create doorways, ceilings, and walls that have realistic measurements but feel extremely cramped when you try playing them out in the game. Your game camera will normally be above and behind the player's head, so you'll need to work out how the camera will behave when the player goes through doors and turns around in corridors. If you leave this until after your levels have been designed, you may have problems that you simply can't properly solve, leading to a jerky and frustrating camera.

Creating buildings can be tough if you're sticking to realism. A real-life hotel can have many hundreds of rooms. Can your player kick open any door? If not, how are the doors locked so that unlocking them doesn't feel artificial? As with any level, creating variety is the key, so you should try to populate your interior environments with as many interesting moving objects and animated characters as possible. Have a couple rowing in a corridor if it fits your setting. The danger is that everything indoors becomes static and you feel as if you are in a lifeless level. Outdoors, it's pretty easy to have birds,

8

swaying trees, objects blowing about in the wind, moving cars, and lots of elements that make a scene feel alive. Inside, you'll need to work hard to try to make sure you pack your level with objects and people that move.

Fantasy Environments

Fantasy environments should be the easiest to create because you don't have any limitations. Here you are relying on your imagination (and the imagination of everyone who plays your game). This has its own problems; if lots of level designers let their imaginations run wild, you can easily end up with disjointed, unconnected levels. You need to create some mock-up artwork of the levels, setting a clear overall style when you create your blueprint. Since the game is fantasy-based, you need to be much more detailed in your description before the levels are designed. Here are some questions to consider:

- What are the rules of your world?

- Are you sticking to real-life gravity?

- Is there magic present in this world, or do things need to behave in a realistic fashion?

- What can the main characters do?

- Does each level need to have a theme, and if so, what are they?

- What is the overall graphical style?

- How realistic will the buildings, objects, and people be?

 Reality Check: Designing fantasy environments can be extremely enjoyable because it allows you to throw the rule book out the window to a large extent. But you need to carefully manage the process to avoid a clunky collection of incoherent levels.

Historical Environments

Creating historical environments is a balance between painstaking research and understanding the gameplay that you want in your game. Simply re-creating actual buildings in a 100-percent realistic way will rarely work. As I mentioned in the section on interiors, you need to think about the camera, especially if it is a third-person game. You may need to widen areas and raise the height of ceilings. You may want to use historical photos as a starting point and then inject your own distinctive graphical style. Don't feel like you need to be totally authentic unless you want to be. Having said that, historical games need to feel right, and research is extremely important. It's important to start off with a decent idea of what the place would have felt like to stand in all those years ago.

Was it bustling? Did it feel magical? Was it a scary place to be? Once you've got an idea of what it would have felt like to your main character, you can design the level keeping this in mind, and use people, objects, sounds, and scripted events to help reinforce the emotional reaction you want to get across.

Space

Creating games set in space is another kind of challenge. Broadly speaking, games set in space can be subdivided into three main areas:

- *Games in which the main character floats around in space:* Since it would be fairly tough to create a character-based game in which you simply float or jetpack around in the middle of space, most games in the first category give you control of a spaceship. Normally they are fast and agile and the gameplay involves combat and often navigation to various objectives, be they planets, space stations, comets, or asteroids. Having played a number of space combat and trading games, I can tell you that one core element is obviously the combat gameplay, in particular, making sure the enemy spaceships put up a challenge and dogfight in an interesting manner, without being impossible to hit. The classic LucasArts title *X-Wing vs. Tie Fighter* is a superb example of this. However, I wouldn't underestimate the importance of designing your version of "space" to give the player some clear references to orientation and direction. This is vital to avoid the gameplay getting totally lost and confused. Older games did this very simply by having a bright sun somewhere in the sky, which the player could use as a reference point. Nowadays, it's possible to be much more elegant. Maybe a beautifully colored dust cloud can wisp its way into the distance, giving the player a large clear reference. You might set your combat very close to a planet, giving the player a real feeling of up and down with the planet's surface stretching below the player. However you do it, try to make the sphere around the player as interesting as possible, and try to include as many small objects as possible near the player (tiny asteroid chunks, space dust, etc.) to help give a feeling of speed and movement.

- *Games in which the main character is within a spaceship or vessel of some kind:* Here the same rules apply as designing an interior level, although you have much more freedom about the size of your environment and it's easier to create huge areas. Think about contrast because contrast is an important element of all games; it keep them interesting as you play. Within a spaceship, you have the freedom to create great contrasts between huge and tiny spaces. Also remember that you can play around with having no gravity, which could make for some excellent gameplay.

8

■ *Games set on the surface of another planet*: Designing the surface of an alien world presents the same kind of design problem creating exterior environments on Earth does. You've got the freedom to create some fascinating things because no one knows what this planet would look like in real life. Again, just make sure that your design is well planned out before any level design begins; get your blueprint created in great detail, and include some mock-up artwork.

So, as with most aspects of game design, the key to creating strong levels and environments is to plan carefully and create a clear blueprint. By following the suggestions in this chapter, you should be able to ensure that your level is varied, exciting, and memorable. And you can't ask for any more than that.

Summary

We've taken a look at how to create game levels and how to make sure each level is exciting and varied and becomes an extremely memorable experience for the player. If you apply these rules to every level in your game, you have a great chance of making the most of your initial game design document. In the next chapter, we're going to look at a rapidly growing area—online gaming.

An Interview with Andrew Oliver

Andrew Oliver is chief technical officer of Blitz Games, one of Europe's largest independent developers. Blitz (formerly Interactive Studios) has been around since the start of the video game industry, and Andrew has worked on hundreds of titles, from the classic Dizzy series right through to its impressive next-gen title, *Possession*.

What do you think are the most important skills that a game designer should have?

AO: The ability to remember that they are making entertainment first and foremost. A game must be fun and engaging to play, but it's so easy to get too close and familiar to a game when you're making it and forget that all players will be seeing it for the first time.

How important is level design in the grand scheme of things when you're making a game?

AO: It's extremely important to lead a player through the story and experience but at the same time not make them feel led. People want to have freedom in games and feel that they can do anything and go anywhere. But if you attempt to give them this in reality, apart from the huge volume of work involved, people actually start complaining because they don't know where they're supposed to go next or what they have to do. So you need to design your game in such a way that it's open enough to give the player a sense of freedom but still contrived enough that you are in control of the wider story arc and progress. If you can balance this perfectly, then the player will have the fullest possible experience.

How closely should a designer think about the challenges of a particular environment (for example, jungle, snow, underground lab, city center) when coming up with level ideas for a game?

AO: The actual structure of a level, rather that its particular environment, should always be the initial focus for a level designer. The overall plot and direction of the game will dictate the environment type that you'll be working with, so it's more important to think about the specifics of what the player will do or learn in that level and then focus on achieving that in a fun and engaging way.

You need to plot out aspects such as where the main sub-objectives will happen and where the enemies will be so that you can theme the streets/tunnels/jungle paths around those goals. While you're doing this, you obviously need to consider the particular constraints or opportunities that your environment will offer you and aim to make the most of them. For example, if you're designing a jungle level, there's much more scope for taking your character up off the floor into new areas than there would be in a city street (unless you're Spiderman!). So think about what the player might want to do if they were in an environment like that and try to match this up with what's technically possible.

Are there any kinds of environments that you'd be very nervous about using as a setting

8

for a game?

AO: Many realistic games suggest a certain environment that would be fundamentally boring with another type of game. An RTS, for instance, may work great in the rolling fields of the open countryside, but for other games, they'd lack much to see or do in an environment like this, so you need to make it more interesting.

As I mentioned earlier, it's all about choosing environments that suit the type of game you're trying to make. There are very few that won't work, and most of them have already been tried in some way or other. Even environments that you would think would present particular challenges (such as airborne or underwater worlds) have been used countless times to great effect.

The real trick is using environments without resorting to clichés. We've all seen games with an ice world, a jungle world, a space world, and so on, but how often are these different worlds treated in an inventive way? As with all aspects of game design, it's all about creating fun worlds for the player to enjoy exploring, so I wouldn't ever say that any type of environment is off-limits; just make sure you make it interesting!

Have you ever played a game where you thought, "Wow, that's a great and very original setting"?

AO: Unfortunately not. I certainly can't think of any off the top of my head but there are plenty of films (notably James Bond and other similar action flicks) that have created huge elaborate sets for final showdowns, and likewise, some of these kinds of sets have come across into games. Games, like films, need to be larger than life, and I think we can all learn a lot about creating great environments by looking at how films approach the same thing. For instance, if you were to create a game environment based inside an old disused factory, you'd be better off looking at Hollywood's version of a disused factory than actually going to one for real. In reality, they'd be empty shells, but Hollywood has realigned our expectations of what we think they should look like, so you instantly get something that's more interesting.

How important are good level design tools when creating a game?

AO: Incredibly important. At Blitz we've put a huge amount of effort into creating a very user-friendly mapping tool that allows everything to be placed in quickly and easily and tried out. We want artists to be free to be artistic and creative instead of spending time fighting with the technology to create the look they want. The easier it is to implement and tweak their work, the better and quicker the final results will be.

What are you most proud of in your career so far?

AO: Making lots of cool games! Dizzy is obviously an old favorite because he helped get us started, but we've worked on so many different games in different genres in different styles with different publishers and for different audiences; it's this variety that keeps things interesting, and the games that our teams now create make me hugely proud.

There's a common misconception in this industry that some of the highest-profile companies are the most creative to work for, but I don't see it. Many of these companies are known for making just one game, or a series of games, but surely there's more scope for creativity if you work somewhere that has a big variety of projects instead of just the latest iteration of a well-established FPS?

People also repeatedly dismiss licensed games as uncreative, but you often need to be even more creative and have more imagination to bring these established universes alive in a new medium.

At the end of the day, I'm incredibly proud of what we've grown here at Blitz, much more proud than I am of any one game. Creating an environment where hundreds of creative people can flourish is definitely our biggest achievement.

What is your favorite ever game (of all time), and why?

AO: That's a very difficult question! There are so many great games in all the different genres. In the very early days games like Elite and Revs were firm favorites. More recently GoldenEye on the N64 has to be one of my top FPSs; it suddenly stood head and shoulders above the rest at that time. The one game that I have probably played the most over the years has to be Mario Kart, on the SNES. It was just so well balanced, very competitive in its two-player split-screen mode and was just so much fun. Donkey Kong Country and Super Mario 3 also deserve a mention here because they were both huge, creative, fun, and broke new boundaries when they were released.

What do you think is the biggest game design mistake that people regularly make with games?

AO: Making games too shallow, and trying to use only one or two simple game mechanics. Games must be "pick up and play," and it would be a mistake to make complicated controls or mechanics as you first start a game, but it can be equally bad to be still using them a few hours in because the player will get bored. There are obviously exceptions to this rule, and some games where a simple mechanic is used over and over again still work and are fun to play. More often than not, though, this approach will simply bore the player as they go through the game. If they invest a lot of time in your game, you want them to continue to feel challenged and rewarded. Stick to one shallow gameplay premise and this won't be possible.

If money and technology were unlimited, what kind of game would you most like to see made?

AO: I get very frustrated at the lack of vision and innovation from most people when a new console is coming out. I don't feel it's enough to just create the same games in the future but with better graphics. One of the biggest things I would strive for if I had unlimited money and technology would be genuinely realistic characters. The limitations we have on the current generation of consoles mean that we can't ever populate our worlds with a realistic number of people, and even

8

the few characters we are able to include can't act or behave realistically. What I would like to see are cities teeming with life—every character would be aware of his surroundings and would react to the unfolding events as the player shaped the environment by his actions. You would be able to have convincing conversations with anyone you met via your gaming headset using speech recognition technology. You'd get sensible responses from them that would be created with realistic on-the-fly sentence construction techniques and genuine lip-syncing and appropriate body language. Visual realism is not something that's very far away on consoles—it's already happening on film—but realism in human behavior is the Holy Grail. And we're talking realistic behavior from virtual characters here—not the "interactive chatroom" that most MMOGs currently offer.

What most people don't realize is that this kind of thing could be much closer than you might think. Most of the technology we'd need has been broken in already in a variety of fields but no one has yet had the time, the money or even the vision to bring them all together into a video game. As I mentioned earlier, we don't actually need to create this completely "real" environment—what we need to do is create the—illusion of realism. Just as we create levels that make the player feel free when actually they're not, we will ultimately be able to use the technology in a clever enough way that all the human interactions the player has will feel real, even if they're not. We don't need to create massively complicated algorithms to pull this off—we just need to think creatively about how the game world works and how we can make it appear to the player.

What do you think is the biggest challenge facing game designers as we move forward?

AO: With bigger budgets, people become more risk adverse, so generally speaking, that means originality and creativity take a back seat. It's the fundamental problem that is dogging development at the moment. Ironically, the accountants, who have the final say, are not the ones with the history in gameplay and very often cannot be sold a vision. Therefore, in order to reduce risk, they go for "predictable" things like sequels and licenses and like to stay in comfortably marked genres that have already been proven in the marketplace. This is killing innovation. We, the developers who know what's needed, try our best to bring originality back to the table, but unfortunately, games are so costly to "prove" to a skeptical publisher. We try and do our bit occasionally, when we can afford to, and we're doing it right now with Possession. I had no doubt that Dreamworks would be successful when it started up because the person at the top, who calls the shots on what gets made or not, is a filmmaker and not an accountant, and when you get someone like Steven Spielberg at the helm, then decisions get made that factor in the creative element as well as the financial.

And finally, if you had one piece of advice to give to a game designer who was just starting out, what would it be?

AO: Dissect gameplay. Understand exactly what makes all the different games fun. Where's the fine line between challenging and frustrating? Don't be led by "they sell well and must be good" games. Most big games are very glossy and hyped sequels that aren't doing anything new or special, so look for the original games that play differently and well. Don't just play the kind of games that *you like—play everything and understand that a game must be designed with its target audience in mind. Play Doom 3 by all means and try to unravel what makes it work, but also pick up something like Barbie and understand why that works just as well for a 5-year-old girl as Doom does for a 20-something hard core gamer.*

8

PART III

Design Challenges

Chapter 9

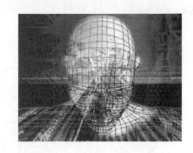

Online Gaming

"It is in games that many men discover their paradise."
Robert Lynd

Online gaming has been around for a while, but it is now getting the widespread recognition it deserves. The growth of online gaming is being helped in large part by the fact that the major consoles are now fully online and broadband Internet connections are becoming increasingly more common, even in remote areas and in countries outside of the United States. Rather than being the domain of tens of thousands of hardcore PC gamers, online gaming is now being played by millions of gamers across the globe, and this figure is increasing daily. Microsoft alone has over 2 million subscribers to its Xbox Live service as I write this, and that figure will grow rapidly over the life cycle of the Xbox 360.

Despite this, online games can be very risky investments for developers and publishers, particularly massively multiplayer online (MMO) games, which tend to be online only and rely on players paying monthly subscriptions. These games are developed with a very different business model than the one used for traditional boxed games and require support and updates on an ongoing basis rather than being finished when the game "goes gold." For every success story like Sony's *EverQuest* (see Figure 9.1) and pretty much anything that NCSoft releases, there is a much bigger list of MMO titles that have been canned after costing their publishers many millions of dollars. Codemasters's ambitious *Dragon Empires* project (see Figure 9.2) is just one example of an expensive MMO that failed to get released, despite several years of work.

Figure 9.1
EverQuest.

Figure 9.2
Codemasters's ill-fated *Dragon Empires*.

Online gaming arguably started with the advent of Multi-User Dungeons (MUDs). The first true MUD was created by Roy Trubshaw in Autumn 1978 at Essex University. It was essentially a very simple text adventure that allowed people across a network to move around locations and chat with other people in the same place. It took inspiration from the superb *Zork* adventure game that was very popular at around the same time in the United States, but it allowed multiple people to enter the adventure together. In 1980, they used an experimental packet-switching system that linked Essex University to ARPAnet in the United States in order to play the MUD with external players for the first time. Online gaming was born.

Key Online Gaming Technical Issues

As a designer, you may be a little resistant about having to learn too many of the technical details of online gaming, but there are a certain number of key questions (which cross into both technical and design areas) that you need to consider when you're designing an online game:

- **How many players will an online game support?** The number of players for a single game could vary from 2 to 50,000. The other issue to think about when designing online games is that not only can a single game have a lot of players to support, but you could also have multiple games taking place at the same time. The big challenge here would be in designing systems so that you have a way to keep these games organized.

- **Will a game be online only?** If possible, you may want to offer a single-player experience to allow players to practice, and to help new players understand the gameplay in a safe arena. This may be as simple as offering players the online game with AI-controlled bots, or you might provide a story-led single player campaign of some kind. Having a single-player element makes it much easier to sell the game in a store, even if the single player aspect is just training for the main online game.

- **How will you sell the game?** Is it going to be a game that people can buy in stores, or can it only be purchased online for some type of subscription fee, requiring that the player register? You might want to send out lots of demo discs with the game and give players a free amount of online playtime before they must pay. Another option is to create a single-player focused game that is sold in stores like most other games, but offer a strong online element as a great additional feature.

9

■ **Will your games be persistent?** Will your games last a certain amount of time before there is a winner and the game restarts, or does the game world persist over time? Games like *Counter-Strike* (see Figure 9.3) demonstrate how well non-persistent online gaming can work, but then other games like *EverQuest* and *World of Warcraft* (Figure 9.4) are both excellent examples of how enjoyable and addictive a persistent world can be.

Figure 9.3
Counter-Strike.

■ **Will you be organizing servers?** Online games are split into two camps—those that require the publisher to set up a large number of huge servers, which host the games that gamers join, or those that rely on players setting up and running servers, often playing on the same machine that is acting as a server. One other option less widely used involves getting your game running on a client-client basis, which essentially means there is no one machine that is the host to the game; all the machines that are playing the game run the game between them. A second issue is how players will find each other. On Microsoft's Xbox Live, for example, the system handles this for you. But on other platforms, you may need to use a middleware solution such as GameSpy or Quazal Net-Z to allow players to find and connect with each other.

Figure 9.4
World of Warcraft.

- **Will you have bots online?** Will you let your online players play against AI bots as well as other humans? Quite often, online games rely on human-to-human interaction, and therefore bots simply wouldn't work well. Some MMO games have a mixture of human and bot players taking different roles in the world. Bots provide training and act as shopkeepers or police the world, meaning that human players don't need to worry about taking on some of these repetitive and dull roles.

- **How will you handle payments and distribute demos?** You'll also need to have a good idea of which financial model you want to use. Some games rely on selling a boxed copy and use the profits to support the online aspects of the game. Some games, such as the immensely popular *Counter-Strike*, require less work after the game is released because users organize their own servers, mods, and tournaments. If you're running an MMO and it requires constant attention from the development team, you'll likely need to charge a certain amount each month as payment from players. Getting players to part with their credit card details isn't easy, and often the best idea is to offer a free demo that hooks the players and makes them want to continue. There are other options you could consider, such as making payments by dialing a premium phone number to top up a gamer's account or selling targeted advertising within the game to fund the upkeep needed.

9

Figure 9.5
Guild Wars.

An interesting model is the one used by NCSoft with the game *Guild Wars* (see Figure 9.5). In this case, no monthly subscription is charged. Instead, the company charges a one-time fee at retail. I guess part of the assumption in this model is that the persistent nature of the world will continue to attract more and more players, meaning that retail sales will continue for a much longer period of time than with traditional games. I imagine that the company can then be less focused on providing a never-ending online experience for people. If you've bought the retail game and played for 30 hours and enjoyed yourself, you should be happy, and there isn't the necessity for the company to generate another 30 hours of gameplay. Shorter persistent world experiences can only be a good thing in terms of introducing a wider audience that doesn't have time to sit online for hours every night, grinding away killing orcs and mining gold.

 Reality Check: However you do it, having a clear business model that makes financial sense is so obvious, but many people seem to miss this crucial point from the beginning!

- Is your game scalable? You need to think carefully about how scalable your online system is or you'll need to have a strict maximum number of gamers that you are going to allow to play or subscribe. Try to design your system so that it's relatively easy to add more servers and increase the number of people who can play the game. It would be pretty bad to have a hugely successful game and not be able to cope with the demand. However, it would be even worse to have the servers go down (crash) because too many people are trying to access them. Rule number 1 is to make sure your servers have a strict maximum number of users so this doesn't happen.

- Will your players be given the freedom to create content? Wherever you can, try to make your game as easily modifiable as possible to encourage online players to create their own content. It should be fairly easy to do this on PC, but on consoles, think about how you can allow people to create new levels or new game rules and swap them with each other. The more freedom you give your players, the more creative they can be, and you will build a bigger community of fans. Bear in mind that you need to be careful legally to make sure that you don't end up hosting artwork and levels that breach other people's copyright. For example, a player might create a Homer Simpson skin for your in-game character. If you inadvertently host this, and allow people to download it, although it might seem fairly harmless, you could be visited by the owner's legal team demanding compensation!

- Do you need to worry about hackers? You will also need to make sure that someone technical in your team gives security and hacking some careful thought. There is nothing more likely to stop people playing a game than if someone else suddenly cheats and breaks the reality of the game world, especially someone who isn't very good and hasn't put in many hours playing. There are many different ways of trying to ensure security with online gaming, but it's definitely something to think about in detail, as is empowering your support staff to ban people who they think are abusing the system.

Understanding the Online Gaming Process

In terms of the functionality behind online gaming, it can be useful to imagine online games as essentially a process that can be split into seven phases. Some of these phases are very easy and are handled by the console manufacture or middleware. But it is important to retain a high-level overview of the entire process and not get so caught up in the actual gameplay that you fail to realize that it's a nightmare for people to actually find a server or simply to meet up with their friends.

Phase 1: Connecting

This should be the simplest phase of all. The player needs to connect their console or PC to the Internet and form the initial connection with whatever server supports the online game, whether it is your own server or a matchmaking service run by Microsoft, GameSpy, or Quazal. Unfortunately, this phase is also quite complicated, particularly in some countries outside of the U.S., where faster connections are less common. Many people struggle to connect their consoles to the Internet; there are a vast number of different types of Internet broadband connections, many quite restrictive, and many that don't offer decent bandwidth. In European countries, for example, 256k and 512k broadband connections are still common! You can make the best online game in the world, but if people can't connect their console online, they'll never play it. It's not your problem insofar as you're relying on the console manufacturers to sort this issue out for you. But don't assume that just because you can connect, everyone can. This issue has been holding up online console gameplay in some countries, and hopefully it won't be such a problem with the next generation of machines.

Phase 2: Validating and Collecting Payment

This phase is optional. For games that are primarily based on single players, and customers have bought a boxed copy of the product, you may want to validate a security code to check that the product is not an illegal copy, or you might simply allow the player straight through to phase 3. With online games for which you expect players to pay a regular subscription (or even a one-off, up-front payment), it is different. At this stage, you need to take the relevant details, log the player in, and charge the player if appropriate. You have to be very careful here because *this is the point at which the most prospective players are lost.* It's often a great idea to offer a limited demo before they need to enter their credit card details. This will help you hook them into the game. Giving credit card details away before players have even tried the game is risky, and many people would be nervous about doing this unless there is strong word-of-mouth about the game. You need to think about this phase and make it attractive. You should be doing a proper sales job on prospective players, constantly reminding them how great the game will be. Too often, this phase simply involves unattractive financial screens demanding personal details, which in turn causes people to go play something else instead!

Phase 3: Matchmaking

Once the player has been validated, it's time to help them find friends that are also playing and get into a game (see Figure 9.6). With a non-persistent game, it's often a

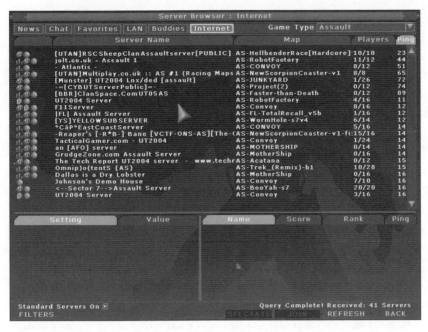

Figure 9.6
A typical matchmaking screen.

case of presenting the player with games that have free spaces available and prioritizing games with friends at the top of this list. But at a more advanced level, you might want to provide chat areas, a way to invite friends to your game, and so on.

With persistent world games, this phase will normally be very different depending on whether the player is playing for the first time or whether they're returning. If they are returning, it may simply be a question of loading their saved data and placing them onto the server that they originally joined. If they're playing for the first time, they'll often be prompted to select a server or "world" to join, and ideally, these will be presented in a useful way. For example, there may be a "beginners" world, which is a useful place to learn about their character, or the servers may be split into different countries so they can play against people who speak the same language they do.

Phase 4: Joining a Server

Once the matchmaking is completed and it's clear where the player is going, they then join the appropriate server. With non-persistent games like *Counter-Strike*, this server is normally not hosted by the publisher; the matchmaking server passes you over to connect to a server run by someone actually playing the game, and from there onward, the players are connected directly with each other. For persistent world games, you are passed to one of several servers set up specifically by the publisher. These servers normally allow a fixed number of players in order to keep the playing experience fast and fun. For this phase, the idea is to transition the player from the matchmaking service to the game as quickly and smoothly as possible. Ideally, the player won't even notice this phase happening!

Phase 5: Starting a Game

Once the player actually enters the game, typically some type of start menu is displayed (see Figure 9.7). This could allow the player to choose sides in a team game or decide on the location at which they will start. The player may be allowed to enter the current game as a spectator, or they may not be allowed to enter the game until the current round is completed. In a persistent world game, the player may be teleported straight into the game world, or they may still be offered a choice of various options such as which equipment to bring into the game, which city to start in, and so on. Again, the aim of this phase is to make things as friendly and uncomplicated as possible. The player should be aware of exactly what is going on and what the current status of the game is. The player should also be able to get into the game using as few button presses or mouse clicks as possible!

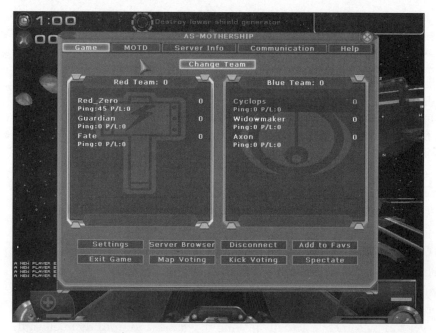

Figure 9.7
Typical game entry screen.

Phase 6: Playing the Game

Finally we get to the fun part—the main phase where the player gets to play the game against other people. The various players' consoles/PCs are constantly sending and receiving information from the server. The server acts as the "boss," making sure no one is cheating and resolving any conflicts that might occur. Some games don't have a server and instead rely on every person's computer doing their own calculations. These kind of games are called *client-client games*, and they bring their own unique problems. I like to think of client-client games as a democracy, whereas server-client games are like a benevolent dictatorship. Although democracy is a nicer idea, in reality, it's easier to get things done if the decisions are being made by one person!

We'll cover some of the most common in-game problems later in the chapter. (The time delays between the various computers and the server are often the most problematic.)

Phase 7: Exiting the Game

Another area that is often not given enough attention is the process used to exit a game. In a persistent world, it may be as simple as storing the current status of the player, putting the player's character "asleep" in a safe area on the map, and then closing the program down. But with non-persistent games, it is important to offer the player a clear choice of what they want to do next. If a game is over, it's not an elegant solution to throw all the players out of the game and make them have to find each other again. You need to allow the players to play again, choosing another map or another set of rules.

If the player has left the game because they have died or lost, this should be made very clear. You need to think carefully about what happens in this situation. Understandably, players aren't going to be happy about sitting around watching a blank screen for a few minutes while everyone else concludes the game.

Creative Idea: Think About Using Spectator Modes

Many games offer spectator modes so that people who have lost can still watch the action. Even better is to provide things that players can do when they have lost. For example, a classic version of multiplayer *Bomberman* allowed people who had been killed to move around the edge of the arena, throwing bombs in at the surviving players. This makes the game more exciting and tense for everyone and means that the game will likely never get boring for anyone. It's a great solution.

However you do it, make sure that when a game is over or when a player has been killed, you make everything very clear and give your players the freedom to do what they want, which will often be to go straight back in and start all over again. I'm also a big fan of providing some kind of facility for randomly choosing things like maps and game types so that players can go straight into the game without having to make lots of selections.

9

Designing One-off Online Games

Some of the most popular games online are not persistent worlds with thousands of people within them, but games like *Counter-Strike*, a first-person shooter that typically consists of up to 40 people split into 2 teams playing 5-minute rounds. Short action games online are missing a great deal of the social play that you find in persistent world games, but they are no less important. By playing against real people, you find richness in tactics and skill ranges that you simply can't mimic with AI bots. People do communicate with each other, and people on the same team typically trigger preset commands such as "follow me" or "go,go,go!" to help direct each other. Some players use headsets so they can actually talk with each other, and when these are set up and working well, they can really enhance the social aspect because you can talk properly as you are playing.

 Reality Check: If you are designing a one-off online experience, make sure you play-test it very carefully. Although *Counter-Strike* gets away with having dead players sitting around doing nothing for several minutes, this is dull, and other games such as EA's excellent Battlefield series (see Figure 9.8) allow players to respawn whenever they are killed. They use a system of capture points where two teams can dominate a map by capturing all the key points. Killed players respawn after a short delay at the nearest capture point that they own. This often means the players start a short distance away from the action. It is enough of a negative that it makes killing people useful while keeping players in the action and giving people who have been killed a chance to regroup in safety. Whichever system you use, test it out carefully and polish it until it shines.

Of course, first-person shooters are not the only type of one-off online game. A huge variety of games can be played for short periods online, and if you go into a game store, you'll find that a large proportion of new titles—whether they are racing, fighting, third-person adventure, or sports—all support online play for a fixed number of people. On the PC platform, systems like GameSpy and Quazal have provided important foundations, helping people find games to join. On consoles, the Xbox Live system has played a major part in making the Xbox console the online system of choice. It will be fascinating to see whether the new systems from Sony and Nintendo can turn this around.

A great example of an online game is a title called *Acrophobia* (see Figure 9.9), currently only playable on the PC. It's a completely unique title, attracting a very different audience to current PC or console games. Several people join a game and are given an acronym (such as P.A.S.) and assigned a subject, such as "politics." All of the players are then given 30 seconds to come up with an amusing or insightful meaning to the acronym that fits the subject. For example, I might enter "Politicians Adore Stupidity."

Figure 9.8
Battlefield 2.

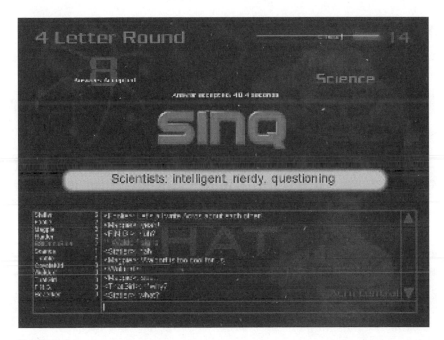

Figure 9.9
Acrophobia.

After the 30 seconds pass, each player is shown all the answers and has to vote on their favorite one (you're not allowed to vote for your own!). The winning answer is the one with the most votes, and the player gets a point. This continues until one player wins. Although it is incredibly simple, I think it is a superb online game design. All the content is generated by the players; the game itself requires very little research. The players score each other, so it's a very fair game. And it's social—players chat away while they are playing and congratulate each other for good answers.

Designing Persistent Online Games

By far the biggest challenge as an online game designer is creating a persistent online world. You rarely get any second chances; once people start paying to enter the world, they expect things to work well and they demand a constantly interesting and immersive experience. You've got to make your world work equally well with brand-new players and players that play eight hours a day every day of the week. In some ways, it's like being a teacher in a class ranging from kindergarten kids up to MBA students. Keeping them all happy isn't easy! And your design often needs to work with very large numbers of players, so it needs to be scalable. It's a really tough but hugely enjoyable challenge. So how do you begin approaching such a task? First, let's look at the different types of persistent world games.

MOs, MMOs, and MMORPGs

MO simply stands for *multiplayer online*, and so MO games (a rarely used term) are titles that are playable online with multiple players. MMOs are *massively multiplayer online* games. The big difference between the two is that MOs might have a maximum of 16 or 32 people, whereas MMOs could have a minimum of several hundred. The difference in scale between the two types of game is very important because it results in fundamentally different game designs. With 16 players, you tend to create non-persistent worlds because, otherwise, if the game carried on for days and weeks, you would probably end up with only a couple of people on at the same time.

MOs tend to be based on time-limited high-action gameplay, with everyone joining at the same time and then playing the game until someone has won. MMOs tend to be persistent because getting several hundred people to all start a game at the same time isn't easy. Having said that, I'm sure that someone will come up with a mass battle game that supports many hundreds of people all fighting a time-limited battle. But at the moment, most MMO games are persistent worlds. In fact, at the moment, most MMO games are also MMORPGs, which stands for *massively multiplayer online role playing games*.

If you're not familiar with role playing games (RPGs), they are a particular genre of game where the player's character develops as the game progresses. The games involve playing a role (hence the name) and originally developed out of the boxed RPG games in the '80s like *Dungeons and Dragons*. The players get stronger, gain levels, get more experienced, and learn new skills, and the game is essentially a long adventure. With many hundreds or thousands of people playing in one world, you need to think very carefully about how the game is designed. One chapter isn't enough to do this subject justice because it is a huge area of highly specialized design, but let's take a look at eight key issues that I think are especially important to consider.

Entry

It's important to think carefully about how a new player starts a game. I'm convinced that the first 15 to 30 minutes of a game will dictate whether the player enjoys the game enough to continue playing. Once there are lots of experienced gamers in the world, new players may feel quite nervous when they start playing. My view is that it's vital to have some kind of clear and welcoming tutorial, disguised however you want, to introduce new players to the world and explain the fundamentals.

War Story: Don't Forget About the New Player

I remember playing an excellent text-only online RPG called *Avalon* that provided a tutorial in a superb way, with an AI character welcoming you, guiding you around for a bit, giving you simple quests, and then slowly letting go as you get used to the world and start meeting other people. Another way is to provide incentives for experienced players to mentor new players. For example, if the game world has various teams (or guilds, races, gangs, or whatever you want to call them), each team would want to get the new players to join them, assuming the game is set up so that new players have a high value. So I could imagine an entry point almost like "freshman week" at a university, where new players are being welcomed by all sorts of people, given advice, and encouraged to join a team. However you do it, don't concentrate so much on existing players that you forget what it's like to be a new player suddenly entering the world.

To Grind or Not to Grind

For me, one of the most frustrating aspects of many MMORPGs is the built-in mechanic of grinding. *Grinding* is the process by which players are forced to spend more and more time fighting creatures or doing other fairly tedious activities in order to grind out another experience level. If you take a look at Figure 9.10, you'll see a typical experience curve. In order to make the game exciting for new players (and to make sure that many players are on a similar level), it is possible to rise through the first few levels quite quickly. However, this rise starts to trail off, and the longer you play, the longer it

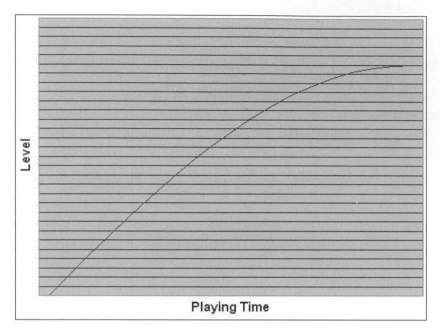

Figure 9.10
Typical experience curve for online RPGs.

takes to get to each new level. The process of grinding forces players to put in a huge amount of hours of repetitive gameplay to progress further. In my view, it is a bad mechanic that does solve some key issues but raises many others. Some new games are being developed to fight against this mechanic, and I hope that they will succeed.

Grinding is a simple way to give players enormously long hours of gameplay, and without it, the challenge is how to retain players who spend many hours in the game world. My feeling is that it all comes down to making the gameplay interesting enough. Standing next to a creature and clicking the left mouse button until one of you dies isn't good gameplay, and that has been part of the problem with some online games so far.

 Reality Check: Try to incorporate a strong random mission/event creator and some really interesting gameplay mechanics that don't get dull, and offer players rewards for being creative as they play your game, rather than rewards for repeatedly doing the same things. Of course, this is all much easier to discuss than to implement, but my feeling is that online games have a long way to go and that we're only really scratching the surface at the moment, especially with regard to grinding.

Keeping Your Game Fresh

One of the toughest design aspects to get your head around is the need to constantly keep a game fresh. With most online games, players can get bored fairly easily if there isn't a constant challenge, and when people are playing a game for several hours a day each day, you need a reason to keep them playing. If you have a maximum skill or experience level that the players can quickly reach, you have nowhere for them to go after this point. You'll probably need a team of designers to keep the product evolving and improving, offering new challenges, one-off events, and tournaments to keep people playing. Adding new content can also be important. For example, you could create new levels or new parts of the world. Adding new weapons, new enemies, and additional missions or challenges can all help to keep your game feeling fresh. MMO games need the most attention, whereas with non-persistent games (like *Project Gotham Racing* or *Counter-Strike*), there is less of a constant demand for new tracks or maps.

Encouraging Social Play

I have seen some online games that are essentially many single-player adventures all happening at the same time, where players go off on solo quests to find money or items and their only aim is to reach a certain level and become the best. Games like these ignore the single most important aspect of proper online gaming—social interaction. On a basic scale, just being able to fight against another human player is interaction, but there is so much more that you could offer. Most online games allow people to chat with each other, but a good online game design will actually provide genuine reasons for players to do so. Encouraging players to go on missions together is a great way of doing this. It gives people a reason to approach each other, and players are able to plan their next adventure together.

Listening to Players

It's extremely important to listen to the people playing your game and understand what they like, what they don't like, and what they want to see in the future. Persistent world games are very different to traditional boxed games. Once a player has bought a traditional boxed game from a store, the sale is done. You will certainly want to find out what players like and dislike if you're doing a sequel, but otherwise, there isn't a huge impetus for you to talk with the people who bought the game. With a persistent game, especially if people are paying a monthly subscription, you need a much better understanding of the players' motivations. If players start canceling their monthly subscriptions, you'll soon find your game running into major problems. So listening to players is one of the most important rules of persistent world games, and although it may sound obvious, you should also make sure that you play the game as a regular player so you get the player's-eye view of the world as well.

Enforcing a Clear Set of Rules

When players invest a great deal of time in a game, they want to feel that the rules are well conceived and they are being given a fair chance to succeed. There is a general game design rule that you never put a "death hazard" (i.e., something that will kill the player) where it can't be avoided by the player the first time they come across it. So for example, imagine a perfectly solid-looking bridge that breaks and drops the player to their death the first time they walk over it. This would be very bad game design because the player wants to feel that they can complete the entire game without dying if they didn't make any mistakes. The same thing applies online. Players need to feel that they can win the game if they didn't make mistakes. Changing the rules and tampering with the world that people have become used to is a bad idea unless you have no other choice.

War Story: Be Careful about Changing Rules Dynamically

Here is a good example that I heard about recently. I can't remember which MMORPG game it was, but one group of people had sailed their ships into a harbor and were blockading the town there, stopping any food or goods from coming in and slowly killing all the people who lived there. This was within the rules of the game. The designers decided that they had to act and broke the rules; they created a new wind that blew all the boats out to sea and saved the town. You might expect that the players were pleased at being saved like this. You'd be very wrong. In fact, a large number of players left the game immediately, and from both sides of the conflict. The people in the boats were angry that they had been cheated because the rules had suddenly changed, and even the people in the town were upset; they were trying to raise an army to fight the boats off, and they would have been much happier for a genuine solution (within the game rules) to have presented itself.

Reality Check: Think carefully about getting the rules clear and solid when the game starts, and avoid changing them unless you have no other choice.

Balancing the Economy

If you speak to people who have worked on persistent world games, they'll tell you that keeping a game economy going is a very tough job. You almost need a degree in economics to do it properly. And it's not surprising—many games have a mini-version of a real-life economy, with thousands of people, issued currency, trade, and new wealth being created as people discover or build new objects. It's important to keep a close eye on the economy in your game because it is possible for a game to be ruined by a player who gets too rich and then uses their personal wealth to damage the game. So make sure you always know how much money is in circulation, and follow the people who have grown extremely rich to make sure they don't abuse their position. How could someone with lots of wealth damage the game? There are many ways. A simple example might be a rich player, who starts paying a large amount of money for food, using his wealth to buy up everything available. This action could easily increase the price of food by several hundred percent, forcing thousands of new players to starve because they can't afford to eat. Maybe your game doesn't use food, or maybe your game allows players to eat from wild trees and catch fish, but the fact remains that players who become too wealthy can use their wealth to dramatically change the market value of any item in the game. You also need to keep an eye on inflation and make sure you're not generating so much new "money" that the value of players' cash falls.

Another interesting aspect relates to players who try to make real-world money from your persistent online game. I've heard about people who actually employ gamers in Asia to play online titles, mining rocks, finding gems, and creating characters that are then sold online (using eBay) for real money. In fact, it's possible to earn a real-life income by playing persistent world games. Now most publishers work hard to dissuade this kind of activity, not the least because they want the freedom to be able to shut the game down when it's no longer commercially viable, and if people are earning money from it, they may encounter a legal problem. Similarly, if the economy in a game crashes due to a change that the game designers have implemented, it could be legally possible for players to sue the company for losing them real-world money. It's a very complicated area, but one you should keep an eye on, and someone at your company should have some kind of strategy for dealing with this.

Solving the Newbies vs. Experts Problem

It's really important to remember that you will soon end up with a mix of highly experienced players along with a constant stream of new players. Think carefully about the kind of experience that new players will have. If you simply let them appear into the world where they are likely to be killed instantly by experts, the game isn't going to be much fun. Some games have safe areas where new players can learn the ropes without too much danger. Other games provide "newbie" servers where new players can play against other new players in relative safety. Still other games will provide a rule that discourages experienced players from killing defenseless new players, sometimes lowering their score, experience level, or money if they do so. Often games encourage players to form teams of some kind, which means that experienced players may find it more useful to protect new players and encourage them to join their side.

Technical Issues with Online Games

There are two major technical issues that affect every online game: lag/ping times between players and the bandwidth that every player has. Let's look at both of these issues next.

Ping Times and Lag

Ping time is the time in milliseconds that it takes a packet of data to travel from the player's console or PC to the server and back again. The data needs to travel down many hundreds of miles of cable or via microwave or satellite links. However the data gets there, there is a delay. Often this delay is less than a 10th of a second (100 milliseconds), but occasionally it is much more, especially if you are playing on a server in a different country. The longer the delay, the less enjoyable the playing experience, because actions like collision and updating of other players' positions start to break.

For example, imagine two players playing a shooter against each other. Alan has a low ping time and Bob has a high one. Bob sees Alan in front of him and presses the Shoot button. But by the time the message gets to the server, Alan has already moved and fired himself. Even though Alan actually moved and fired after Bob, the game will receive that data before and the result will be that poor Bob actually gets killed as he sees Alan miraculously leap sideways and fire.

As you can imagine, lag can be a major problem. Your game needs to be designed in such a way that it minimizes this. It's quite a technical issue, but it normally involves letting the computers predict where their opponent will be based on their current path, direction, and speed and then, if they don't get a packet of data, using this predicted position instead. Although it is still not perfect, it's normally much closer to reality than assuming the player has stopped and is standing still, particularly in games with vehicles (where instant stopping is extremely rare!). Close combat games are the worst; anything that involves split-second timing and players close to one another will suffer badly from lag. As the Internet backbone gets better, hopefully this issue will become much more manageable.

Bandwidth

Bandwidth is the amount of data that you are able to send back and forth to a game. If you imagine that your connection to the Internet is like a water pipe, then bandwidth is the diameter of that pipe. Broadband connections allow a PC or console to send lots of data across the link because the pipe is very wide. If you use a modem (and many people still do in some countries and rural areas), you'll have very limited bandwidth.

So how does bandwidth affect gameplay? Well, imagine you have 20 people in a game. So that every computer playing the game knows where the players are, the server sends around the location of each player along with their current actions. Let's say that all this information is sent 30 times each second. With 20 players, and 30 times each second, that is 600 chunks of information being sent every second across the Internet. If your bandwidth is small, it simply might not be possible to send this much information so quickly. In that case, some of it will be delayed, and you'll quickly get a backlog. The game will start to have problems. If you have a broadband connection, it's fairly easy to send all this information and avoid the problems.

For this reason, many online games now support only broadband-equipped players. The installed base for broadband is increasing rapidly, and it is now a necessity for decent online gaming. Bear in mind that what one person might call broadband (which can be as low as 256k in some places!) is very different to what another might call broadband (2 or 4mb minimum in other places!). So even broadband-equipped players can suffer from low bandwidth if the Internet is busy and they're using a 256k connection. Who said that technology was getting easier?

Digital Distribution and Steam

I'll finish this chapter by discussing digital distribution, which is a very hot topic at the moment and something that is certain to grow in the future. The best example of digital distribution is Valve's technically superb but controversial Steam system (see Figure 9.11). Steam is controversial because you can't run the games without an online connection and you need to give Valve your personal details; it also scares the hell out of game retail outlets who can envisage a future where all games are bought and downloaded from the Internet!

This system allows players to purchase and download games from the Steam servers. It automatically patches and updates games with new content, making it an excellent system for people who don't want to travel into town and buy games from a store. However, Steam is also required to authenticate both downloaded and store-purchased copies of Valve's games. This means the following:

- If you have a PC upstairs in your house, or in your study, or you live somewhere without Internet access, you can't play any of their games.

- Some people have experienced technical problems getting this authentication system working and have therefore become frustrated.

- Many people have been banned from the system. I assume most of them were pirates using copied or cracked versions of the games, but a small number may have been normal users who had their registration code copied or cloned by others.

9

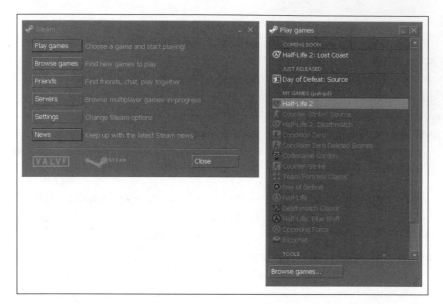

Figure 9.11
Steam.

Steam is a superb system that is well ahead of its time. I have no doubt that the arrival of consoles with built-in wireless networking and the increasing level of broadband adoption will lead to more systems like this, but hopefully with some of the teething troubles solved. You can already use 3G Mobile Phone network cards in many countries to connect a PC remotely to the Internet from almost anywhere without any need for cables. I suspect that publishers and console manufacturers will be making this kind of system a priority moving forward, and like it or not, I believe digital distribution will become an increasingly important element in the games industry as we move into the future. From a financial point of view, a huge percentage of the money that customers pay for games at the moment goes to the retailers—often somewhere between 30 and 60 percent. If this money can be saved, along with the cost of manufacturing discs and manuals, developers and publishers will find it much easier to afford the kind of stunning next-generation titles that players expect.

Summary

In this chapter, we've taken a good look at the challenges involved in designing both one-off and persistent online games—something that is only going to become more and more important. Next up, we're going to explore a very common but uniquely tricky aspect of game design—creating strong sequels to successful titles.

An Interview with Raph Koster

Raph Koster is a veteran online game designer, and was responsible for the design of ground-breaking online titles such as *Ultima Online* and *Star Wars Galaxies*. Raph started gaming on the original Pong machines, and found the online gaming bug with his involvement in MUDs (Multi User Dungeons) in the early 1990's. Raph is now Chief Creative Officer at Sony Online Entertainment where he is continuing to push the boundaries of online gaming. This makes Raph the ideal person to ask about online gaming.

Where do you see online gaming going in the near future? Do you feel it still has a huge way to go?

RK: I do think there's still a long way for it to go. When I look at the history of online games, it's rather closely paralleled the current trends on the Internet in general. When the Net was the province of academic geeks, the games were heavily demanding of math and smarts; they were erudite places that dug into big topics of virtual sovereignty, and so on. Once the Net became the land of giant online services like AOL, Genie, Prodigy, CompuServe, and so on, the games did too—they were walled gardens on those clunky services, somewhat clunky themselves, with gameplay paid by the minute. Then came the MMO revolution, in tandem with the Internet revolution. This is marked by all you can eat subscription fees, just like the ISPs, designed for modems and lowest common denominator users. Today, the Net is all about lightweight web services, feeds flying everywhere, and active user participation even in the big media outlets and commerce sites. I feel the games will follow.

Both the Net and the online worlds are aiming at the same kind of thing which is that lofty dream of cyberspace. We both have a ways to go.

How important do you feel consoles are becoming to online gaming?

RK: Very, but we shouldn't forget that online gaming is about the online part, and that means its true platform is a network, not a console or a PC. An inevitable part of the future is the platform-agnostic game.

What are the key differences when you're designing a persistent world game for consoles as opposed to PC?

RK: Interface is the biggest. A game in many ways boils down to the way you interact with it. If the interface is bad, the game is going to be bad, regardless of how beautifully designed the game might be behind the scenes. Consoles offer a limited interface, and critically, it's an interface that is poor in specifically the strengths of online games: communication and diversity of activity. The rise of voice tech is of course going to ameliorate this, and it's going to be interesting to see the impact of this on a gaming culture that has valued anonymity so much.

9

There has been some recent debate about the "grinding" mechanic in many online games where players have to repeatedly carry out the same action in order to get to the next experience level. Do you feel this mechanic will be consigned to the history books at some point, or is it a fundamental part of online gaming?

RK: The challenge is that online games demand a huge amount of content. Players play them endlessly because playing with their friends is fun. The game is the excuse to play alongside other people (not always with them). So there has to be a lot of game there. This is why developers have been driven to the repetitive content that exists today.

I think it's going to fall away, but gradually, as we get smarter about how we fill the games with things to do, which may not mean our traditional notions of content.

What is your favourite ever game (of all time), and why?

RK: Probably M.U.L.E. on the Atari 8-bit computers. It was the quintessential multiplayer game, in many ways it still is, plus it's smart, and not just a button-mashing fest.

What are you most proud of in your career so far?

RK: Oh, gosh. I have no idea. Probably connecting people, actually. That's what these games can do so well. When I look back on it, it's not so much about the cool features that actually worked out, but rather about how people used them, and how they ran with it all and formed into communities, often leaving the game far, far behind.

What do you think is the biggest game design mistake that people regularly make with online games?

RK: Treating them as single-player games.

If money and technology were unlimited, what kind of game would you most like to see made?

RK: The metaverse, of course!

What do you think is the biggest challenge facing game designers as we move forward?

RK: The fact that the technical and artistic obstacles to creating a game are getting so high. The industry pushes more and more towards committee-built games that can earn back their investment, and that makes life hard for game designers, who by their nature want to do new things.

How do you feel about non-persistent online games where people play a single game for 20 minutes or so at a time? Is this an area which you believe will become more or less important in the future?

RK: There's a zillion of these out there already, of course—all the multiplayer gaming is like this. So it's important now, and it will continue to be. If anything, though, I think we will see the addition of more and more persistent elements to those. People like having standing, accumulation of trophies and ranks, and so on.

And finally, if you had one piece of advice to give to a game designer who was just starting out, what would it be?

RK: Make as many games as you can. You can make games by yourself very cheaply. Do it constantly. Don't get hung up on graphics and music—that's not the core of your job. Do it with index cards and dice and go boards and beads and cut up paper if you have to. Do it on a computer if you can. But do it. It's the core of what you do, and all the most important lessons can be learned that way.

9

Chapter 10

Designing Sequels

> "You have to measure your success by the way your audience responds to your games. No matter how small that audience is, it's yours. Your game is part of the lives and the memories of those people in a way that WordPerfect or Lotus 1-2-3 or Windows can never be."
>
> *Orson Scott Card*

For this chapter, I had to squeeze in a quote from my favorite author, Orson Scott Card. He makes a very valid point: you can measure how successful you are as a game designer by finding out how people react to your games. Even if your game doesn't sell well, you can be very proud of your achievements if it has touched people and you know that gamers out there will be able to recall it fondly in 20 years' time.

If, however, it does sell well, you won't have time to be proud because you'll be too busy working out how the hell you're going to resurrect the lead character you killed off and create an even better sequel!

In this chapter, I'll take you through the process of designing sequels. We'll start by looking at the issues that make creating sequels so challenging, and we'll look at some of the great (and some of the awful sequels) that have been created by others. Then, I'll show you how to work through the process of planning out the design for your own sequel. As you'll learn, it's important to do your homework up front so that you'll know what to focus on when you create your sequel. In the second part of the chapter, we'll look at some of the boundaries and trade-offs that you'll want to consider as you design your sequel. The big question you'll always need to ask is: How much can you change an existing game to make a sequel?

The Challenges of Creating a Sequel

Designing a sequel to a successful game can be one of the toughest challenges you'll ever face. Sometimes it feels as if you are stuck in a catch-22 situation. Make changes and you'll be slaughtered by the reviewers for ruining the magic of the original. But if you just add new content and don't mess with the game, the reviewers will criticize you for rehashing the first game without moving it forward!

The chances are that previous versions of the game will have built a strong brand that your company will be concerned about harming. If anything happens to damage the brand, guess who will be blamed? Everyone will have a different opinion about what should be done. Fans of the original will be the most vocal, demanding all sorts of impossible improvements and closely critiquing every interview and screen shot that gets released. People internally will probably exaggerate their part in the success of the original product, and you can guarantee that everyone will have a strong opinion about how that product should move forward. And heaven help you if you didn't work on the original. People from the original team may well feel that only *they* properly understand why it did so well. As soon as you want to make changes that they don't feel are right, they'll question your understanding of the brand ("...*but you weren't there; you don't get it...*").

War Story: The Challenge of Reinventing Old Brands

Sometimes the hardest sequel to design is one based on an original title that is more than five years old. I have spent large portions of my working life coming up with all sorts of ideas to reinvent old brands, and it's not easy. Sometimes the game market has simply moved on. Great game mechanics *can* transcend across the years, but this certainly isn't always the case. Often, unique features from the original game have been copied and improved on by other games that have come out in recent years. At times like this, you need the strength to either innovate radically or be honest and advise that updating the original simply isn't going to work.

If that hasn't scared you enough, it can be very hard to come up with original ideas for sequels because most of the best ideas are often used in earlier versions. It is an even bigger problem if you're working on a fourth or fifth iteration, late in the technology cycle. If you have created three or four previous titles, coming up with a new approach is going to be really tricky. This is especially true when the programmers are struggling to create any new technology for the game engine, as is often the case late in the life cycle of a console.

Is that enough of a challenge? Well, if you have a game that takes place in a constrained setting (such as a sports game), coming up with the next unique selling point will be twice as hard.

Phew. But take heart. Before you decide to give up before you have even started, I should tell you that despite the challenges, creating a sequel is actually a great thing to do.

Why Creating a Sequel Is a Great Thing

When you're creating a sequel, you start with one enormous advantage. You know that players loved the original game, and enough of them bought and enjoyed it to make a follow-up game worth doing. Working on completely original titles can be a scary experience because you're never quite sure whether people will love your game or whether it will go over like a lead balloon. Working on a sequel can be reassuring; people out there are looking forward to what you're making, and you know that the core gameplay experience has a big customer-tested stamp of approval.

The chances are that you have a great foundation to build from, including some fun and addictive gameplay that works well and a technical engine that can handle the core game. This is a superb starting point for a sequel; much of the hard work is done, and you can hopefully spend the development time working on innovation and making the game shine (as opposed to spending all your time on the basics and getting the engine running, as is often the case with a new title).

Lots of gamers are probably looking forward to your sequel already, including everyone who enjoyed the first game. The press will give a sequel more respect and opportunity than they give to a new title because it has an existing track record. You will have a fan base to draw from, and you can ask them questions; in some cases, this may be a massive number of people with fan Web sites around the world. You can also use all the magazine reviews from previous versions to identify the most common criticisms and decide what improvements to concentrate on.

Reality Check: There are plenty of reasons to be confident and excited about working on a sequel. It's your opportunity to create the perfect version of the game. You can design something that can build on a great foundation and turn it into a masterpiece.

The History of Sequel Games

Game sequels have been around since almost the birth of video games themselves; titles like *Asteroids Deluxe* in 1981, *Stargate* (the sequel to the superb *Defender*) in 1982 and *Ms. Pac Man* in 1983 set the scene for what was to come. Creating a sequel to a successful game has always been a very obvious route for game developers. If a game proves successful and people enjoy it, the players tend to want more of the same. They know the name, so creating a follow-up title is less risky than creating something new from scratch. And as technology was changing rapidly from the 1980s onward, there were always new technical aspects that could be brought to bear.

Great Game Sequels

Although it's more difficult to create a great sequel than it is to create a bad one, many good ones have been developed over the years. Let's look at some of my favorites.

Splinter Cell: Pandora Tomorrow

This game is an extremely solid sequel that was enhanced by a revolutionary design for the online gameplay where third-person camera stealth characters play against first-person camera shooter characters (see Figure 10.1). It's a great example of how to push a major brand in the modern games marketplace.

Figure 10.1
Splinter Cell: Pandora Tomorrow—a great sequel.

Grand Theft Auto 3

This game is truly one of the most important titles of modern times (see Figure 10.2). It created a genre-defining game that was a revolution when compared to the previous two games. The previous games featured a top-down 2D viewpoint of the cities, but GTA3 moved this into 3D with stunning effect. The developers took lots of risks but did it superbly and made it one of the biggest selling game franchises of all time.

Figure 10.2
Grand Theft Auto 3.

Final Fantasy VII

This is still seen by many as the definitive version of the Final Fantasy series, with an outstanding storyline and superbly rich characters (see Figure 10.3). The Final Fantasy games are excellent examples of how much variety is possible between versions because they normally feature totally different characters and storylines each time.

Jet Set Willy

Despite a few bugs, this game was a big improvement over *Manic Miner* (see Figure 10.4). It also was one of the few times that a sequel didn't share the same name as the original, yet everyone knew it was the sequel, and it achieved immense success.

Donkey Kong Jr.

This sequel turned the original concept completely on its head (see Figure 10.5). Instead of playing Mario, you played as Donkey Kong Jr., trying to rescue Donkey Kong from Mario. And it was also a superb game.

Curse of Monkey Island

This sequel turned a graphical text adventure into a real visual experience while keeping the same magic (see Figure 10.6). It's one of the best adventure games ever created.

10

Figure 10.3
Final Fantasy VII.

Figure 10.4
Jet Set Willy.

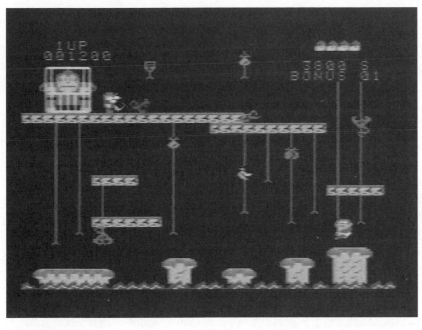

Figure 10.5
Donkey Kong Jr.

Figure 10.6
Curse of Monkey Island.

Awful Game Sequels

Sensible World of Soccer

The move to 3D just didn't work at all for this sequel, and the developers managed to take an enormous step backwards in terms of fun and gameplay.

The Legend of Zelda: The Wind Waker

A controversial choice, since the gameplay was great but the decision to turn the main character, Link, into a cartoon caricature lost many of its fans.

Rise of the Robots 2

This sequel turned out to be one of the worst games of all time due to the lack of any decent gameplay that made the game fun to play. It was also a spectacular marketing achievement; they used the graphical style and some clever ideas to sell a total turkey.

Tomb Raider: Angel of Darkness

This sequel was a real travesty. The developers managed to damage the control system and produce something that was far worse that the previous Tomb Raider games in terms of the core gameplay.

Starting Your Sequel

The question you might be asking now is where's the best place to begin when starting a sequel project? Before you invest in any design work or have your developers write any code, you should spend some time doing your homework to get prepared. As you'll learn in this section, this involves playing and studying your existing game and doing as much research as you possibly can.

Play All the Previous Versions

It sounds obvious, but before you begin thinking about designing a sequel, make sure that you have played all the previous versions in their entirety. Make notes as you play, writing down anything that annoys you and any ideas that crop up for making the experience richer and more immersive. This is just as important if you worked on the original product. You'd be amazed at how many people who develop a game never really play it *properly*. By properly, I mean from beginning to end without any cheat codes. Ideally, it will be at least a month or two since you've seen the previous game, and you'll now have a level of detachment that will allow you to notice things that you didn't see previously. If you did work on the game before, try to find someone with fresh eyes to play through it with you. This will be invaluable, as you do become blind to certain aspects of a game when you work on it for a long period of time.

Questions to Ask Yourself

Here is my list of the most important questions you should try to answer as comprehensively as possible to help identify the weakest areas of the original game.

GAMEPLAY

Did the camera system work well in all situations?

Were all the controls intuitive, or were some actions hard to carry out?

Were any characters, items, vehicles, or weapons unsatisfying?

Did the save-game system work well?

How powerful were the first 30 minutes of the game?

Can you make the first 30 minutes more impressive and exciting?

Was any part of the core game experience frustrating?

Did the multiplayer modes work well? What could make them better?

Was the front end clear and intuitive to use?

Was it quick and easy for players to select the options they wanted from the front end, or was the process unnecessarily long?

Were there any key gameplay differences between any different platform versions of the game? If so, which platforms worked best and why?

LEVELS/ENVIRONMENT

Are there any levels in particular that were better or worse than the others in how they worked?

If so, why were they stronger or weaker than the other levels?

Was the game too short or too long?

Were the individual levels/stages (if applicable) too short or too long?

Can you come up with ideas for reusing levels within an additional game mode?

Were the environments interactive enough?

Were there lots of objects that the player felt they should be able to interact with but weren't able to?

Was there any reason for the player to replay parts of the game? If not, would this have helped add to the longevity?

10

DIFFICULTY

Were new players adequately taught how to play the game?

If not, how can you create an exciting way of training in the sequel?

Did the gameplay in general seem too hard, too easy, or just right?

Did the game allow both expert and novice gamers to enjoy themselves?

GRAPHICS

What were the worst graphical areas of the game?

Did the characters look great and animate well?

Did the levels/environments look cutting edge?

If applicable, were the weather effects really good?

Were any particles used (fire/water/sparks, etc.) and did they look realistic?

Was the front end as impressive as it should be?

Was the on-screen display clear and intuitive?

Was there anything on the on-screen display that wasn't really needed?

Was there anything missing from the on-screen display that could enhance the game?

Were all the cut scenes or FMV sequences good enough?

Were there too many cut scenes or not enough?

If the game was on multiple platforms, did each version take full advantage of the possibilities provided by its platform?

WRITING

Was the storyline powerful enough?

Was the dialogue well written?

Could players relate to the hero, or did they find him/her annoying?

Did any of the key characters fail to work as planned?

Was there too much or too little dialogue and storytelling in the game?

AUDIO

How good was the sound?

If you used Dolby surround sound, did it work as well as it should have?

How strong was the music?

Was the style of music the best choice for the game?

If voiceover artists were used, how did the quality compare to other top titles?

Were the audio levels well balanced?

Did the audio enhance the gamplay, building tension and providing release when it needed to?

MIDDLEWARE/PHYSICS

If the game used any middleware solutions, did they impact the gameplay negatively at all?

If the game used some kind of physics system, did it work as planned, and did the results look realistic (if this is what was intended)?

There are many more questions you could consider, but this checklist will get you pointed in the right direction.

Research, Research, Research

Once you've started to answer the questions I just introduced by playing your existing game all the way through, you should spend time doing some serious research. Some people believe that research is wasted time and that you should be focusing on working on the design or technical specifications for your sequel. In my experience, research is very rarely wasted time. A good analogy is building level editing tools or a game scripting system. While creating these tools might seem like a lot of time-intensive work, and you don't get anything obvious back, in the long run, spending time to create a great editor or a clear and powerful scripting system will pay you back significantly. Design research works the same way; sometimes just one line from a review somewhere can spark off a new idea that dramatically impacts your game design.

Let's next look at the types of research that you should be doing.

10

Read Magazine Reviews

Try to get your hands on as many reviews as you can from all versions of the previous games. You might find the negative ones harder to study, but dig deep. A large number of reviews are now available online, and a friendly call to a game journalist at a key game magazine might help you locate an old review. Look for common themes and criticisms that appear in the different reviews, but be careful not to leap to quick decisions based on individual reviewer comments. Just because one journalist thinks that your modern-day shooter would be much better if it was set in sixteenth-century Paris, it doesn't make them right.

Talk to the Development Team

Speak to the development team who worked on previous versions of the game, but don't just talk to the designers. Spend as much time as you can interviewing the different people involved in the game—programmers, level editors, musicians, and so on. Ask the programmers what frustrated them (but be prepared to cut their answer short if you want to escape alive!). Find out if there is anything cool they can do for a new game but haven't done yet. Often programmers create an engine that is capable of some really incredible and unusual features but they never get asked about these features by the designer. (Designers often assume that features that don't appear in the game aren't possible.) Find out whether any programming shortcuts were taken during the development of the existing version of the game that hurt the final product. Ask the level designers what their biggest problems and constraints were. Ask the lead artists if there were any fundamental problems that stopped them from making the animations, characters, or environments as strong as they'd have liked. Ask the musicians what they'd have liked to do if they had the time or the budget.

Subject Research

There are no two ways about it—unless you are making a fantasy game set in a completely original universe, you must get to know your subject matter inside and out. You need to totally immerse yourself in your game's theme until you become an expert. If you're creating a soccer game, you need to know and love soccer. If your main character is a special-forces soldier, you've got to know what kind of people they are, what drives them, and how they operate. The more information you can gather, the better. Use books, DVDs, TV programs, and movies, and never be afraid to approach real-life experts for their advice.

Reality Check: One of the best additional expenses on a project can be to employ a real-life expert as an advisor, even if your project has a tight budget. Getting an expert involved for even half a day will allow you to ask lots of questions and get a much better feel for the subject matter. Don't ever assume that you and your team have all the experience you need with the subject matter you are working with. If you use an outside expert, make sure you set aside time and other resources so that you'll be able to follow up on at least some of the advice you receive. It's easy to fall into the trap of collecting good advice but then simply ignoring it because you have other things to do.

Try to gather as much first-hand experience as you can about the subject matter you are working with. If you're making a rally driving game, for example, take a rally driving course so you can actually get a feel for the handling, the noise, the viewpoint, and the hundreds of other things (often very tiny) that you'll notice subliminally and end up putting into the design. If you're making a game with a baby as the lead character, spend some time watching babies: how they act, move, talk, and interact with their environment. It sounds so obvious, but so many development teams rush headlong into full design and development and the most critical research is ignored or not done properly.

Player Research

Since you're making a sequel, you are in the enviable position of knowing that many hundreds of thousands (or hopefully millions) of people have played the original game. These may be devoted fans of the game who are running fan sites on the Internet and posting on discussion boards about the game. But they will also be people who played the game and didn't enjoy it as much—critics, if you will. Don't underestimate the importance of genuine feedback from both types. The fan is someone who is almost certainly going to buy the sequel, and this player knows the original game extremely well. Find out what they liked, what they missed, and what they would like to see in the next game. The critic won't buy the sequel, but their feedback may enable you to appeal to people like them next time around.

Reality Check: If you design only for the fans, it will be hard for your sequel to gain new ones. That doesn't mean you should turn your back on what made the first game successful, but it does mean that you need to identify and fix the problems and annoyances that the fans may have overlooked.

Many game publishers still put feedback cards inside boxed games, and some of these cards ask the gamers for their views on the game. If you can get ahold of these cards, they can be very useful. Most publishers will also have a database of e-mail addresses from people who registered an interest in the original title. You may be allowed to contact some of these people for some more specific feedback. However you do your

10

research, please don't fall into the "only I know best" mindset. Companies that don't listen to their customers are the first to go bankrupt, and there is nothing special about a game designer that violates this rule.

Consider Using Early Focus Groups

Focus groups are normally used later on in the development cycle of a game, when gamers from your target demographic can play the game and give you some early feedback about things you may have missed. However, in many cases, it can be useful to have a very early focus group, either getting people to play the original game and comment, or running ideas for the new game past them to see which ideas appeal the most.

Do the Needed Market Research

Many people think that performing market research is the same thing as using a focus group, but it isn't. Focus group studies are carried out on a very small scale; for example, one study might involve putting together three groups of six people and asking them detailed questions. Market research is carried out on a much larger scale; normally more than 100 people to get a statistically useful result. Market research can be by done by e-mail, regular mail, or telephone, or by attending conferences or even just standing in the street outside a video game store asking questions to people who walk by. Market research is not as in-depth as focus groups, but it can deliver much higher-level infor-mation. For example, do PlayStation 2 gamers prefer having a male or a female main character? Would people consider buying your sequel if it was set in Antarctica or Africa? What are their initial thoughts when they hear the name of your brand? Be-cause so many people are being asked, you can get a very good idea of whether you're heading in the best direction or not. But make sure you pick your candidates well. If you ask a mailing list of hardcore PC gamers how much depth and complexity they like in their games, don't be surprised at their answers. If you're designing a game aimed squarely at the hardcore PC audience, their answers will be just what you need to know. But if you're designing a multiplatform game for the mass-market audience, you're going to get results that are misleading. Speak to your publisher's marketing team; they will know exactly what kind of customers you should be aiming for.

If You Didn't Work on the Original

Life can be much tougher for you as a sequel designer when you didn't work on the original game. In many ways, having fresh unbiased eyes on the game is a great thing, but you may find that the less-enlightened people in the development team don't share this view. If you get yourself in this situation, here are some tactics that can help you out:

- Speak to the development team before you begin, and listen to their thoughts.

- Do your research and decide what changes and improvements you want to make.

- Explain the changes to the team, and be firm but fair about the changes needed.

- If there is anything that they disagree strongly with, use your research to show them why it needs to be done. If necessary, organize a *feature test*.

What Is a Feature Test?

Get a small team of gamers in. Depending on what aspect of the game you'd like to test, you may need to get people who have played the original game or new players who haven't experienced it at all. Set up a couple of different versions of the game—one with the change/feature you want to include and one without. Agree in advance on some non-leading questions, and then sit back and listen to the results. Be big enough to admit it if you were wrong, but hopefully, seeing gamers appreciate the changes you want to make can be an excellent way of proving your point of view.

Laying Foundations for Further Versions

If your game has a storyline, it will normally be important to try to leave the story open for another sequel. You may have a professional scriptwriter creating the storyline for your game, in which case, they will be used to this requirement, but make sure you mention it in their brief. If you're writing the story yourself, make sure you don't kill off the lead character unless your publisher is happy with this and understands that it may limit the potential of a follow-up game. There is a skill involved in leaving some story threads unanswered and open for a follow-up without leaving the player wondering what happened and feeling unsatisfied by the game ending. If in doubt, get the story working well for this game and worry about a follow-up game if and when it happens.

10

Creative Idea: Create a Design Wish List

Store all the design ideas that you don't end up implementing in a wish list for later versions of the game. This will prove really useful for you (or another designer) when the time comes. Get used to having a wish list on the wall during development, and write on it whenever anyone wants something that just isn't possible given the time frame, budget, or current technology available.

How Far Can You Go?

One of the toughest issues you will face when creating a sequel is how much you should change the current game. Your players have likely enjoyed the game, so you have to make sure you don't lose the magic ingredients that made it work well. In my view, there are three fundamental laws of great sequel design that every designer needs to follow.

Law 1: Don't Mess with the Magic

Don't try to radically change the core gameplay if it worked well. Know what people liked about the current game, and don't break it. As I mentioned before, research is really important so that you understand why people liked the game. Don't try to turn an action game into a stealth game. Don't try to fundamentally change a control system or camera that worked well. Don't mess with the magic.

War Story: Don't Mess with the Magic

The first law of sequel design is "Don't mess with the magic," and the third game in the successful Conflict series, *Conflict: Vietnam*, arguably suffered from this very problem. The core gameplay behind the success of the previous two titles was the four-character squad control and the ability to use your squad intelligently—for example, splitting them up, flanking the enemies, and covering advancing squad members with your sniper. Some of this was lost in the thick, claustrophobic jungle of Vietnam, and too much of the game ended up with narrow linear paths without the freedom to use your squad effectively. Rather than being a useful tool, the squad members became in many ways just extra lives running along behind you.

Law 2: Fix It

You need to find and fix any problems or issues that players had with the current game. Make sure you polish any rough edges. Again, research will help you identify these areas. Look for the issues that reviewers all came up with. Watch new players playing the current game without any assistance from you. What annoys them? Fix it.

Law 3: Add Fresh Ideas

Come up with some new ideas that will add to the whole package and make your sequel feel fresh. Brainstorm sessions can be useful. Bear in mind that even the smallest little feature can make a big impact. One of the Colin McRae Rally sequels seemed to highlight the windscreen camera view as a big new feature and how the rain/water drops moved across the windscreen. It's a pretty small element in the grand scheme of the game, but it was still something that managed to get them lots of coverage in the press.

Adapting Your Brand to New Technologies

My three laws are important for anyone who is creating a standard sequel, but what should you do if your sequel needs to be on a brand-new platform? Well, all three laws still apply, but you'll now have a big opportunity for much more innovation and risk-taking. If you are dealing with the next generation of computing and graphical power, you will be able to achieve things that weren't previously possible. Even if you are developing your sequel for another platform with a similar technology level, you can try to do things a little differently and play to the strengths of the new platform.

Let's assume for now that you're being given the chance to take a successful brand onto a new generation of technology. What kind of improvements and changes should you consider? Broadly speaking, you can break things down into five main categories: graphics, sound, controls, gameplay, and multiplayer/online.

Graphics

It's a fact: gamers and the gaming press in the United States and Europe are obsessed with graphics. So while we (as designers) understand that it's the gameplay that makes a game magical or not, you're going to have to help push the graphical level of the game as well. And while some might argue that designing the graphics isn't part of the designers' role (it's an artist thing!), a great game design comes from understanding roughly what is possible and designing around the capabilities. So, if you're developing for a powerful new console or a PC with a stunning new graphics card, use that to your advantage. You'll probably have more memory to use, so you can ask for more animations. Do you want your main character to have five different run animation cycles and switch between them at random to make the character seem less rigid? Concentrate on the animations that the player will see throughout the game. (It's amazing how many games have a brilliant set-piece animation that will be seen only rarely, yet an awful run animation that the player sees for 90 percent of the game!)

Reality Check: Create your design to work best with lots of on-screen characters or loads of particles that form part of the gameplay. Don't limit your scenarios. If you want a 50-character fight in the middle of an erupting volcano, ask for it. It might not be possible, but if you don't aim high, you're not going to break any new ground.

10

Sound

Sound hardware in the latest consoles seems to be approaching the limit of what is possible. Make sure you include a small section in your design covering what you'd like to hear, sound-wise. Sounds that are occluded by walls and objects are now possible. You should expect full Dolby surround-sound support, environmental effects processing (such as rooms that produce echo or deaden normal sounds), and so on. Understand what is possible, and push your sound engineers to use sound fully.

Controls

Look carefully at the controllers for the new platform. Is there anything new that you can exploit? Have any changes/improvements been made to the previous controller?

Make sure you know which buttons are analog and which are digital. Is there support for force-feedback or vibrations within the controller? Think about using the analog nature of the buttons. This can be done in a very subtle way, making the main use largely digital, but just adding a little effect depending on whether the button is pushed hard. When people are panicking in a game, they tend to press the buttons harder. So why not use this to your advantage and make the player character use more desperate animations when the buttons are pushed really hard?

Gameplay

Having lots of processing power on a new platform can allow you to do many things with the gameplay that you wouldn't have considered previously. It allows you to have a larger number of characters or objects on screen. A great example of this is the Dynasty Warriors series, which used the power of the PlayStation 2 when it first came out to have huge numbers of warriors in an environment.

New technology can also let you have much smarter, realistic AI characters, using the processing power to be really ambitious about what you want them to do. Working on a new console may allow some very clever ways of doing things you wouldn't have thought were possible.

Creative Idea: Brainstorm for a Unique Gameplay Idea

The best way to come up with unique gameplay ideas is to brainstorm. Sit around a blank sheet of paper and try to come up with everything that your character could possibly do. Don't think about any limitations when you're coming up with ideas; try to write down every single crazy thought you can come up with. If you're trying to simulate real life in your game, think about everything your character could do in the same real-life situation. Then sit down, and every time you want to cross out an idea because "you could never do that," try to figure out a way to make it happen (which may mean sitting down with the programming team and bashing the idea around a little).

Multiplayer/Online

Now that all the current consoles have an online capability, the interest in online gaming is likely to grow significantly, and we should see new platforms that have even better and more intuitive systems for connecting and playing across the Internet. I suggest taking a close look at the online specifications for the new console you are considering designing a game for and see what has changed. Does the platform provide a voice-communication headset as standard? Is there an EyeToy style camera that you could use as part of a multiplayer game mode? Don't just copy other online games and throw in a simple deathmatch mode unless your game merits it; try to come up with a unique approach that will help make your online game stand out from other titles out there. For example, look at *Splinter Cell: Pandora Tomorrow*'s unique asymmetrical online gameplay, which greatly helped this game stand out from the crowd.

Summary

Hopefully, this chapter has given you some insight into the unique challenges inherent in designing a sequel to a successful title. As long as you remember to do your research, retain the gameplay magic while fixing flaws, and add a handful of really fresh ideas, you're heading in exactly the right direction.

Creating a sequel can be an immensely rewarding design experience, so enjoy it, and remember how many people out there will be looking forward to what you're creating! Next up, we're going to look at the rising trend for in-game advertising and how to embrace it without selling your soul.

10

An Interview with Alex Ward

Alex Ward is creative director of Criterion Games and is the man behind EA's phenomenal Burnout series and the innovative *FPS*, *BLACK*. Alex previously worked at Acclaim and has an outstanding track record as one of the leading game designers in Europe. With the innovative improvements that he has made to the Burnout series, Alex is ideally placed to comment on the challenges of designing game sequels.

What do you think are the most important skills that a game designer should have?

AW: It has to be the ability to communicate. It sounds stupid, but it's actually pretty hard to do well. The world is full of players. Everyone can play games. But playing games and enjoying them doesn't mean that you can design them. The best designers I have met happen to be excellent communicators. They speak clearly and confidently and get you excited about their ideas.

If a game designer is asked to create a sequel to a successful title, where should they start?

AW: It helps if they were part of the original development team. This isn't always the case, but it's a great starting point. Just like the movie business, a great sequel is about providing something new, but also staying true to the original. It helps to identify the core values of the original game and then stick to them religiously. And I mean religiously.

Burnout, for example, has always been about high-speed driving. Nothing else. This is the core, the essence of the game. We've never attempted to move away from this focus. Our original "rip-o-matic" (a montage of images from games, films, TV shows, and adverts intended to communicate the flavor of the experience before any work has begun) was all about high-speed car chases from movies, in particular a chase from the film Ronin. We set out to create a game experience that mirrored this in every way—from the way the cars were driven to the sounds you heard from the engine.

Once the core values are identified, it's necessary to innovate within these values. After all, a sequel is only a success if it's bigger than the predecessor. No one will buy a game that's weaker than the original. Players are looking for how it's better, how it improves upon the first, and how it brings something new to the table.

Thinking back to 2002 when we were working on Burnout 2 : Point of Impact, we went into the development process armed with having just made the first one. The team remained intact. We wanted the new game to be faster, bigger, and above all, be more accessible to a wide range of players. We all admit our first game was just too damn hard. Chris Roberts, one of the designers, argued strongly that some players just wanted to crash cars and weren't necessarily that interested in any of the racing experience at all. Thus, a new game mode was born and that was how Crash Mode began.

When designing a sequel, how do you judge the balance between adding innovation and retaining the gameplay that made the original so popular?

AW: It's very difficult. There has always been a time during the development of the Burnout series where we have physically set up side-by-side comparisons of the previous games and the current game in development. Do they "feel" right? Which is faster? Is the new one way, way better? Would you have to be nuts to choose the older ones? We always try to adopt the mindset of the consumer to help us focus. And we try to be the toughest consumer of all. I think the hardest thing I've ever learned in game development is having to be the person who says, "That just isn't good enough yet." Being able to say the game is bad is really important.

What are you most proud of in your career so far?

AW: It has to be starting the Burnout series back in 2000. It got started in a hotel bar in downtown San Diego. The team consisted of about four people and we all disagreed with each other. None of us had ever made a good game before. I'd not even made a game before, so I had no idea of what was to come. But I'd played a lot of hits, so I had a feeling for what a good game should be like. And I'd always been a racing game fan. So I had very definite opinions of the type of game I wanted to play and also a strong sense of what commercially was happening. I'd worked as a publishing A&R guy for a few years, so I'd seen a lot of developers getting it hopelessly wrong. Looking back, it hardly sounds like a recipe for success. But I met up with some incredibly talented programmers and artists. Everyone was hungry for success. We were four guys in Guildford and we were taking on the world.

When you're designing a sequel, do you carry out research or focus groups with people who bought the original game, or do you rely solely on your own knowledge of the brand to guide your design decisions?

AW: I think the best mine of information is usually the development team. They know what they did inside and out. If you have to rely on focus groups, then this is usually a sign that the development team has no idea and is not fully committed to making a good video game. That said, focus groups can be useful once a development has begun. We did not use focus groups for the first two Burnout games. We did for the third game, but that was only once the game was really taking shape and this was more to reconfirm a few things rather than look for inspiration.

A surprisingly high number of "third games" in a series disappoint. Why do you think that is, and how did you manage to avoid it with Burnout 3?

AW: This is probably because we are very tough critics of what we develop. And we hold a very thorough and open postmortem process at the end of each game. This is a real "Chinese parliament" situation with anyone able to express their thoughts and feelings about what went well and what went not so well. We had a bit of break between the second game and the third one. (This

10

was the time when we secretly began development on *Black*.) During this time, we were able to reflect on where we wanted to take the series. I'm talking here specifically about the network experience. We never wanted to go online with the game until we could perfectly capture the offline single-player experience and offer it seamlessly online. No other games had managed to get their traffic system online. To us, it was absolutely crucial. It just would not have been *Burnout* without all of the speed, all of the traffic, and all of the crashes. Another reason why we managed to keep everything fresh was our focus of always trying to bring a new game mode to the table. In *Burnout 3* we looked to merge the new battling/fighting/takedown mechanic we were introducing with the instant gratification of Crash Mode. We tried several iterations out before what we christened "Road Rage" was born. So the third game came to market with a whole heap of new features and it became a "must-buy" for fans of the series.

What is your favorite ever game (of all time), and why?

AW: It's a real split between *Asteroids* and *Time Pilot*. But my "desert island" game would probably be *Asteroids*. The best machine in the U.K. is located at Archer Maclean's house in Banbury. I know because I've played it! The machine looks and feels like it just rolled off the line at Atari back in 1982. It's such a simple and hypnotic game. It's easy to get into yet it has a great depth to it. It was one of the first coin-op machines I ever saw. And it never ends! It's the sort of game you keep coming back to. And I keep coming back to it. I really should know better but I just can't help it and it's 2005 and I am still playing it.

What do you think is the biggest game design mistake that people regularly make with games?

AW: This is an easy one. I have strong feelings about this. The biggest mistake has to be making the game far too hard to play. Game designers so often get this completely wrong. And I openly admit it, we fell victim to this on our first game.

Burnout wasn't particularly the biggest game in the world so we deliberately made it pretty challenging. And "pretty challenging" quickly became too hard for most people outside the development staff. It's really important that we encourage gameplay testing and feedback early on in the process. One way to find out if something will work or not is to quickly get it working in the game and move from there. No elegantly written design document or carefully honed PowerPoint presentation or press sound bite can save you. At Criterion we're particularly interested in seeing reactions from our test audiences that included wives, girlfriends, parents, and children of the team—mostly people who don't play too many games—having a first look or play. This stuff has been invaluable to us over the past few years.

If money and technology were unlimited, what kind of game would you most like to see made?

AW: There are three movie experiences that have had a profound impact to me.

One is seeing Tron back in 1982. It was amazing, and it was difficult to stay excited about VIC-20 software for long when I got home from the cinema. Although the coin-op game of the day was great, I don't think anyone has truly exploited the potential for a beautiful Tron experience.

The second is seeing the movie The Last Starfighter. I would love to be recruited by the Star League and enjoy a deep space-trading/shooting experience. David Braben's seminal Elite sparked a lot of imaginations back in the early 1980s and to this day has never been rivaled. A game where you could have the experience last over several years would be very powerful indeed.

The third is seeing the Terminator 3D ride/movie at Universal Studios in Hollywood. I found the whole experience so astonishing and was so overwhelmed by what I saw and experienced in the movie theatre that I had to sit down outside and try to get to grips with it. The effect was incredible. I started to dream about the prospect of gaming in true HD with movie-like image quality coupled with 3D imaging. It sounds silly but you really do have to see it to believe it.

What do you think is the biggest challenge facing game designers as we move forward?

AW: Making games for a broad audience is something a lot of teams will struggle with. As the potential gaming audience grows now to the tens of millions, the software experience will have to be many things. It will have to cater to a wide range of abilities and offer a compelling and rich experience. The games business is already 10 percent greater in revenue than the movie business, but continually beating them in terms of global mass-market entertainment will be pretty difficult.

And finally, if you had one piece of advice to give to a game designer who was just starting out, what would it be?

AW: Communicate!

10

Chapter 11

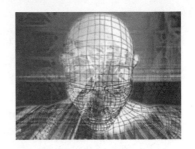

Advergaming and Sponsorships

"Ads are the cave art of the twentieth century."

Marshall McLuhan

In the clean and pure world of a game designer's head, the idea of selling advertising space within a game, or having the logos of sponsors cluttering up a perfectly designed GUI, is often a horrible thought. It's very easy to feel that you're "selling out" by having in-game advertising. But it's something that you need to address, and in the modern world, where it's starting to cost more and more money to develop games, it can often make sense to raise some money back in return with some advertising if done subtly and tastefully.

In this chapter, we'll start by looking at the challenges of advergaming and the gray line that exists between licensing and advertising. You'll learn how to use various techniques, from including brand names on your product packaging as a credibility enhancement to putting branded objects into your game. Throughout, I've tried to introduce a number of different approaches to stimulate you to come up with some of your own ideas. Advergaming is a fairly new field, and the opportunities and constraints are likely to evolve and change drastically over the next few years.

The Challenge of Advergaming

Just as with the movie business, the challenge is to take advantage of the opportunity of using advertising without going overboard. You've probably seen a few movies (a recent James Bond film comes to mind) in which the advertising has been overdone and the final result becomes a never-ending lineup of overt car and mobile phone brands. But for every film like this, there are countless more that have successfully achieved in-film advertising and branding, and few viewers are put off by it. The trick is to keep the advertising as subtle as possible. Even back in the older days of film, when a lead character performed an action such as jumping into a Lamborghini, the action helped advertise the Lamborghini brand despite there being no payment or connection between the companies at the time; the director just wanted a Lamborghini because it looked cool on film.

Another example involves characters in films having conversations in bars. If the actors have a particular brand of beer in their hand, it's not going to look odd unless there is an obvious close-up on the label. Yet many people will still subconsciously notice the brand. This kind of brand placement in games isn't going to ruin the experience if it's done carefully. In fact, in many ways, it can make a game feel more realistic and authentic. If you're being chased down a street in New York, wouldn't you rather see real store names as you pass by them rather than obviously fake ones? If your character has a PDA that you access to get new information, wouldn't it feel more realistic if the PDA was one that actually exists?

Reality Check: The argument for and against advertising in games is one that will continue on and on. I'd advise you not to take a position that you become completely against advergaming. Try to understand that in some cases advergaming can make a game feel more realistic, as well as help to pay for that awesome orchestral score you want to get written. The field for advergaming is relatively new, so there are many unique ways to incorporate advertising with games. This means that you can get very creative with how you work with sponsors and incorporate marketing messages into your games.

Selling Your Soul?

From my point of view, it's up to you as the game designer and person responsible for the "heart and soul" of a game to be careful about what kind of in-game advertising you allow into the product. As I just mentioned, I feel that it's a balancing act. You need to be careful that any advertisements you include don't tip too far in one direction. If people pay $40 for your game, they don't want to be bombarded by blatant product promotion. Don't sell your game's soul, but keep an open mind, and try and find the balance that is right for you.

A Gray Line: Licensing vs. Advertising

You might encounter a rather gray area when it comes to licensing. At one end of the scale, you'll likely need to pay to license any major brand for inclusion in your game, and at the other end, the brand holder will pay you to feature its brand in your title. This gray area usually depends on how much clout you have with your game or brand, the relative skills of your licensing team, and the attitude of the company involved. By and large, the distinction tends to be about who really benefits the most. The question becomes: Does the addition of the advertised brand significantly improve the quality and overall impression of the game, or does advertising the brand in the game mainly benefit the owner of the brand?

Let's look at an example. Assume that you're creating a racing game and you want to include a Ferrari. This brand of car is probably much more widely known than your game. It increases the attraction of your game to consumers, so it's clearly a great thing for you. It makes your game feel special, and players want to drive the best cars. But the benefit Ferrari receives for being in your game is much smaller. The folks at Ferrari might feel that being in your game isn't going to help them sell very many cars. In fact, the risk of being in your game (which from their point of view might not be very good) is probably much more important to them than the reward of seeing their cars in yet another video game. Because of these circumstances, you may well have to pay Ferrari a considerable sum to include its car in your game.

On the other hand, including Red Bull drink cans within your game environment is unlikely to add much to your game at all. In fact, you may feel that unless you also include Coke, Pepsi, and a host of other brands, having a specific brand may look like an obvious advertising ploy and therefore make your game weaker rather than stronger. However, the makers of Red Bull, providing that your game is a high-quality one, might view your game as reaching an important demographic that they can't easily reach using other advertising vehicles. The message of linking fun quality entertainment with their drink could be an important one. Clearly, in this case, you'd expect them to pay you to feature their brand in your game. I'm using Red Bull as an example only because it has been in a large number of games (hopefully this has been successful from the company's point of view), and I'm sure the company would agree with me that its product is very different than Ferrari's in terms of what kind of advertising deals it could command. Unfortunately, neither company is paying me to mention them! (I wonder if you can get in-book advertising deals?)

11

Reality Check: Most licensing calls are rarely very clear, so it's worth pushing the brand owners by explaining just how many copies of the game you expect to sell and highlighting your track record and the demographics of the people who will purchase the game. Even if you don't manage to get some money for in-game advertising, you may end up with a deal that doesn't cost you anything and benefits both parties greatly.

Advertising in Games

Let's take a look at a few real-life examples of how in-game advertising has been implemented very well and some in which I think it has been implemented badly.

Good Examples of Advertising in Games

I chose these games because the advertising is fairly subtle and, when they were released, the games broke new ground for using advertising. One important lesson to be learned here is that you can make your in-game advertising more palatable and effective if you find new and clever ways to incorporate it.

Wipeout 2097

The Wipeout series has always been at the cutting edge, with many new ideas. In-game advertising was one of them. *Wipeout 2097* (see Figure 11.1) advertised companies like Red Bull on in-game billboards and was one of the first games to do so. What's more, because the game is about a futuristic racing championship, the advertisements seemed in keeping with the game, so they never felt out of place. Along with the great licensed music tracks, they made the game feel very cool.

Crazy Taxi

Crazy Taxi (see Figure 11.2) was one of the very first games to really go to town with in-game advertising. It featured a whole load of national chain stores, such as Tower Records, KFC, Fila, and Pizza Hut. The advertising made the city feel realistic and

Figure 11.1
Wipeout 2097.

Figure 11.2
Crazy Taxi.

definitely enhanced the gameplay. Again, the advertising was totally in keeping with the game, and because there was such a variety, it never really felt like you were watching an advertisement.

Bad Examples of Advertising

In certain respects, advergaming gets such a bad rap simply because it has been done poorly in so many games. I would imagine that you have your own list of games in which the advertising really annoys you, and here are a few that I would also put on the list.

Zool 2

Zool 2 (see Figure 11.3) didn't just have a few advertisements or product placements for Chupa Chups sweets—the game was basically an entire advertisement for them. Whole levels of the game were based around the sweets, with signs, banners, and products everywhere. If there is a line that you shouldn't cross as a game designer when it comes to in-game advertising, *Zool 2* not only crossed it, but flew across it with a rocket pack on. Frustratingly, it was also a great game, but the advertising ruined it for many people.

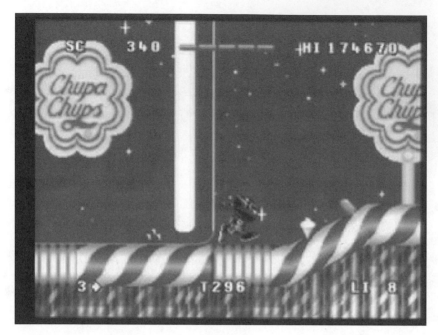

Figure 11.3
Zool 2.

Judge Dredd: Dredd Vs. Death

Red Bull's Australian arm bought advertising within the game and then insisted on having a huge amount of presence. Not only are there big crates of Red Bull all over the place, but there are moments where an in-game character throws a can, which bounces and lands right in front of camera, filling the whole screen with the brand name. I suspect that the developers probably didn't have a choice in the matter and were forced to do this by the publishers. Oh dear!

War Story: How Far Will You Go?

After giving Judge Dredd such a hard time over its use of Red Bull in its game, I should even things up a little by pointing out that I also had a major soft drink in one of my games, with the main character even drinking it at one point. I'm ashamed of myself. But some of the things they wanted us to do went far beyond this. For example, they wanted the main character to mention the brand name and say how good the drink was. Hmm. Maybe not!

Techniques for In-Game Advertising

There are many different ways to advertise brands in video games. Some are subtle and some are more obvious. Let's look at a few paths that are becoming increasingly well trodden. Often, games will use a combination of these techniques to keep a good balance between gameplay and broadcasting marketing messages.

Reality Check: The online game *EverQuest II* allows players to order a pizza in-game from Pizza Hut, and Pizza Hut will deliver it to your door (see Figure 11.4)! Press a certain key and a special pizza menu pops up in the game. Here you can select what you want, key in your address, and get it delivered within 45 minutes. Now that's in-game advertising! This approach worked so well, even though it was a very obvious advertisement, because it was so unique that it generated a lot of extra "word of mouth" attention from players of the game.

Figure 11.4
EverQuest II Pizza Hut advertisement.

To start, you'll want to review the various advertising opportunities listed in Table 11.1. Here I've compiled the types of advertising that are used for various categories of games.

Table 11.1   Some in-game advertising opportunities.

Game Type	Opportunity	Description
Sports/racing	On-screen timer	Brand the on-screen timer with a real-life clock/timing company as they do in athletics coverage on television.
Any	In-game item	Use a real-life product as an item in the game, perhaps a drink can, a pair of trainers you can buy, a mobile phone, and so on.
Any	In-game audio	Announce a new product on a PA system or in-game TV.
Any	Loading screen	Feature the company or brand on all the loading screens somewhere.
Sports/management	Stadium/sponsorship	Have the brand or company name as the name of a stadium, or in a management game, use the brand or company as an in-game sponsor.
Sports/racing	Car/vehicle customization	Place a company's logo onto cars in the game, and allow the player to use the logo as a decal.
Character games	Customizable character	Have a company's logo on the character's clothing or as a decal that can be applied as a tattoo.
Any	Storyline/plot	Include the company/brand in your storyline; in a similar way that FedEx was included in the story of the film *Castaway*.
Sport/racing	Reward screen/medal ceremony	Have the company sponsor the reward screen or the podium that the winning athletes stand on.
FPS	Watch	Have a watch company sponsor the watch that your in-game character wears. In an FPS, the watch should be visible a great deal of the time.
Any	Compass/map	If your game uses an in-game map or compass, why not get a real-life mapping company or compass manufacture tied in, with a small logo on them?
Any	FMV/cut scenes	Place companies' products subtly into your FMV sequences or cut scenes

(continued)

Table 11.1 Some in-game advertising opportunities *(continued)*.

Game Type	Opportunity	Description
Any	In-game pickup	Advertisers love this; picking up their product in the game has a positive effect on the gameplay. Not a very subtle example, but say if your character is getting tired, finding some Jolt cola could help keep them awake.
Any	Locations	If a particular building is likely to attract visitors, why not get them to pay to be in the game? For example, you could set a level of your stealth game in the Natural History Museum in London at night and lots of young gamers globally will be made intimately aware of the museum.
Adventure	Reference	If your adventure game features any kind of reference section (where the player can go to look up facts), why not base this on a real-life reference book?
Any	Tutorials	Include a real-life person or company in your tutorial section so they are helping train the player.
Racing/action	Vehicles	Include a particular vehicle in the game, and use it in a cool way. *Tomb Raider: Legend* has a tie-in with Jeep that works in this way.
Any	Building frontages	If your character or car is moving through a city, you can make it feel realistic while generating revenue by getting sponsors on board—banks, fast food establishments, gas stations, and so on.
Sports/racing	Billboards	Most racing games can get away with advertising billboards and signs, just as in real-life races. The same goes for sports games, especially those that take place in stadiums. So why not fill these up with real brands?

11

Understand the Brand

No matter what specific techniques you use to convey advertising messages in your game, you first should spend some time researching the brand that you are using. Really get to know it and make sure that you and your team understand all of the important implications. Here are some questions to ask yourself:

- What do people first think of when they come across the brand?

- What demographic does the brand appeal to?

- What are the strong and weak points about the brand?

- Are there any negative aspects that people associate with the brand?

- What types of advertising does the brand holder do with the brand?

- Does the brand have staying power?

- Will the brand be compatible with the "theme" of your game?

Take a look at how the advertiser has promoted the brand in other areas. What do its advertisements look like? Is there a consistent theme running through the promotion? Take a look at the company's Web site and see how it perceives the brand. If you understand the brand, you are more likely to use it in the right way within the game. This has two benefits: it keeps the advertisers happy, and if they're happy, they are less likely to insist that you do more in the game with their brand, thus reducing the chance of people noticing overt advertising in the finished title.

Branding a Game

One obvious route is to get a brand name either in the name of the game or on the box or packaging. Adidas did this with soccer games a few years ago, and Nike is apparently working with Sony on a fitness product as I write this. In order for this to be worthwhile from a game designer's point of view, either you need to be offered lots of money or the brand needs to help you sell your game. If you are developing an unbranded athletics game, for example, adding *Reebok* might help you sell the game, but it does add authenticity and is therefore a good thing regardless of whether the company pays you money or not. Having a brand attached to the name can damage games, though. If journalists feel that you've slapped on a brand name to try and sell a bad game, word may well get round, and you could end up with a more negative public reaction than if you hadn't used the brand.

Reality Check: The Adidas soccer game didn't do very well, but this was almost certainly due to the fact that the game itself wasn't great. The lesson is that you can't make a poor game sell by adding a well-known brand! In fact, if you use a brand that is perceived as being very popular and of very high quality, you need to go the extra mile to make sure that your gameplay is really good (of course, you'd be doing this anyway!). The people who buy a branded game are likely to purchase the game having very high expectations, especially if you are using a high-end brand.

War Story: Fixing a Dull Game with a Cool Brand

When I was at Codemasters we created a game called *No Fear Downhill Mountain Biking*. In this instance, the "No Fear" brand was added to provide authenticity. At the time, this brand represented a very cool high-status extreme sport image, and it fit the game very well. The company who owned the brand was able to use the game to help promote itself, and we had a cool label attached to an otherwise fairly dull game name, so both of us won in this situation.

In-Game Logos or Signs

A more traditional route involves getting a brand logo placed into the game. This is done in sports and racing games using standard advertising techniques just as in the real world, but game designers are starting to get smarter about other ways of using logos and signage. Fortunately, games don't have to copy real-life, and there is no reason why you can't allow the player to tattoo the Nike logo onto the virtual golfer when he's being created at the start of a game.

In–Game Objects

Using in-game objects involves the placement of products into the game. These objects could be anything from a bottle of beer to a Mercedes sports car. The idea is that the object is visible and recognizable to the player and the player sees it in a positive light. Ideally for the advertisers, the objects have a constructive use that benefits the player. For example, Pepsi might want its cans and bottles to be available from in-game vending machines to boost the players' health or skill level. From a designer's point of view, objects that add authenticity to an existing game design are good. For example, if you already have a gun in the game, branding it with a Heckler and Koch logo is probably a good thing because it will make the player connect more with the object. Objects that feel out of place and contrived are not good, and I'd encourage you to fight any pressure you receive to use such objects as strongly as you can. If you suspect there is a chance that an average gamer will see a branded object and think, "That's just a blatant advertisement," then don't use it.

Music and Audio

Another underused way of advertising is through sound effects, audio, and music. If your character runs through a shopping mall in the game, for example, you may be happy letting real advertisements play over the PA system. Many games have strong musical sound tracks, and rather than paying large sums of money to license them, you might be able to get a talented new band to appear for free or even pay you to feature their name in the game and play their music to lots of new customers. There are also several examples of music being written specifically for games by well-known musicians or DJs. For example, Paul Oakenfold wrote an original track for a rally game that I worked on recently and has just been signed up exclusively for EA. I've heard that many new artists who are featured in major EA titles have had album sales jump massively, so there is no reason the same effect can't happen in your game.

Blatant Advertisements

You may decide to have proper advertisements in the game while the game is performing functions such as loading screens. You could also play video commercials on the walls in the game. Some online games have advertisements taking up part of the screen in the "chat foyer" when players are waiting for new games to begin. If you think you can get away with it and it won't annoy players, this kind of advertising is something you might want to consider.

Other Games

It's amazing how rarely publishers use their games to cross-promote other games. I believe that as our industry continues to get more professional, more and more titles will include trailers for forthcoming games and hopefully playable demos as well. By having a "trailers" section in the front end, it's fairly simple to promote other games that you are developing and help develop some hype. You need to be careful to stick within the guidelines of the console manufacturers (which includes not advertising Microsoft games on a Sony game and vice versa). Some publishers bundle in a second disc, which is a standard promotional DVD of their lineup. But it's easier and cheaper to include the trailers on the game disc if you can do so. If you have a realistic game world, why not include poster advertisements for your other titles rather than making up fantasy advertising?

Online Updates

One interesting aspect that has come about due to the rise in online-enabled consoles is the ability to download new content from a central server. In terms of in-game advertising, this offers fantastic possibilities. Say your game sells a million copies. That's a million people who will be playing the game at various points over the next two months (or probably more, since some people will share a copy). Assume the game lasts 10 hours—that's 10 million man-hours of advertising potential. With the facility to download advertising from a server, you can keep the in-game advertising fresh and attract multiple companies and brands. In a racing game, for example, the player can come back to a track to find that the billboards have changed. The sponsor on the loading screen can alternate each time the player starts up the game. And this also introduces the ability to show advertisements within certain time slots. If a TV company wanted to promote a particular show, there is no reason that anyone playing the game within a couple of hours of the start time couldn't be shown an advertisement somewhere (maybe just in the front end or on an in-game banner) that tells them the show will be commencing shortly.

Of course, I'm not suggesting that you should consider destroying your carefully created feeling of immersion by peppering your gameplay with real-world advertisements. But there are certain types of games that aren't about creating immersion and telling a story. One example would be sports and racing games. By considering the power and flexibility that online advertising updates offer you, it's possible to earn quite a bit of revenue that you can then spend on making your game even better.

Using In-Game Advertising Agencies

If all this sounds too much like hard work, there are companies that offer to manage in-game advertising for you. Some companies will even sort out the online updating of advertising I mentioned previously. Ideally, you should hook up with one of these companies at an early stage—you may find that a couple of tiny tweaks to your design allow new possibilities. Again, it's vital to keep a balance between revenue and not ruining the game, and you need to be careful when talking to agencies not to get carried away! But the advantage of using companies like this is that you can tell them about your game, who is publishing it, how big you expect it to be, and most important, what opportunities there are within the game (and packaging) for companies to sponsor or advertise. Video games are growing in terms of their reach and demographics. As more people ignore TV adverts, or skip past them after recording shows onto hard disc, advertisers need to look elsewhere to hit carefully targeted customers. Video games offer that, and I strongly believe that in-game advertising is going to grow rapidly over the next few years. I just hope it doesn't get too blatant!

Adding Authenticity

One excellent reason for adding licenses to your game is to build its authenticity and realism. The first step is to make a list of exactly what licenses/brands you'd like to use in your game. It's worth trying to push yourself. There is no harm in approaching massive companies; the worst they can do is say no. What is important is to have fallback options and to set a date at which, if you don't have the licenses, you will use something else. I've been in many projects where the licenses take much longer than you'd think, and the last thing you need is a license holding up your gold master. In fact, games have been pulled from the shelves after manufacture because the right permissions hadn't been received, which, as you can probably guess, is an extremely devastating and expensive situation to be in. Try to think about all the places in your game where a real-life brand might help. To convince these companies to get on board (and ideally pay for the privilege as well), print out some in-game screen shots with their logo put in, showing them the kind of result they'd get. You will find that you need to pay for many licenses—cars, real race tracks, some real-life buildings, and so on. But ideally you'll be able to convince the brand owner that they will benefit from the association, and you can reach a deal that benefits both parties.

Creating a Version of a Game for a Company

The ultimate destination when talking about working with other companies is to actually create a game for them. More realistically, this might be to create a special version of an existing game for them, since most companies can't (or won't) pay the $4 million to $12 million needed for a high-quality console game. If you're creating a racing game, you might want to consider developing special versions for some of the car manufacturers that you're working with, featuring only their vehicles and putting their branding on the front end and loading screens. If you're talking to a company about in-game sponsorship, then why not bring up the idea of a unique version just for the company and see if it is something it would be willing to pay for. Bear in mind that if a company wants a console game, you'll need to submit the extra version to Microsoft/Sony/Nintendo in order to manufacture gold discs, so you need to check this out before signing the deal and find out whether you'll be charged extra for QA and whether you can get a low-volume run manufactured. Otherwise, creating a tailored PC version of your game is obviously much simpler, and this route makes a lot of sense. Many companies have trade shows, and it's great for them to be able to run a game that features their brand at these shows to inject some entertainment and excitement. For them, it's a case of having something very cool and exciting attached to their brand—video games are great at attracting young consumers. For developers or publishers, it's simply a case of making some additional profit from their existing game engine.

Summary

Hopefully, you've seen the different kinds of in-game sponsorship and advertising that you might want to consider at some point. Although it may feel overly commercial, remember that you need to make money with your game, and by using advertising in the right way, you could add authenticity to your project while also earning revenue. This could mean that you wouldn't need to sell as many copies to start making royalties, or even that you have additional money to do a better audio recording or to employ a couple more level designers. Just don't sell your soul.

11

An Interview with Maryam Bazargan

Maryam Bazargan is the Founding Director of New Street Media, one of the leading players in the in-game advertising arena. New Street Media brings together publishers, developers, advertisers, and gamers in this rapidly expanding industry. Publishers and developers receive the benefit by an additional source of income for their games, and advertisers are able to dynamically advertise to a vast audience of gamers or develop joint events and marketing campaigns. New Street Media works with companies such as PlayJam, Sony Computer Entertainment, Eidos, Konami, Ubisoft, and Vivendi Universal. Maryam is the ideal person to ask about in-game advertising and the benefits it can bring.

In-game advertising seems like an area of rapid growth. Do you think it will eventually become standard in every new title?

MB: The market is certainly set to grow for a number of reasons:

- *As development costs spiral, developers and publishers will look to recoup some of their investment from advertising revenue.*

- *Games are becoming ever more entertaining and immersive and the number of platforms and handheld gaming devices are increasing. This means the gaming audience will increase. At the same time, gamers are likely to spend more time playing games, which ultimately translates to less time spent consuming other media. This means that an advertisers' best route to consumers will be through in-game advertising!*

- *As games become more realistic, this will offer more in-game advertising opportunities to brands. However, at times the games will also need to have the brands in the games for realism purposes.*

Is there a strong demand from companies wanting to advertise their products to gamers?

MB: Today, brand holders have realized how much time their audience spends playing games, and they see the value of having their brand in those games to reach gamers so that their brands will be associated with games. With new ad-serving technologies that allow geo-targeted and time-specific in-game advertising campaigns, more and more brand holders are looking to get involved.

Other than financial, what benefits are there to developers who include dynamic advertising in their titles?

MB: Dynamic advertising technologies can be used to update other game information, such as always having the latest car models in a game. A game designer could even have a character's wardrobe change depending on the season, which would help keep the game fresh. And obviously all this could be paid for by advertisers anyway.

Dynamic advertising technologies track the gameplay of the game, so developers can see exactly how long gamers are spending playing the game and interacting at each level, which could ultimately aid in future game development.

Do you feel that most kinds of games are applicable for in-game advertising, or are there only certain genres where it works best?

MB: We have to keep the advertising real. If a gamer has paid $60 for a game and they are presented with a brand's ad in a Sci-fi environment of a game, which adds nothing to the gameplay, then it is obvious to the gamer that this is a paid-for placement and could have a negative impact on their perception towards the brand and the game developer and publisher. The player might feel cheated.

I certainly wouldn't say most games can take in-game advertising today, but I think more and more will. As publishers and developers realize the potential size of the in-game advertising market, they may concentrate more on the urban, driving, and sports titles that tend to present the most obvious advertising opportunities.

There are always routes available for in-game advertising that don't lend themselves to this and brands who want the association with particular games, such as joint events, co-marketing, promotions, and so on.

What are you most proud of in your career so far?

MB: Being able to really enjoy my work!

If money and technology were unlimited, what kind of game would you most like to see made?

MB: I'd like to have a game that creates a full scale version of a chosen city, say New York, London, or Paris with the choice to personalize the characters, your own face, perhaps a few friends, and a few celebs to download. Basically, I'd want to be able to live my dream life through the game. That could be a bit dangerous too. If you spent too long playing the game, I'd imagine you'd be in danger of mixing reality and the gaming world! But it would be fun.

Do you see the opportunity for in-game advertising to get even better and smarter at targeting consumers in the future?

MB: Of course, just like the internet has created lots of opportunities. Today we can totally track an internet user's surfing habits and target them by that. We'll get to a point where we know which games a gamer is playing and target them through various games with corresponding messages. We'll be able to give absolute reach for every campaign and little advertising wastage.

11

Better targeted ads and geo-targeting means more and more brands can consider the medium for the campaigns, not just the big global brands.

And finally, have you got any advice for designers who are nervous about placing advertising in their game?

MB: Don't worry, go for it. It is definitely here to stay so you might as well have a piece of the action. Just ensure whoever is looking after the in-game ad sales for you has the interests of the gamers at heart. Always look to add to the gameplay through realistic advertising.

Chapter 12

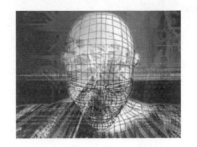

Audio

"Music expresses that which cannot be put into words and that which cannot remain silent."

Victor Hugo

Some game designers are adept at working with audio, and they understand how important it is to work closely alongside musicians and sound engineers. But unfortunately, time and again, audio is an area which many game designers put little effort into. The argument usually goes something like this:

"Surely that's a job for the musician or audio guy? It's nothing to do with game design; we create the game, and the audio engineers put some sound effects and music over the top."

This is a dangerous point of view, and one that I believe often results in average audio at best. Why is this? Well, because the issue of giving the player good feedback gets overlooked.

In this chapter, we'll look at why audio is so important for games. I'll recommend how you can work with musicians and audio engineers to get the best results. I'll then present the different types of techniques that you can use to incorporate music and audio into your games, and hopefully make them an important integral part of your designs.

The Magic of Audio

In the real world (assuming you are lucky enough to have all your senses intact), you are constantly being bombarded with thousands of pieces of information every second. Throughout your field of vision, hundreds of things are moving. You're constantly smelling and tasting the air. You're feeling your feet touch the floor and your clothes move against your skin. You're getting input from all over your body on how hot or cold you are. Your inner ear is telling you which way is up, and whether you're off-balance. And most importantly, you're listening to many sounds in 3D: Distinguishing different voices, the rumble of a plane overhead, a washing machine next door, or a lawnmower further down the street.

As a game designer, you have a small number of ways that you can give feedback to the player. Hopefully, you'll agree that giving feedback to the player is a pretty fundamental part of good game design. So without using sound and music, what can we use to give feedback?

- You can print text on the screen for the player to read.

- You can use the TV screen or monitor to show something visual happening (either in the 3D game world, or within the 2D GUI).

- You can rumble the controller if it has this facility.

- You could even turn on and off the analog light on the controller.

That's it. If you ignore audio, you have no other ways of giving feedback to the player. And since the player can generally only look at one thing at a time, exclusive use of graphics for feedback (for example, having your character limp when he's been injured) will restrict how immersed the player can get.

That's why sound and music are so important. You don't have access to touch, smell, and balance, so you've got to take full advantage of what you *can* use. Consider a standard action adventure game, for example. Simple things like having different footsteps on different surfaces will immediately give the player feedback of what they are standing or running on. With driving games, a basic sound effect indicating that the car is losing traction and is starting to slide will make a massive change to how the player controls the vehicle. It's hard to visually notice a car sliding until it's too late, but by using a subtle sound effect, you give the player instant notification to take action. Scratch beneath the surface of a really great game, and you'll see lots more audio invention and creativity.

Music is equally important; go back and play the original *Tomb Raider* games and you'll find a basic but still very powerful implementation of dynamic music. The player quickly learns that music (and in particular, changes in music) give them lots of information. When the fast action music plays, it means an enemy has spotted the player. The adrenaline kicks in, and the player darts into cover, looking around for the attacker.

When the player enters a beautiful new location, they are treated with some magical music to highlight this fact. The music is saying, "Wow! Look! A massive new area for you to explore!" Hopefully, *Tomb Raider: Legend* is going to move this musical experience to the next level.

Reality Check: As a designer, you need to be involved with both the sound and music in your game, helping it enhance and affect the gameplay, rather than just sit over the top of it. So in this chapter, I'm going to cover some of the things that you should think about when you're sitting down to work out what kind of music, sound effects and voices you want to have in your game.

Good Examples of Games with Audio

Before we get into the details of how different audio and music techniques work, let's look at a few games that have good audio.

Medal of Honour

The *Medal of Honor* series (particularly the first two titles) demonstrated a hugely impressive soundscape which helped build up a fantastic atmosphere. The soundscape would often consist of distant shouts, dogs barking, and tannoy announcements. None of these came from specific characters or distinguishable locations, and therefore didn't represent an immediate threat to the player. However, they really helped make the environments feel much bigger and more dangerous than they were in reality.

Tomb Raider

The *Tomb Raider* games have consistently used music in an interesting and dynamic way. Although many games include dynamic music, I still believe that this series has some of the simplest and most effective. By reusing particular pieces of music, the game designers have used music to create apprehension about what is around the next corner, or to help make the discovery of a gorgeous new area even more special.

Wipeout 2097

The *Wipeout* series was, for me, the games which defined licensed music, and just how great licensed tracks can be in games. *Wipeout* was the first major game to feature a truly cutting-edge series of tracks, to mention the track names in the game, and to actually market this. The combination of stunning graphic design, great gameplay, and a fantastic musical selection made it such a big success.

12

Some Not-So-Great Examples of Games with Audio

When audio is done badly, players really notice and might even feel that the audio (or lack thereof) really hurts the gameplay. Here are a few games that have audio that significantly impacts the gameplay.

ISS Pro Evolution

This otherwise fantastic soccer game series fails consistently to implement in-game commentary in a professional manner. It has become a running joke now among fans, and if you compare the standard of in-game commentary with its major rival, *FIFA*, they are like chalk and cheese. Long gaps between words, and different parts of a sentence being spoken at different pitches are common problems that occur almost all the time.

Hugo

The PlayStation game, *Hugo*, is a perfect example of a very common audio problem; having an annoying and repetitive piece of music that plays all the time. After a few hours of playing the game, you end up wanting to strangle the developers! If you can't afford enough variety in the music, you should allow most of the game to be played without music, and make the sound effects superb.

Need 4 Speed Underground 1 & 2

With this game, it looks to me that E.A has tried too hard to be "street." They have targeted the game music at a specific demographic group, and put in a whole load of breaking new rap and techno artists to appeal to this demographic. But it's such a specific style of music that everyone else ends up hating it, and turning the music off. I wouldn't be surprised if more than half the global purchasers really disliked the music on the game because it was so specialized.

Working with Musicians and Audio Engineers

As I mentioned, it's very dangerous to leave the audio design solely in the hands of a musician or audio engineer. But it's even more dangerous to try and do it yourself. As a game designer, you should have the best understanding of how audio can be used in a game to enhance the gameplay and immersion, and how music and voices can be used to empower the storyline and emotional impact of the game. But you need a musician to deal with the type of music you'll be using, how it works, what time signature and tempo to use, and how best to link dynamic sections of music together. The musician needs to decide the content of the music, but you need to decide when and how it is triggered. Likewise, your sound engineer needs to decide which sound effects to use and in what combination. But *you* need to decide how they are placed in the world, and make sure that all the gameplay-enhancing sound effects you need are present and of a high quality. Ideally, if you can build a good working relationship with your musician/engineer, you'll get a much better result. If the two of you work closely together, it will be much more effective than splitting the work into two separate sets of elements which you each do on your own.

Designing Your Music

Music has the ability to get inside people and dramatically affect their mood. Why do you think so many people own iPods and portable CD players? Music really can touch the soul in ways that visual pictures and moving images struggle to do, and it is one of the greatest tools that you have available to help direct your player in a particular way. Try watching tear-jerking endings in films such as *Titanic* or *Gladiator* without the audio playing, and you'll notice what an amazing difference the beautiful musical scores make.

There are many different kinds of music that you'll need to consider using. Do you go for original or licensed music? Should it have modern R&B artists or use a classical orchestral score? Do you want dynamic atmospheric tracks or heavy rock covers?

Getting the style right is your first challenge. I would strongly advise that you start by trying to remove any preconceptions you have. If you take away just one piece of advice with regards to music it should be this:

> **Take some footage from your game, or a similar title, and try playing a variety of different musical styles alongside it.**

You'll be amazed how often people fall into the trap of using modern licensed music without considering whether there might be a more interesting and unusual approach.

Reality Check: The style of music may be forced upon you by your publisher. If you're working for E.A, for example, you're unlikely to get the freedom to try something too different, especially if you're working on a sports or driving game. But, for me, the most interesting game music isn't modern licensed tracks by next year's big rap star, although that certainly has its place. Music can be used to get emotion from players, and it is extremely unlikely that you'll get this from modern licensed music unless you choose very carefully. Big budget blockbuster movies rarely have 50-Cent rapping over the emotional climax!

One thing I want to hammer home right away is that you shouldn't automatically go with what you like. It sounds obvious, but many designers put their favorite style of music into their game without any kind of focus testing. If you're considering a few different styles or types of music, get a few people from your target age group in, and see how they react to it. With film-style orchestra scores, you're on pretty safe ground, but if you want to go with 1920's big band music or hardcore jazz, you really ought to make sure it isn't going to alienate your potential customers.

Think about Demographics and Incorporate an International Focus

It is important that you have a very clear idea of what age group you are aiming at, whether your game is aimed at men or women, and what territories your game will be sold in. For example, Country and Western music might work with a certain audience in America, but it will not work with most audiences outside the United States. The latest sugar-sweet teen pop star might be famous, but won't attract older gamers if you're creating a PC-only strategy game. Think carefully about the kind of music that will appeal to your audience. If certain territories are particularly important, why not try and license at least one local track for them? Fortunately, most countries are used to English-language songs, but if the lyrics are important to the game, you'll need to localize them too, or at least provide subtitles. Localizing games is a real art, and too many games treat localization as an unnecessary evil. When it is done well, it can greatly increase sales. Leaving music to one side for a second, a great example of localization was when Codemasters launched a cricket game in the late 1990s. They kept the same game, but changed the name from *Brian Lara Cricket* in Europe to *Shane Warne Cricket* in Australia (Shane Warne was a famous and talented Australian cricket player). With this small change to the code (and his face on the box), Codemasters were able to retain the number 1 spot in Australia over many huge rival products. So think carefully about localization, and if you only use local American, British, or European bands, bear in mind that they may not work in other territories.

Using Original Music

Let's consider original music. You'll need to find a composer to write the score for you. Assuming you have decided the style of music you want to use, there are hundreds of very talented musicians available for you to choose from. The best idea is to get some recommendations, contact a few, and get them to send samples of their work in.

To get the best out of a composer, you'll need to give them as much information as possible. This can vary depending on how musical you are, and how much depth you want to get into. It might be as simple as "I want four ghostly atmospheric tracks that are similar to this piece of music" (and give them a CD that you've found with a great example on it). Or it may be as complex as breaking your storyline down into individual elements, and getting a complete score written to coincide with the individual highs and lows in your storyline.

We'll talk about dynamic music a little later, but you need to decide at this stage whether you're happy with a fixed number of tracks, or whether you want dynamic music written for your game. The word "dynamic" simply means that the music is going to change quickly depending on what is happening in the game.

Ask the composer to send you rough cuts of the tracks as soon as they are written, so you can give feedback and direction straight away. And if you don't feel that you are musically qualified to give feedback, get other team members to sit in and listen to the music with you, and summarize their feedback.

Let's take a quick look at the most common types of original music that you might want to use in your game:

Use a Band to Create Original Music

One of the more creative approaches is to talk to a band that has the right kind of musical style, and ask them to create original music for your game. If you get along with the band, and can show them the game and explain the kind of thing you want, it's possible to get some very well tailored tracks. Writing brilliant tracks isn't a simple process, and if you want a superb piece of original music, they may need to work on a few different tracks until you get what you are after. I used this approach with a rally driving game that I worked on called *Richard Burns Rally*, where we got Paul Oakenfold (before E.A snapped him up exclusively) to write an original track for us. We were actually very pleased with the result, but it did take a few small revisions until the track was right.

Pros: The biggest advantage of this approach is that you're getting something fresh and new; who knows, it could even end up being used on their next album. Having a well-known musician or band compose your music could also create extra interest in your game. You might find that you are able to reach new markets, and they help get your game talked about in the non-specialist press (i.e. non-gaming mags such as *Loaded!*)

Cons: The biggest disadvantage is that the band could easily create something that just isn't as good as the amazing single that attracted you to them in the first place. They might not be as talented at writing music that will work for a game as you might think.

12

Use a Solo Composer to Create Original Music

Many games take this approach, as it is normally the easiest. There are a large number of very talented composers and song writers who specialize in creating music for interactive games. Many of these writers have worked on literally hundreds of titles, and have a huge amount of experience. The normal way of working is to provide a brief (ideally along with some examples of similar music), and then to listen to the resulting tracks in draft and then final form.

Pros: The biggest advantage of using a solo composer is that he will have done game music many times before. You are very likely to get good music on time that fits the purpose you want. The composer will also be able to give you a realistic time and cost estimate because they know what it takes to get the job done.

Cons: If you're looking for something unusual and unique, it is less likely that you'll get it from this approach, unless you sit down with the composer and deliberately request him to try off-the-wall ideas. Composers that work this way are basically "work for hire" and they are likely to have only so many ideas. They basically make their money by cranking out work and thus they may not put in a lot of "creative time."

Use an Orchestra

Working with orchestras can allow you to produce some fantastic and high quality musical scores that sound extremely professional. It is possible to get extremely realistic results without an orchestra using some of the latest orchestral sample CDs, but you'll never get the feel of a live orchestra; having a room full of extremely talented musicians gives something extra that is very hard to replicate otherwise. Your musician will probably need to employ a professional orchestrator to translate the music into the right format for the various instruments. The most important rule of using an orchestra is to make sure you're totally happy with all the music before the session. If you decide later that some of it doesn't quite work, or you need some extra stuff record, it will get very expensive very quickly.

Pros: You should get a fantastic professional result which will sound like a major feature film if done properly.

Cons: It will be expensive, and orchestral music might not fit the game you're working on. Using an orchestra will also take a lot more time and could delay your game if you are on a tight schedule.

Creative Idea: Use Musical Themes

One thing that movies do very well is to use musical themes for major characters. When the main villain comes on screen, a particular sinister piece of music is played, and this section of music is replayed again when the villain reappears each time. The viewer subconsciously associates the piece of music with the villain. The director can use this approach to their advantage later on. For example, they could play the villain's theme quietly behind an otherwise happy scene to add a huge element of tension, as the viewer knows that something bad is likely to happen. If you have a character-based game, think about using themes, and discuss these themes with your musician.

Using Ambient Music or No Music

It is not necessary to use music at all within a game. I've seen several examples of games that don't use music. If you decide to go down this route, you have to make sure the sound effects you use are really top-notch. One alternative approach is to use ambient music to provide a "soundscape" for your game. These fall short of being proper musical tracks, but may have musical elements; maybe just some quiet strings or a choir. The subtle approach can work extremely well. Some of the music in *Full Spectrum Warrior* by THQ demonstrates this approach.

War Story: Leave Out the Music

If you play the latest Conflict game, *Conflict: Global Terror* (as known as *Conflict: Global Storm* in Europe), listen to the in-game music. More appropriately, take notice of the lack of it. By dropping the in-game music from this version, the gameplay has become a little more immersive, since you can now properly hear the great audio effects, shouts, and enemy sounds. The fact that no journalist picked up on the music being removed was also very interesting, and I think that shows the decision to take it out was the correct one. So don't feel you have to have music in your game. You should only use it where it is genuinely going to improve things. Also, remember that you can use powerful music occasionally for key moments, and then have either no music, or just a quiet ambient soundscape playing for the rest of the time.

12

Pros: Having very little music in your game allows the player to focus on the audio effects. If you're creating a stealth game where it's important to listen for enemies making noises, music can be a big distraction. Ambient music can set the scene perfectly, while remaining in the background.

Cons: Music can help build emotion, make storylines more powerful and add real pace and excitement to game levels. By not having any real music in your game, you're missing out on a great way of adding polish.

Using Licensed Music

Another popular type of music that you can have in your game licensed music from bands or individual artists. This is often used in sports and driving games, or in free-roaming games with vehicles, to simulate in-car radios or CD players.

Working with Record Companies

If you want to use licensed music from established pop stars or bands, you may want to contact a record company directly. You'll normally get a better deal if you use one or two companies for all your music; picking and mixing individual tracks from a number of different companies can turn out to be quite expensive. Try and give the record company as detailed a brief as possible; some are happy to search around and recommend artists in a particular style, whereas others will only respond to specific requests.

Working with New Stars (The E.A. Approach)

By buying a record label, E.A has been able to go direct with certain artists like the Black Eyed Peas. However, they also try hard to identify artists of the future, to listen to up and coming bands and to link them into new games so that new bands are "breaking" at the same time that they are featured in a game. E.A's approach is also a useful reminder that by featuring a new band in your multi-million-copy selling game, you can actually be giving them a large amount of publicity to exactly the right audience, particularly if their name appears in the game somewhere.

 Reality Check: Don't assume that you should be paying bands lots of money to appear in your game, when there is a real case for them paying to be featured in games. This is especially true for big sequels, where a band will know they will be getting lots of exposure.

Using Musical Licensing Companies

One other approach to licensing music tracks is to use a musical agency. Companies (like Couchlife in Europe) provide a service where they will take your brief and put together a range of tracks for you to listen to. They normally take a set budget, and will get you tracks that fit within that budget (obviously taking a small percentage themselves for this service). If you don't have the time or the contacts to go direct to record companies, this kind of service can be very useful and time-saving.

Designing Sound Effects

In the early days of video games, sound effects used to come from one of two different sources: either creating all the effects in-house with various items and a microphone, or by using a sound effects library on vinyl or tape. Stock sound effects libraries still have their place, but if you're serious about quality (which you should be), you won't want to have the same car engine or machine gun sound as other games.

Creating your own sounds (providing you have some decent recording equipment and someone who understands sound) is still a route that is worth considering for a few key sound effects; it's one way to guarantee a unique sound that no one else will have. I've been involved with several projects where this has been done well; from recording a variety of weapons at a gun range to dropping a melon down a five-story stairwell and recording the splat (but be prepared for a major clean-up job afterwards!).

Unfortunately, it's easy to get sound recording wrong, and most companies now use professional audio studios to create sound effects for their games. The real professionals still like to create sounds from scratch wherever possible, but they will also have vast databases of sounds that you can draw from. I've been fortunate enough to work closely with Air Studios in London, who provide an excellent example of this quality approach. Air Studios is responsible for much of the audio and musical recording for some of the biggest films around (including the recent Bond films and *Gladiator*). They have an excellent track record with regard to sound effects, and they are passionate about creating surround sound effects which are unique and extremely realistic. They have a props room which is full of objects that can be trodden on, hit, smashed, and scratched, and it is great to see people taking the time and trouble to create new sounds, rather than relying on reusing existing samples.

One sound effect that you need to think about carefully is what I call the background sound layer. This is the ambient sound that plays in the background, which you'll hear all the time in a particular game location. Not all games have this, but it helps avoid silence, and I feel that an ambient sound loop is important. It is often a long, looping sound effect. Done well, it can add a great sense of realism to your game; the *Medal of Honour* titles are an excellent example, with their background loops including distant speech and alarms to keep you on your toes. But remember that this loop will have to work behind everything that the player can do in the game. Sometimes the background sound layer is almost a halfway house between sound effects and music, with musical undertones helping to create an atmosphere. And many games won't use a background sound layer, but will just have music playing throughout the gameplay, especially if the game provides an "arcade" kind of experience where reality isn't important.

Using Variety

I'd like to touch on the importance of variety when you're creating sound effects. It's very easy to do the minimum amount of work required, particularly when you're working with a tight audio budget. But if you want to create a game that's going to score 10/10 with respect to audio, you need to make sure you've got more than enough variety in the audio. Variety is important in almost every aspect of audio, but sound effects are especially important. Let's look at an example such as footsteps. The most basic implementation would be one footstep sound that plays whenever a character's foot touches the ground. Many games do this! They'll simply play the same sound effect a little quieter if the player is walking, and louder if he's running. A much richer implementation which enhances the realism and immersion effect would be to have different footsteps for each surface type, and different footstep sounds depending on whether the character is walking or running. Another level up would be to have individual footstep sounds for some of the characters. For example, you might have a footstep sound for an old man who has a limp, or the main villain in your game who has a unique footstep. By giving the main villain slightly different-sounding footsteps, you add a whole new level of terror to the gameplay, as the player will be able to hear the villain approaching, and know that it's him.

Reality Check: Try to use variety across all your sounds effects wherever possible. And if you can only have a certain number of sounds per level, use different sounds for different levels to give each level a unique audio feel.

Tips on Sounds for Cars

Getting car sounds right is a unique and tricky skill. Really good car engine sounds are a dynamic combination of many different channels of sound, all playing at the same time. You've got the cylinders in the engine, the noises created by the car body moving around on the suspension, the boom of the car exhaust, the sound of the clutch being engaged, and the noise of the wind outside the car adding to this cacophony. Add in the sound of the brakes and the tires running over the current road surface, and you've got quite a lot going on. If the player switches from an internal to an external camera, the sound should change accordingly; you'll know from experience that the noise of a car engine sounds quite different inside the car to outside. You can also use sounds to improve gameplay as I mentioned before, by adding audio feedback if the tires start to lose friction or the brakes lock. By doing this, you give the player a much better idea of what is going on, and more chance to skillfully control the situation. A good example here is the *TOCA/Pro Race Driver* series (which has a particular place in my heart, since I started my career as a programmer working on the first TOCA game!). They have a huge number of different vehicles in the game, and each sounds unique. They blend a whole load of different sounds together, and if you damage your car, you can actually hear parts of your car start to go wrong. Another great example is *Richard Burns Rally*, a game so realistic that if you drive up a hill, the altitude (and slight reduction in oxygen) will affect how the engine sounds. A nice feature in this game is when the car idles.

Most games have a constant engine sound when a car is idling, but if you listen to a car in real life, you'll notice that the pitch of the engine goes up and down slightly due to natural variation. Since the car engine in *Richard Burns Rally* is modeled so accurately, this effect came for free.

Tips on Sounds for Cities

Take a walk through the nearest busy city and listen. Take a recorder with you, and record the sounds as you walk around. Cities are full of all kinds of noise; some close and some far away. In my view, every game set in a city should have some really varied ambient sounds constantly playing in the background (depending on where you are within the city). Road noise, car horns, people shouting in the distance, occasional ambulances or fire engines going past; all these sounds will make your city come alive, and feel like there is more going on than just what the player can see. Why not put in some special one-off sounds as a treat to the player. So for example, have a sound of a couple arguing coming from a first-story window. The player will not be able to get in there, and it's nothing to do with the main story, but it will help bring the place alive. As the player walks past the window, it'll help him feel like the city is living and breathing.

Tips on Sounds for Jungles/Forests

If you have a jungle or forest handy, again, why not take a walk through it, recording what you hear. I'm not suggesting that you should use the recording you make in your game; just that it will provide a great reference source for you. Jungle and forest can be claustrophobic and it's easy to get lost in them, which makes it relatively easy for you to make them quite a scary experience. Wildlife (especially birds) and trees moving and swaying form the key part of your ambient sound. But don't forget the importance of sound for building tension. Unknown animal cries in the distance, or the sudden snap of a twig and branch behind the player, can be very unnerving.

Tips on Sounds for Battlefields

On a battlefield, your key audio challenge is often to give the impression that you're one soldier in the middle of a massive battle. Ambient sounds playing in the background (sounds that aren't emitted by a particular unit or person, but are just playing generally) can make a real difference. Use the noise of artillery firing in the distance or gun shots echoing from above a hill. Bombard the player with all sorts of sounds when you want to simulate a full-scale assault. Make sure you include a specific sound for a bullet that whizzes past the players' ears. This can be a great gameplay device that tells the player "someone nearly killed me," and can be used to encourage him to find cover. Sometimes games can be very harsh—one headshot from a distant sniper and you're dead. Having a few bullets narrowly miss you is a great way of preparing the player, and giving him the chance to take evasive action.

12

Working with Voices

You can have the best music and sound effects in the world, but if you have poor quality voice actors, it can drag your game right down. Bad voices are very obvious, whereas great voice acting often goes unnoticed. Let's take a look at some of the things to keep an eye on when recording voices.

Voice Recording

Most games require voiceover artists to speak the lines of your main characters. Many a great game has been ruined by casting really bad voiceover talent, so it pays to be very careful and exact about the kind of people that you hire. You'll need to be as specific as possible with your descriptions of the characters, and the kind of voices you are looking for, and don't be afraid to say if something isn't right. Generally, the process is very similar to that of casting voice actors for animated films; you're looking for someone who fits the character perfectly, and ideally, if you can afford a well known actor, then that will really help your PR team promote the game.

War Story: Use the Right Accents

I've noticed that most children's TV shows and cartoons in the U.S. are actually dubbed with new English accents for the UK. It might be worth considering recording both US and UK voices if your game is aimed at young kids, as parents on both sides of the Atlantic are happier with their kids learning to speak their own version of the language!

The Voice Recording Process

The first thing that you need to do is to ensure you've got a clear and fully complete game storyline. Once you have the storyline in place, you can get the dialogue written, which will normally consist of both in-game and cut-scene dialogue. Hopefully you will use a professional writer. Unless you have written scripts and dialogue professionally and are very confident in your ability, it is much better to use an expert. Go over the dialogue carefully, and make sure it all fits, and that you're not going to change it.

Once the dialogue is complete, go through your game in detail and work out if there are any other miscellaneous voices that you're going to need. For example, you might need voices for public address system announcers, people talking in the street, and so on. Once you have done this, make a list of every different character in your game, and approach a voice recording specialist to arrange for your characters to be cast. In my experience, what tends to happen is that you'll get maybe three or four voice actors recommended for each major part, and the specialist will provide you with samples of their work. If possible, try and get them to record a few test lines of the actual in-game dialogue, so you can judge them with the actual material. If your game doesn't have a big audio budget, you may not be able to do this. Try and fight the urge to recommend your friends and colleagues in the roles. Professional voiceover artists are extremely good, and very adept at doing different voices/accents, as well as "acting" with their voices. They know how to put just the right level of emotion into their performance. It is extremely unlikely that your friends (unless they are all actors) will be anywhere near this standard when they're being recorded on their own in a cold recording studio booth with several engineers staring at them through the window!

Listen to the samples, and rule out any actors you feel are not right. Then get some other people to listen to the remainder, after explaining each character and their role in the game, and get their opinions. Then decide who you want to use, and book the session.

The Session

Although it is possible to do pickups later on, in reality, you only really get one good shot at doing a recording session, unless you're willing to waste money and risk the wrath of the guys paying you. So make absolutely sure that you're not recording the voices too early. If it is likely that your levels will be changed, and the final storyline might be altered, you really should wait until later on. Having said that, many games that require early playable demos are forced to do two sessions: one for the early demo (since placeholder voices aren't good enough), and another later on when the dialogue and levels are totally locked down.

Prepare carefully, making sure you have a clear script for every piece of dialogue you want, with the character's names next to every line. Where possible, provide some guide to the characters and their personalities that the voice talent can read. Try and bring in some video footage of the characters in-game so that your actors can see the people they're voicing. But when the recording starts, try and leave things to the experts.

Reality Check: You should say when you don't think a line works, but you also need to remember that the producer, engineer, and voice artist do this every day, and the last thing they need is being asked to redo every line three times. Even worse is when a game designer tries to tell the voice actor how they should say a line. You might get away with doing this a few times, but if you start telling the actors how to act, you're going to have an uncomfortable day.

Localization and Voices

You need to think carefully about how your game voices will work in different territories. I'm not just talking about countries that don't speak English, but also the differences between the U.S. and the U.K.. I work in the U.K., and we always try and get an American to listen to our voices before we start recording as a sanity check. In fact, we have often recorded voiceovers in the United States even though the development team is based in the UK if the characters demanded it. If your characters are supposed to be American, there really isn't anywhere else you should be looking. But there are cultural differences, and what can sound quite funny in one country often doesn't work at all in other countries. Think about the writing style as well; lots of cultural jokes simply won't work in other countries even when they are translated. A great example of this is the television show *The Office*. Take a look at the original UK version and then the US version. It's fascinating to see the differences, and observe how much the sexual undercurrent has been toned down for an American audience.

War Story: Use the Right Accents, Take Two

I worked on a game where one of the key voices for some important marketing material was chosen by one person. Unfortunately, that person wasn't a natural English-speaker, and the accent he selected (which sounded fine to him) was really quite bad. So, if English (or Anglo-American) isn't your primary language, always get someone else to double check the casting of voice actors.

Try and keep the quality levels up if you're recording foreign voice talent as well – although you personally might not care as much about the German voices—the gamers in Germany certainly will, and you owe it to them to make sure that you use professionals who will do the job well. You also need to decide whether to use subtitles, or to localize everything. Some European countries are used to seeing films and games with subtitles, and you can save quite a bit of money by doing this. However, it's rarely the best option.

Using Variety

In a similar way to sound effects, you need to think carefully about the amount of variety that you use with the voices. With voice artists, it is about striking the perfect balance between varied voices (so that it is easy to tell the characters apart) without making them so diverse that they don't jel. A good example of this for me is Microsoft's otherwise excellent game *Fable*, which had an enormous number of different accents and voice types to try and differentiate all the villagers that you meet. Unfortunately for me, they took this slightly too far, and I know a couple of people who found the voice acting annoying because of this. Having said that, variety is extremely important in another way—in can help avoid repetition. Take a squad based game or an RTS where you order people to go to a certain place. The player is going to do this action an awful lot during the game, yet I have seen games that just have one voice sample in response; something like,—"Yes, sir!" After about ten minutes, this becomes annoying, and after ten hours; well, it could easily be frustrating enough to drive a player to take the game back to the shop. As a designer, you need to take note of the voice samples that are likely to be repeated again and again, and make sure that you capture a large variety of them which can be chosen from randomly. So instead of just repeating "Yes, sir!" every time you place an order, use variations such as "On my way," "Affirmative," and "Okay." You should be able to come up with 20 different variations; even if they are just the same phrase recorded again with slightly different pacing and emphasis.

Audio Technology

Understanding the basics of audio technology and how in-game audio works can be a really useful skill for a game designer. You don't need to be an expert, but a basic knowledge can help you understand the limitations that your sound engineer/musician has, and can assist you in raising the audio bar in your next title.

Analyzing Audio in Games

It's worth getting a few top titles, sitting down with them in a room with a proper surround sound setup, and just listening to how they use audio. Listen to how they take advantage of surround sound. Take note of which sounds are used, where and when they use music, and immerse yourself in the audio environment that the games create. It's one of the best ways to learn what works well, and what doesn't.

Dolby 5.1

Supporting Dolby surround sound in your game is becoming more and more important, and with the next-generation platforms, surround sound support is a standard which you'll need to meet. Creating surround sound is actually easier in many ways for games than for any other media, since our games already contain all the 3D information necessary. So it's not much of a design issue, although you should think about placement of enemies and sound sources to best scare or shock the player. A sudden whispering voice from behind the player can have an amazing effect! You may want to consider supporting 5.1 mixes of your music as well, although most games so far only use the surround speakers for sound effects.

12

Sound Filters and Effects

It's possible to use some quite advanced effects in relation to sound. Having walls and objects that muffle sound can make an environment feel much more realistic. If music is playing in the distance and you close the door, it really does sound excellent when the closed door muffles and changes the tone of the sound. Also, proper reverb (echo) is very useful, and can make a large tiled bathroom or empty building sound perfectly accurate. You should speak to your sound programmer, and see what effects and filters are available to you. Then think whether you can use these in the game to good effect. For example, you might consider having a room where the reverb level gradually increases as something scary happens which could sound highly unusual and very cool. You should think about filters and effects regardless of what kind of game you are making. They are just as applicable in racing and sports games as they are in a stealth-based action game.

Stereo

Although it's important to think about surround sound, it's equally important to consider how the game plays in stereo. Proper use of the left and right speakers can really add to the game, so make sure that your sound programmer uses them properly. For example, if you're making a squad game, and you have an AI character on each side of you, make sure that the stereo separation works well, so you hear each character distinctly. You might also consider using the stereo effect for special sequences in your game—for example, having noises move from left to right to create a disturbing feeling.

Adjusting the Various Levels

There is one thing you must remember to schedule in with regard to audio, and that is proper level balancing. Too many games don't do this properly, and you end up having a loud intro sequence followed by quiet front-end music, a medium volume level FMV and then really quiet in-game sound with very loud character dialogue. It's important to check that all the different types of audio in your game are well balanced, so that players don't need to constantly adjust the volume of their TV. Check this with all the different setups: a stereo TV, a mono TV, headphones and a full Dolby Digital 5.1 setup.

Summary

Hopefully, this chapter has helped you realize just how vital in-game audio is. It's important that you appreciate that audio is not just something to be layered on to improve your production levels; it's something that can genuinely improve your gameplay. Sound effects and music can make a real difference to the gaming experience; they can help the player realize and react to what is going on more quickly, and they can deliver tension, fear and excitement. Getting the audio right can be the element which makes the difference between a good game and a great game. So spend some time listening to other games, and make sure your next title is even better!

An Interview with Chris Nuttall

Chris Nuttall is in charge of game audio at Air Studios in London. Not only does Air Studios create video game audio, but they are also a key player in the film and music industries, with film credits such as *Gladiator* and most of the James Bond films, plus key albums for artists such as Coldplay and George Michael.

Chris has worked on the audio of many major games including Harry Potter and *The Italian Job*, and is uniquely positioned to comment on the challenges of audio design.

How strong a knowledge of audio do you think a game designer should have? Do you prefer working with designers who leave all the audio to you, or with designers who have created the gameplay with audio in mind from day one?

CN: Finding out the game designer's mission statement about how the sound is going to work within the game and its uses is always the best starting point from the audio team's point of view. How is the audio to be used, is it there to heighten drama, keep the pace and tempo of the action moving, what parts of the design can be enhanced by the soundtrack, what parts are needed to provide gameplay guidance?

From this it is an advantage if the designer knows the fundamentals of what can be achieved in a game with the various middleware and bespoke tools available to the project, and this can then be further developed into the audio design document.

The more a designer can express their vision for the game and has access to the in-progress work throughout the project with the audio team, then so much the better, although as with any medium, it may not be the designer who has the final sign-off of the audio assets, so a good agreed design and good communication amongst the team are essential.

Do you feel that musicians and audio engineers should be involved earlier in the design process than typically happens at the moment?

CN: Just as a technical artist should be attached to the design process, so should the equivalent for the global audio of the game. This should be a dedicated audio producer and/or lead sound designer contributing towards the completion of the design document, who then continues during pre-production to bring the design elements of the game onto a working level with the technical aspects of each platform, along with planning abilities for team size, workflow schedules, artist relations, and outsourced materials as appropriate for each stage.

As with every other development department, good, early planning and constructive involvement is paramount.

12

Quite often it seems that game designers and audio engineers/musicians work fairly separately. Have you got any views on this, and whether it's a bad thing or not?

CN: Communication is the most important factor throughout any project. Firstly, to put in place the assets and skills that the audio design requires, and secondly, the creation of the material along with implementation. There will always be periods of time where there will be separated working groups, but with clear planning from the start, there's no reason why this should alter the quality of the work provided.

What are you most proud of in your career so far?

CN: The times where the audio has done its job and worked to create a moment of experience without consciously making the player have to listen to the sounds, but just react naturally as if immersed within the playing environment.

With the increasingly widespread use of Dolby surround sound in video games, do you feel people are using this facility properly?

CN: The games & teams that have used surround sound should ALL be applauded; it's a natural partner in complementing the visual side to bring the players into the game, and with all platforms supporting some form of surround audio, it should be now considered the norm for games.

Having said that, from a creative standpoint, I don't think we have heard the last of 3D audio, stereo and mono moments being used in conjunction with each other as perspective elements and points of view within the gameplay vehicle.

The multi-speaker arrangement should be seen as the canvas on which the audio sits, the content and how it is used is the creative element to the soundtrack.

Do you feel that in-game audio has reached a pinnacle, or are there still major advances to be made in the future?

CN: As the technology of each platform moves forward, with greater amounts RAM, number of audio voices, and streaming techniques, along with the use of real-time effects and modeling, the creative team will always find new ways and methods of utilizing these techniques, along with developing new tools for the creation and manipulation of the assets.

Complementary skill sets from other related industries will be amalgamated where appropriate, brought in by open dialogue and personnel changes and outsourced work, but better technology doesn't equally make better sounding content. It is the creative talent involved that will be the main driving force in pushing for any further advances.

What do you think is the biggest game design mistake that people regularly make with games?

CN: Most games are designed for a number of purposes, bringing a great game design idea to fruition, to bring a new IP into market, to be released and complement other products or media events, to reach certain demographics for branding requirements, and for these and many more reasons, it has to answer the dreaded double question that can sometimes get lost during production: What's it about and why would anyone want to play it?

And the killer question: Yes, it's a good idea, and yes, it's a great design but is that any reason to actually make it?

If you can't answer these then there's a mistake.

If money and technology were unlimited, what kind of game would you most like to see made?

CN: Episodic content where various elements of the plot are experienced via the most appropriate delivery platform, cinema and television for linear, game platforms for non–linear story–play and mobile devices where appropriate would be interesting if the quality, depth of plot and continuity was a seamless experience within the story.

My personal answer in terms of genre would have to be a good old–fashioned horror game where the player is left feeling that they have enjoyed an experience that only the non–linear platform can provide.

What do you think is the biggest challenge facing game designers as we move forward?

CN: All industries continually change simultaneously in a number of directions, and the working models and practices will change accordingly. Along with changes of team sizes, the new producers (internal, external, third party and associate), project (artistic) directors, area specialists (script writers), marketing teams, representatives of the financiers, IP owners, and the other related media partners, it is important to remember that they are all there for very good reasons.

At times, the games industry can seem like its own singular entity but is part of the global entertainment industry, and the importance of the new roles created will bring a changing influence to the balance of decision making. All of these people will always want to work with the best game designers and so maintaining their originality, creative and design skills, and (maybe) having to stick up for their role and importance in game creation is (maybe again!) going to be a challenge. Of course, that's if we're thinking that the role of the designer stays as it is and doesn't also evolve!

And finally, if you had one piece of advice to give to a game designer who was just starting out, what would it be?

CN: Find your natural balance between the creative and business sides of your work, learn from the other skill sets of the people you meet, bring every experience you have into your work, and above all, enjoy every moment of it, because this is what you've always wanted to do.

12

PART IV

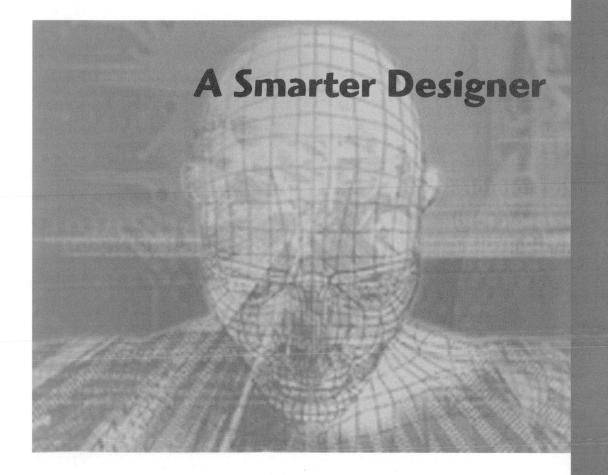

A Smarter Designer

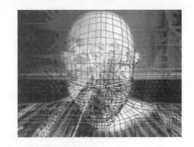

Chapter 13

Market Research and Focus Groups

"Research is the process of going up alleys to see if they are blind."

Marston Bates

I used to be very suspicious of market research and focus groups. After all, *I* was the game designer, so what good were the opinions of people who had never designed a game in their entire lives? To defend myself slightly, I think my suspicions were due in part to having seen market research used in highly dubious ways to try to justify indefensible decisions. But over the years, I've come to realize that market research and focus groups can become important tools for game designers when used wisely.

In this chapter, I'll start by relating to you a couple of stories that I found extremely eye-opening concerning market research. Then we'll look at the various techniques that game designers and developers use to conduct market research. In the last part of the chapter, I'll switch gears a little as we look at focus groups.

The Value of Market Research

Like any kind of information, market research can be easily distorted. The problem is that those doing the research can show you just one side of the picture. But this doesn't make research a waste of time. In fact, it can be one of the most useful weapons in your game design armory. If you do your research well, it will give you the confidence to try out new ideas and run with the ideas that you really believe in because you've tested them out. Your research will also help you uncover new ideas that you might be overlooking.

Sesame Street

I imagine that pretty much every reader will be familiar to some extent with the kid's TV show *Sesame Street*, which has been broadcast worldwide since the Children's Television Workshop was founded in 1968. The show was created to address a very real problem—the underachievement of preschool children from poor areas, particularly within ethnic minorities. The entire foundation of the show was based around research, using educational psychologists and sociologists. They would test elements of each episode over and over again using groups of at least 30 children to identity when the children got bored, the best number of times to repeat items, and how to keep the kids' attention. When an episode was broadcast, the producers would measure the reactions to that episode, and if a particular segment didn't work and children wandered off to do something else, they wanted to know why. Children were observed as they watched to see how they reacted, then interviewed and tested to see what they learned. Parents were interviewed to get at feelings or reactions the kids may not have been able to articulate. The entire process was very detailed.

But did it work? Well, I think the success of the show (broadcast in 120 countries and having won more Emmy awards than any other) is a testament to their approach. Not everything can rely on the sheer amount of research done to formulate this show, but it seems clear that preschool children are learning lots from it, and yet it keeps their attention day after day, unlike most other educational shows. Without research, *Sesame Street* simply would not have been possible.

Moneyball

There is a fascinating book titled *Moneyball: The Art of Winning an Unfair Game,* which a clever gentleman from Electronic Arts told me about. The author, Michael Lewis, tells the true story of a baseball coach named Billy Beane. His team, the Oakland A's, was short of money and talent and was heading nowhere. Billy had the genius to try something no one else had thought of. He spent months looking at very detailed statistical analysis of baseball matches and came upon some surprising results. Traditional theory was blown out of the water as Billy went after players that other teams would have left on the sidelines. For example, he specifically targeted a left-handed receiver, looked for batters with a high "on-base percentage," and looked for pitchers who were good at getting lots of "groundouts" (apologies if you don't understand baseball terminology, but you'll see my point in a second). By spending no more money than normal, Billy was able to assemble a team that was totally contrary to what would be assembled with normal thinking. The fans and other managers laughed at him. And the result? The team consistently exceeded expectations. They didn't win the World

Series (why do they call it a "world series" when it's just American teams?), but they came very close, and the point had still been proven.

Reality Check: Do some research, analyze the information you have, and you can come up with some revolutionary new directions and ideas.

Useful and Useless Research

Of course, research is useful only if it is factual and relevant. A simple example would be to pick 30 people at random off the street and ask them what kind of video game they think it would be cool to make. At first glance, it seems like a sensible idea. Although the sample size is very small, a survey like that should help you get a feel for what the public wants and hopefully generate some ideas that are likely to sell.

So as an experiment, I've just done exactly that. I took my pen and a clipboard yesterday and asked the question to 30 random people walking in Clapham Junction in London. The most interesting answers I got were as follows:

- *Star Trek*

- *The Sims* but with kittens

- *The Simpsons* because there has never been a decent Simpsons game

- A game about fighting fires

The most popular answer was *Match of the Day* (a British weekly soccer TV show), which was mentioned by two men.

Now picture the scene: I've produced a summary of my research, and you're in charge of deciding what game to spend $10 million developing next. Two people mentioned *Match of the Day*, so that's twice as popular with the public as *The Simpsons* or *Sim Kittens*. Fantastic. So you spend a sum of money buying the *Match of the Day* license and then spend $10 million creating a soccer game. The game is launched, and it flops. Not only does it flop in every country outside the U.K., but sales within the U.K. aren't great, either. What went wrong?

What the research summary doesn't indicate is that, in actual fact, one person overheard the other saying *Match of the Day* and then said the same thing because they didn't know what to else to say. My research was flawed in that one person influenced another, but this fact didn't get put into the summary. Although this is a very small example, it's very easy for a flaw in the research process to greatly alter the answers you get. For example, questions can be easily tailored to get more yes or no responses (we'll talk about this later). By picking people in London, I'm certainly not getting a good feel for the variety of views across the U.K., let alone Europe or the U.S. By standing close to a railway station, I've ended up talking to lots of commuters, who tend to be middle-aged. So already, my "random" selection of 30 people has ended up consisting of 16 middle-aged commuters who have just left the nearby station. I asked a couple of other questions as well to help give an insight into how inaccurate my research was. It turns out that 19 of the 30 people don't buy video games. So although they came up with some interesting answers, none of them buy any games, so they're not the people I should be asking (unless I'm trying to create a game to appeal to non-gammers)! Only 11 of the 30 people bought games at all, and only 6 described themselves as regular gamers. Both people who answered with *Match of the Day* were not gamers, and were middle-aged. It may turn out that people in the more relevant 16-to-28 age group don't like *Match of the Day* or are such big fans of *FIFA* or *ISS* that they wouldn't touch another soccer game regardless of the license.

 Reality Check: Here's the lesson learned from this exercise that got me out of the office for a few hours: We need to carefully analyze who is being asked questions and what they are being asked. Market research can be extremely useful, but if it's not done properly or if it's misunderstood, it can be downright dangerous.

Focusing on Useful Research: Market Research vs. Focus Groups

Now that you know how *not* to do market research, I want to spend the rest of the chapter discussing how market research should be done to get good results from it. But first, let's start by looking at the difference between market research and focus groups.

Focus groups are sessions in which a small number of people come into a room and are given a presentation, maybe shown a game or some images, and then asked a number of questions, either individually or as a group. A number of these small sessions will be held; each one could typically be as small as 5 people or as large as 25 people. Focus groups allow you to get feedback from small groups of people on specific issues and to ask them in-depth questions to help understand why they feel the way they do. They are sometimes set up to contain the right demographic mix of people, and sometimes they are simply groups of close friends who are interviewed in their own homes. With groups of friends, you get much more openness (as they are comfortable talking in front of each other), but since they all share similar interests and are normally the same demographic, you hit a much narrower section of the market.

Market research involves a much larger number of people who are asked questions individually, normally on the phone, by e-mail, by post, or in the street. Market research normally canvases the opinion of upwards of 100 people and is better suited for asking more general questions and gauging the general views of the wider public on certain issues. We'll spend time looking at each of these activities in detail and you'll learn how they can be useful to a game designer. We're going to start by looking at market research.

Doing Good Market Research

Market research can be an extremely useful tool to help you make key design decisions, particularly at an early stage in your design process.

The only reason you wouldn't need market research would be if you're perfect (you know everything and understand everyone in the world) or if you're designing the game for yourself (you are the target audience).

Reality Check: Designing a game for yourself is one of the most common reasons for poor-selling games. Many designers are guilty of creating a game that they'd love to play. When the game is finished, they understandably think it's brilliant. And then hardly anyone buys it.

Ask yourself whether you are a typical game buyer. Being in the game industry, you're probably quite a hardcore gamer who plays a large number of games. This immediately stops you from being a representative of the average console gamer. You're quite possibly older than the core audience you're aiming at. You certainly only live in one country, whereas you'll want to appeal to people across the globe. If you had a perfect knowledge of what an average gamer wants in every key territory, you might stand a chance of designing a game for them without any kind of research. But I know a lot of people in the industry, and none of them would profess to having that kind of knowledge.

Doing Your Own Market Research

There are two routes to producing market research: one involves hiring an outside professional company to handle it for you, and the other involves doing it yourself. I'd first like to show you how to conduct market research yourself. I'm not necessarily recommending this route, but if you don't have a large development budget, it may be the only way to get the information you need, and it can be done for virtually no cost. In many ways, it's fairly simple. You want to get the views of a hundred or more people—probably gamers who regularly buy games, unless your design is targeted at a different demographic. First of all, you'll need to decide if you want to target people from different territories, or whether you're happy just to focus on your country.

13

You then need to find 100 or more people. The four methods you can use to communicate with your selected group and do your research are e-mail, phone calls, standard mail, or just going out on the street. Your company may have put reply cards in previous games, in which case you may already have the contact details for lots of gamers. Compose a nice e-mail with a few clearly worded questions, and maybe offer to send a prize at random to one of the respondents (check this with your legal guys first because there are rules in various countries about offering prizes to the public). You might want to go onto online discussion/bulletin boards and find people, one by one, to assist you; this can be a very good way of finding people from overseas to help out. Or you may want to go into a shopping center, stand outside a video game store, and ask people to fill in a quick survey (maybe print 100 T-shirts to give away to encourage people to take part). However you do it, carefully analyze the type of people who have replied, and make sure there aren't any patterns that make the research less valid. Always get their age, sex, and favorite game platform as part of the information you collect so you can break the results down.

Using Professional Research Companies

By using a company that specializes in market research, you should be able to reach exactly the kind of people you want, in whichever countries you want. Also, you should get an excellent report back, one that breaks all the information down and hopefully highlights the most interesting results based on the considerable experience the company has in conducting research. That's the ideal scenario. As with any kind of outsourcing, some companies are superb (and you can build up a long-term relationship with them), whereas others are poor. If you use a professional research company, you can be sure you'll get the most accurate and unbiased results, providing you give them lots of clear information up front and understand what you want to find out.

Methods of Getting Market Research

Let's look at the various methods that are used to collect market research data. For most research projects, you'll likely use a combination of two or more of the methods. For each method presented, I'll point out some of the tips and techniques I've learned over the years for getting the best results.

E-Mail

Send clear, well-worded e-mails to people, ideally offering them the chance to win a prize or giving them a money-off voucher for answering your questions. The great thing about e-mails is that, providing you've got enough e-mail addresses, it's easy to reach large numbers of people and get a huge amount of research data. The important thing is to think about what format you use to send your questions. Don't assume that everyone has Microsoft Word on their PC. Keep the file size as small as possible or it might bounce from lots of e-mail inboxes.

Phone

Cold-calling people on the phone is a tough job, and you need to be prepared to get lots of harsh responses because most people don't like being phoned up for research out of the blue. People are much more likely to respond when a reward is involved. The great advantage of phone calls is that you can press the respondents for more information in particular areas, depending on what they say. So, for example, if you are creating a dinosaur game and someone says that they really hate dinosaurs, you can ask them why and get to the real reasons. In comparison, with e-mail or mail, you might just get an "I hate them" response with no further elaboration. One main downside is that it takes a long time, especially if you are cold-calling. You may get an answer from only 1 in 10 people, meaning that you'll need to call 1,000 numbers to get the 100 that you want!

On the Street

Stopping people on the street is also a tough job, and just as with cold-calling people, you need to be prepared for people who are unpleasant. It helps if you're a natural salesman, and having a beaming smile can make a huge difference. As with phone calls, the advantage is that you can press people for more information. However, it does take quite a long time; not quite as bad as cold-calling on the phone, but it will probably take you an entire day to get 100 people to answer your questionnaire! Also, you're likely to be fixed in one location, which means you won't get a very good spread of answers (unless of course you travel to various cities, asking questions in each city).

Mail

Using snail mail is another useful way of getting people to respond. I understand that you can get quite different response rates in different countries; some places get so much junk mail that it all goes in the trash however interesting and unique you make it. However, a clear and interesting letter accompanying the questionnaire, along with the chance of a prize or reward, can really help your response. Also, it's quite flattering to be asked for your thoughts about a video game idea. This is certainly very different than the usual credit card mail shots. As with e-mails, it's possible to get lots of research back with little effort, providing you have up-to date-mailing addresses and you've created an interesting package for people to read and respond to.

13

Deciding Which Questions to Ask

Market research is good for asking general questions about your game design and concept. The kind of questions I'd recommend that you ask involve the theme, your one-sentence elevator pitch, and the game name. You might also give a detailed description of a key game mechanic and see if your respondents find it interesting or not. As an example, let's take my rather dubious game design from Chapter 7, *Mole with a Mission*. What kind of questions would I ask? Well, you need to be careful not to ask too many questions or you will find that people get bored and might not get to the end of the questionnaire. You want to keep them interested and make sure they answer everything or the results won't be accurate. So I'd probably ask at least 12 questions, half of which are specifically designed to get information about them to help qualify the responses:

1. What is your age?

2. What is your sex?

3. What game platform (e.g., Xbox, PSP, PC) do you play on the most?

4. Do you buy games yourself, and if so, how often?

5. What are your favorite kinds of games?

6. What are the first thoughts that enter your mind when you hear the word *mole*?

7. How interested would you be in playing a game in which you are a mole?

8. In the game, you will be able to dig underneath objects and cause them to fall down and collapse with real physics. Does this make the game more appealing to you? What do you think of this idea?

9. The mole is very angry and is trying to get back at the humans who are endangering his family. He's a super-cool, pissed–off* mole with an attitude. Does this make the game sound better or worse that you'd imagined so far?

10. Given no limitations at all, what would you like your mole to be able to do in the game?

11. Do you think the mole should be male or female?

12. Do you think the game should look highly realistic or be unique and stylized?

    * Note that I wouldn't use the phrase "pissed-off" if my research group included children!

With more time, I'd probably add on another five questions, and if I was doing the research by e-mail, post, or on the street, I might show them a mock-up of the character (since he is so important in this concept) and get their views on the character design. Although it's not strictly game design related, I might also show them a mock-up of an advertisement or the game packaging to get across the kind of marketing angle that might be used.

Analyzing the Research

The most important part of the process by far is the actual analysis of the data and deciding what actions to carry out based on the analysis. Too much market research is analyzed and then promptly ignored. Also, many people like to read market research in a way that supports their own opinions. That's why it's a good idea to use an external company, one that will be able to analyze the results in a completely unbiased and independent manner. If the results to any question are unclear, consider doing more research to find out more. If any question has a pretty clear answer, you need to weigh that against other research you have and take action based on your findings. For example, in the "Mole" questionnaire I just presented, say that people are largely negative about the design until question 9, where I mention that the character is a super-cool, pissed-off mole with bags of attitude. At this point, people change their minds and think that they'd really like the game. So it's clear that the mole's personality should be a very important part of the gameplay. It may also make sense to make the product name reflect this, maybe even being as radical as calling the game "P***ed-Off Mole," which would immediately get the attitude across. Don't jump to conclusions based on inconclusive research, but don't ignore something that lots of people are saying. It's much better to try to address problems now than to find your game not selling once it's in the stores.

Also remember that questionnaires can be written to force certain answers. The so-called "halo effect" describes the phenomenon where respondents who give a favorable answer to one question let their positive opinion spill over into subsequent areas of a survey. For example, it's possible to run a number of clearly positive questions together (such as, "Do you wish you had more money?" or "Do you disagree with violence?") and then follow with a controversial question, hoping that the positive responses generated will encourage more people to say yes to the controversial question. And it does work, so make sure your questionnaires are generated by people whose interest is neutral and who have no advantage in getting biased results.

13

Getting the Most from Focus Groups

Focus groups work in a very different manner than market research. In general, they are not as accurate, because you normally work with a much smaller number of people. They are beneficial, however, because they allow you to dig a little deeper and perform research that you wouldn't be able to achieve with a questionnaire-type interview. Because focus groups are not as accurate as other types of market research, you do need to be careful about jumping to new conclusions when you use them. However, if you know that you have a problem area, or if you're concerned about a particular aspect of your game concept, they can be particularly useful.

Focus groups tend to consist of small groups of people who get together with a facilitator somewhere quiet and are talked through a concept, shown artwork, or allowed to play an early build of a game. Because the session might be from 30 minutes to 4 hours, you can spend a great deal of time with each person, asking them lots of questions both before and after you present them with information and hopefully understanding exactly why they feel the way they do. Where market research is a broad tool that gets a wide range of opinion but doesn't dig too deep, a focus group is a narrow tool that digs deep and gets to the bottom of the opinions of a small segment of people.

Holding Your Own Focus Group

Running focus groups by yourself is fairly easy to do. First, you need to decide what demographic group you want to talk with. You may choose to do a couple of focus group sessions, each one with a different age group. For each session, you need to find between 5 and 10 people who fit your target demographic; they might be friends, colleagues, friends of friends, or whoever. You also need to decide in advance exactly what you want to talk about and what the aim is. If possible, don't talk or present your own opinions, but listen without interfering. In fact, you may be able to hire a room with a one-way mirror, which allows you to closely watch and listen to the focus group without getting in the way and risking biased answers. Or you could film the sessions and watch them yourself later. Give the people present some kind of reward for taking part.

Using Professional Companies to Conduct Focus Groups

As with market research, getting a professional company involved can make a big difference in terms of the suitability of the people chosen to take part and, more important, the analysis of the session(s). It's very hard not to be slightly biased about the questions you're asking, regardless of how hard you try to be neutral. By getting independent people to judge the feedback, you can avoid affecting the results.

Types of Design Focus Group Sessions

There are a number of different types of sessions that you can use, whether it's asking different kinds of questions about the design or getting people to play the game at different stages during its development. Here are a few particularly useful things that a focus group can help you with.

General Concept

You can use a focus group to get detailed feedback on a particular game design concept that you have. If possible, do a short, clear presentation of the game design, using photos, artwork, and videos that you have created or that were taken from a variety of movies to provide an idea of the mood and style of the game you're proposing. Stop the focus group after you mention the title and the one sentence "hook," and get their opinions at that point. Then explain the game to your group and get their opinions after they've heard the full concept. Find out what grabs them, what they like, and what they dislike. You may find that what you thought was your hook might actually not be the most appealing element of the game.

Gameplay

It can be extremely useful to get feedback on gameplay issues from focus groups. Bring along a build of the game, ideally playable without the need for instructions or external input. Watch people play the game without interrupting them, and see what they find frustrating, where they get confused, what makes them laugh, and when they get excited. Break down the game afterward into various components (front end, controls, camera, main character, levels, and so on) and get detailed feedback from the focus group on each element. It's so easy to get too close to a game when you've been working on it for a long time, and you'll often find that people completely miss a key element or fail to understand the controls because they're not obvious enough or not explained well.

Difficulty Balancing

Balancing the difficulty levels in your game is a key part of the game design process, and it's often done between the traditional alpha and beta milestones, if not before. Focus groups are an excellent way to assist with this, provided you can get people to play the games for a decent length of time. If you are using standard difficulty levels, make sure that easy, normal, and hard (or whatever you call them) are indeed easy, normal and hard. If new players struggle with easy, you've got a problem. If experienced players breeze through hard, you've also got a problem. If you're using an adaptive difficulty system, try it with both poor and excellent players and make sure it reacts well.

13

In addition, within each difficulty level, you need to try to identify any frustration points. If you look at Figure 13.1, you'll see a typical game difficulty chart. You're trying to find the points at which the player finds the game too difficult and throws the controller down in annoyance. Obviously the game needs to provide a challenge, but if a

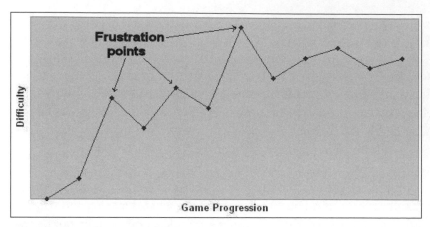

Figure 13.1
Difficulty curve showing frustration points.

section is simply too hard, people will not enjoy it and may take the game back to the store. Watch people playing through the game, and get them to write down any point that they find frustrating. By comparing the results of several people, you can quickly identify areas that need to be toned down a little.

You can do exactly the same thing with boredom points. These are literally the places in the game where the player gets bored and starts to lose interest. Again, get people to play through the various difficulty levels, and mark down any places where they got bored. By comparing the answers, you can see if any area needs to be trimmed or made more exciting. Great games are put through this kind of process several times to make them as perfect as possible.

Dangers of Focus Groups

Despite the many positives that focus groups can provide, there are number of common traps that are easy to fall into when you're running focus groups. Let's take a look.

Leading the Focus Group Members

One very real danger of having people from your studio actually involved with the focus group is that it's very easy to accidentally affect the results. For example, if you see a player getting stuck because they don't know the right button to press, it's second nature to say, "Oh, just press Circle there." The player will then proceed and will probably fail to mention that it was a problem, whereas in reality, players who buy the game are not going to find a free game designer in the box with the disc!

Dismissing Stuff You Don't Like

I've been to a focus group session where two sets of people saw exactly the same people play the game and yet one group came away saying, "It's way too hard" and the other group said, "It's a little too easy." That's why it is important to record some verbal feedback with the people afterward, asking them clear questions like, "Was it too hard or too easy?" Also, by using a professional company, you'll hopefully get an unbiased report that will tell it like it really is. Listen to the results, and even if you don't like the sound of something, think about it properly before dismissing it. Why did the people say that about the game? Could there be some element of truth in it? Even if you disagree, see if you can improve it anyway, just in case the focus group respondents end up being right.

Misrepresenting the Data

Whenever anyone tries to draw a conclusion from focus group data, make sure you look at all the data in total to make sure the conclusion is correct. For example, say I don't like the way the car handles in a vehicle game. I could pick out two or three negative comments about the car handling and make a case for altering it: "Look what the focus group is saying. See these three people's comments. We've got to change it!" However, if you actually look at the data as a whole, you might find that out of 20 people, 17 actually really enjoyed the handling. It's a very blatant example, but it's possible to pick pieces from any kind of research to support a particular case. So make sure you check out all the data before making big changes.

Summary

I hope that you've now got a clear understanding of exactly what market research and focus groups can offer you. As a game designer, they may be your only link to the people who are going to buy your game. And the *only* way to make a successful game is to create something that people are going to want to buy. Like grenades, market research and focus groups can be dangerous in the wrong hands. But used properly, if you want to beat the competition, they're a very important piece of equipment in a game designer's armory.

13

An Interview with Ian Baverstock

Ian Baverstock is business development director (and co-founder) of Kuju, and has been responsible for the continued growth and success of one of Europe's leading independent game developers. Ian is responsible for sales and business development at Kuju, including new business areas and creative strategy. He played a major part in the launch of Kuju Wireless, now one of the fastest-growing wireless publishers in the U.K.

Do you feel it is important for game designers to understand the market they are designing for?

IB: Absolutely. I think designers need to understand who they are designing for. They don't necessarily need to pander to that market, and often the most inspired and original titles come from not listening to the market, but doing something the market might not expect. However, I think designers and designs always benefit from the context of understanding the market.

How do you decide what consumer demographic you are aiming for with a new title?

IB: We are generally designing games for one of two audiences: the core gaming demographic of 18- to 30-year-old males or we are designing games for absolutely the widest possible audience—this is more because of the history of the studios and the types of games we create. The key demographic questions for us are usually, "Are we making an 18 rated game (and is that sensible?)" and "are the mass market games successfully appealing to everyone (male and female, all ages)?"

How would you suggest that designers go about learning what the game-buying public wants?

IB: I think the key thing is for designers to recognize that they aren't the target market (or at least might not be!). The designers have to learn the skill of making games for other people, and that leads to market research, focus groups, and a willingness to listen to other opinions about a design.

What are your experiences with focus groups? Have you found them useful?

IB: We have found focus groups to be particularly useful for refining game designs and implementation. So far, whilst they have helped form ideas about which games to take from concept to publishers for development funding, this is in general still enough of a commercial black art to be of limited value.

What are you most proud of in your career so far?

IB: Of the released titles, the one that I am most proud of is Microsoft Train Simulator. Whilst it isn't everyone's idea of a game, the reviews and players of the game all universally come back with comments like "surprisingly addictive." The reason is that we took a simulation and built a lot of very well-disguised gameplay into the title and people enjoy that game without even noticing they are playing one sometimes. I think that helped a lot in the huge success of the title.

What is your favorite ever game (of all time), and why?

IB: I find it difficult to choose between Populous and Age of Empires, but probably Age of Empires wins it. The game had a surprising amount of depth, and this came entirely from the fundamentals of the design. I lost a large amount of my life to the Age of Empires series but hardly ever played the "canned missions." The random maps and the multiplayer mode were enough on their own.

What do you think is the biggest game design mistake that people regularly make with games?

IB: Designers are always making games too difficult; either the game balance is simply too hard or there are challenges that take too long placed too early in the game. My view is that it is not about maximizing the time people spend on a game but maximizing the amount of fun they have. Not being able to get through a level or a puzzle is not fun no matter how long it takes.

If money and technology were unlimited, what kind of game would you most like to see made?

IB: I think a lot of people are waiting for good online multiplayer cooperative gameplay. The isolation of individual online gaming puts a lot of people off. Unfortunately, cooperative play (especially online) is more technically challenging—especially with the large number of players that I'd like in the same world.

What do you think is the biggest challenge facing game designers as we move forward?

IB: I think that the next generation will be essentially online-only machines. This means that we will be able to start collecting detailed statistics for what real players actually do with a game once they have taken it home. At that point, the design craft will be transformed into something with a lot more data and a lot less "black magic."

And finally, if you had one piece of advice to give to a game designer who was just starting out, what would it be?

IB: Learn to listen to everyone about what they like about a game. Even if you don't agree with them, if they're having fun, then they must be right!

13

Chapter 14

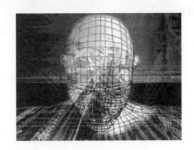

Design Teams, Prototypes, and Pitching

"Once the game is over, the King and the pawn go back in the same box."
Italian Proverb

I have a theory that I believe in passionately: the greatest entertainment product (whether it is a game, TV show, or film) comes when a talented creative person comes up with a clear vision and then works with a team of other talented creative people, without any ego or competition, polishing, improving, and re-polishing the vision until it's a winning game design, shooting script, or screenplay. If you are like many designers, you might find this to be a difficult guideline to follow, especially at first. This approach might go against what you've experienced so far in your own game design work. You might be thinking about projects that were ruined or significantly compromised because they were designed and developed with too many of the wrong people. It would be easy to conclude that the more people that work together to design a product, the greater the chances of failure. Before you convince yourself of this reality, give me a chance to show you the other side.

It took me a number of years to fully embrace using a team approach for designing, prototyping, and pitching games. Once you experience the benefits, you won't want to return to using the "lone wolf" approach. It's too easy to become protective about your own design or storyline, not wanting other people to mess with it. And many games are created in that way, with a good designer coming up with the idea, crafting a game design, and then sticking to it until the project is complete. The major work, in a sense, remains driven by a solo vision. Over the past few years, I have become more and more convinced that this isn't the best way to design and develop games because games are getting far too complex, and a person working solo (no matter how talented they are) can't do everything.

In this chapter, we'll start by looking at the value of using design teams. You'll see how you can benefit by learning from professionals in other creative industries (such as TV and film) that are more mature than the games industry. These other professions readily embrace the practice of relying on design teams throughout their development cycles.

The Value of Using Design Teams

Let's start by looking at the TV industry, which is similar to the games industry in many ways. Just as with games, the creative TV people try to come up with a powerful idea that is entertaining, has both a great storyline and great characters, and captures the imagination of viewers. If I plugged in the process of how I incorrectly designed games for many years, it would translate to designing a TV show like this:

- A TV writer would come up with an idea.

- The idea would be written down and fleshed out a little, with the writer doing all of this work in some back room, all on his own.

- The writer would create the scripts for a 12-episode series all on his own. (After all, the writer came up with the idea and knows what he wants more than anyone else, so he is in the best position to create everything that is needed for a series of shows.)

If you were a TV producer, would you fund a project that was designed and developed like this? I don't think so. You'd probably give the project the big thumbs-down, no matter how good the initial idea was. You'd probably look for a project that involved a more team-based approach and be confident that the team would be able to develop their ideas into a successful show.

The solo approach doesn't often happen in TV now; the experts have learned that however talented one person is, you just don't get a consistent quality without having other people involved. Don't just listen to me; listen to the people responsible for the most successful shows in the world.

Mike Scully, executive producer of *The Simpsons*, describes the writing process they use as follows:

> "A writer will come up with an idea. Then, we get together as a group and flesh the idea out. The writer will then write a detailed outline of the story and we will offer notes on the outline. After the writer finishes the script, we all come back and tell him how much we love it, and then, we all tear it apart!"

David Chase, writer of *The Sopranos*, explains just how much reworking goes into a script:

> **"Scripts may go through 10 drafts, revised with notes from (several people) before they're seen by any of the cast or crew."**

Both shows use a "writing room"—a big meeting area with a large team of talented writers. In this place, they bounce ideas around and go over and over a script, making it better each time. The key to these writing rooms is to avoid ego; they all understand that everyone can come up with both good and bad ideas. By being free to criticize anything they don't like, and by listening to everyone's views, they can create a show that ends up getting as close as possible to perfection. Pick almost any successful TV show, and you'll find they use a writing room of some kind.

So how can we apply this approach to game design and production?

My view is that game design should work in exactly the same way. You need a creative lead who will be the one person with overall responsibility for the project. But you also need a strong creative team of designers with whom you can hold regular meetings to revise, polish, and improve your game design, your level design, and your story. If you work at a development studio with more than one team, I'd advise you to include the best designers from other teams in your "writing room." Include people who are not working on the game day in, day out and therefore will look at the design with fresh eyes, which often uncovers obvious things that people closer to the project may have overlooked.

Creative Idea: Use Objective Designers

At the publisher I work for, we use mainly external development teams. But several years ago, I introduced a team of designers who work alongside the designers at the studios. They work on a couple of projects and are able to dip in and dip out of projects to a certain extent. Far from seeing them as a pain in the neck, the development teams have almost unanimously found these designers to be extremely useful. Since they are not living with the game as it is being designed every minute of every day, they are able to take a step back and see things that aren't obvious when you are too close to a game. They're also able to deliver feedback directly to the team after the game is demonstrated to retailers and distributors. This allows the team to get a much better idea of what the people who end up buying the game are thinking.

Get Over the Pain of Working with Others

14

Don't be afraid to share your idea with others. This is easy to say, but I've certainly had to learn this the hard way. People who are ultimately unwilling to let other creative talent look at and give input to their "baby" may throw out statements such as

> "Too many cooks spoil the broth!"

or

> "Design by committee never works!"

Let me address these two comments head-on. In my experience, it is correct to say that design by committee can be a problem. But this has always resulted from either one of the following:

- A project team that has no clear lead designer who could draw views and summarize the results

- A team that has people involved who don't understand game design or are just not very good designers

Reality Check: All designers have their own unique eccentricities. Everyone has a slightly different outlook on life, and no individual can claim to understand the games market perfectly. So what's the best way to avoid letting any flaws that you have influence a game? Use other designers, and double-check things with them every so often. Hopefully, they'll agree with you most of the time. But there will always be the occasional time when they all say, "No! That's crazy!" If several people whose opinions you trust are all saying the same thing, then this is probably one time you're wrong!

The answer to both the negative statements is to look at the proof. And when you see the sheer quality of shows like *The Simpsons* or *Frasier*, it's clear that the "writing room" approach works. And although I haven't asked any of the guys from Valve, I'd be prepared to bet money that they used a similar process to polish the game design in *Half-Life 2*. More and more game development studios are recognizing the value of using design teams.

Reality Check: As with many rules, this one isn't absolute. There are always exceptions. For example, the series *The West Wing* was largely created by one person, but once the show was established, a team of writers and creators was needed to keep it going at its high level of quality. There are a few U.K. television shows that have been largely written by one person. But when you're looking at the success of programs like *The Simpsons*, one-man ideas are few and far between. I'm convinced that the "writing room" approach is the route to quality.

Design by Formulas

As an aside, you might be interested to know that many TV shows use a very formulaic approach to creating their plots. A great example is *The Sopranos*, which uses a writing room to great effect. In the writing room, the main writer works alongside the show's other writers/producers to flesh out the story for each episode. They make a list of the "beats" within the episode, each beat effectively being a scene. Each episode consists of around 35 beats, and there are 4 story strands. Each of these 4 strands has a beginning, a middle, and an end. The main 2 strands (labeled A and B) get 13 beats each and form the basis of the story for that episode. The C strand (normally a much less important but interesting subplot) gets 5 or 6 beats, and the D strand (normally a comic character) will just have a few beats. The team sits around in the room using a whiteboard to sketch out how each of these 4 stories will work, and then they piece them together into a show. The lead writer is quoted as saying, "I firmly believe that the more time a filmmaker has to edit, the better a piece will be." So don't skimp on time when you're finalizing your game design or storyline; you can always make something better.

If you're responsible for hiring designers to be part of your team, try to work out what the current strengths and weaknesses of your existing team are. The strength of a team is more than a combination of the individuals, and I have found that getting an interesting mix of talents is the best approach. If you've got several designers that love sports games, don't get another. Find someone who is a big RPG or adventure game fan. If you're all incredibly creative but disorganized, find a designer who can help organize the team and actually get things finished.

Prototyping Games

All the games that we create have what I call a prototype phase. This is essentially a preproduction phase that we fund, normally lasting between three and six months, in which time a small team will work on the core elements of a game, proving risky areas (parts of the game design which are innovative and haven't been done before) and generally creating a strong foundation that they can build the main game on.

Why do we do prototypes? There are two main reasons from my point of view:

- Risk management: For a publisher, committing many millions of dollars to a game is a very big risk, one that is getting greater as game development costs increase. One way to decrease this risk is to spend a much smaller amount trying out some of the key ideas to see whether they're going to work or not. If they don't work, and the gameplay at the end of a prototype isn't fun, a publisher will lose a great deal less money finding this out than if they had finished and released the game.

- Good planning: It's crazy to dive into full development with a huge team without proper planning. The British Army has a saying: "Proper planning and preparation prevents piss-poor performance." And it's very true. As part of the prototype process, we lay down a very detailed design document, complete level breakdowns,

14

the final storyline, a detailed schedule, risk assessment, and all the other key documents that form the start of a professional multimillion dollar project.

Planning a Prototype

You need to start off by deciding exactly what you want out of a prototype. For me, it's normally proving the core gameplay, along with any particularly unusual or unique game mechanics that are risky. We'll also try to produce at least a small section of a level to near-final graphical quality to demonstrate what we're aiming at.

Prototype periods are the time to try things out. If you think a completely new kind of rendering might give your game a unique look, give it a go. For this reason, it is sensible not to overload your prototype plan with too many things; otherwise, you'll never have any time for experimentation.

Reviewing a Prototype

As you begin to build the prototype, it's sensible to clearly lay out your goals and what you're expecting. This way, you've got some way of measuring the final prototype delivery and seeing how close you are. If you don't lay out clear goals at the beginning, it's very easy to get sucked into the magic of the game development process and lose sight of what you were really after. Try to step back and evaluate the prototype with other people who haven't seen the game before and don't know the design. If the prototype is fun, and people genuinely enjoy playing it, you've got yourself a strong foundation. If it isn't fun, I'd recommend that you either stop the project then and there or else extend the prototype period, try to identify why the gameplay isn't working, and then sort it out.

War Story: Don't Get Carried Away Early On

Too many times I have seen a prototype that honestly wasn't really fun get green-lighted for full development because key people (sometimes including myself!) got carried away with the potential and what it might be. Sometimes you need to forget the final game that you can see in your head and take a look at the real game in front of you on the television screen.

With most products that fail, most people involved often comments at the end, "I knew that this game wasn't going to be successful." Yet during the design and development process, most get so carried away by the passion of the work that they don't speak up. If you are aware that things aren't going right, don't just sit on the sidelines. Get involved throughout the entire process and provide your feedback when it's needed to help keep the project from getting into trouble at the end.

War Story: Don't Be Seduced by the Potential of Your Prototype

I remember a prototype we did that featured guys on dinosaurs racing through the jungle hunting each other. The project didn't actually get past the prototype stage (quite rightly), but it was a very close call, and I was on the wrong side of that call! As a designer, I had become obsessed with the gameplay possibilities and what I might be able to do with the game in the future. Therefore, I wasn't really judging what was in front of me—a pretty average game with a subject that just wasn't going to appeal to the market and would struggle to fill a 10- to 15-hour game experience. My mind was off dreaming of incredible AI routines, hunting with smell trails, destructible trees and bushes, none of which were practical at the time (on PS1), and all of which were a million miles away from where the game currently was.

Pitching a Game to a Publisher

If you work for an independent development team, you'll probably find that you need to present your great game concept to a publisher at some point. Even if you are owned by a publisher (or work directly for one), you may still need to pitch new concepts at some point or another. So how do you go about presenting your great new idea and making a great impression? I've assembled some tips here to help you plan your pitch and present it to a publisher or management.

Planning Your Pitch

As with most things in life, preparation and planning are absolutely vital. If you don't plan properly and end up trying to "wing" a presentation, you'll never do your best, regardless of how good a presenter you are. Let's take a look at some of the things you ought to think through when you're preparing your pitch.

The Hook

As I have said several times already, one of the most important things you need to focus on is what EA used to call the "Razor X"—a clear one-sentence description that sums up what makes your game so special. Another way of thinking about it is how you would respond to "Describe your game in one sentence." If you can't come up with a response, it's unlikely that your game will do well. Of course, there are exceptions to this rule, but most successful new franchises have had one key hook that grabs people.

If you find that your hook is too complicated, it might also indicate that your game idea is too complex. Try to simplify things as much as you can and keep working your pitch until you can boil it down to a one-sentence description. If you are having trouble, start by making a list of the four or five really important features of your game and see if that will lead you to a main focus. Often, going through the painful process of throwing out

14

things at the beginning will help you keep your game focused. It will also save you valuable time during the development process and help you avoid having features that just clutter up your game and stop you from focusing on the really important stuff.

Here's an example of a typical hook: "The game is all about explosions, bigger, more varied, and more intense explosions than ever seen before, with real physical blast effects on every object, character, and element of the environment."

Actually, this hook is actually not a long way from the hook that develops Criterion/EA must be using on their shooter *Black*, which is essentially all about guns, bullets, and intense gun-based carnage.

In this case, when someone first hears about your game or first sees it in the stores, or if teenagers are talking about it in the street, you want them to have "explosions" in their mind. If you've got to choose between implementing fully destructible buildings or the ability to drive cars, refer back to the hook. Clearly, having destructible buildings would reinforce your hook, and therefore, for this game, it would be the better feature to include.

Videos

Some of the best product pitches that I've seen have used short, well-edited video clips, showing key areas of game prototype footage (or even movies, TV shows, or other games) to help get the concept and gameplay across. Rather than showing a long chunk of game video, they break it down into a number of smaller videos, each of which demonstrates a specific point. For example, one key feature in a game might be the most realistic snow ever seen in a video game. In this case, you could show a short video clip demonstrating why it's the most realistic, or you might show what kind of effect you want to get by taking incredible snow footage from movies or documentaries. At this stage, you don't need to spend a lot of time or money making the sample videos. The point is to help the person you are presenting your game idea to better visualize some of its key features and selling points.

USPs

You need to understand the key features and unique selling points (USPs) of your game concept. The definition of the word *unique* can vary a little depending on whom you talk to. I know some pretty anal producers who insist that a certain USP isn't unique because an obscure Japanese game from 11 years ago used that feature in some way. My definition of *unique* is that most people who are potentially going to buy the game won't have seen that feature in a game before.

Reality Check: Of course, if you are presenting your game concept to someone who is very knowledgeable about the industry, make sure that you also do your homework and that you really know how your game is unique and compares to the competition. There is nothing worse than making a presentation when you haven't done your homework and being brutally exposed. I always try to guess what difficult questions might come up, and I bring along the relevant facts on sheets of paper just in case.

Gameplay Examples

If you're not able to show early prototype of the gameplay, a good way to help get the game across to people is to describe what a typical five minutes from the finished game will be like. Explain where the camera will be, what the character looks like, what the player will be doing, and what makes the game interesting and exciting. Try to talk through a practical example of the main unique feature. If you have any sketches you can provide, this could help show some of the features you are planning.

Gameplay Demo

Ideally, you'll actually have an early section of prototype gameplay to demonstrate. Nothing beats demonstrating something playable. It will show off your key USP, will look visually impressive (at least have a small section of the level looking incredible), and will impress the people present. I've seen products signed up on the strength of a great concept tied with a stunning video of mocked-up final gameplay, so it doesn't have to be playable (but it helps!).

Doing Something Unique

If you want to get your pitch noticed, try doing something unique. I'll mention a couple of real-life examples later in the chapter, but the key strategy should be to get your ideas noticed. This is particularly important if you're sending a pitch and/or demo through the post. It's important that your pitch makes an impression as soon as the acquisitions person opens the package.

If you're giving a presentation in person, try to make it memorable (for the right reasons). You might want to start with an unusual opening. Let's look at an example. Imagine you're demonstrating a game featuring booby traps. As preparation, you place a few simple booby traps around the room while you are setting up, simple things like placing a plastic file with a smaller firecracker underneath the desk. As you mention your USP (the booby traps), casually ask one of the people to pass you your file. When the firecracker goes off, and everyone has recovered, explain how easy it is to place booby traps and how easy it is to trigger them. I guarantee no one in the room will forget your USP and your demo. Of course, be careful you don't use anything too

14

powerful; you're unlikely to get a contract if you've blown off the index finger of your prospective CEO!

Presenting Your Pitch

I have 10 rules I think you can use as a guideline to make sure your pitch is going to be as good as it can possibly be. Of course, don't just follow these rules blindly. Make sure you think through the presentation of your pitch and fine-tune the rules to work for your particular needs.

1. Refine the Hook

Have a clear message and a product hook; you must be able to explain what makes your game special in one sentence. It's what makes your game stand out. If you remember this all the way through the development of your game, you stand a much better chance of sending the consumer a clear message about your product. If you want to introduce new features, bounce them off the hook. If they don't link in with your hook, don't use them.

2. Use the Best Presenter

The person presenting must be knowledgeable, trustworthy, and enthusiastic. I've seen presentations of great concepts ruined by a disorganized, confused, and amateur presenter, who inspired very little confidence in either the design or the development studio. If you are not sure about who you are planning to use as your presenter, audition them and perhaps a few others. Assemble some of the members of your team and have the candidates give a short sample presentation. Be very selective and pick the person who really stands out.

3. Present the Features

You need to have a clear understanding of the features and USPs and be prepared to explain them in detail if asked. Try to make sure that they're not clichéd. For example, everyone says, "The game will have the best artificial intelligence ever seen in a video game" or "It will be a cross between *GTA*, *Halo 2*, and *Metal Gear Solid*." Prepare for your presentation with the mindset that the people you will be presenting to have heard it all already and try to give them something that really gets them to take notice.

4. Don't Forget the Detail

Provide a sensible and realistic time frame and budget. Don't underbid, don't pick a figure out of thin air, and try to avoid nice round numbers for project budgets (they look suspiciously like they've been rounded up).

5. Show Off Your Technology

Demonstrate that you already have strong technology. Most publishers won't sign a project with a developer unless they can prove they have strong technology. Even if it's for their first title on a new generation of machines, it's still important to demonstrate existing technology, editing tools, and so on to prove that you have the skill set. Make sure you can clearly explain how your technology is different and better than what other developers have. Use examples that are easy to follow. If you are proposing to use middleware, make sure you've got an evaluation version, have worked with it, and can ideally demonstrate something on it that looks visually impressive.

6. Discuss Your Strengths and Weaknesses

Acknowledge your strengths and weaknesses, and explain how you will work around the latter. Don't be arrogant. By being honest up front, you will likely win over the person you are presenting to. As you discuss your weaknesses, just make sure that you introduce a plan to show that you have thought through your situation and that you have a solution.

7. Present Your Track Record

Demonstrate your track record. If you're an established studio, run through your product history. If you're a new team, run through the key individuals and their track records at other companies. Have any of your team members worked together before? If so, mention it!

8. Detail Your Structure

You must have a strong team structure. This would include having an experienced producer and designer and perhaps a separate project manager. Explain how your studio is structured. The CEO shouldn't also be the lead programmer. Personally, I always try to look for situations in which design and production have equivalent "power" and importance within a company. I've seen too many programmer- or art-driven products created in an environment where the designers are not treated properly and don't get any say in the game (which invariably leads to a weak gameplay experience). I've also seen very design-focused studios continually changing the game and falling down technically or artistically. Make sure that the structure you present will look balanced.

9. Communicate Your Passion

Show that your team has passion for this project. However you do it, you need to get across that this project is important to you and that you're excited about it. If you don't care about a game and it's just another work for hire job, that attitude is likely to come across in your pitch. Including something special in your presentation will go a long way in putting out the message "We really want to develop this game." You don't need to

14

say it; your actions will do the talking for you.

10. Provide Good Market Analysis

Make sure you analyze the competition. Understand where and how your game will fit into the market. If you come with a great original concept but haven't even looked at competitive products and whether anything like it has been tried before, you won't look very professional in the pitch meeting! Provide charts and visual examples to show how your approach stacks up against the competition. If you are pitching a game in a crowded genre, make sure you really can explain how it will be able to compete. Heavy competition can scare people, but if you have a good plan, you'll have a fighting chance of getting someone excited about your game.

Perfecting Your Presentation Skills

As a designer, being able to present in a professional and enthusiastic manner is an extremely useful skill. I mention enthusiasm because it is vitally important when presenting. When you're doing a pitch, you need to convince people that your game concept has the potential to be a massively successful game. If *you* can't get excited about it, no one will. The games industry has some superb presenters, people like Phil Harrison at Sony and J Allard at Microsoft. So if you want to be really good, watch the guys at the top and analyze how they present and what they say. Videos of Phil and J presenting at their respective console launches at E3 2005 should be available on the Web if you hunt them down.

Here are five tips that I think are vital if you want to be a really great presenter:

Practice, Practice, Practice: You can never practice enough. Rehearse your presentation a number of times (and that includes the technical bits, like switching between programs or running videos).

Try Not to Read off a Script: Many people find it hard to present without having every word written down on paper. But if you can, try to reduce your prompt sheet down to a few key sentences, and then talk in your own natural way.

Creative Idea: Use Smart Techniques for Your Presentations

When I'm presenting, I tend to use PowerPoint to bring up a few short bullet points, and then I flesh these out as they come up. It's down to your own personal presentation style, but I find that when presenters speak off the cuff, it shows that they are knowledgeable and comfortable talking about their subject; they appear to be in control. Conversely, when presenters hold a script up to their noses and read out their pitch word by word, it is much harder to create a powerful impression.

Show Something Visual While You Are Talking: There is nothing more boring than someone waffling on about a game for five or more minutes without any kind of visual cue. If you want to talk about something that is important to your game design, give the audience something to look at (but make sure it doesn't distract from what you are saying). This might be as simple as bullet points appearing on a slide, or it could be a looping, in-game video or some entertaining photos that you make appear at appropriate moments while you talk. You might want to use a real object—perhaps a balloon, some juggling balls, large photos, or even a giant flaming kangaroo—to make a visual statement and help people remember what you're saying. (If anyone manages to use a giant flaming kangaroo in a pitch, please e-mail me and let me know, and I'll buy you a pint).

Often, people don't remember exactly what you say once a presentation is finished, but they will remember visual things as well as humor. If you are presenting to a group that is also listening to other presentations, try to give them something visually unique so that they will remember your project

Don't Talk and Play at the Same Time: It is almost impossible to play a game and talk about it eloquently at the same time. One or the other suffers, and either your character hurtles to their death for the fifth time or you stumble through a key USP because you're concentrating on the controls. If you are good at presenting, let someone else play the game (having practiced with them carefully before) while you talk over the top. If you're not a good speaker, play the game while someone else describes what it going on and what makes the game so special. Choose an exciting section of the game that is representative, and if you have any slow, boring bits, don't play through those to get to the exciting stuff. Take the time to create some kind of save position or teleport location so you can jump straight into the action. Also, you may want to use an infinite health cheat because it can be frustrating when you are killed just before the spectacular ending of a level!

Don't Dress Too Smartly: I have seen many people present, and when people turn up in a smart suit, it's often possible to tell whether they wear that kind of clothing day in, day out (in the games industry, the answer is normally no). You certainly shouldn't look too scruffy, but when I see a presenter, I want them to appear honest and I want their natural personality to come shining through. For me, the best presentations are when the passion and enthusiasm of someone who clearly knows their stuff come through clearly. Dressing up in clothes that you're not comfortable in is a bad start in my book. Be yourself.

14

Two Great Pitches and One Big Loser

I thought I'd finish off this chapter by telling you about a couple of pitches that have really stood out in my career so far. To balance things, I'll also tell you about one of the very worst pitches that I've ever had to listen to. Don't worry, however; I'm not going to mention any names.

Reservoir Dogs

When we were looking for a development team to create the *Reservoir Dogs* video game, we had a number of teams come in and pitch to us. One of the teams arrived at our office dressed in black suits, thin blacks ties, sunglasses, and gelled-back hair; just like the characters from the film. They admitted afterward that they were going to sprinkle fake blood over their shirts but were worried that our receptionist would call the police! By having the balls to do this, they made a great first impression with us and helped get their pitch off to a great start, showing us that this wasn't "just another pitch" from their point of view.

Body Parts

Continuing with the blood theme, one developer pitching for a different game sent me a big plastic packing box. I opened it and found a whole load of fake body parts wrapped in cling film (that's plastic wrap to Americans) and covered in fake blood. It was a pretty horrific discovery on a Monday morning when I was still half asleep, but it was a great way of introducing a pitch (at least it was once I'd realized that the fingers and ears were fake!). As an aside, I had a hell of a job getting rid of the box. I couldn't put it into a trash can in the office in case the cleaners found it and called the police. I ended up giving it to one of our QA staff, who I believe used its contents for practical jokes for the next six months.

Tiddlywinks

I was pitched a licensed Tiddlywinks game, which would feature the world Tiddlywinks champion, and all the "stars." If you haven't heard of Tiddlywinks, you're probably not alone; it's a kids game in which you flick a plastic counter into a pot using another plastic counter. The person pitching had gone into too much detail and was really passionate about Tiddlywinks being a major sport. He felt deep within his soul that if only this game was commissioned, it would be competing with *Madden* and *FIFA* within a few years, yet unsurprisingly, he had no supporting research to demonstrate this. Needless to say, I didn't share his opinion. It took me two hours to get rid of him (I'm way too polite sometimes!).

Summary

You've now learned that I believe the best games most often are a direct result of working with other talented people. Today's complex games, which need to reach wider and wider audiences to be commercially successful, can't be designed and produced using the "lone wolf" approach. It's really hard to go it alone as a designer, and it's important to have someone else who is creative to bounce ideas off of. Working as a design team is about sharing ideas, accepting criticism, and polishing a concept until it shines. When a talented design team is in full flow, magic happens.

14

An Interview with Tim Heaton

Tim Heaton is senior development director at EA Partners Europe. Tim has a strong track record, having worked at Gremlin and Warthog. He has been in the games industry since 1994, and is currently working with some of the best development studios across Europe.

What do you think are the most important skills that a game designer should have?

TH: Oh, that's easy. They should be creative. They should have inspirational leadership skills. They should understand contemporary popular culture. They should have a technical appreciation. They should be logical. They should be innovative. Personality traits that most psychologists say are almost guaranteed to be mutually exclusive.

Some designers like to think of themselves as solo designers, coming up with a vision on their own. How important do you feel teamwork is when designing computer games?

TH: I think design probably splits into two different roles—the vision and the implementation. Vision (i.e., the general concept for the game) can be one person, or a well motivated team, although getting real innovation is likely to come from one focused, obstinate person. Implementation should always be a team effort—you're looking for the best methods to provide the vision, and that comes from a collection of skills and approaches.

How important are prototypes in the game development process?

TH: The most important thing! The theory is obvious—sort out your risks early, play and refine with a cheap small team, and be able to communicate the key areas of your game. Actually making theory reality is much tougher for many varied reasons, but it pays off when you can do it right.

What are the biggest mistakes you see when developers pitch new concepts to you?

TH: Not understanding the market.

What are you most proud of in your career so far?

TH: Being involved with Actua Soccer at Gremlin (early use of mocap, simulated 3D, etc.... ahh, the good old days), and now being part of EA's highly motivated production teams, which I do believe are defining the next generation of consumer entertainment.

What is your favorite ever game (of all time), and why?

TH: Elite (BBC Micro)—emergent open world, emotionally involving. Sounds like a next-gen game!

What do you think is the biggest game design mistake that people regularly make with games?

TH: Making games too "big." Do less better.

If money and technology were unlimited, what kind of game would you most like to see made?

TH: *That is actually really difficult. I look forward to GTA and other open-world games that aren't restrained by technology.*

What do you think is the biggest challenge facing game designers as we move forward?

TH: *Keeping creative vision whilst working with very large teams and strictly maintained budgets.*

And finally, if you had one piece of advice to give to a game designer who was just starting out, what would it be?

TH: *It all boils down to communicating your ideas. Hone those skills.*

14

Chapter 15

Designing Seriously Serious Games

"Take everything you like seriously, except yourselves."
Rudyard Kipling

An exciting new area of game development involving serious games has emerged over the past few years. This movement largely started in the United States under the direction of the Serious Games Initiative and is growing rapidly on both sides of the Atlantic, with more and more games and conferences being introduced each year. In the spirit of full disclosure, the founder of the Serious Games Initiative is Ben Sawyer, who is also one of my editors for this book. Ben has become a successful champion of designing and developing successful serious games for industries such as health care, education, technology and so on. I owe Ben a huge thank-you for helping me out a great deal with this chapter.

The serious games movement is a fascinating area and a growing one that uses game technology for practical purposes in unique ways. As a game designer, this is an area that you may have overlooked, but it is one to consider because more and more opportunities are emerging every year. Designing games that will be used for more "serious" applications also introduces different challenges and requires an alternative mindset and range of skills.

In this chapter, I'll introduce the serious games movement and show you some of the types of games that are currently being developed. I'll also provide you with some design tips to help you get started in this new and exciting area.

A Quick Look at Serious Games

You might be wondering what exactly are serious games? They are essentially projects in which game technology and gaming mechanics are used for training people, educating kids, creating business simulations, helping people recover from poor health, simulating real-world events, and hundreds of other applications other than providing entertainment. Serious games have been around in one form or another for some time, but only recently has there been an organization available (**www.seriousgames.org**) to help focus all the different companies and developers involved in this area. The serious games organization provides a unique forum for discussing this growing area and sharing ideas and resources.

 Reality Check: To understand the serious games niche, you have to shift your thinking about the game development business. While society in general needs to realize that games can be used for purposes other than entertaining their kids, it also takes some adjustment on the developer side. It's a very different operating environment and calls for some unique thinking.

Let's first take a look at a few examples of how game principles can be used for more serious projects, and then we'll discuss some of the unique design challenges involved.

Games for Education

Traditional video games have been shown to increase decision making, reaction time, dexterity, and hand-eye coordination. So when video games are created especially for use in education, it's hardly surprising that the results can be extremely impressive. And these games are not just for kids—serious video games can be a useful educational tool for adults. One example is the Education Arcade.

The Education Arcade (**www.educationarcade.org**) is a research initiative dedicated to making and exploring the use of video games in education. It works with the Games-to-Teach Project, an initiative developed by Microsoft and MIT. As an example of what it gets involved with, there is game called *Environmental Detectives* (see Figure 15.1) that allows educators to investigate a range of environmental issues, from radioactive spills to toxic chemicals and dangerous particles spread in the air. A particular version runs on a Pocket PC with a GPS unit attached. It simulates underground toxic spills so that students need to physically walk around sites, sampling the ground. The program allows the player to use the GPS to tell them what the sample results are at a particular location. The game provides the closest possible simulation to a major toxic spill without doing it for real (which obviously isn't possible!).

Figure 15.1
Environmental Detectives running on a PDA.

Games for Business

Since a video game is a fun and interesting way of presenting information, it's not surprising that many companies use video game mechanics as a basis for training staff. Intel's *IT Manager* game is a great example (see Figure 15.2). The game simulates an IT department within a company. The idea is to test the entire skill set needed to be an IT manager and help managers realize what their strengths and weaknesses are. It involves hiring and training staff, buying and installing equipment, dealing with problems, using office space efficiently, battling virus attacks, and even coping with crazy CEOs!

British Telecom created a similar experience called the *BT Better Business Game*, in which the aim was to show people how to manage social and environmental issues in a business. You play the role of a CEO as you get to try to keep everyone happy by making decisions on various problems and opportunities that arise. The game shows you that there is no easy answer to these problems. Keeping shareholders happy while making decisions that suit your employees, business partners, and environmental pressure groups is very hard indeed. But if you think through the problems carefully, it is possible to come out on top.

15

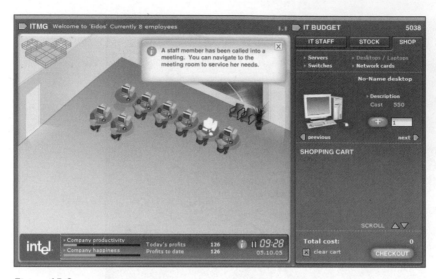

Figure 15.2
Intel's *IT Manager* game.

Games for Health

One very exciting emerging area of the Serious Games Initiative is the Games for Health organization (**www.gamesforhealth.org**). This group holds a conference each year in the United States (Baltimore, Maryland) and its focus is to bring together the top talent in game development and the medical profession. The goal is to apply cutting-edge games and game technologies to a range of public and private policy, leadership, and management issues for the health care industry.

The Initiative founded Games for Health to develop a community and determine the best practices for the numerous games being built for health care applications. To date the project has brought together researchers, medical professionals, and game developers to share information about the impact that games and game technologies can have on health care and policy.

In addition to the Games for Health conference, the Initiative is working to catalog the games that are used in health care, assist current development, collect best practices, share research results, and explore ideas that might improve health care administration and policy.

Currently, there are two sides to games for health: personal treatment and professional practice. The former includes treatment, disease management, physical therapy, exergaming (or gaming that promotes exercise), mental health treatment (VR/psychotherapy), cognitive learning (*Brain Training* for the Nintendo DS is an example), and

Figure 15.3
Fighting cancer cells with *Ben's Game*.

other applications that people personally purchase. The latter includes health messaging, modeling, simulation, and training.

One of the more interesting games that have been created for health care is *Ben's Game*. The game was developed for a young boy, Ben Duskin, who was diagnosed with leukemia at age 5. At age 8, Duskin submitted a wish to Make-A-Wish to make a game about fighting cancer. The game (see Figure 15.3) allows the player to control one child as they combat cancer by fighting cancer cells. The game started out as a more personal mission but has become quite popular. It has been downloaded over 170,000 times and continues to generate a lot of traffic for the Make-A-Wish Foundation Web site.

Designing and Developing Ben's Game

As I mentioned earlier in the chapter, designing and developing serious games does take a different mindset than developing traditional entertainment-style games. A game like Ben's Game requires some extra steps throughout the project simply because of the nature of the project. I'd first like to acknowledge the contributions of Dr. Ian Bogost to this sidebar; he provided a detailed posting about Ben's game at the Gamasutra.com site. (Dr. Bogost is also featured in the interview at the end of this chapter.)

15

The game was developed by Eric Johnston of LucasArts. It took six months to make, with Johnston and Ben Duskin working one evening per week and Duskin also on weekends. The developer indicated that it was difficult to make the game because of the time required. (Creating a game in six months is a tough job for anyone.) The first step is usually to acquire funding, but they skipped that step. When Johnston made his first game, he accomplished it alone and in only 10 weeks (*Pipe Dream*, a classic puzzle game). Since then, the scale of gaming has increased considerably, so Johnston used this new opportunity as an excuse to get back to his short, independent approach. The project budget included a USB flash drive to allow Duskin to take the game home after every meeting and 16 liters of limeade. Johnston was surprised and impressed by the child's involvement and guidance.

The second step would be to ask LucasArts for permission to make the game, and Johnston says he also skipped that step. He just started making the game, realizing that in the worst case, he could simply make it at home. After getting some traction, LucasArts allowed him after-hours access to the office, including the sound studio, which was a huge help in the development process. The company's legal and PR departments allowed the game to be released for free; the company also facilitated a tour of Skywalker Ranch and the archives for Duskin, places that Johnston had never been himself in more than a decade working for LucasArts.

One question Johnston found himself bound to ask was, "How can we design a game about cancer?" Clearly, the player can't lose or die. The two decided to focus on distraction and entertainment for kids undergoing cancer treatment. Distraction is a big part of pediatric medicine, as there's very little patients can do in treatment.

Every Tuesday, Johnston and the young Duskin worked on the game (except one week when Duskin was grounded). Johnston has photos of the two working on the game, demonstrating the child's detailed involvement in the design as a primary driver. He shared his experience watching Duskin play the game, which he cited as a tremendous help in the iterative design process.

The game's development started with the concept of a field of cells, an abstract and stylized approach. The field has mutating cells that grow, similar to John Conway's game *Life*. *Ben's Game* uses a shield (to protect against side effects), health, ammo, and attitude as markers of the player's health level. But when attitude runs out, Ben instructed, you keep fighting, living beyond what the level says you can.

Mutating cells aren't very understandable, and kids don't see them during treatment; they see the nasty side effects of treatment. So in the game, you fight monsters that are manifestations of seven side effects: fire represents fever, cue balls are hair loss, "ro-barf" is vomit, vampires represent bleeding, the tornado stands for rashes, snow monster are colds, and the evil chicken represents chicken pox. The game allows players to choose from a number of playable characters or create their own.

Figure 15.4
FreeDive by Breakaway Games.

Another unique serious game that has been created to help with healthcare-related issues is *FreeDive* (see Figure 15.4). This game is a basic scuba diving simulation created by BreakAway Games that helps kids distract themselves when they are receiving uncomfortable treatments. The irony of this game is that many people complain that video games are bad for kids because they distract them from doing other important things (such as homework), but here is a game that flips this issue on its head. The distraction that the game provides turns out to be a successful cognitive pain killer.

Games for Military

As so many soldiers have now grown up playing video games, it is obvious why games make an ideal tool for training military personnel and for providing experiences in a memorable and enjoyable format. Several military simulation "games" are also created by BreakAway. A good example of such a game is a project in which the company developed an anti-terror simulation for the U.S. Navy. The aim was to create a training tool that would simulate real-life missions that the Navy's antiterrorism group would carry out. The multiplayer 3D game would let players perform tasks and interact with AI- or human-controlled ships and boats.

15

Figure 15.5
America's Army game.

Other higher-profile examples include the game *America's Army*, which was funded entirely by the U.S. Army (see Figure 15.5). This game, which has a slightly more realistic slant than traditional war games, has proved an extremely successful recruiting tool for the army, attracting more than a million players in the first 10 months alone. Although Army officials are nervous about saying so, *America's Army* is clearly seen as a recruitment tool, and I have heard that overall application levels have risen significantly since the introduction of this game. One sign of the success of *America's Army* is that the Ministry of Defense in the U.K. is already looking seriously into the use of the video games medium to assist with its own recruitment.

Games for Government

Many people in and out of government are increasingly recognizing that games can provide a way to allow constituents, elected officials, and government workers to explore and play with policy decisions that can have far-reaching effects.

Toward those ends, a few efforts have been developed, including some budget simulators (*MassBalance* and *BudgetUtah* are two). As this book is being written, several agencies inside the American government are looking at some game-based simulations for homeland security and environmental policies.

The government market is broken into three levels: federal, state, and local. Federal (or national) governments are usually the most flush with funds and large-scale problems that might more readily make them customers for game projects. State (or provincial) governments would be the next logical group, and finally local governments would be next. The problem with these smaller governmental areas is that while they may represent more workers, issues, and even larger sums for spending, they don't have the ability to so readily allocate funds for unusual things like games.

However, local governments/regional councils are more accessible and they can be good places to start. Often local governments will seek grants for nontraditional projects rather than fund them with their own money. In addition, various officials at the local level often have the contacts and knowledge of central government that can be incredibly useful. So while they don't have a lot of their own funds, they can be a good place to start.

Creative Idea: Creative Funding Sources

What some developers have learned is that if they can get a product funded by a central (federal) source, they can offer smaller governments a free or subsidized product and then have them pay nominal fees for customizing that product to their locality. So, instead of paying $1 million for a new game, a local government might pay $15,000 to implement a specific scenario, map, or other content that makes the product more relevant to them. If you had 100 customers paying $10,000, this would give you $1 million in additional revenue.

A final point about government customers is the CYA (cover your ass) factor. Government staff and elected leaders will usually refrain from taking huge risky chances on things because they don't want to create an easy target for their detractors or stir up controversy. It doesn't mean they'll be staid and off-putting, just that you need to work closely with them to arm them with a very strong case so any attacks can be properly repelled. For example, a game-based project that runs on state-of-the-art hardware may look fantastic, but if detractors can show that only 5 percent of a government's computers can run it, then it's an easy target for criticism. Likewise, if a game only allows for one point of view, it can be attacked as potentially controversial and highly biased.

Reality Check: Remember also that the attacks may not come just from other portions of a government; they could come from nongovernmental organizations, average citizens, and the media, as well.

15

Other Types of Serious Games

I've focused on a number of different kinds of serious games, but there really is an almost infinite variety of uses that games can be put to. Table 15.1 shows a number of notable serious games products, and details of where you can find out more.

Table 15.1   Some notable example products.

Name	URL	Comment
Virtual U	www.virtual-u.org	Teaches university management principles
Incident Commander	www.incidentcommander.net	Used by municipalities to train in emergency response management
Hungry Red Planet	www.hungryredplanet.com	Helps inform people about good nutrition
VRPhobia	www.vrphobia.com	Provides direct treatment of major phobias using video game technologies to immerse patients in environments they fear
A Home of Your Own	www.mediaop.com	Helps people learn how homes are built, bought, and sold
Hazmat	www.etc.cmu.edu/projects/hazmat	Trains firefighters in hazardous material and terrorism incidents
BT Better Business	www.btplc.com/Societyand environment/Businessgame	Provides experience managing social and environment issues at a major business
DarWars	www.darpa.mil	Uses game technologies to create a multitiered all-encompassing military training simulator
Close Combat Marine	www.tecom.usmc.mil/techdiv/ ITK/CCM/CCM.htm	Uses the Close Combat engine to help marine commanders practice tactics
Intel IT Manager	www.intel.com/cd/corporate/europe /emea/eng/114556.htm	Tests how you'd cope as an IT manager running a growing business
Virtual Leader	www.simulearn.net	Teaches leadership issues to corporate managers
Full Spectrum Warrior	www.fullspectrumwarrior.com	Real-time strategy game that teaches rifle platoon leadership tactics

(continued)

Table 15.1   Some notable example products *(continued)*.

Name	URL	Comment
America's Army	www.americasarmy.com	Exposes potential recruits to the training and roles of Army soldiers
Environmental Detectives	http://cms.mit.edu/games/education /Handheld/Intro.htm	Lets you take on the role of environment protection officers dealing with a major toxic spill

The Market for Serious Games

There are essentially three distinct non-entertainment markets right now. The first is the traditional educational game market. It's the market that is most similar to the regular games market. Products are developed, published, and sold at retail. The target customer is mostly the parent, although young kids will certainly have some favorite brands like Lego or Rugrats that they can be attracted to. This market is almost as old as the games market itself. It's dominated by a few large publishers like Riverdeep and Infogrames/Atari and a huge number of smaller independents.

The second market is the non-retail educational market. This includes teaching tools for schools and higher education, corporate training, and e-learning. Despite its gargantuan size, it's not an easy market. School budgets are tight, e-learning is all over the place, and selling into these markets is either an expensive proposition or one that takes a lot of patience. I think it's changing for the better, but slowly. Unlike the traditional edutainment business, this market involves either direct development for a specific project (e.g., developing a training solution for Big Oil, Inc.) or a packaged product aimed at a specific area or subject (e.g., an MBA marketing simulation sold to business schools).

The third market is a collection of markets that involve other non-entertainment applications of games. These include policy games, health games, advocacy games, advergames, and other problem solving systems. Most of these games can be seen as providing some variant on learning and exploration from a game design view, but the market they sell in is less defined than the education market.

Specific Markets

Within those three broad outlines are hundreds of separate vertical markets and classes of games. I've outlined some of the biggest vertical markets in Table 15.2.

15

Table 15.2 The biggest vertical serious games markets.

Market	Comments
Military	This market has lots of hoops that you need to jump through to get contracts, and many times you need to pair up with an established military contractor.
Corporate	Corporate training is a large market but is also very splintered and cost-conscious. It involves not only training games, but also advergaming ideas and the use of games and game technologies in the analytics area as well.
Elementary	Most elementary schools are too hard up to spend funds on software. The home market is better but is limited by its retail sales model.
High school	Unlike elementary school, high schools have a bit more money but it's still very tough. The home market for educational games is nearly nonexistent. When was the last time you saw a 16-year old playing *Reader Rabbit*?
Higher education	This market is helped by the fact that students may be made to purchase games like they are textbooks. Universities won't spend funds on games themselves, but professors can be encouraged to recommend them. Once you are an adopted part of a syllabus, you're usually golden for multiple years.
Games for health	If your game will be used in patient care, it may need to go through clinical trials and get regulatory approval before it can be adopted for use.
Home school	An interesting market with ready funds for products for the increasing number of parents who want to educate their children either wholly or partially at home. Although originally it was closely tied with religious conservatives in the United States, the market is slowly becoming more mainstream.
NGO market	Projects specific to nongovernmental organizations (NGOs) are tough because obtaining the funding can be difficult. Some NGOs can self-fund, but others will need third-party help to get projects off the ground.
Government	The military gets games, but many other segments of most governments are clueless on gaming and its positive use for training, analysis, and problem solving. Don't forget governments split into distinct markets: central government (federal), regional (state), and local.
Individuals	This is a less-distinct market because it is an area of the hobbyist. The individual development scene is exploring using games to make individual and political statements.

A Typical Serious Game Project

So what does a typical serious game project look like? Here's a quick rundown:

- The mission of most projects is to effect some sort of change (often behavioral) or provide an insight in relation to a problem.

- The development usually requires a combination of pure game development skills with major subject matter experts who can ensure that the information the game provides and teaches is accurate to whatever level of detail the solution requires.

- Such a project often requires many major disciplines to work together, not only subject matter experts and the development team, but also potential implementers (i.e., teachers, professors, trainers, and so on), potential co-marketing types, and other consultants.

- Often these projects are funded directly by the client or a third party. It can also be a business-to-business sale, but most projects are decidedly not a consumer retail model.

- Developers working on serious game projects commonly avoid state-of-the art target platforms. Since many target players may not own high-end computers or game consoles, you have to aim for a wider and less-capable platform of computer hardware.

- The opportunity for revenue (aside from construction funds for the developer) may not be in the software itself but in a suite of services that the game provides. This could be customization of the product, training seminars with the product, advertising, or scenario subscriptions. Often it is smart to shift the perceived item people are paying for away from the game itself.

- Serious games usually involve some unique engineering needs. This can include substantial printing capability, output of game statistics to spreadsheets, or special features for teachers and trainers to use. These kinds of things will be new to most game developers.

- Serious game projects usually feature long (and at times arduous) sales processes as you work through layers of decision makers in order to get to a go decision for a project. This may dissipate in time as organizations become better at understanding games and the best practices take a more standard shape. However, it won't ever go away completely.

15

Design Challenges for Developing Serious Games

Although I haven't worked personally on any serious game projects, I've talked at length to people who have, and it seems that the biggest design challenge is retaining the gameplay and general feeling of "fun" that video games have while hitting the specific targets for a project in terms of accuracy and relevancy. Games like *The Sims* or *Theme Park* are great fun. It's easy to say something like, "Let's make a game like *Theme Park*," in which you manage a supermarket so Wal-Mart can use it for training. But you need to properly understand what a game like *Theme Park* offers that makes it so enjoyable. Otherwise, you risk creating something that lacks the gameplay magic you need.

That's why it's so important for experienced game designers to get involved in creating serious games. They are the people who understand why a game works and can take this practical knowledge and apply it to non-game applications. When simulations are created by people who have never worked on games, many of them are dull and people often don't enjoy playing them. For me, that's the difference between "serious games" and business and military simulations. Serious games are *games* made by *gamers*.

One specific challenge that you might come across if you're designing a serious game is a general aversion to the area, as well as poor public perception fueled by people unfamiliar with games. A lot of people simply don't understand how many people play games, and they don't know how game development works or understand the breadth of how games are used. There are some common reasons for this:

- Many critics see games as "kids stuff," not useful or attractive to older audiences.

- There is a common feeling that the costs associated with developing games are too high.

- Another common complaint is that the time frame of development is too slow. Games take longer to develop than other training materials such as books or videos.

- The industry hasn't helped defend public perception of games. Some of the high profile mainstream games such as *Grand Theft Auto* and *Postal* have damaged the perception of the games industry, and unfortunately, the press is much less likely to talk about the many positive games out there.

- Because of the high profile that some military uses have had, there is an incorrect perception that the use of games for various training purposes is primarily a military exercise.

There is a general inexperience with game technology by many decision makers and their organizations. Not everyone speaks "game," meaning that often you are dealing with potential customers who need lots of orientation. Also, production management is not the forte of most potential clients, making it a risky decision for organizations not used to engineering games. This all adds up to the fact that the conventional wisdom on games being used outside of entertainment is that this practice is a fad that will go away soon. And essentially, you're a fad until you're not, and the tipping point hasn't been reached quite yet.

That tipping point may well be approaching, though.

Today, the technology and the market is much better prepared for the release of more serious games. A lot of this is being driven by a combination of the growing mainstream interest in games and the large gains made by game technologies. There is not much doubt these days that game programmers are among the best programmers in the world. The games industry has the cutting-edge visuals, interface design, AI techniques, and storytelling capabilities that put most other mediums to shame. Even more important, games are very widespread, so not only are the visuals amazing, but they run on hardware that costs a few hundred dollars.

The technology and the appeal games are having to a new generation are the core drivers that are forcing researchers and decision makers to take a new look at the potential for games as tools and platforms for education and training. What projects like the Serious Games Initiative are doing is helping to make it clear that if you want a game-based solution, you need to engage the right people. You don't hire a landscaper to build a house for you.

Key Pointers for Designing and Selling Serious Games

I thought a useful way to end this chapter would be to set out a few key points that can help you navigate the opportunity to expand into games outside of entertainment markets. As with much of this chapter, these come courtesy of Ben Sawyer, who heads the Serious Games Initiative:

- Solve the problem: If you can't identify a problem and solve it really well with a game, don't do it.
- Focus on comparative advantages: The comparative advantages of a game over other learning and training products are where you will make the best impact during a sales pitch; games are great fun, can look stunning, and present very well.

15

- Don't sell transference; sell skill, process, and insight: Don't make people believe your solution will have all the same stuff that makes *Half-Life* or *Mario Kart* fun, compelling, and amazing. Turning something into a game does not involve magic pixie dust. Instead, sell your skills, the processes you take, and your unique insight on a problem as a game developer.

- Build networks, lay foundations, and partner: The successful serious game developer builds a network of contacts and partners that lets them more readily develop business and deliver great solutions to particular customers. It is not a market to go it alone in.

- Be as creative with your project as you can: Don't forget that while your game is important, the creativity of a great delivery solution, great supportive teaching materials, or novel ways of applying your game to a problem can have a large impact on how well the entire effort succeeds. This is where you come in as a designer.

- Beware of other ways problems can be solved: If your game isn't a greater solution than most others, it's probably not a good idea to do it.

- Don't retail: The fact is retailers are barely stocking many commercial entertainment PC games or large amounts of console titles. If selling your serious game at retail is a key part of your business model, you're likely to get into trouble.

- This is not the game business as you know it: By now, this should be fairly apparent.

If the world becomes convinced that the best people to build a new generation of learning software and simulation tools are game developers, then there will be a whole new world of customers available to studios and independent developers. Coupled with the ability to work on subject matter that may be novel, interesting, and maybe even socially conscious, developers will have a compelling set of reasons to bring their skills to this arena.

Creative Idea: Research More About Serious Games

If you want to learn more about serious games, take a look at Water Cooler Games (www.watercoolergames.org), a useful Web site that looks at video games for all sorts of serious uses, or the official Serious Games organization site (www.seriousgames.org).

Summary

Hopefully, this chapter has given you a brief insight into the rapidly growing area of serious games. It's a really broad and exciting area full of unique design challenges, but most of the core game design skills are still very applicable.

In the next chapter, we're going to look at what to do if you're placed onto a "disaster project" —a game that is already well into development and is heading downhill rapidly. You'll learn how can you turn things around and make the project a success.

15

An Interview with Dr. Ian Bogost

Ian Bogost is a game designer, academic game researcher, and educational publisher. He is assistant professor at The Georgia Institute of Technology, where he teaches and conducts research on video game criticism and video game rhetoric. He is also co-editor at Water Cooler Games, the online resource about games with an agenda, and has published and spoken internationally. Ian is also the founder of two companies: Persuasive Games, a game studio that designs, builds, and distributes electronic games for persuasion, instruction, and activism; and Open Texture, a publisher of cross-media education and enrichment materials for families. Prior to his academic and game development career, Ian was CTO of one of the top interactive marketing companies in Los Angeles, where he worked on early experiments in advergaming. All this makes him the ideal person to talk about the subject of serious games.

Why do you feel that serious games seem to be such a rapidly growing area at the moment?

IB: Video games are an expressive medium like poetry, art, and film. Finally, after 30 years of games as a leisure activity, we are making strides in moving games into the sphere of art, critique, and social change. Serious games are one example of how this change is taking place. The idea that games can not only entertain but also educate, influence, and train is a step in the right direction. But we still have a long way to go. As a "movement," serious games still represent only a fraction of the possibility space for non-leisure games. I have been using the phrase "video games with an agenda" to refer to games that seek to do more than reinforce existing social structures— but also to challenge those social structures themselves.

To be sure, the growth of "Serious Games" is not solely motivated by profit. Working for educators, nonprofits, and similar institutions does not yet yield the hand-over-fist profits of commercial gaming. But there is great potential, and I think we'll only see this market grow. More than just the market growing, we'll see more artists and activists using games for social change, and that's one sign of a maturing medium.

Do you believe that games can be a force for changing the way people think and for helping create change in our societies?

IB: Video games are different than other media; they can simulate experiences and processes, something that no other mass medium can claim to do. Video games are uniquely positioned to help us understand the systems that structure our lives. When we play games, we explore (and often change) the rules of behavior in specific situations. There is no precedent for a medium that allows us to critique the fundamental assumptions we make about the world so easily.

What are you most proud of in your career so far?

IB: In 2003 Gonzalo Frasca, and I designed and developed the first ever official video game for a U.S. presidential candidate. The candidate was the ill-fated Howard Dean, and the game was admittedly small—we created it in a mere three week's time. But The Howard Dean for Iowa Game represented the first time a politician, let alone an American presidential candidate—had used video games as a part of their communications plan. Many other officially endorsed campaign games emerged in the aftermath of the Dean game; some of them I created, and others were developed by candidate and political party organizations. So I'm happy to have helped usher in a new possibility space for video games as endorsed political speech.

What do you think is the biggest benefit that game developers bring to training and educational software? Is it the immersion that comes with realistic technology, the fact that they can create an immediate and enjoyable control system, or something else?

IB: Educational software has been in a rut for years, for decades, perhaps. Game developers are finally bringing a new perspective on educational software—namely, that it can do more than skill and drill. The best educational games aren't pedagogical, and the best educational games don't drill rote learning. Rather, the best educational games teach students of any kind to understand a situation—from the way TCP/IP works to the operations of a business to the conditions that underlie the American Revolution—as a set of processes rather than a set of facts. As more students, young and old, learn to ask why the world works the way it does, we'll build a more engaged and successful population.

What do you think is the biggest game design mistake that people regularly make?

IB: When you make games for the general public, you have to take into account the varying video game experience of ordinary people. I think the biggest game design mistake is assuming that your players will understand more about gameplay and the user interface than they really do. As gamers, designers tend to assume that players have as much game literacy as they themselves do. I've been guilty of this myself, and it's one of the biggest challenges I find in my own design practice.

Where do you see serious games going in the future?

IB: Serious games are one example of a whole range of expressive video games—games that challenge the world around us just as literature and art have done for millennia. Personally, I'm less interested in the future of pedagogy and corporate training (valid though those areas may be) and more interested in the expressive power of video games, their ability to make people ask difficult questions, to change their views, to inspire and impel them to make the world a better place.

15

If money and technology were unlimited, what kind of game would you most like to see made?

IB: I'm most interested in the future of games about the human condition. We've seen a lot of games about fantasy and role-playing, but not so many about what it means to be a human being in our world. I'd like to see a game that opens new doors to players' understanding of the world and their place in it. What I'm suggesting here is the video game equivalent of the novels of Gabriel García Márquez, or the poetry of Charles Bukowski, or the philosophical works of Edmund Husserl. I'd like to see a video game that could garner its creators a Nobel prize.

And finally, if you had one piece of advice to give to a game designer who was just starting out, what would it be?

IB: Play more games, but don't just play games. Read literature, read poetry, watch film, view art. Immerse yourself in the five-millennium history of human expression. Find your place within it, become inspired, identify a problem you want to illuminate or a situation you want to change. Find something to say about the world. Don't be content to design games because you enjoy playing them. Tackle hard problems, and strive to break new ground in human experience, not poly counts or unit sales.

PART V

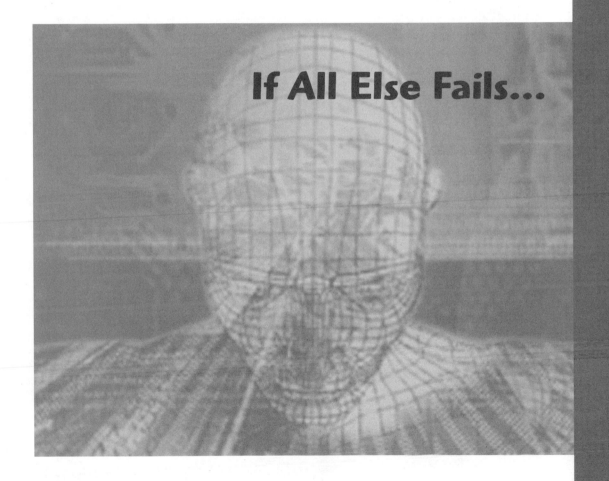

If All Else Fails...

Chapter 16

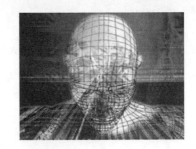

Disaster Management

"There's no disaster that can't become a blessing, and no blessing that can't become a disaster."

Richard Bach

This chapter is all about worst-case scenarios. As you build a reputation for being a good game designer, the chances will increase that you'll find yourself on a project heading downward faster than a plummeting elevator. Everyone around you will share the desperate hope that you'll be able to work your magic and turn the game into a best seller. This may feel like a death sentence. If you had your way, you would be moving on to some brand-new project, designing the next big thing from the ground up. Instead, you feel stuck working on the game from hell, with a demoralized team and a publisher wondering where the exit door is. You'll probably think that this is the worst thing that could possibly happen to a game designer.

Well, not necessarily. Working on a troubled project could turn out to be a very rewarding experience. (I bet you knew I was going to say that, didn't you?) Such a project will give you the chance to be a hero as you help to rescue the day. In theory, it should be a no-lose situation. Since people may have mentally written the game off in their minds, it should come as no surprise if you're unable to turn the project around. But if you do manage to set it in the right direction, your credibility and reputation will be greatly enhanced.

Surviving a Project from Hell

Back in the real world, working on a project that is greatly troubled (and possibly saving it) is not easy. People may forget that you came onto the project *after* it was in trouble, and when it fails, you may become the "poster boy" for the failed project. If you become involved in a project like this, make sure everyone knows from the outset that it will be hard to turn the project around, and if the project doesn't work out, remind the people who count that things may have been very different if you'd been involved from day one.

 Reality Check: The smartest thing to do is put on your best positive face and throw yourself into making the game better. If you have a positive attitude and believe in what you're trying to do, you should find that morale on the title will improve across the board and you'll be able to get the team focused and optimistic again. Accept the challenge, but don't let anyone pass the blame onto you for what has gone on previously.

So, what should you do if you've been dumped onto the next *Daikatana*? Here are the steps you should take to try to turn the project around:

1. **Analyze and identify all the problems within the project.**

   Walk through all the different aspects of the game, and make a list of everything that isn't good enough. Broadly speaking, split the game up into the following areas:

   - Overall theme/concept/title
   - Characters
   - Storyline
   - Level design (both general and specific)
   - Cameras and controls
   - Character actions and interactions
   - Overall level of fun
   - General graphical quality
   - Animations
   - Front end
   - Music
   - Sound effects
   - Variety
   - Difficulty

16

- Ease of entry/tutorials

- Major bugs

- Length of the game

- Replayablity

- Other game modes

- Multiplayer/online gameplay

- Project staff (are any team members causing a problem?)

We'll take a look at all of these areas in more detail later on. The key thing to remember is that, for each area, you should take a close look at the current status of the game and write down the problems. Ideally, jot down a few possible solutions. For example, if the ease of entry is a real problem (new players find the game too hard and impenetrable), you might consider redesigning the first level, adding pop-up tutorial boxes, or creating a new tutorial section outside of the main game. If you know an area has problems but you're not sure how to improve it, take a look at other games that work well and note what is different about them.

2. **Order the problem areas in terms of importance.**

   Decide which issues will make the most difference if they are addressed. Concentrate on areas that are easiest to deal with and those that will give you the biggest improvements. In the real world, you won't be able to do everything that you want to. So rate all the problems with the game according to how bad they are and what effect they will have on the final review scores if they're fixed.

3. **Come up with a plan of action to fix the most important areas.**

   To get the most bang for your buck, focus on the issues that will have the biggest effect on the final review score for the least amount of work. Gameplay issues should always take precedence; getting the core gameplay working well is the single most important aspect of your role. An easy way to do this is to give each issue a score from 1 to 10 that represents how big you think the problem is and what impact will be made if you fix it. Then give it a score (again, from 1 to 10) for how easy it will be to fix. Add the two scores together for each issue, and start working on the highest-scoring ones (which will be biggest problems that are easiest to fix).

Let's look at an example. Assume that you've decided there are four big problem areas on your new disaster project:

- The in-game camera is truly dreadful.

- The game is way too hard, difficulty-wise.

- The online multiplayer gameplay is weak.

- The main character makes everyone laugh (and not in a nice way).

For each problem area, score the importance, using your best judgement as to how big an effect the improvement would make on the final game. Then score how easy it will be to fix each problem, speaking with individual team members to help you get a realistic estimate of how long it might take to make changes if necessary.

Table 16.1   Assessing which areas to focus on.

Fix	Importance (10=high)	Is it easy to do? (10=simple)	Total Score
Implement a new in-game camera	10	6	16
Alter the difficulty level	8	9	17
Add new gameplay mechanics to online	7	4	11
Create a new main character	9	5	14

Looking at Table 16.1, it appears that it would be much more sensible to target the difficulty level and in-game camera rather than sorting out the online gameplay. Obviously, you really ought to tackle all four areas, but again, in the real world, you might not have the time and budget available to do this (that doesn't mean you shouldn't fight hard to try to make it happen!).

Remember the 80:20 principle, which often holds true for video games; a small amount of effort can often result in large improvements.

4. **Don't be afraid to use other games for reference.**

There is no point in continuing to try to fix your unique combat system that just won't work when there are perfect examples out there that work really well. Don't be precious about it because you've got to turn this game around as quickly as you can. Often, the best way to do this is to use other games for inspiration. Imitation is the sincerest form of flattery, and it's not copying (unless you're taking a very unique feature that has only ever been done by one game). Ask yourself, "Will reviewers say that we copied that game when they write the review?" If not, add it in.

16

5. **Focus the project—cut, trim, and slash**

A short but really enjoyable game will always review better than a long sprawling game that isn't fun to play. Most people agree that modern games are probably too long. As long as the game doesn't end up being ridiculously short (which I would define as less than 8 hours of gameplay), you should seriously consider cutting the amount of content and focusing on the quality of what is left. If a feature isn't working and you feel the game can survive without it, cut it out. It's a little like horticulture; sometimes in order for a plant to survive, you need to trim it back harshly.

There are also lots of tricks that you can use to increase the length of gameplay (and replayability) without adding more levels and content. Put in pickups for the player to collect, to give players a reason to explore your environment. Add in a new game mode that allows you to replay the existing levels but with a different purpose. A great example of this is the *Max Payne* "New York Minute," which gives you the chance to replay the levels, but with a time constraint (see Figure 16.1). It reuses the whole single-player game and adds a timer on the screen, and die-hard players have a whole new reason to play the levels again as

Figure 16.1
Max Payne.

the frenetic pace forced on them by the timer leads them to try things differently and sprint through the levels. You can also add a really challenging difficulty mode. One of the best examples of this is the classic N64 game *GoldenEye* (Figure 16.2), in which moving up to a harder difficulty level not only gave you a larger number of tougher enemies, but it also added extra objectives within the existing levels, encouraging you to explore further and find areas that you hadn't visited before. Making your difficulty levels this polished will add a bit of time, but this may give you more confidence about trimming the number of levels from the game and save much more time on artwork and level construction.

Figure 16.2
GoldenEye.

My advice is don't be afraid to cut, and to cut hard. It's something that film directors have to get used to when their 4-hour epic has to be edited to a more reasonable size. Film editor Sally Menke recently said, "…cutting a film can be about 20 percent editing, 80 percent politics…,"and unfortunately the same is true for games. It can be really horrible cutting levels that you love and that some poor level designer has spent months of their life working on, but if the project is headed for disaster, you can't afford to become emotionally attached to anything. You'll need lots of tact, but it's much easier to make major changes like this when a project is obviously in trouble.

Case Study: Fixing *JetPack Jim*

16

Turning a bad game around involves almost everything that I've written about in this book: understanding cameras, working with control systems, developing characters, working with different platforms, and so on. To help you see what is involved, let's take a look at a sample case study that illustrates some of these points. The game that we will be trying to save is

JETPACK JIM
"Have jetpack, will travel"

To avoid offending anyone, we're going to look at an imaginary game (as opposed to a real game). *JetPack Jim* is a title that is designed for the PSP and the PC and is due to be completed in three months' time. Unfortunately, it's way behind schedule and much work is still needed to finish it so that it will be ready for release. We've also heard through the rumor mill that the game really sucks. We've been put onto the project to try to turn it around. It's day 1, and all we know about the project is as follows:

Jetpack Jim **is a game that has been designed for 12- to 24-year-old males. You control Jim, our brave hero, who uses his jetpack to fly around the sky, leaping from one place to another as he tackles criminals and makes the city a safer place to live. As well as being able to fly, as Jim you can also carry out hand-to-hand combat with the criminals and pick up and drop objects on their heads, which is one of the few enjoyable aspects to the gameplay currently.**

WEEK 1
TASK LIST
Always start a new project by finding out as much as possible about its status; listen first, speak later. I suggest we spend our first week doing the following:

- Meeting one-on-one with the team members, listening to their concerns and the problems they have had.

- Playing the latest version of the game on both platforms, and analyzing it using the list at the start of this chapter.

- Doing some research on jetpacks.

- Speaking to a few people to see if they think the title and tag line of the game is as bad as I think it is.

- Playing other games that are similar in style. Of course, you'll only know which games to look at once you've seen what *Jetpack Jim* is like.

- Compiling a list of all of the critical areas of the game that still need to be completed or redone.

RESULTS:

- After talking to the team, it is apparent that they have very low morale. Most of them think the gameplay is awful, but they don't know why. They don't feel that they can get all the levels done on time. One of them thinks the game is brilliant and can't see what all the fuss is about. The producer has just had a baby and isn't around much. Some team members feel that the game design is missing something special.

- After playing the game, it is obvious just how bad it is. The camera is solidly attached three feet behind the main character and never moves from that position. The controls are awkward and unresponsive. Some of the weapons are fun, but some are dreadful. The game lacks anything really unique and the levels don't use the jetpack very much, which is the one interesting thing about the design. The game is also way too difficult.

- The jetpack research produced lots of interesting facts. The most useful ones are that jetpacks have a limited altitude and that they run out of fuel. There aren't many real ones around, but a very interesting jetpack called the SoloTrek is being developed. They're currently very dangerous and hard to steer. Most of them use small jet engines, which get extremely hot. If you run out of fuel in the middle of the air, you'd need a parachute or ejector seat to survive.

- Everyone we spoke to felt that the name was really bad. It wasn't just us! So we resolve to try to get the name changed as soon as possible.

- Having played the game, we took a look at some other games that involve vertical takeoffs, including *Pilotwings* (Figure 16.3), the old ZX Spectrum game *Jetpac*, and the influential *Thrust*.

WEEK 2

We're now ready to make some major recommendations. In order to turn this game around, some major decisions need to be made and some critical tasks need to be completed. We've written up a clear plan of action that we believe can turn this game into something much stronger. We're going to present this plan to the person who put us onto this project and make it clear that this is the only way to make this game work.

Figure 16.3
Pilotwings.

PLAN OF ACTION:

- We will need more time if the game is to reach a decent quality level. After talking with the producer, it seems like an extra three months is achievable, giving us six months until completion. (Of course, you may not be given more time, but if you feel it is the only option, and it is always a last resort, then ask for it.)

- The design needs a big boost. To this end, we've trimmed some of the game mechanics that weren't working and identified fixes that should help the camera and control system. When playing *Pilotwings*, we found that it features a jetpack, so we've been able to directly compare our controls and the controls in *Pilotwings*. Since our control system is currently so bad, we're going to implement some of the features from that game. We're also going to use the jetpack much more in the game.

- We've come up with two new gameplay elements that should help add uniqueness to the game without being much extra work to implement. First, the flame from the exhaust of the jetpack can be used to set fire to things as well as to burn enemies. The length of flame depends on how much power is being used. The lead programmer has a great idea about how to make everything and everyone in the world flammable! Second, we'll need a way keep the jetpack fueled. If the player runs out of fuel in midair, they can pull their parachute (which they have to quickly do manually before they plummet to the ground) and then run to the nearest refueling station.

- We want to trim the scope of the game down to a more sensible size. It currently has about 30 huge levels, many of which aren't finished. By playing through them all, we've identified 10 that just don't work well and don't offer much in the way of gameplay fun. By trimming the game down by a third, we can focus on making the rest of the game stronger, as well as adding in objects to set fire to with our new jetpack feature.

- After speaking to the team and holding a very small off-site focus group of a few younger gamers we know, we're recommending changing the name. We'll just call it *Jetpack* because this name sounds cooler and much less like a cheap shareware game. We'll also recommend that the marketing team rewrite the awful tag line to fit in with the new design. *(By the way, this name is probably trademarked in the real world, but this is a hypothetical project!)*

- We'll present the new plan and revised design to the team members to try to boost morale. Having spoken to them all previously, we know what they are concerned about and can focus on addressing these issues to help everyone feel more positive. We think that the name change and the new focus of the game will really get them excited and help to breathe new life into the project.

- We need to focus on the differences between the two platforms. Thus, we put together a PC-specific brief with the programmers, concentrating on making sure that the PC controls are carefully thought out and that the game will work as well as possible on the PC.

WEEK 3 ONWARD

We've now got buy-in from the key people for the changes we want to make. There are some people in the team who are opposed to the changes, but we spend time with them to justify what we want to do. If they don't listen, then we're not going to lose too much sleep over it; it's rare to get everyone in total agreement when you're dealing with designs.

We're now ready to move into the stage of implementing the changes and working with the team members to get the key gameplay changes in as early as possible.

Summary of the Project

Dealing with projects that are heading for disaster is the biggest design challenge you can face. As long as you do your research (listening to people on the team), identify carefully what isn't working, and are prepared to make tough decisions (including dramatically cutting content), you should stand the best chance of getting something good out at the end. Remember that something short but sweet is infinitely better that a long, soulless game.

Keep in mind the following key tenets of disaster management:

Research: Play the game, talk to everyone, and get as much information about the subject matter as possible. Find out everything there is to know about the project.

Plan: Formulate a clear and realistic plan that you believe will help turn the project around. Make sure there are no gray areas and that everyone will be able to understand exactly what is required. Keep in mind that one of the reasons the game is in the state that it is in is likely an inadequate plan. In order to get the game out of the big rut it is in, a good plan is absolutely necessary. Otherwise, you run the risk of having the team fail again, and that would be really demoralizing. If you want to add new features, make sure they are realistic, and if you have a fixed time frame, see if there is any other remaining work that can be cut to make room for the new elements.

Communicate: Explain the plan to the team, individually if necessary. Use your knowledge of their concerns to help them buy into the new plan. If the project has been going badly and you are offering a route to make the game better in parallel with a plan for finishing the game in a sensible time frame, they should be very keen to jump on board. If the project has been dragging on, many team members might just want to get it finished, so you need to present a clear idea of where the finish line is.

Implement: Make sure your plan is implemented. Devote the time that is needed to helping the key programmers, artists, and designers get the core elements focused in the right way as quickly as possible. Use focus groups to check the difficulty, and make sure the game is more enjoyable than it was before. Keep talking to people and hopefully, you will find that morale will improve as the team sees the game coming together.

Focus: As I've mentioned, the best way to avoid being swamped by a disaster project is to break it down into individual sections and try to identify fixes from each separate problem area.

Common Problems You'll Encounter with Fixing Troubled Games

Now that we've worked through the process of trying to improve a game, let's step back and look at the most common problems that you might come across when getting involved with a troubled game.

Poor Elevator Pitch or Razor X

As I've mentioned several times in the book, it is vital that your game has a clear "hook"—a simple one-line description that summarizes what will make the game so special. It's often called an "elevator pitch" because if you were trying to describe the game to another person while going up in an elevator, you'd have about twenty seconds to do so. If someone asks you why they should buy the game, what would you say? If the game's key features are not clear, you are in big trouble. It may have had one long ago and the project has since taken a turn in the wrong direction. In this case, you need to carefully steer it back on course. Or the game's original designers may have never worked out the game's key hook. Hopefully there is one, so look through all the features of the game and see if one of them jumps out at you. If so, focus on this element and make it even better.

 Reality Check: If a game really doesn't have anything that makes it stand out, you'll need to create something. Take a look at the gameplay, hold a brainstorming session, and try to come up with something new that fits the existing game but will offer gamers and magazine reviewers something unique. Make sure that everyone understands that the game's hook is arguably the single most important thing you can contribute to a project that is in trouble.

Bad Camera Work

Bad games often have really bad in-game cameras. These are either a result of someone wanting to try something new (which didn't work) or just that they have been implemented by someone who doesn't understand how in-game cameras are supposed to work. The easiest thing to do is to find a similar game and use that as a reference point. If you can show your programmers how the camera is supposed to be by letting them play another game, there is a good chance that they can replicate that. Although originality is great, when your project is in trouble, copying something else is the best way to quickly get an area like the camera up to scratch.

Poor Control Systems

As you already know, the control system is incredibly important. The in-game character or vehicle needs to react instantly. When you pick up the controller for the first time, the game needs to feel intuitive. With troubled projects, the controls are often a nightmare. As with cameras, the best way to improve things quickly is to pick a similar game with a good control system and make your programmers copy that. Then, if you have more time, you can work on making your control system more unique.

Lack of Fun

Quite often, problem games just aren't fun to play. If you fix the cameras and control systems, things will often get better, but the real problem may be that the core gameplay has been designed badly. There is no easy answer to making things fun. You should definitely play the game through and see if any of it is enjoyable. If so, you should concentrate more on the enjoyable gameplay and try to replicate it throughout more of the game. If the gameplay isn't fun at all, I'd advise you to take a look at the most similar game you can. If you're creating a platform game that is dull and lifeless, take a look at a top platform game, such as a Mario game or the Prince of Persia series, and see what they are doing differently. The key is to break the gameplay down into components. Here are some questions to ask: Do you spend too much time running around with nothing to do? Is the combat dull? Is your character too slow? Does the player need to use his brain, or is the game too linear and obvious?

War Story: Games That Aren't Fun Fail

If you'd like a real-world example of a game that isn't fun, get ahold of a title called *Trespasser* by Dreamworks Interactive (see Figure 16.4). My apologies if any of the development team is reading this, but it was a title that promised a great deal and delivered a poor and unexciting experience. At some point, someone should have sat down, played the game, and said, "Hey guys, this game just isn't any fun!" It's a good example of where developers can get so caught up in the details (such as the "revolutionary" physics puzzles that unfortunately never really worked) that they lost sight of the bigger picture.

Demographics or Platforms Issues

Does everyone know what kind of player your game was created for? Is it a kids game, or are you creating a mature title for older gamers? Are you trying to create a mass-market title for all sorts of people, or is it a hardcore game? Does everyone know what the lead platform is? Are you trying to create a console game, a PC game, or a handheld game?

Staff Problems

Quite often, there will be at least one problem person (and maybe more) on a project and they are a main reason the project has been going so badly. If you are able to identify problem people, you need to think carefully about how to deal with them. If

Figure 16.4
Trespasser—a game that got off track.

they are vital to the project, you need to bring them around; go out with them for a drink and find out why they are negative. Is there anything you can do to bring back some enthusiasm? If they aren't vital to the project, you need to speak with the person who put you onto the game and suggest that they consider making a change. You're never going to have a whole team full of super-enthusiastic geniuses, but having a problem person who is extremely negative can bring an entire team down. Use whatever power you have to try to resolve the situation as quickly as you can.

Reality Check: When you have staff problems, it's easy to procrastinate and hope for the best. But the real truth is that problems like this don't go away on their own. It's also likely that a problem person is really affecting the rest of the team, even though the person might seem popular. In my experience, the sooner you replace the person, the sooner things will get better. You'll likely look at the situation a few weeks later and remark, "Why didn't I make a change sooner?" If your gut instincts tell you that you need to replace a problem person, follow your instincts.

Poor Title

Check the title of the game. Does it work? Do people understand it and feel it is a good name? If not, find a load of alternatives, do some focus group work, and try to get the men in suits to agree to make a change. Often a change of name can do wonders, particularly if the project has been in trouble for a while; it can feel like a breath of fresh air. A game's name is a hugely underrated element in my view, and although having a great name clearly won't make up for poor gameplay, I have seen many strong games damaged by having names that confused people or didn't give them any idea what the game was about.

War Story: Make Your Game's Name Match Its Hook

I'm a little biased in telling this story because it relates to a game series that I'm now responsible for, but I've always felt that the Hitman games have an extremely clear hook, mainly due to the name. The name Hitman is just so obvious to consumers; they know exactly what they're going to be doing. Just by hearing that one word, they understand that they're going to be experiencing the life of a hitman, carrying out assassinations and contracts. Compare this to, for example, *Wild 9* by Shiny Entertainment. The game itself was an enjoyable platform game, but I don't think the name did it any favors. What does *Wild 9* mean? As a consumer, why would that excite me? Of course, there are many examples of games that have names that don't really mean anything; *Half-Life* is a typical example. But I believe that a name that allows people to understand your hook is equivalent to a huge percentage of the marketing money you would otherwise need to spend to educate consumers about your title.

Poor Storyline

If you are developing a story-based game, go through the storyline carefully. Is it great? If not, can you make any changes without having to redo vast amounts of the game? Don't only read the storyline on paper; see how it has been translated into the actual game. Often I have read a great plot on paper only to see that vital bits of the story have been missed in its implementation. The only storyline that counts is the one that players see when they play through the game. It needs to be rich and powerful and make the player want to keep on playing to find out what happens next.

Problems with the Game's Difficulty Level

Bad games are often insanely hard. Make sure that average gamers who have never played the game before can get through the game on the normal difficulty level without having major problems. Ensure that you have an easy and hard level as well, so that the game can be played by players with skills that fall within a wide range of skill sets. Make sure that the first level or section of the game is easy yet exciting. Also make sure that new players are shown the core controls and taught the mindset that they need to have to play the game. For example, if you are working on a stealth game, it's useful to start the game by reminding players of this and showing them how to use stealth to their advantage. Otherwise, they may have come straight from an all-action shooter and their default actions will be to plough into the enemy with guns blazing. Make sure that there are not any major difficulty spikes—places where the game gets so hard that people are likely to give up.

Inadequate Pacing

Look at the pacing within the game. Are any sections that are too dull or calm? Are any sections too exhausting? Try to mirror the roller coaster effect that you get in great movies, rising up to a huge crescendo, then calming down before building up to the next peak.

Need for Licenses

If the game has any licenses, make sure that they have been signed up, that the licensors are happy, and that you are using the licenses to your greatest advantage. If the game doesn't have any licenses, think about whether it would help to add some. In some cases, adding a license can really help define a product and provide a hook that wasn't present before.

War Story: Make Sure Your Licenses Are Secure

Making sure that licenses have been signed up sounds like a very obvious thing to do, but it has badly burned more than one company. A classic example is the publisher Psygnosis who released *Formula 1 '97* without properly checking its license agreement with the owners. The result was that the company had to remove the games from the shelves and remaster a whole load of new discs without the offending material included. The cost of creating all the discs that had to be scrapped was significant. The figure was never revealed, but I would imagine it was well over a million dollars.

Unappealing Characters

Make sure the main character is appealing to the player. If the average player doesn't like the main character, your game isn't going to sell well. Make sure the character is well animated. Also, if you are fixing a third-person game, make sure the character's back has been really well modeled, since the player will be seeing this viewpoint most of the time. Think about other characters that you meet in the game. Are they interesting and varied enough? Are they two-dimensional, or are they genuinely intriguing individuals?

Inadequate Levels

Are there too many levels or not enough? Are they varied enough, or are they incredibly similar to each other? Make sure the levels make full use of all the core mechanics; it's no use having a stunning night-vision camera if none of the levels are set in the dark! Think about whether all the levels look visually impressive. Are any of the levels clearly worse than the others? What makes each level special?

Online Problems

If the game features online play, make sure it is playable online and then test it. Is the online play fun? Do the online game modes fit in with your razor X? If the online mode is not unique and is the same as in many other games, try to come up with a unique way of playing the game online. Think about having a cooperative game mode. How about making the two sides nonsymmetrical? So, in the case of *Jetpack*, rather than having a eight-character deathmatch where everyone has a jetpack, why not have seven characters on foot (or in ground-based vehicles) all competing against each other to hunt down the one player with the jetpack. Give the single player a height limit, and force him to return to the ground regularly (to collect objectives or refuel). Try to make your online game mode unusual, while of course playing it thoroughly to make sure it's great fun. And yet again, if you don't have much time and your online mode isn't working, copy a similar game!

Problems with the Front End

Take a close look at the front end to your game. Often the front end lets a whole game down; it's the first thing that new players see, and if it looks poor or is confusing, people might just stop playing straight away. Now is not the time to create an elaborate front end, so make it as short and simple as possible, but make sure it has a professional and attractive graphical look. If you don't have a strong 2D artist on the project, make sure you find one from somewhere!

Audio Issues

Listen carefully to the music and sound effects. Quite often, with disaster projects, these will be cheap, limited, and of poor quality. Find out exactly how much space and room you have, and then identify the biggest problems. Are there certain sound effects that you hear all the time? If so, it's worth tackling these first. Is the music dreadful? Then consider removing it and focusing purely on sound effects. If you need music, find some prewritten music that fits.

Real Gaming Disasters

Here is my list of the worst games ever made. These games represent total disasters that even the best designer in the world would struggle to fix. My condolences if you have had the misfortune of working on any of these titles. If you have been involved on any of these games, I strongly advise you to remove any reference to it from your resume and consider psychiatric counseling to help you get over the trauma!

William Shatner's Tekwar: I've just come out of a building. Aaarggghh! I'm being shot. But I can't see who is shooting me. They must be miles away. Aaarrrgghhh. I'm dead.

Trespasser: We're going to create the most amazing physics-based game ever made. Oops. None of it works. Quick, throw in a pair of breasts for the main character, and hope no one notices....

Daikatana (see Figure 16.5): "Jon Romero is going to make you his bitch."*

   *As long as you like low-resolution brown textures and being attacked by lots of very small creatures that are really hard to shoot.

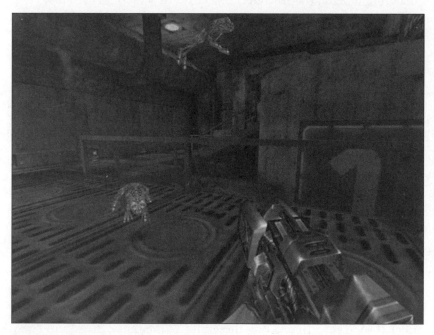

Figure 16.5
Daikatana.

E.T.: This has gone down in the annals of gaming history. Not only was the game awful, but the manufacturer allegedly made more cartridges than there were consoles in existence at the time. Most of those cartridges are apparently now buried deep beneath the desert.

16

Driver 3: It must take real effort to create a sequel considerably worse than the previous two games. Gameplay-wise, it's even worse than *Driver 1*, and that was on the original PlayStation. Just don't mention review scores and allegations of impropriety.

Nighttrap: This game was supposed to be "The definitive multimedia experience." As with so many other games at this time (it was on the ill-fated 3DO machine), the designers wanted to be film directors and ended up making something totally noninteractive yet much worse than a straight-to-video film.

Toonstruck (see Figure 16.6): An anonymous source told me some of the chaos that ensued with this project, which was a live-action/cartoon melange much like *Who Framed Roger Rabbit*. Virgin allegedly spent many millions on it, even building a big budget chroma key studio especially for the game. After many disastrous years, they only ever released half of the game, which promptly sunk without trace because it was rubbish.

Figure 16.6
Toonstruck.

Summary

I hope that this chapter will prove useful if you ever find yourself on a project that needs turning around rapidly. It's a challenging and immensely satisfying experience if you can pull it off.

So, we're now almost at the end of the book. In the final chapter, I'm going to attempt to summarize all the key points and consolidate all my advice throughout the book into 10 game design commandments. But first, a brief diversion to meet a fictional friend.

Dan the Disastrous Designer Has a Job Interview

I didn't feel I could ask any real-life designer to be my expert on disaster management without risking major offense! So therefore, I'm going to interview Dan the Disastrous Designer, who is a fictional character I made up. I have created him for the sole purpose of demonstrating a number of key flaws that I have come across when meeting or interviewing designers. Dan the Disastrous (and Depressingly Dreadful) Designer is without a doubt the worst game designer ever to be given the title, and if you can try to avoid his general attitude, arrogance, and obvious mistakes, you'll be on the right track.

Let's interview Dan for a lead designer role and see how he stacks up.

Your resume says that you have worked on "a number of top titles." Can you elaborate? Have any of your games reached number one?

DD: Well, I have worked on lots of great games. They didn't reach number one, though, but they should have.

They didn't actually enter the charts at all, did they?

DD: They did! Space Badger Extreme reached number 19 in Lichtenstein. Well, okay, they didn't chart anywhere else. But that wasn't the games' fault. The games were really incredible; we were let down by our publisher, who didn't market them at all. If only they'd had a big TV advertising campaign (preferably during the Superbowl), then they would have sold millions.

So you feel the games were strong in terms of gameplay and overall quality?

DD: Yes. Super Mech Racer was easily better than Gran Turismo! If only we'd had their sales!

But *Gran Turismo* has averaged review scores of 95 percent, whereas the highest score that *Super Mech Racer* received was 30 percent, and I'm told even that was because the reviewer was too lazy to actually boot the game up.

DD: Ah. But that's the gaming press for you. They didn't understand my game design. It wasn't demonstrated well to them, and none of them "got" what I was trying to do. Without sounding arrogant, I think my concepts were ahead of their time. My artistic vision went over their heads.

Why do you think these titles didn't do so well, and what lessons have you learned from them?

DD: You know what they say: If at first you don't succeed, try, try, and try again. So I'm not steering from my course. I know my designs are fantastic, and one day I'm going to get the recognition I deserve.

You seem to have designed only for the PC. What is your view on console games?

DD: The PC is clearly the most important platform for games. Look at games like Daikatana and Star Wars: Force Commander, both of which were hugely underrated.. Therefore, I don't believe in supporting consoles. They're a cheap man's PC. I mean, I don't play console games, and I don't see why I should constrain my design and sell my creative soul to the devil by working on a console. It's the one thing I feel very strongly about.

What do you think are the most important elements of a great game design?

DD: Clearly graphics are the most important thing. But I believe in creating emotion in the people who play my games. More specifically, I like to create confusion and a sense of mild panic. By keeping the player unsettled, never really understanding what is going on, I feel that a game becomes even more immersive and the player is forced to sink or swim.

So do you like to include difficulty levels in your games?

DD: I'm a big fan of difficulty levels. My last title, Major Snake Bandits, had four of them: hard, very hard, ultra extreme, and a special "Impossible Ninja" option that opened up if you completed the game on ultra extreme. Admittedly, none of the testers could get past "hard," but I know that real fans of the game with true persistence will, and they are the guys I care about.

Okay. Let's talk about other games. What do you think about the Grand Theft Auto series? Why do you think it has been so successful?

DD: That's one game that really annoys me. Let's face it, the games are really crap. The story is poor, the character animation looks bad, and it's all a big con by the magazine reviewers who are in the pockets of Take Two. If only the 15 million people who buy each version of the game understood proper game design, they wouldn't buy them. They're all idiots. But things will change.

So when you're creating a design, what kind of person are you creating your game for?

DD: Well, that's obvious—the general public. Fortunately, I think I'm pretty representative: I'm medium height, I like eating Mexican food, and I'm a gamer. So I normally find that if I like the game, it's going to appeal to the mass market out there. I definitely don't believe in focus groups or market research. That's all bull from men in suits. None of the people they ask are game designers, so of course they're not going to be able to give sensible opinions!

So why are you looking to leave your current job at Arty Electronic Games?

DD: I'm having, erm, let's call them "creative differences" with my team. I'm working with people who don't understand my vision, and I'm not prepared to compromise. They just don't realize what I'm trying to do, and they're so corporate. They keeping talking to me about money and time when it's obvious that quality is the only important element that makes games successful!

I'm not sure I should ask this question, but I will anyway. Do you feel you're a tactful person and a good team player?

DD: Totally. Tact is my middle name, and I get on well with pretty much anyone. Admittedly, I've had a few problems on each project, but everyone has that, right? I mean, I've had the odd fight, but it's all part of the games industry, right? As long as everyone does what I say, doesn't argue with me, and just lets me get on with the creative process without any limitations, then I'm a complete angel to work with.

Chapter 17

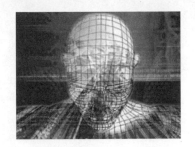

The Final Chapter

"The best way to predict the future is to create it."
Jason Kaufman

I thought I'd start this final chapter by donning my mystical hat and cape, dusting off my crystal ball, and giving you a few of my predictions for gaming technology as it moves forward.

The games industry moves more rapidly than almost any other. The raw power of our consoles increases exponentially every five or six years. More people than ever play video games as part of their lifestyle, and the average age of gamers increases annually. Now, there are as many people in their 30s and 40s who regularly play games as there are children who play. Game publishers, developers, and retailers have evolved over a relatively short period of time from naïve enthusiasts into a highly professional industry turning over a huge amount of money. Gaming is getting seriously grown up.

But one thing is certain. We still have a long way to go, and there will be many spectacular changes as we move into the future. I'd like to begin the final chapter by suggesting some of the exciting things that may lie in store for game designers. As a designer, it's important to develop your own sense of where the market is headed so that you can try to design for the future. The last thing you want to do is design an incredible game only to find out once it is completed that game players aren't interested in playing your style of game or that you've made a game for a platform that is becoming obsolete.

The Top Trends in Gaming

When taking out our crystal ball to peer into the future, the best place to start is to look at the trends that are now driving the industry. In certain respects, where the market is headed will likely be directly or indirectly pushed by what game developers and technology companies are producing today. We can also learn a lot by looking at related industries.

The Demise of Platforms

In the long term, I think it is inevitable that gaming technology will reach a level where you cannot discern any further improvements to graphics, sound, or processor power. Already, Dolby surround sound is approaching the ultimate audio experience. Once the graphical power of processors allows game environments that are almost indistinguishable from reality, the power of the hardware manufacturers will end. There will be no advantage to a particular platform when your washing machine has enough processing power to run *Final Fantasy 25*. With the almost unlimited power predicted if quantum processors become a reality, content and gameplay really will become king.

Once this becomes the case, control of the industry will belong to the people who own the brands and licenses and to those who can develop the enormously complex and detailed game worlds demanded by the consumer. The "wow" factor in our games will become the amazing content, playability, and interaction, instead of the impressive 3D graphics.

So, what will games in the future actually run on? Well, the games industry is one of the few industries that actively encourages multiple standards, or platforms. Most other industries have one fixed format, such as DVD, which all manufacturers support. I believe it is highly likely, with technology rapidly converging, that a standard will emerge. This would most likely happen by the time the processing power available starts to outstrip our ability to improve the graphics, physics, and connectivity of our home consoles (why buy a particular console when they all have the same features?). However, this transition may occur even earlier. And who is best placed to provide that standard? Well, I wouldn't bet against a certain large American company that already provides the operating system for several of the biggest-selling game platforms.

The Aging of Video Gamers

Let's face it: the secret is out. The population around the world is aging. The "baby boomer" effect is not just something that impacts the types of cars, homes, or golf clubs that are being purchased. The demographics of video game players will continue to change rapidly, ultimately ending up almost identical to that of film and movie viewers— extremely mass market, and available in every household. Games will no doubt be developed to appeal to the new niches this creates. In much the same way that many companies specialize in kids games today, companies will specialize in creating games for older gamers. These types of games will probably involve less emphasis on twitch gameplay and more emphasis on mental challenges and puzzle solving. This changing demographic will also likely encourage more successful "serious" games. Now is a good time for all of us to start thinking out of the box and look for ideas and designs that might appeal to more mature gamers.

Distribution Channels Are Going Digital

Gamers are still likely to purchase their games at video game stores for the foreseeable future, but the tides are changing. Shopping in physical locations is a fun thing to do and provides a social component that many people still can't live without. But each year, sales continue to shift to the Internet for most types of media- and entertainment-related projects. This is like a train that is going downhill that will simply keep picking up momentum.

Games provide a unique opportunity over other types of media, such as books, because consumers can use digital distribution channels like the Internet and purchase and download everything they need. The Internet also provides advantages because players can get extra features and updates that they can't readily get in stores.

It's likely that digital distribution will become the leading distribution channel for gamers, with people buying and downloading games online from home. Already Valve's unique Steam system has delivered *Half-Life 2* online to many hundreds of thousands of customers, cutting out retail. But will it happen across the board? Much will depend on the film and music industries, from which we often take our lead. In the late 1980s, people claimed that no one would be reading printed books in 20 years' time; that books would all be electronic. E-mail hasn't stopped us from writing letters or receiving mail, but it has rapidly become the most regularly used form of communication for much of the population.

For the same reason that people like to own printed books, I think some people would miss the thrill of buying a game and opening it on the way home to thumb through the manual in anticipation. In the same way, I believe that it's possible that digital distribution may end up complementing retail, with stores selling more of a physical package such as a T-shirt, stickers, complementary novel, and a hint book all bundled in with the game. For certain, the Internet will provide a quick and easy way to update games, buy new levels, and download demos. Whether it will end up being the medium that everyone uses to get the latest new game is still a question that needs to be answered.

One thing that could cause digital distribution to become a standard would be if a console manufacturer decides not to release games at retail and makes all software downloadable from its central game server. There has even been talk of future game platforms that have all the processing power at the server end, and people in their houses have just a controller, a television, and a fast Internet connection and the game is played and processed in a huge server warehouse, with the visual images sent back to the player's TV. Whether this will happen in the near future is highly debatable; the amount of processing power needed would be staggering. But it's an example of one route that the industry could take moving forward. Looking at Nintendo's plans for the Revolution, it wants to make all previous Nintendo games available online to download and play. So we're definitely heading in this direction!

Sound and Vision Is Going Immersive

Most people who have experienced the headache-inducing virtual reality (VR) headsets of the 1980s will have glimpsed the potential for an incredibly immersive experience. The ability to turn your head and look around in full 3D within a computer-generated world is a remarkable one. For those that haven't experienced it, I would suggest that the leap from a 2D TV screen to true 3D immersion is greater than the difference from mono to stereo sound or from black-and-white to color television. If hardware manufacturers manage to develop either truly 3D televisions or a 3D headset the size and weight of a pair of sunglasses, I believe that the next revolution in gaming (and film-making) will occur.

True Dolby Digital 5.1 surround sound is a very impressive experience. Currently, for an exorbitant price, you can buy headphones that provide you with a full surround sound experience. At some point soon, surround sound may well become a standard that everything will support, from personal stereos to all home entertainment devices.

Getting Connected

There has already been much comment made about Sony's vision of the future, with its "cell" architecture that allows a number of Sony devices to not only communicate with each other, but to assist each other with processing if necessary. The time is coming soon when everything that can communicate with each other will, and this should make life much easier for consumers. Devices will automatically connect to the nearest wireless network, talking to other devices, downloading the latest drivers, and keeping themselves up-to-date. The advent of broadband is already proving an extremely exciting way for game players to play their favorite games. I'm a strong believer that there will always be a place for both online and single-player games, and that the

17

average gamer will spend about 50 percent of their gaming time online, competing against others. So I wouldn't stop designing single-player titles. Online RPGs will develop into online worlds, where players can temporarily forget that the real world exists as they become immersed in licensed universes. Where trolls, swords, and dungeons once reigned supreme, the most successful online communities will be created with guns, fast cars, and film licenses, bringing persistent online gaming to the mass market.

Advancements in Gameplay

Hopefully, the future will see the end of difficulty levels. Games will recognize how the player is playing and adjust the difficulty on-the-fly, providing every player, regardless of how good or bad they are, with a constant challenge. Speech generation is another very interesting area that will allow big advances in gameplay. Once our consoles are capable of generating realistic human speech from computer-generated text, we will be able to have truly lifelike AI characters within our games, who can discuss things that you have done within the game, offer advice, and help dynamically, depending on how you are playing the game. Combine this with voice recognition and you will be able to interact within environments in a highly realistic way, chatting freely to computer-generated characters in order to get clues and solve puzzles.

Artificial intelligence is an area that currently lags behind more glitzy game aspects like visuals, physics, and sound. With big increases in processing power, hopefully more believable AI techniques will come to the fore, focusing on conversations and subtleties of character, rather than just dodging bullets and running away convincingly.

Over the past 10 years, the length of games has been continually increasing to the point where it takes some part-time players a year to complete the latest version of *Final Fantasy* or *GTA*. Fortunately, developers are beginning to realize that there is a limit to the length of gameplay that needs to be in a game. Hopefully, as we move into the future, single-player games will increase in quality rather than duration of gameplay, and we will provide 10 to 20 hours of a brilliant gaming experience. Otherwise, game development teams may grow to many hundreds if consumers expect 40 hours or more of real-world quality environments and characters.

I also expect to see a big increase in "mega" games, costing upward of $30 million in terms of licenses, development costs, and marketing. There may have been several of these already; games like *Gran Turismo 4* and *GTA: San Andreas* must be close to this. But expect more, as games get more expensive, more extravagant, and even more mass market. Another interesting recent shift is the move by companies like EA to break new ground with big licenses. Instead of simply piggybacking their games on new film releases, publishers are experimenting by creating original new storylines for existing franchises, such as the Bond series. Maybe the day will come when the tide turns and the film industry starts using our storylines and following our lead on these big licenses? Many of our games are now being made into films, as Hollywood has woken up to the creativity that is going on in our industry. Bungie has managed to get director Peter Jackson working on its *HALO* movie, and the movie *Doom* (which is just being released as I write this) is another example. My company, Eidos, has had two *Tomb Raider* movies released, and hopefully, more of our brands will be coming to a cinema near you in the future.

With one ultra-powerful platform, true 3D photo-realistic worlds, believable AI characters, and mega-sized titles, the future is really something to look forward to. But to ensure that our companies are best placed to thrive as the industry moves forward, we have to ensure that we don't take anything for granted.

Don't Let Others Put You Off

There have been many times in my career when people have told me that an idea of mine wouldn't work or a game mechanic wasn't worth bothering with. That would often put me off initially. But I soon learned that, more often than not, they were wrong. Saying no and finding a flaw in something is the easiest thing in the world to do. As a tribute to all those designers who ignore these negative thoughts, here is proof that the naysayers don't always know what they are talking about:

"Drill for oil? You mean drill into the ground to try and find oil? You're crazy!"
-Drillers whom Edwin L. Drake tried to enlist to his project to drill for oil in 1859

"Everything that can be invented has already been invented."
- Charles H. Duell, director of the U.S. Patent Office, 1899

"Who the hell wants to hear actors talk?"
-H.M. Warner, Warner Brothers, 1927

"A rocket will never be able to leave the earth's atmosphere."
-The New York Times, 1936

"That rainbow song's no good. Take it out."
- MGM memo after first showing of The Wizard Of Oz, 1938

"I think there is a world market for maybe five computers."

- IBM chairman Thomas Watson, 1943

"Television won't last because people will soon get tired of staring at a plywood box every night."
-Producer Darryl Zanuck, 20th Century Fox, 1946

"You ain't going nowhere, son. You ought to go back to driving a truck."
-Jim Denny to Elvis Presley, 1954

And a special mention to the King of Negativity, Royal Society President Lord Kelvin. Lord Kelvin made three very clear statements between 1897 and 1899:

"Radio has no future."

"X-rays are clearly a hoax."

"The aeroplane is scientifically impossible."

Remember these misguided "words of wisdom," and please don't let negative people stop you from being creative and trying new ideas! You won't be right all the time, but it's better to try something new and fail than to stay within your comfort zone and never innovate. If Will Wright had listened to the first publisher feedback he got on *The Sims*, he would have scrapped it. The fact is that he didn't let them dissuade him and had the balls to stick with his vision. Twenty million copies later, guess who's had the last laugh!

I can think of countless times in my career when I have seen negativity result in bad business decisions. Someone I used to work for turned down two titles that each went on to sell over seven million units because he felt they were too risky. It's very easy to say no to something. But having the bravery to get behind something when you've seen that spark of something special is the mark of a great designer, in my opinion.

The 10 Game Design Commandments

Before we finish up, I wanted to try to consolidate all the tips and hints that I have been giving throughout the book into 10 game design commandments that you can readily put to work. These commandments are simple and straightforward, and if you take the time to follow them, I'm really sure that you'll see noticeable results in your own design work.

1. You Must Have a Hook

Year after year, I have seen first-hand the importance of having a clear hook. You must be able to summarize what makes your game idea distinctive in a sentence. A clear hook attaches itself to everything, ending up ingrained in the marketing campaign, the box, the trailers, the game demo, and the product name. A clear hook is an addictive idea; a "meme" that infects everyone. (Evolutionary biologist Richard Dawkins describes a "meme" as an idea that can be spread through people like a virus; for example, a catchy song that crosses the globe or a new design of sports car that makes a huge impression on car designers everywhere and is used subconsciously in future car designs). Start your game with a clear hook and focus on it all the way through development. If you actually end up with a game that delivers on that hook, you've done your job well. If the sales and marketing team hear about the hook early on, and understand it, the chances are that your marketing will match the game and together, everyone on your team will speak one clear and powerful message.

Also, don't ever forget the importance of your title. As I mentioned earlier, I have come to believe that the name of a game has enormous importance. If you have a clear hook, make sure that the name reflects this and you'll find that interest and sales are much larger. For example, let's pick up on an idea I mentioned earlier in the book. Let's say that your clear hook is "The first full 3D game to feature a perfect jetpack implementation." Rather than calling your game *The Adventures of Boris* as you were planning to, it would be much better to call your game *Jetpack*. Having a game name that contains a reference to your hook is by far and away the best thing you can do, in my view. If your clear hook is "stunningly realistic earthquakes with buildings falling down," make sure your game title has some reference to quakes or natural disaster. Even something a little subtle, such as *Richter Scale*, would help give people an idea of what makes the game special before they have even picked up the box. There are always exceptions to this rule, but I believe that having a good hook and using it to name your game is a very sensible way to increase the odds of your game being successful.

2. Don't Ever Be Afraid to Innovate

Please don't ever be afraid to innovate and come up with new ideas. When designers try things that haven't been done before, the industry moves forward. Playing it safe and not doing anything new may result in fairly decent sales if you do a great job and market it right, but the products that sell millions and are remembered in the future are always innovative. If you want to be known as a brilliant game designer, you need to have innovation in your game designs.

17

Reality Check: Don't get stuck in the trap of being a design copy machine. Copying ideas that others create is a good way to get started and learn, but it's also important to move past this stage and develop your own ideas.

That doesn't mean that every design should be completely unique or that you need to create a new kind of game with every product; if that were the case, you would probably never end up getting a game made. But it's possible to add highly innovative features and game mechanics into otherwise traditional and popular genres. Let's look at a few simple examples. The physics gun in *Half-Life 2* made an enormous difference to a traditional linear first-person shooter experience. The bullet time in *Max Payne* single-handedly made the game stand out from other third-person action titles at the time. Trying to create the most expensive and spectacular crashes in *Burnout 3* added a whole new way of playing a traditional city-racing arcade game. You get the idea.

As I mentioned at the start of this chapter, too many people are ready and willing to be negative. For every single great idea, there have been people standing there, shooting it down before it even started to grow. But if you have the confidence to innovate when you can, to try new things out while keeping a commercial understanding, you stand a chance of being the next Will Wright, Peter Molyneux, or Shigeru Miyamoto.

Reality Check: I mention having a commercial understanding because you can't innovate all the time. Once a project is heading toward the finish line, you have to make sure the design remains locked down. Knowing when to innovate and when to stick with tried-and-tested techniques so that you can quickly finish a product is a challenge in itself. And it is a challenge that many fantastically original designers have problems with. But the rule is clear: Don't be afraid to innovate.

3. Research, Research, Research

As you learned earlier in this book, research is an extremely important aspect of being a game designer, and one that is too often forgotten or left lingering on designers' to-do lists. The term *research* covers a whole host of different areas, including fully understanding the subject matter of your game, playing lots of other games in the same genre, speaking to people in your target audience to get their views on your design, conducting large-scale market research, and finally, using focus groups and difficulty-balancing groups.

Properly understanding the subject of your game is an obvious but often forgotten rule; if you're making a game based on Vietnam, you must understand the Vietnam War, have seen the major movies and TV shows, have read books by people who were there, and so on. Without that, you risk creating a crass, half-baked attempt to replicate a complex period of history. The same is true of almost any game design unless it is 100-percent original. It's also vital to play all the competitive games and have a good understanding of what other titles are doing. The average person who buys your game will probably be aware of the other titles or will have read a review written by someone who was.

Game design is a very subjective pursuit, and it is all too easy to become so totally wrapped up in a game design that you lack the vision to see the forest for the trees. If you play your game every day, how can you make a balanced call on the control system when you've become so familiar with it? You're never going to be able to get back the feeling of trying it for the first time. So don't be afraid to use other people and get their reactions, whether it's one to one, a small group of gamers, or a big market research campaign asking for people's thoughts on a particular hook or game title.

 Reality Check: If you don't make time for research, it will turn around and bite you in the backside. The more research you do, the better prepared you will be for all the decisions you'll need to make over the course of developing your game.

4. Get Your Camera Right

If you have a strong understanding of how the in-game camera behaves in the best games on the market, you'll have a real advantage as a game designer. It's a major asset being able to identify what a camera is doing, what it's actually revolving around, whether it's jerking and needs to be smoothed, and so on.

As I discussed in Chapter 5, the camera is incredibly important. You look at every game through the camera every second that you play it. Any judders, jerks, and annoying camera movement bugs are going to become very frustrating. The camera needs to be carefully set up based, on the game you're making; there isn't a "one size fits all" solution. You need to think about what the player needs (and will want) to see and find a solution that is immediate, fairly invisible to the user, and practical for the purpose.

I'm also a big fan of trying to avoid user-controlled cameras wherever possible; there are always reasons why you might want to provide this option (so the player can investigate his surroundings, for example), but I have a personal dislike of games that require the player to constantly center the camera back behind them rather than the game doing it. If you want your game to be played by the biggest number of people, you need to make it easy to get into, and intuitive to pick up and play. Many, many people cannot cope with a two-stick control that requires you to move not only the character around, but also the camera at the same time!

17

As I've mentioned, the key to understanding cameras is to play the best games out there and analyze exactly what the camera is doing. Many great games have been ruined by bad cameras, and if you design your camera carefully and early, you'll have a strong foundation on which to build a great game.

5. Get Your Controls Right

Getting your camera just right is critical, but perfecting your control system is even more important. A great control system means that your character and game responds immediately and predictably to the player's control inputs. People talk about "pick up and play" games, and this means using a control system that is simple, obvious, and immediate. Don't ever have delays when using key controls. Shiny's Dave Perry explains it very succinctly:

> **"Don't ever take control away from the joypad/keyboard unless you really want to piss off the player. When you press jump, make him jump. Fight animators or anyone else who tries to get you to do anything else. Instant response is key."**

As with cameras, the best way to learn about control systems is by playing other games. Rent a whole load of games and try them out; see which ones feel right when you pick them up and which ones are a real struggle. Analyze what it is about the controls that you find frustrating. Try to determine which games have the best control systems and how different genres of games use different control systems.

6. Never Forget the Importance of Sound and Music

As we've discussed in the chapter about audio, sound and music, these elements are often neglected by game designers. There is too often a large division of skills that makes designers leave everything to the engineer or musician. But this is wrong. The best way to make sure that sound plays a fully integral part in your gameplay experience is to design it in early and work with your engineer/musician. Start with simple ideas, like the squealing of tires when they start to lose grip, or make sure that a different kind of footstep sound is played when the player walks over a hidden trapdoor. Although simple and obvious, they have a fundamental effect on the gameplay. If you can hear your car starting to lose grip, the player has extra time to react and try to control the car.

More complex ideas include things like having a musical theme for evil characters that you can then use to introduce tension later in the game or having music linked in with the gameplay in some way so the player triggers off new channels by completing sections of a level, building up the musical score to a crescendo. However you do it, make sure you give attention to audio, and give it real thought when you create a design document. Too many game designs have an audio section that effectively says, "We'll support surround sound, and we'll license in some music." Audio is a lot more important than that!

7. Good Teamwork Pays

It's really important to know your own limitations and to understand that a one-man design rarely works. Even the greatest designers in the world bounce ideas off other talented people, and all the really good ones know their own strengths and weaknesses. Knowing your weaknesses makes you a better designer; there is no harm in getting the assistance of someone for an area in which you're not strong. Imagine if Steven Spielberg started composing his own music, or acting in his movies, or editing the sound, or trying to do the makeup. Don't ever be afraid to use experts to advise you or assist you!

Remember that some of the greatest creative projects have resulted from someone having a great idea and then refining it with other talented, creative people until it shines brightly. Remember the writing teams who create some of the greatest television in the world. By using a combination of great creative people, they can create products having consistently high quality. Get the best designers in your company together and have a brainstorm with them. Get them involved with your original concept and bounce around ideas for making it better, for adding new features, and for polishing it. Don't put up with an okay design or an okay storyline or okay music. Try as hard as you can to push each feature, using other people where necessary, until they are each excellent.

8. Story Is King

If you can, order a copy of *The Writer's Journey* by Christopher Vogler from Amazon. Having a decent knowledge of the story writing process is a great asset. Make absolutely certain that you use a professional writer for creating your plot and dialogue. You may need to create an outline within which the writer will work, but try to give the writer as much freedom as possible. Unless you have a writing background, don't fool yourself in thinking that you can write dialogue as well as people who do it every day professionally.

Try hard not to let your story and plotlines get swamped by the game and go missing. It's easy to start off with a great storyline but to see bits changed, cut, and moved into different places. Before long, the story isn't recognizable and players don't understand what is happening. Identify the key moments of your story (for example, when a plot twist is revealed or a main character is killed) and ensure that these moments in the

17

game are clear and dramatic. Use all the tricks you know with regard to cameras and editing to make the game as emotional as possible for the player.

9. Remember the Magic 30 Minutes

The magic first half hour is the most important section of your game. You need to strike a careful balance between showing off a visually stunning and extremely exciting environment and keeping the actual gameplay fairly simple. Use the first half hour to gradually introduce the core game mechanics to the player. Remember that most players, journalists, distributors, and retailers will judge your game largely based on the first 30 minutes. You need to show off your key USPs and demonstrate how incredible your technology can be while making sure that all players will be able to get through the level fairly easily. The ultimate trick is to set the game up so that every player (regardless of whether they are good or not) feels that they just made it through the level in one piece due to their skill.

10. It's All about the Gameplay

Your core gameplay is the single most important element of your game. I have seen games that looked average sell extremely well because they were fun. And I have seen even more games that looked stunning sell badly because they played like a dog. Ask any great game designer and they'll tell you that it's all about the gameplay. For example, listen to two veterans of the games industry, Larry Kaplan and Sid Meier:

> "We used to spend so much of our time on gameplay, and today's games seem to put too much emphasis on graphics and sound. It's the gameplay that makes a game fun; sometimes they forget that."
> *Larry Kaplan*

> "I like games that are simple, not games that are trivial, but also not games that require you to invest a week or to relearn something. I like games that you can just pick up, sit down in front of, and get going."
> *Sid Meier*

If your game is fun, you will be forgiven a great number of sins. If your game isn't fun, nothing you do will redeem it.

So there you have it. I hope you've found at least some of this book useful. I've tried to stick to practical, common-sense design that you'll be able to use in the real world, and I have deliberately avoided going down theoretical and academic routes, however interesting they can be. If you remember my 10 commandments of game design and make a real effort to make sure you try to maximize each of those areas in every game you work, you won't go too far wrong. As a friend of mine says, "It ain't brain surgery."

A Final Thought

One final thought to finish on, and it's about emotion. Great films make people cry; they stir up strong emotions and the climax to a great film can be the most exhausting and exhilarating experience. Millions of people watched the film *Titanic* again and again to experience the emotional highs and lows. But films are a non-interactive medium. Surely video games should be capable of doing even more since the player is actually taking part. Players should have a stronger emotional connection to a game, and the characters within it, than they do to a film. It's pretty obvious.

Yet this doesn't happen at the moment. The fantastically underrated game *Ico* on the PlayStation 2 came close, as the two characters are dramatically drawn apart after being together and relying on each other for so long. But other than that, we're still quite a ways off. There is a great quote from Philip Price about this very subject:

> **"To me games have an extremely great and still unrealized potential to influence man. I want to bring joy and excitement to people's lives in my games, while at the same time communicate aspects of this journey of life we are all going through. Games have a larger potential for this than linear movies or any other form of media."**
> *Philip Price*

If game design is going to move to the next level, we designers need to understand why films can be so immersive and emotionally powerful. We need to make sure our game storylines and characters are created by people as good as or better than the scriptwriters and directors in Hollywood. We need to do even more professional preproduction, planning exactly how the game will play out in detail. Too many games play a beautiful but flat cut scene and then play a section of gameplay that doesn't carry that plot or storyline on. You get a sequence of "cut scene–unrelated gameplay–cut scene–unrelated gameplay" and so on. Great games will need to build on the in-game cut scenes used so well in the Half-Life series and develop new and better ways of encouraging the player to develop bonds and attachments with AI characters. I've got my own ideas about how to do this, but I've got to have some secrets left.

If you've got any views on this book, positive or negative, please send them to me at **patrgol@yahoo.co.uk**. I'd love to hear your thoughts. I hope you've found something useful in here, and if I help just one person in their journey to becoming a great game designer, then all the long nights will have been worthwhile.

Appendix

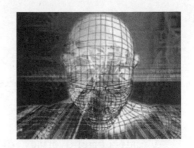

Game Design Template

The game design template presented in this appendix demonstrates a typical layout for a game design document. If you go through this template and fill in each of the sections, you should end up with a strong, detailed document that covers all the relevant areas, and hopefully ensures you don't miss anything important. What it can't do is make your game design superb; the originality must come from you!

The template obviously doesn't include artwork. It's important to make sure your design documents are visually attractive, so try and include any sample artwork you have come up with, or even just reference photos you've found on the Internet to help give a feel for atmosphere and style.

The template is split into four sections. The first provides a key overview to your document. Many people will just read this section to get a feel for what your design is about, so it needs to summarize everything that makes your design unique. The second section goes into much more depth about the gameplay and the general game mechanics. The third section provides more detail about other aspects of the game. Finally, the fourth section details project risks. This section isn't strictly necessary as part of a game design document, and is sometimes found in a separate document. However, I have included it here because I feel it's really important that the lead designer/creative director understands these risks, and that they have considered them when creating the design. Risks are not just something for a producer/project manager to worry about; they affect the whole project and the entire team.

Section 1: Overview

Design Summary

Create a brief overview of the game design, including the key design aims, and your "hook." This overview should be a paragraph or two that grab peoples' attention and makes them want to read on. If you can't grab people with this section, your design is very unlikely to work. Here, you need to discuss what makes your game design so special and why the reader should be excited about your game design.

USP List

Arguably, the USP is the most important element of the design. It consists of a list of any unique selling points that set your game apart from the competition. I'd suggest that you list out each USP, and write a paragraph or two on each one, summarizing how you want them to work.

Game Objective

In this section you need to answer questions such as:

- What is the players' key objective in the game?
- What is the goal?
- Why should the player care about progressing?

Visual Style

In this section you need to answer questions such as:

- What kind of visual style are you going for?
- Are you designing a game to mirror reality?
- Are you trying to create something visually unique?

Target Audience

The two key questions to address in this section include:

- What kind of age group are you aiming at?
- Are you aiming at a mass-market gamer, families, older gamers or hardcore players?

Target Platforms

List all the platforms that are being considered for the game, and specify which, if any, are the most important.

Expected Age Rating

List any controversial/adult content in the game, and the expected American or European age rating. Details on how the ratings systems work (and what game elements are likely to lead to a higher rating) can be found on the ESRB and PEGI websites, respectively.

Section 2: Gameplay

Typical Gameplay Example

Write a few pages of narrative describing a typical five or ten minute section of the game from the player's point of view. Pick a exciting section from within the game that you feel will help the reader understand the vision that you have in your head. Once the reader has read this, they should have a much better idea of where you are coming from.

Game Modes

Write a brief description of all the game modes in the game and how they will work. Will they all be available from the start of the game, or does the player need to unlock them?

Key Gameplay Mechanics

Write a detailed description of all the key gameplay features and mechanics. You can cover the unique features in more detail here. You should also include any other key features which aren't unique, but are still important to your design.

AI Description

If your game includes other characters/cars/objects which need to act intelligently, write a brief overview of the AI behaviors that will be needed in the game.

Difficulty Systems

In this section, you need to answer questions such as:

- How will the varying abilities of players be addressed?

- Will you use various difficulty levels, or will the game try and adapt the difficulty automatically?

Controls (on All Platforms)

Create a clear description of the control system for all parts of the game and for each platform. Where possible, give an example of another game that uses a similar system. It's helpful here to have a picture of a controller, labelled with your controls.

Camera Descriptions

Write a description of all the different types of cameras used in the game, with particular attention to the main default game camera. Where possible, give an example of another game that uses the same system.

Interface/GUI

Create a brief description and a rough drawing of the in-game GUI. What information do you want to display? Will it appear all the time, or just fade up when needed?

Audio/Music

Create a detailed description of any music that you'll need in the game, along with any suggested musical style, plus key sound issues and how a cutting-edge audio experience will be achieved.

Multiplayer/Online

Describe any split-screen, hot seat, network, and online multiplayer game modes. You should also indicate if the game will have downloadable content and whether it will support online stats.

Front End

Create a clear flowchart of the front-end menu system, plus a description of the visual style that you'd like to aim for. How will the game begin? Will you have an intro FMV?

Saving/Loading System

Create a clear description of how the saving/loading system will work. Can the player save at any time, or are there checkpoint saves or a fixed number of saves per level? Does the game automatically save, or does the player need to choose themselves when to save the game?

Section 3: Game Detail

Back Story

Write a clear and detailed description of the background history of the main characters/ game world.

Game Storyline

Summarize the game storyline from beginning to end. You don't need a full script at this stage, but you should provide a story overview so that the reader understands what is going to happen over the course of the game. If you plan to use a professional writer, and they haven't started work yet, put down the current, sketchy storyline, and explain who will be re-writing it, and when.

Mission List/Game Geography

Create a list of all the missions/levels/tasks in the game, plus rough maps of any key areas. Although you should have a level design for every part of the game, it isn't necessary for an initial game design document.

Key Character Descriptions

Write a description and graphic mock-up of all the key characters in the game.

Key Vehicle/Objects

Create a description and graphic mock-up of all the key vehicles and objects in the game.

Section 4: Project Issues / Risks

FMV/Cut Scene Technology

Describe the types of FMV and/or in-game cut scenes that will be used and how they will work. How will the camerawork be handled, and do you have someone on board with a good understanding of camera direction/editing/cinematography to do this work?

Licenses/Product Placement

List any licenses that need to be signed for the game (including music), plus any opportunities for product placement. Try and prioritize these licenses if possible to assist the licensing team.

Languages/Localization

Write down a complete list of languages that the game will be translated into, along with any specific localization issues. How can you help this game sell in other countries? Can you alter the design at all to boost sales in any key territories, and if so, is this worthwhile?

Schedule Overview

Here you should provide an overview of the game schedule, with the key target dates, including "first playable," when the core features will be playable for the first time.

Team

In this section you need to answer questions such as:

- How big will the development team be?

- How will this vary over the course of development?

- Who are the key people?

- Do you/they have enough designers and level designers for such a project?

Middleware to Be Used

In this section you need to answer questions such as:

- Will middleware be used for any versions of the game?

- Will the game require physics middleware?

- Do you know which middleware will be used?

New Technology

List any key new technology that will need to be developed by the team, and doesn't currently exist. How will this be done?

Key Project Risks

Create a list of all the key project risks (i.e., practical, project-based items, especially schedule-related) and how to minimize them.

Key Design Risks

Create a list of all the key design risks (i.e., gameplay items) and how to minimize them.

Section 5: Summary

Summary

Summarize your game design document, and why you think it has the potential to be a great game. Leave the reader excited, and desperate to play the game!

Index